SPEAKING IN SOVIET TONGUES

SPEAKING IN
SOVIET
TONGUES

LANGUAGE CULTURE

AND THE POLITICS OF VOICE

IN REVOLUTIONARY RUSSIA

Michael S. Gorham

NORTHERN ILLINOIS UNIVERSITY PRESS

DeKalb

© 2003 by Northern Illinois University Press

Published by the Northern Illinois University Press, DeKalb, Illinois 60115

Manufactured in the United States using acid-free paper

All Rights Reserved

Design by Julia Fauci

Library of Congress Cataloging-in-Publication Data

Gorham, Michael S.

Speaking in Soviet tongues : language culture and the politics of voice in revolutionary Russia /
Michael S. Gorham.

   p.   cm.

Includes bibliographical references and index.

ISBN 0-87580-313-X (alk. paper)

1. Soviet Union—Languages—Political aspects. 2. Language and culture—Soviet Union. 3. Oral
communication—Soviet Union. 4. Soviet Union—Politics and government—1917–1936. I. Title.

P119.32.S65 G67 2003

306.44'947—dc21

2002040955

For Veronika and for my parents

CONTENTS

ACKNOWLEDGMENTS

This book is the product of research and training in three related fields—Russian literature, linguistics, and cultural studies—integrated here under the general rubric of "language culture." It first took shape in the embryonic form of a doctoral dissertation in 1994 and has since undergone major revision and expansion.

The list of individuals to whom I owe thanks reflects the interdisciplinary nature of the topic itself. For their support in the earliest stages of this project, I thank Boris Gasparov, Viacheslav Ivanov, and Irina Paperno. Aleksandr Etkind, Larry Holmes, John Murray, Maksim Shapir, Victor Zaslavsky, and Viktor Zhivov all provided thought-provoking comments in their respective areas of specialization. I am particulary grateful to Konstantin Polivanov, whose philological acumen, bibliographic and archival prowess, and unfailing friendship proved invaluable to my research stays in Moscow, and to Lazar Fleishman, Stephen Moeller-Sally, Richard Stites, William Mills Todd III, and Andrew Wachtel for their detailed and insightful comments on the work as a completed dissertation.

Revised and expanded drafts of the manuscript benefited from thorough readings by E. C. Barksdale, Sheryl Kroen, and Galina Rylkova, and from the reactions of scholars at the numerous interdisciplinary conferences and workshops at which portions of the project were presented. Alexander Burak provided expert advice on many of the more challenging Russian-English translations. Special thanks go to Frederick Corney and Kevin Platt for their close readings, their ability to pinpoint fissures and faultlines, and their friendship, and to Gregory Freidin, whose guidance, insight, and inspiration made this whole endeavor possible from start to finish. While expressing heartfelt gratitude to all, I nevertheless assume full responsibility for any errors, omissions, or oversights that may appear.

· · ·

Research on this book was made possible in part by the Research Scholar Program of the American Council of Teachers of Russian and the American Council for Collaboration in Education and Language Study, with funds from the Department of State and the U.S. Information Agency; a Post-Doctoral Fellowship from the Davis Center for Russian and Eurasian Studies at Harvard University; a grant from the Eurasia Program of the Social Science Research Council, with funds provided by the State Department under the Russian, Eurasian, and East European Training Program (Title VIII); a grant from the International Research and Exchanges Board, with funds provided by the Department of State (Title VIII program) and the National Endowment for the Humanities; and financial support from the Humanities Scholarship Enhancement Fund at the University of Florida. None of these organizations is responsible for the views expressed.

I am additionally indebted to the numerous staff members at Russian and U.S. libraries and archives who facilitated access to the mounds of resources required by this ambitious project. These institutions include the Stanford University Library, the Hoover Institution of War, Revolution, and Peace, the Harvard University Library, the Library of Congress, the University of Florida Library (Alena Aissing, in particular), the Russian State Library, the Ushinskii State Pedagogical Library, the Russian State Archive for Literature and the Arts, the Russian State Archive for Social and Political History, the State Archive of the Russian Federation, the Institute of World Literature, the Academy of Sciences' Institute of Russian Language, and the Archive of the Russian Academy of Education. I am likewise grateful to Mary Lincoln, her outside readers, and her staff at the Northern Illinois University Press for their comments, professionalism, and attention to detail in the final stages of production.

Finally, I extend my deepest gratitude to Veronika and to my parents for years of support, confidence, patience, and understanding.

▪ ▪ ▪

Earlier versions of sections of this book have appeared in "*Natsiia ili snikerizatsiia?* Identity and Perversion in the Language Debates of Late- and Post-Soviet Russia," *Russian Review* 59, no. 4 (October 2000): 614–29; "Mastering the Perverse: State-building and Language 'Purification' in Early Soviet Russia," *Slavic Review* 58, no. 1 (spring 2000): 133–53 (used with permission from the American Association for the Advancement of Slavic Studies); "Coming to Terms with the New Writing Citizen: Soviet Language of State in the Diary of Kostia Riabtsev," *East/West Education* 18, no. 1 (spring 1997): 6–21; "From Charisma to Cant: Models of Public Speaking in Early Soviet Russia," *Canadian Slavonic Papers/Revue canadienne des slavistes* 38, nos. 3–4 (September–December 1996): 331–55; and "Tongue-tied Writers: The Rabsel'kor Movement and the Voice of the 'New Intelligentsia' in Early Soviet Russia," *Russian Review* 55, no. 3 (July 1996): 412–29. I am grateful to all for their early support and permission to reprint.

NOTE ON SPELLING AND TRANSLATION

I use the Library of Congress system for transliteration except where proper names may be better known to readers in other spellings: for example, Maxim Gorky, Roman Jakobson, Lev Tolstoy, and Lev Trotsky. I have retained the Russian original of most literary texts quoted owing to the centrality of language in this discussion but have done so in English transliteration at the request of my editor. All translations from Russian to English are my own, unless otherwise noted.

SPEAKING IN SOVIET TONGUES

В оный день, когда над миром новым
Бог склонял лицо Свое, тогда
Солнце останавливали словом,
Словом разрушали города.

["On that day, when God bent His face over the world, the sun was stopped by the word, and by the word cities were destroyed."]

—Nikolai Gumilev, "Slovo" ("The Word," 1921)

"If I come to you and speak in tongues, what good will I be to you, unless I bring you some revelation or knowledge or prophecy or word of instruction? . . . Again, if the trumpet does not sound a clear call, who will get ready for battle? So it is with you. Unless you speak intelligible words with your tongue, how will anyone know what you are saying? You will just be speaking into the air."

—1 Corinthians 14:6–9

INTRODUCTION

In the life of the word, a heroic era has arrived. The word is bread and flesh. It shares the fate of bread and flesh: suffering. People are hungry. Still hungrier is the state. But there is something even hungrier: time. Time wants to devour the state. He who lifts up the word and shows it to time, as a priest lifting up the Eucharist, shall be the second Joshua. There is nothing hungrier than the modern state, and a hungry state is more terrifying than a hungry man. Compassion for a state that denies the word—this is the civic path and heroic deed of the modern poet.

—Osip' Mandel'shtam, "The Word and Culture" (1921)

In the new conditions of our life, anyone who has not gone off into their shell altogether must from time to time be an orator. By orator we mean not only individuals giving speeches at large gatherings, meetings, etc., but also anyone who has had the occasion to address in words even the smallest group of congregated people. To convince, to explain something, to calm, to encourage, to appeal—these are the obligations which life is constantly placing on us.

—From a popular public-speaking manual (1926)

Debates over language figure centrally into public discussions of identity and authority even in the most stable times. In just the past decades of American history—marked by relative economic prosperity and political stability—the American English language culture has featured a government-led interest in "Plain English," a brief but nationalized debate over the foreign-language status of "Ebonics," and a more sustained and culturally divisive battle over the notion of "political correctness." The last offers the best contemporary example of the essential linguistic roots of broad-based "culture wars." Seemingly innocuous forms of address and naming become volatile signals of political affiliations—implicit or explicit—concerning broad concepts like class, race, and gender. Such language-based political battles challenge traditional assumptions about who we are and who is in charge, and the conflicts offer alternative visions of power relations by redefining the verbal landscape. Prominent even in times of relative calm, this sort of "metalinguistic" discussion, discourse on language, or "talk about talk," becomes even more intense during times of radical social and political upheaval.

In the following pages I examine the proliferation of such discussions of language in early Soviet Russia, the manner in which they helped give shape to what eventually emerged as a stable language of state, and the role in that process of the institutions most involved in the production and dissemination of public discourse. While avoiding reductionist claims that everything comes down to language, I nevertheless assume that much of the legitimacy of an emerging power is judged, conferred, and perpetuated based on how its representatives articulate its ideas, goals, and promises in writing and speech and how, through debates about those ideas, the basic language and images that are used become either reinforced, redefined, or undercut.[1] Simply put, the degree to which a population accepts the "imagined community" of an emerging state depends largely on how effectively that state identifies itself with a set of ideas, principles, and traditions; authorizes itself as the best means of realizing them; and provides its citizens with both the means and motivations for embracing those ideas and their mode of expression, or discourse.[2]

The idea that the relationship between meaning, authority, and identity is mediated by language is certainly not new. Plato and Cicero expressed the dynamic interdependence largely in connection to the uses and abuses of classical rhetoric.[3] Proponents of the doctrine of Adamic language saw language as divinely inspired, the path to knowledge and the source of Truth.[4] Condillac and the French Encyclopedists wrote about the social origins of language and its formative role in the expression of national culture "from the simplest everyday events to the most exalted creations of man."[5] Karl Marx likewise acknowledged the power of language when invoked to bring credibility and authority to revolutionary movements.[6] And Friedrich Nietzsche underscored the creative potential of language and the human ability to "consciously will" it into a force and into action.[7] In the twentieth-century thought of Mikhail Bakhtin, Roland Barthes, Pierre Bourdieu, Michel de Certeau, Michel Foucault, and Stuart Hall—to list only some of the primary theoretical sources that have inspired my study—this age-old recognition of the interdependence of language, identity, and authority has become an a priori assumption and, largely as a result, has given rise more recently to a wealth of culturally sensitive studies of language (and linguistically sensitive studies of culture).[8]

Several language-oriented studies of early Soviet Russia published in the past decade are particularly worthy of note. As an interpretive description of some of the basic "vocabulary" of revolution in 1917, Orlando Figes and Boris Kolonitskii's book on the language and symbols of the Russian revolution offers an engaging collection of source material and analyses, sheds important light on some of the basic symbolic fields that helped shape public discourse in this time of transformation, and advances the instructive thesis that, the more flexible the political discourse—capable of accommodating a variety of different idiomatic views—the more likely that discourse is to establish itself as an authoritative and lasting power.[9] Jeffrey Brooks, in the early chapters of *Thank You, Comrade Stalin! Soviet Public Culture from Revolution to Cold War*, uses his close reading of newspaper language over the first decades of Soviet rule to elaborate on some of the key metaphors and narratives that dominated that medium and documents the shift within it in dominant speech acts—from persuasion in the immediate postrevolutionary years to compulsion by the late 1920s.[10] In his case study of Magnitogorsk, Stephen Kotkin has brought the term "speaking Bolshevik" into the common parlance of Soviet historians. While the term itself as used conflates what I argue are two distinct discourses (the language of Bolshevism and the language of the Stalinist party-state) and thereby oversimplifies a more complex development in revolutionary language culture, it does offer a useful metaphor for Kotkin's important contention that a variety of domains in everyday practice under Stalin (language, dress, etc.) were critical for establishing, negotiating, and acquiring "the new terms of social identity" and that they served as a kind of "barometer of one's political allegiance to the cause."[11] Katerina Clark, in her book on Petersburg and cultural revolution, introduces the compelling notion of "Promethean linguistics," which she uses to describe the tendency of leading cultural figures in Soviet Russia to use language as a touchstone for confronting an array of broader cultural and ideological concerns.[12]

My study not only confirms the special ability of language to serve as an object for debating broader issues of identity and state building but also demonstrates that such practice was by no means limited to the big names in contemporary language politics; it took place as rigorously and as instrumentally on the "front lines" of language—the newspapers, the schools, in literature, linguistics, folklore, and ethnography. Michael G. Smith's *Language and Power in the Creation of the USSR* has made this task easier with regard to the institutions of linguistics and language pedagogy, offering a rigorously researched analysis of the language theories, policies, and practices that, in most cases, were imposed upon the schools, the academy, and the non-Russian nationalities (with varying levels of success) during the first three decades of the Soviet era.[13] Smith's discussion of the evolution of Soviet language policies with regard to ethnic minorities (a topic I ignore entirely in this volume) provides a particularly insightful window into the critical role of language in the shaping, distorting, and reinventing of national identity.[14]

This book offers the first interdisciplinary examination of the dynamics, forces, and voices involved in the emergence of a coherent language of state in the aftermath of the Bolshevik uprising of October 1917. It likewise presents the first in-depth study of the fundamental role of literature in that process. Strongly reflecting my own training in language, literary, and cultural studies, it operates on the premise that narratives and the voices used to articulate them are largely cultural constructs and that who we are is largely defined by how we write and speak.[15] Discussions about and representations of language, therefore—particularly in times of radical social and political change—frequently reflect broader attempts to articulate visions of state authority and national identity.[16]

The term "language culture," as I use it here, has its roots in the formulations of the Russian linguist Grigorii Vinokur, whose book, *Language Culture (Kul'tura iazyka*, 1929), is most commonly credited with having laid the groundwork for modern Russian scholarship in the social and cultural history and theory of language usage.[17] Vinokur used "language culture" to refer to the linguistic practices of a society and its members on all levels of verbal production, from poets and politicians to the so-called "masses," the "people on the streets." In later Soviet usage, the term came to assume a narrower, more didactic, meaning more akin to "speech etiquette" or "proper usage" (also known as *kul'tura rechi*). Rejecting that narrower usage, I use "language culture" in a manner reflecting more recent trends in the sociology of language (referred to above) that link language to issues of power and authority. My understanding of "culture" is likewise influenced by more recent discussions of cultural studies that place as much emphasis on "practice" as on structure or system. William H. Sewell, Jr., for example, defines "culture" as "the sphere devoted specifically to the production, circulation, and use of meanings," adding that "the cultural sphere may in turn be broken down into the subspheres of which it is composed: say, of art, music, theater, fashion, literature, religion, media, and education. The study of culture," Sewell continues, "is the study of the activities that take place within these institutionally defined spheres and of the meanings produced in them."[18]

Equally critical to Sewell's notion of culture is the manner in which that system of meaning-making is used and employed in practice, for it is this second element that accounts for the evolutions, revolutions, and transformations—both intended and unintended, predictable and unpredictable—that a culture experiences during periods of radical social change.[19] By this understanding, then, "language culture" would constitute a subsphere in which the primary institutions responsible for "the production and circulation of meanings" in the early Soviet context are linguistics (including ethnography of communication), literature (including folklore), journalism, and education. And, within that subsphere, those meanings evolve, develop, and transform as they are filtered through a variety of sometimes competing, sometimes complementing, linguistic and cultural practices.

FAULT LINES IN THE CULTURAL HISTORY OF THE RUSSIAN LANGUAGE

The events surrounding 1917 may have brought about the greatest jolt to Russian language culture up to that time, but they by no means triggered the first such crisis in voice. Central to Peter the Great's campaign to modernize and westernize Russia at the turn of the eighteenth century was an overhaul of the official language of the state and the newly burgeoning press—not only in an attempt to make it more generally accessible and efficient but also, more fundamentally, "to give the new culture a new means of expression."[20] Peter's personal involvement in the reforms attest to their political importance, as does the rancorous reception his reforms received from ideological foes, particularly those affiliated with the Church, who looked upon them as further signs of an "impure" and "diabolic culture."[21] Both the replacement of some of the "arcane" Church Slavonic letters with Latin (Western) ones and the mandate of a "simpler" Russian in all but liturgical publications graphically symbolized the tsar-turned-linguist's revolutionary politics. Obedience to these reforms became an indication of allegiance to the monarch: as in matters of dress and shaving, Peter's reforms rendered the very act of writing and reading politically charged behavior.

It took a century to reconfigure the literary language itself. After Peter's advocacy of a style less dependent on the cumbersome morphology and syntax of Old Church Slavonic and after later attempts by Vasilii Trediakovskii and Mikhail Lomonosov to at least differentiate among "high," "middle," and "low" writing styles—each corresponding to appropriate literary genres—it took Nikolai Karamzin's epistolary and short prose to introduce the language of "polite society" into Russian belles lettres. Much of that new style borrowed words, phrases, and expressions from western European languages (primarily French, but also German and English) to articulate moods and emotions inadequately expressed by existing Russian options. In other cases, the foreign loanwords reflected more of a social fashion for things Western. Fraught with new underlying implications regarding national affiliations, traditions, and identities, the changes led to the next significant episode of language-culture shock in Russian history: the early-nineteenth-century debate between the "archaists" and "innovators." Representatives of the former group, such as the writer and statesman Aleksandr Shishkov and the poet, critic, and Decembrist Wilhelm Küchelbecker, believed that the infusion of loanwords polluted the national language and, by association, the Russian nation. (That their own models for the restoration of an "authentic" national language were themselves grounded in a largely imaginary vision of that language was commonly ignored by the archaists.) For the innovators such as Karamzin, the influx represented a necessary modernization and expansion of the literary language along similar lines to those mandated in civic discourse by Peter the Great a century earlier. As in the case of Peter's reforms, the link between language ideology and broader attitudes toward national identity was direct and clear. In this very early battle between two of the more resilient forces in Russian cultural history, one's allegiance to the camp of "Slavophile" or "westernizer" was in no small way gauged by one's stance on the language question.[22]

Although the nineteenth century witnessed substantial evolution of the literary language, it was not until the turn of the twentieth century that Russian language culture experienced its next serious shock as a result of its intersection with broader social and political transformations—this one caused by the same combination of factors that, in many ways, later fueled the language crisis of the Bolshevik revolution. In the closing decades of the nineteenth century, the industrial revolution brought about demographic shifts that changed the linguistic profile of the nation. It witnessed growing numbers of workers and peasants migrating to urban areas and enrolling in schools.[23] Previously located outside the bounds of print culture and public speech, these citizens brought with them their own language traits and reading habits, which were alternatively mimicked or ignored by various populist-style campaigns to "enlighten" them, and sparked a surge not only in didactic literature but also in popular adventure, science fiction, and romance novels.[24] Some of them even took pen in hand themselves, the pioneers of the "proletarian culture" that was to stake its claim in the cultural establishment after 1917.

Together with the forces of industrialization, the advent of modernism in the arts—and new voices in literature, in particular—contributed substantially to the linguistic instability and tumult of the times. Decadent and symbolist poets turned away from the romantic and realist modes of expression canonized by Turgenev, Tolstoy, Nekrasov, and Chekhov in search of a voice that more aptly expressed the anxieties of the day, the profound sense of uncertainty in the traditional institutions of church and state, the anticipation of radical transformations, and the new power and influence that all this brought to these creators of the Word. Among the more powerful representatives of this new logocentrism was Andrei Bely, who in his 1909 essay, "The Magic of Words," wrote of language as being "the most powerful instrument of creation."[25] Following in the tradition of Aleksandr Potebnia, and Wilhelm von Humboldt before him, Bely singled out the "creative word" and "living speech" as those aspects of language that had the capacity of creating the world anew.[26] Like those earlier celebrants of the creative word, Bely endowed poets with the supreme power of creation, due to their ability to both conjure up and penetrate the "deep secrets that lay in language."[27] In an essay on poetic glossolalia written on the eve of the Bolshevik takeover, this capacity assumes apocalyptic proportions: "There will, indeed, be a brotherhood of nations: the language of languages will destroy languages, and the second coming of the Word will come to pass."[28]

Like Bely, the poet Velimir Khlebnikov viewed the creative act of poetry making as a form of prophesy, and language innovation in general was the key to solving the ills of humanity. "Let a single written language be the companion for the future destinies of mankind and let it be a new collecting vortex," he wrote in 1919, "a new collector of humankind. Mute graphic signs will reconcile the polyphony of languages."[29] While his "transrational language," or *zaum*, was offered as a utopian, universal language that lay hidden beneath the mundane surface of everyday language, the keys to the perception and reproduction of the language belonged, at least in its formative stages, to only the most privileged of poets.[30]

The modern combination of anxiety and innovation was further complicated by the political upheavals brought about by the suppressed uprising of 1905 and its aftermath. Terms such as *revolutsiia, ideologiia, agitatsiia, miting, proletarii,* and *burzhuaziia* cried out from oppositional pamphlets and papers like magical incantations of some vague but better future.[31] In contrast to the great ruptures in language culture during the Petrine reforms and the debates between the archaists and innovators of the romantic era, this early-twentieth-century verbal tumult had an enormous breadth and depth, extending beyond the restricted limits of the educated elite, to directly affect—if not engage—the interests, concerns, and voices of the mass reader and speaker. Newspapers and publishing houses made concerted efforts to bring the language of politics to the people, publishing scores of dictionaries, glossaries, and pamphlets with definitions of the new vocabulary of revolution.[32] For better or worse, the convergence of technology, democratization, and industrialization gave rise to a nascent imagined speech community of previously unimaginable proportions.

SPREADING THE BOLSHEVIK WORD

After a decade or more of activity in underground circles, the language of Bolshevism burst with added force into the public sphere with the revolutions of 1917, flooding newspapers, journals, pamphlets, banners, textbooks, rallies, speeches, classrooms, and contemporary fiction. In part a product of the need for new words to describe concepts that simply had no Russian equivalent, in part a result of the utopian mentality that the entire social landscape—language included—could be redefined from scratch, the verbal mix of neologisms, bureaucratese, nonstandard slang, and high Marxist rhetoric imparted a linguistic jolt to the reading and listening public like none Russia had ever experienced. The growth of the printing industry and the socialist underpinnings of the Bolshevik message itself meant that a much greater portion of the citizenry would, like it or not, be brought into the grand renegotiation of meaning that defined the language culture of early Soviet Russia.

That citizenry's active involvement, in fact, was a matter of political survival for the Bolsheviks. When they seized power in October 1917, they sought to create a "dictatorship of the proletariat" in a country dominated by semiliterate peasants. The violence and famine resulting from a divisive civil war dramatically reduced by 1921 an already insignificant working-class population, exacerbating the Bolsheviks' already precarious position of "a superstructure in need of a base."[33] The First World War and the violence following the revolution plunged the lagging nation into economic chaos. The political tenuousness of the situation was complicated by the ideological dubiousness of the New Economic Policy (NEP) in 1921, a broad-based policy shift that moved away from the militarized, command-style economy of "war communism" preferred by Trotsky, Lenin, and others.[34] Seen by the leadership as a necessary evil on the road to the greatest good, the NEP offered perhaps the greatest compromises to the peasantry, in the form of personal property rights and the freedom to sell agricultural goods on the open market. In short, for a ruling party intent on establishing firm control over the power structure of the emerging state, made vulnerable by the sheer paucity in numbers of its proletarian constituency and wary about a (largely peasant) population exposed to pernicious bourgeois practices and sentiments, the need to establish firm ideological control only intensified in the aftermath of the fractious civil war.[35]

Lacking the material and social bases, the new Bolshevik leadership was forced to depend primarily on *ideas* about the proletarian state and revolutionary world order to legitimate its power symbolically. Just two weeks after assuming power, Vladimir Lenin, recognizing the ideological clout of the printed word, issued decrees authorizing government control of all newspapers.[36] The country's high illiteracy rate in many respects eased the Bolsheviks' task of molding both language and citizens to shape their ideas. Under the direction of the "Commissariat of Popular Enlightenment," or Narkompros (the Bolshevik reinvention of the Ministry of Education), the state intensified its literacy campaign "[w]ith the aim of providing the entire population of the Republic the opportunity of conscious participation in the political life of the country," as a 1919 decree signed by Lenin openly declared.[37] Party directives made no attempt to conceal the specifically ideological goals of press and education policy. The resolution on press and propaganda from the Eleventh Party Congress in 1922 stated outright: "The press is one of the mightiest weapons in the Party's struggle for influence over the masses, for their Communist enlightenment and organization."[38] In that same year, the Soviet censorship apparatus was institutionalized in the form of Glavlit.[39]

The urgent need to get out the Bolshevik word was confounded, however, by broken channels of mass communication. Despite the party's early control over the press, the printed word was not reaching its audience—particularly in the countryside. A combination of low literacy levels and problems in production and distribution led the rural populations to depend on other, oral sources for information about the "outside world."[40] As the journalist and propagandist Iakov Shafir wrote in his pioneering study of the reception of Bolshevik newspapers in the countryside, these sources often assumed the disturbing form of "talk, rumor, and gossip" and were almost completely dominated by "counterrevolutionary" forces—"popes, sorceresses, . . . nepmen, former landowners, and various other white-guard gangs."[41] In the tales about Lenin as the Antichrist, anti-Soviet miracles, and wonder-working icons and in rumors of war, taxes, UFOs, meteorites, and the end of the world itself, Shafir detected a degree of consistency and overlap that suggested organized campaigns against the Bolsheviks and urged in his report that, particularly in those regions where the paper was little read, more attention be directed toward what he called "oral literature" *(ustnaia slovesnost').*[42]

For a variety of practical reasons, then, the early battle for verbal authority took place largely through oral modes of communication. Bolshevik agitators, orators, and political activists canvassed factories, villages, Red Army divisions, and town squares, traveling to outlying regions on "agitational trains," delivering news, information, and the party message to the periphery. One of the more common methods for communicating with the masses was the "living newspaper" *(zhivaia gazeta)*, a generic hybrid that combined the public reading of the daily news with factual and ideological elucidations. Oftentimes (much to the dismay of the more orthodox party officials), these "performances" more closely resembled variety shows than agitational sessions.[43] But the basic principle was the same—to disseminate information and interpretations of recent events through a medium readily accessible to more remote and less literate members of the population. One agitator's report appearing in the trade magazine *Red Journalist* suggests how the forum functioned as a kind of linguistic indoctrination, or at least elucidation:

> You should have seen how the public crowded around me from all the train cars and all sides of the platform. In a minute, a crowd of 150–200 people had gathered. Sitting on the stairs, I began to read slowly and precisely. No matter how popular the newspaper style, some fairly difficult sections nevertheless arose, especially in the articles. When this happened, I would provide explanations right on the spot. They listened to me with great attention. When I finished reading the summary of operations, some in the audience unfamiliar with our military affairs began to question me in detail about the front-line effort. Others asked questions on general political

themes. Five-to-ten minutes of such discussion passed. During this time, some of the surrounding crowd dispersed, while new people approached. They began to ask me to read the paper again, which I did. As a result, I served 300 people with one newspaper.[44]

Beyond their practical advantages, such intermediate forms of public discourse—halfway between the literate and educated world of newspapers and party speeches, on the one hand, and the illiterate and "dark" world of the masses, on the other—proved exceptionally effective at both articulating and appealing to the spirit of revolution. The symbolic appeal of such public "talk" caught the eye of the American journalist John Reed, who in his famous documentary of the events of October 1917 described the sense of import and urgency surrounding the spoken word: "Lectures, debates, speeches. . . . Meetings in the trenches at the front, in village squares, factories. . . . What a marvelous sight to see Putilovsky Zavod pour out its forty thousand to listen to Social Democrats, Socialist Revolutionaries, Anarchists, anybody, whatever they had to say, as long as they would talk! For months in Petrograd, and all over Russia, every street-corner was a public tribune. In railway trains, street-cars, always the spurting up of impromptu debate, everywhere."[45]

Oratory and public speaking became both a medium and symbol for a revolutionary zeal that not only called for the abandonment of old, canonical ideas but also demanded "fresher" and "livelier" forms of speech by which to escape the world of dead institutions and thought. As one contemporary commentator put it, the reemergence of the spoken word had begun to reclaim the rightful place of the divine Logos from the previously dominant (bourgeois) bureaucratic, written word.[46] Lenin, Trotsky, Zinoviev, and other Bolshevik leaders—following in the great tradition of orators stretching from antiquity to the French Revolution—demonstrated the power of eloquence in inspiring, persuading, and inciting the masses. In a society in the midst of fundamental social and political transformation, it was essential that those masses take an active role in the construction process—at most, by becoming "activists" themselves; at least, by sacrificing time and energy toward realizing the visions of a new society.

THE INSTITUTIONALIZATION OF THE "LIVING WORD"

Beyond the popularity of the "living newspaper," a number of institutional changes point to an overall renaissance of what, in early Soviet parlance, was referred to as the "living language" *(zhivoi iazyk)* or "living word" *(zhivoe slovo)*. Although the terms themselves date back at least to the nineteenth-century lexicon of the populist writer Vladimir Dal', they acquired new prominence and mystique in the context of revolution.[47] In the realm of higher education, "Institutes of the Living Word" appeared in both Petrograd and Moscow, each dedicated to research and training in various spheres of public speaking. Beginning in 1918, the Petrograd-based Institute offered more than 800 students a year a curriculum divided across four disciplines—oratory, pedagogy, literature, and drama.[48] In a speech at its formal opening, the commissar of education, Anatolii Lunacharskii, asserted the central role of such institutes in "returning the living word to the people" and enabling a "gigantic dawn of speech," because "a person who remained silent in a time of political crisis was only a half-person."[49] At primary levels of training, grammar textbooks trumpeted the arrival of the revolutionary era of the living word.[50] Grade-school children and adult-education groups attended classes in politically correct storytelling (rasskazyvanie) and the "collective declamation" of poetry.[51] One of the more popular Russian language textbooks of the decade echoed the theme of citizen participation in social construction in its section on "Protocols," emphasizing both the increased importance of public gatherings and the empowerment afforded those who participated in them. Participation in such meetings accustomed the "masses" to "collective activity" and permitted them "to change living reality."[52] In literature classes, teachers were encouraged to complement fictional readings with organized conferences replete with orators, socially relevant debates, and even trials of fictional heroes and villains—all in order to "draw [students'] attention to the thick of life" and "stimulate their involvement in it."[53]

Outside the academy and schools, the Proletarian Culture movement (commonly referred to by the Soviet-style stump-compound, "Proletcult") was the most established venue for the cultural development of new Soviet citizens, providing forums for workers and peasants to read and develop their writing skills.[54] Though it became subordinated to the central government in 1920, the organization's grassroots activity continued throughout the decade, making fiction more accessible to a population previously marginalized by its inability to read and write. The literary products of the organization, though limited and largely mediocre, nevertheless reinforced the symbolic force of the spoken word, often casting it in mystical overtones that have come to be recognized as a characteristic feature of Proletcult prose. A 1918 story appearing in the Proletcult journal The Future (Griadushchee), for instance, described factory halls transformed into mighty sanctuaries where the speech of orators "poured over the crowd evenly and flowingly in a mighty, vigorous stream."[55] An orator in a 1919 sketch used his voice to convert masses antagonistically disposed toward Bolshevism ("mighty, like thunder, it engrossed the entire factory") and to "weld" the crowd into a united whole by articulating its "most secret thoughts." ("In another few minutes, the meeting was listening to his speech as if bewitched [zacharovan-noe], and every word escaping the lips of the comrade poured out beneath the hot blue sky and struck against the soot-covered factory walls; every thought shrouded by him in words was the most secret thought of everyone").[56] Yet another sketch, appearing in *The Flame (Plamia)*, described how a poorly educated worker-protagonist named Antonov was swept up by an orator's speech, the words of which he could barely understand (a kind of proletarian glossolalia):

> The thoughts, like rocks, turned heavily in his impoverished, beaten head, and it was hard for him to keep up with the speech of the tall, agile man in glasses and understand what he was talking about. While the word was pounding itself into Antonov's brain, becoming lucid and alive, the man in glasses had already gone far ahead.
>
> But one thing was clear: the man was talking in radiant, colorful words about him, about his beggarly life.[57]

The journalistic venue for upstart writers, often referred to with the ungainly stump-compound *rabsel'korovskoe dvizhenie* (the "worker-village correspondent movement"), took shape entirely under the direction of the state, and it brought hundreds of thousands of peasant and working-class writers to the pages of local and central newspapers. Spearheaded at *Pravda* in 1919 by such influential party leaders as Mariia Ul'ianova (Lenin's sister) and Nikolai Bukharin, the movement ostensibly sought to give "the voice of the people" direct access to the pages of the state-run press. Newspapers encouraged worker and village correspondents *(rabkory* and *sel'kory)* to send letters describing the everyday conditions of their homes, communities, and workplaces and often assigned specific themes for investigation.[58] By publishing the letters, editors hoped both to make the papers more appealing to the "mass reader" and to flush out growing instances of local corruption in the countryside. Over the course of the 1920s, the movement mushroomed in size and demographic scope, soon giving rise to *voenkory* (military correspondents), *zhenkory* (women correspondents), *iunkory* (youth correspondents), and even *pikory* ("Pioneer" correspondents).[59] As the first serious state-run organization of "popular" language centered around the press, the movement became a particularly important battleground for competing models of writing for the new Soviet citizen.[60]

As with specialists in the fields of education, literature, and journalism, linguists and philologists also demonstrated serious interest in the living language of revolutionary Russia. Although the turn to a more sociolinguistic approach to language study predated October 1917 and extended beyond the borders of Russia, it assumed an increasingly prominent, even urgent, appeal in the context and spirit of social reconstruction.[61] A 1920 budget proposal of the Moscow Linguistics Circle, whose members included many of the leading young linguists and philologists of the day, declared that "the drive toward studying living, contemporary phenomena that has always characterized the work of the circle has now found broad application."[62] Meeting notes from 1919–1922 back up that somewhat self-serving pronouncement with more reliable evidence of its active interest in the study of the living word. The circle dedicated two of its weekly sessions, for example, to a report on the revolution's influence on contemporary legends and their link to politics, delivered by the folklorist Iurii Sokolov and attended by the likes of Grigorii Vinokur, Petr Bogatyrev, Osip Brik, Roman Jakobson, and Mikhail Peterson.[63] It also hosted talks on "Factory Neologisms," "Contemporary Words Formed from Acronyms," and the need "to study the language processes connected to the war and revolution," the last of which sparked plans to create an archive of "contemporary living language."[64]

Although only scant evidence of the project's realization can be found, several of the group's members wrote about the language of the war and revolutionary epoch in separate works published during the 1920s, and even more contributed to the new but growing body of scholarship with a sociolinguistic orientation.[65] In a similar spirit, the faculty of the Institute of the Living Word declared as its main research goals the formation of a discipline devoted to "the art of speech" and "the study of the influence of the war and revolution on the Russian language."[66] The State Academy for the Study of the Arts provided another center for specialists interested in the study of public speaking, where commissions dedicated to "The Study of the Living Word" and "The Study of the Effect of the Persuasive Word" met regularly to discuss both historical and theoretical aspects of oratory.[67] The second group organized its agenda around oratorical models from various historical periods, beginning with antiquity, continuing through the French Revolution and the tsarist Duma, and including the oratory of great contemporary speakers, such as Lenin, Trotsky, Lunacharskii, Grigorii Zinoviev, Lev Kamenev, and Klara Tsetkin.[68] Among the main psychosocial processes identified at the commission's opening meeting as being key to effective oratory were the orator's ability to facilitate the individual's loss of "attributes distinctive to his personality and enter into the ranks of the collective 'I'" and the orator's ability, through "praise, picturesque speech, mimicry, gestures, [and] the mastery of verbal rhythm," to "lull the criticism of vigilant consciousness and gain access for suggestive influence on the subconscious."[69]

WHEN WORDS GET IN THE WAY

The logic of academic commissions did not always correspond to the messier realities of a language culture in flux. With the new Bolshevik ideology came a manner of speaking and writing that was equally new for most citizens and, oftentimes, most confusing. Its more prominent features included an array of neologisms, acronyms, stump-compounds, and loanwords, extant Russian words with changed meanings, and an odd stylistic mixture of bureaucratese, nonstandard slang, and high Marxist rhetoric. As the discourse became increasingly productive, so, too, grew the evidence that it was either incomprehensible to, or—still worse—misinterpreted by, large portions of the population. What to the "revolutionary vanguard" had been no less than a charismatic "gift of tongues" was, for many peasant and working-class citizens, little more than a mystifying babble. Instead of adopting the language as their own, peasant and working-class citizens in particular expressed frustration, alienation, and mistrust toward the "language of authority" *(iazyk vlasti)* and turned away in great numbers from newspapers, agitators, and the party itself.[70]

Even those who welcomed the new language structures as a source of newfound empowerment often invoked it in inappropriate ways, thereby impeding the process of legitimation. Both accidental and intentional parodies undermined the new leadership's search for verbal authority and subverted its self-fashioned revolutionary identity. This essential conflict between the need for a new, authoritative "tongue" befitting the state and citizens of the future and the need for a semiliterate population to understand and identify with the message of that discourse created a profound political, social, and cultural dilemma. Before every orator who boasted the fiery eloquence of a Lenin or Trotsky—two of the most celebrated Bolshevik rhetoricians—there stood an army of tongue-tied citizens, either entirely deaf to the emerging discourse of power or inadequately versed in it. How does a reborn society go about bridging such a fundamental communication gap? How do leaders and institutions with the authority and influence to do so cultivate, out of the chaos and rubble of war and revolution, an authoritative language of state that is both capable of articulating its ideas and accessible to common citizens who not only must comprehend the ideas but acquire and reproduce the language themselves?

The interdisciplinary discussions, representations, and resolutions of that dilemma form the focus of this study. Using material from a wide range of sources—from literary, linguistic, and journalistic debates to school curricula and how-to manuals for beginning writers and orators—I describe the contours of sometimes competing, sometimes overlapping models of language that coexisted in the early years of state building. In the process of tracing these voices, I discuss the underlying implications of their characteristic notions of authority and identity and, in the end, suggest how each contributed to the more uniform language of state that became firmly established by the mid-1930s. While the institutions central to this discussion (journalism, education, linguistics, and literature) were by no means the only ones involved in the production, dissemination, and legitimation of authoritative language, they do account—in the case of early Soviet Russia—for the vast majority of the discussion about language and voice that took place.[71]

Given the prominence of newspapers in the Bolshevik mobilization campaigns, the language of the press drew considerable attention from cultural leaders and trade specialists alike. Newspapers were at once the most common printed channels of official communication for a majority of the population and, quite frequently, the sources of the most extreme examples of language innovation or mutilation (depending on one's perspective). Compounding the importance of style in the press was the postrevolutionary boom of amateur journalists with either working-class or rural roots and, more often than not, an imperfect knowledge of both standard Russian and the new Bolshevik phraseology. The need to educate these cadres of *rabkory* (worker correspondents) and *sel'kory* (village correspondents) posed fundamental questions of voice (What language[s] were they to employ in constructing their reports?) and led to still broader problems concerning the linguistic identity and authority of the new Soviet state itself.

For similar reasons, the language problem captured the attention of the educational establishment. Very early on, language and literature textbooks and curricula began to incorporate and reflect the new language of Bolshevism, and teachers and pedagogues openly debated the problems they encountered in the classroom with respect to the sudden shifts in acceptable standards and codes. As in other spheres, the models for speaking and writing presented to students generally reflected specific ideas as to where authority should or did lie. The question of how a student was to speak and write became integrally linked to the more general task of shaping young Soviet citizens. The interrelationship was acutely felt, because a large portion of the "student" population consisted of nonreading adults whose education through literacy programs was of paramount importance for the successful transmission of Bolshevik ideas.

Linguists likewise had an influential hand in the reformation of language identity and authority. The Russian philosopher of language Valentin Voloshinov expressed this influence most aptly when he wrote that "[h]istory knows no nation whose sacred writings or oral traditions were not to some degree in a language foreign and incomprehensible to the profane. To decipher the mystery of sacred words was the task meant to be carried out by the priest-philologists."[72] It was linguists and philologists who compiled dictionaries and glossaries, wrote grammars, and defined and redefined "standards" and "norms" and, in so doing, helped determine, in effect, what "counted" as legitimate language and what did not. It was they who generated analyses of the new language culture of the day in books, pamphlets, and articles that frequently ventured beyond relatively neutral, scientific description into the realm of *proscription*.[73] Most of the leading linguists of the period actively contributed to the discussion and transformation of early Soviet language culture and encouraged—with a variety of motives—the contextualization of those discussions within the broader issues of authority and identity.[74]

Finally, given their special adeptness at verbal representation, writers played a critical role in making symbolic sense (or nonsense) out of the often chaotic, conflicting, and incoherent values and ideas cluttering the postrevolutionary landscape.[75] Russian literature of the 1920s, in particular, exhibited wide and conscious experimentation in language and voice and was charged with a sense of urgency and import that stemmed from Russia's traditionally high regard for the writer and the power of the word (as expressed in the Mandel'shtam quote serving as epigraph to this introduction) and compounded by the "hunger of the modern state" and its race against time.[76] To a degree often difficult to appreciate in Western society at the turn of the twenty-first century, early Soviet intellectuals representing a broad range of movements and ideas were keenly sensitive to the power of the pen and the writer's responsibility in giving voice to revolutionary culture and society.

The breadth and depth of their awareness largely accounts for the eclectic array of fictional works discussed in these pages. While they all share, implicitly or explicitly, a common concern for the interrelationship between language, authority, and identity, I have purposely taken care to select a body of literature that most aptly reflects the diversity of voices that helped shape the language culture of the times. For this reason, alongside such well-known writers as Isaac Babel', Vladimir Maiakovskii, Boris Pil'niak, and Andrei Platonov, the works of largely forgotten authors—such as Aleksandr Arosev, Soph'ia Fedorchenko, Nikolai Ognev, and Lidiia Seifullina—also appear, as do representative excerpts from the often broken and coarse voices of the novice writers who sprouted and were nurtured in the hothouse of early Soviet letters. For similar reasons, I make no attempt to offer comprehensive readings of the collected works of any of the writers at hand: instead, I limit my discussion of fictional works to the specific issues of language, narrative, and voice. How does an author's narrative voice contribute to the construction of its fictional world? How do speech traits and writing styles reflect and comment on the identity and authority not only of the characters depicted but of the storytellers themselves? Who is bestowed with the "gift of tongues," employing the language of state in appropriate contexts with authority and conviction? Who, in contrast, is verbally mocked, condemned to babble, or silenced altogether?

This focused set of questions imposes a political and historical dimension on my literary analyses that may make some students of literature squeamish. In the context of a study of language culture, however, such an approach is not only justified but should also provide insight into the uneasy mutual determination that characterizes literature's relationship with other institutions responsible for the production and legitimation of language as well as insight into the negotiation of meaning in times of radical change.[77] As sensitive as state authorities were to the didactic function of literature—exemplified by their direct participation in literary debates and by the scores of state-sponsored readership studies of the 1920s and early 1930s—so too were legions of writers keenly aware of the state's pervasive influence on the broadly manipulated and highly vulnerable Russian literary language. The state depended as much on the traditional authority of the literary language as early Soviet writers depended on the emerging language of state for their own narrative expressions. It was an uneasy, often contentious, relationship that inspired some of the best and some of the most perverse narratives of the day.[78]

After documenting, in chapter 1, the linguistic features most commonly associated with the early revolutionary language culture as well as the broad dimensions of the resulting communication gap, I dedicate the rest of the book to the proposed solutions to that crisis and the processes by which the linguistic order and authority of the mid-1930s came to eclipse the chaos that characterized the postrevolutionary years. In doing so, I posit four primary models of language—revolutionary, popular, national, and party-state—which emerge from an analysis of the plethora of printed material addressing the issue between 1917 and 1934. As with any hermeneutic system, these models, or "voices" as I also call them, are abstractions, or "ideal types": no single document represents the perfect expression of any one model, nor are all the models mutually exclusive.[79] In fact, one often finds overlap between the voices and, at times, even total agreement. The differences, nevertheless, are salient enough to identify overall distinctions in the implicit assumptions a given model makes as to where and with whom lies the greatest linguistic authority, which modes of communication, or "speech genres," are most appropriate for expressing that authority, and which speakers and writers best articulate the desired collective identity of the Soviet state and its citizens.[80]

My differentiation of ideal-typical models finds further justification in the degree to which one can detect rises and falls in the authority, or "linguistic capital," of the different models during the period in question.[81] The revolutionary model, for instance, with its emphasis on language's revitalizing and inspirational potential and its ability to empower speakers and writers by articulating novel visions and ideas, enjoyed its greatest amount of authority in the years just before and after October 1917. The popular voice, to the degree that it also envisioned a radical upheaval in the social distribution of linguistic authority, shared some of the utopian features evident in the revolutionary model. But, with its greater sensitivity to the communicative strengths *and* weakness of the "voice of the people," or *glas naroda*, its peak in linguistic authority followed that of the revolutionary model (in the early to mid-1920s), just as, in the terms of Max Weber, the mundane reality of everyday life tends to simplify, or "routinize," the high-flying eloquence of charismatic authority. The national voice grew in authority in the mid- to late 1920s, embraced by a growing number of cultural leaders as a much-needed antidote to the excessive experimentation and mediocrity of writers writing in a revolutionary or popular vein. In its vision of a "standard" national language rooted in the Russian realist "classics," moreover, the national model of language marked a fundamental shift in authority from oral to written modes of communication, from a revolutionary culture bent on innovation to a more established culture of canonical norms. Although the national voice proved a particularly potent tool for establishing verbal authority in the new Soviet society, all three of these models of language strongly influenced—both ideologically and stylistically, by both positive and negative example—the party-state model that emerged as the dominant, authoritative language of state by the middle of the 1930s. More than the result of a decade-long process of centralized control of information and the channels of communication, the language of the party-state proved so powerful largely owing to the effectiveness with which it discarded the weaknesses and absorbed the strengths of the competing models of public discourse that preceded it.

• • •

Without doubt, the Bolsheviks' early reliance on oral modes of communication such as oratory, the "living newspaper," storytelling, and recitations arose largely out of a practical need caused by the breakdown of print media and the high rate of illiteracy among its would-be citizens. The need to "get out the word" was especially acute at a time when little else but language and ideas could be offered as a concrete sign of the new social and political order. The "living word" thus gave citizens more direct and immediate access to the language, symbols, and visions of the new society and encouraged their active participation in its verbal construction. Yet the new emphasis on "living language" arose from more than just rational pragmatism. In addition to its numerous genetic links to prerevolutionary Russian language cultures and influences, it reflected the general utopian spirit of the time, the belief that all aspects of society, including speech, could and must be leveled and built anew. Particularly in light of the social, political, industrial, and aesthetic transformations witnessed by Russia since the turn of the century and culminating in the onset of Bolshevik rule, it was a vision with symbolic breadth and depth far greater than even Peter the Great could have imagined.

Precisely for that reason, it also carried with it potential dangers unimaginable in previous periods of language crisis. As much as they enabled the vision of a radically new linguistic order the advances in technology, shifts in demographics, and angst of modernization greatly complicated the possible verbal permutations of that order, giving rise to a variety of voices competing for authority and power in defining the verbal contours of the new state and its citizenry. Especially when it became clear that the language of Bolshevism was indeed assuming altered forms and that those forms were being consumed and reproduced by the population in often unanticipated and undesired ways, all who enjoyed positions of influence over the emerging language of state recognized that the problem at hand went far deeper than accidental slips of the pen and tongue.

One of the essential ingredients to all instances of language cultures-in-crisis is the tension between contradictory attitudes toward the nature and function of language itself, a tension aptly captured in the concept adopted for the main title of this book. "Speaking in tongues," the "gift of tongues," or "glossolalia" all contain a range of meanings that extends between the opposite poles of divine understanding and mundane confusion. In one sense, the terms refer to the miraculous power of communication bestowed upon Jesus' apostles (after a visit from the Holy Spirit on the Pentecost), whose prophesies to a crowd of "God-fearing Jews from every nation under heaven" were immediately understood in the native tongue of each individual listener.[82] Theirs was a universal language with the power to convey a revolutionary message to the as yet unbelieving, in both an authoritative and meaningful way. A second sense of the term denotes a similarly ecstatic language, but one whose meaning is shared only by a chosen few of a given community and is perceived as gibberish by all the rest. This is the sense used in modern charismatic movements such as Pentecostalism and in Paul's first letter to the Corinthians, in which the apostle acknowledges the divine inspiration of such language but questions its didactic benefit. Like the first, this second sense of "tongues" implies a language of power and authority, but one predicated primarily on membership: if you belong, you have access to the gift; if you do not, it is at best a power-wielding babble. Indeed, a third, more secular, understanding of the term deprives it of any ecstatic or charismatic roots whatsoever: "speaking in tongues" or "glossolalia" in this sense simply means "unintelligible speech, gibberish."[83] The metaphor swings to the opposite biblical pole—from the ubiquitous and prophetic utterances of the Pentecost, to the chaos and confusion of Babel.[84] By mapping out the institutional forces, the critical debates, and the fictional representations of the language culture of early Soviet Russia, this book explores the process by which the utopian visions of a revolutionary, charismatic "tongue" became mired in a sea of Babelian confusion and, eventually, evolved into a more restrictive, membership-driven cant of sacred authority.

THE CONTOURS OF THE

COMMUNICATION GAP

In the very act of linguistic expression our perceptions assume a new form. They are no longer isolated data; they give up their individual character; they are brought under class-concepts which are designated by general "names." The act of "naming" does not simply add a mere conventional sign to a ready-made thing—to an object known before. It is rather a pre-requisite of the very conception of objects; of the idea of an objective empirical reality.

—Ernst Cassirer, *The Myth of the State*

"He's speaking incomprehensibly—must mean he's a Bolshevik."

—Comment overheard by *Rabochaia Moskva* columnist in 1926.

According to the book of Genesis, the first instance of "naming" was also the most perfect. After creating man and woman in his image, God bestowed upon Adam the power of giving names to the animals and trees in the Garden of Eden. Later interpretations of the event elaborated on the nature of this "Adamic language" used before the Fall, citing as its most important feature the direct correspondence between name and thing. With their succumbing to temptation and subsequent discovery of good and evil, humans lost the ability to capture the essence of a thing in its very name; language became a conglomerate of arbitrary signs, even a source of Babelian incomprehensibility.

Bolshevik efforts to rearticulate postrevolutionary public discourse reflected a cognizance of the Adamic power of the word in giving shape to reality. Though some of the bolder philosophers of the word, such as Andrei Bely and Velimir Khlebnikov, experimented with ways of rediscovering the essence of a concept through renaming, more conventional Bolshevik "Adams" set about the more humble task of merely redefining the verbal landscape to symbolize, with greater success and immediacy than they could hope for in other spheres, the coming of a new age, a new authority. While in many ways they were successful at redefining both the landscape and the terms of debate, they nevertheless fell notably short of restoring the Edenic link between name and thing. First, and most important, they were only one of many sources of linguistic influence—and a source, given their tenuous hold on power and the shoddy state of mass communication, that was imperfect at best. Second, the Bolshevik party, especially in the early stages of revolution, by no means presented a single voice or even a coherent "party line" all through its ranks. And, finally, even when the message from the "top" reached the population in a more or less unadulterated form, there was no telling how that message then would be received and transformed by speaking and writing citizens.

The language of Bolshevism, then, was largely a symbolic work in progress, an unfinished piece of fiction whose style and direction were subjected to influences far beyond the directives of the Bolshevik leadership. Although there is no doubt the Bolshevik party, by virtue of its power over the channels of communication and the flow of information, had greater influence than any other actor in the battle for linguistic authority, it was still one of many contributing to the cacophonous mix of linguistic raw material that formed the early revolutionary language culture—and from which a more coherent, more authoritative (but no less fictional) language of the Soviet state would eventually emerge. A better understanding of the dynamics of that process lies in the language of revolution itself and in the early reactions to it from key portions of the population. What were the distinguishing features of the linguistic raw material that, despite its complex origins, came to be associated with the new Bolshevik order and served as the source of such volatile confusion, reappropriation, and debate?

CATALOGING THE LANGUAGE OF REVOLUTION

One of the more common forms of linguistic practice engaged in by Valentin Voloshinov's "priest-philologists" was the basic description of the changes that had taken place in the Russian language since October 1917 (and earlier, in some cases). Despite the relatively large number of such accounts appearing between 1919 and 1929 and the variety of interpretive biases, they show considerable overlap in their views of the defining features and their origins. Of the dozen or so books and articles published by trained linguists and dedicated specifically to the changes in contemporary Russian, seven are of particular note for both their insight and their prominence in the broader language debates: Barannikov (1919), Mazon (1920), Jakobson (1920–21), Kartsevskii (1923), Polivanov (1927), Selishchev (1928), and Chernykh (1929).[1]

When describing the defining features of the language of the revolutionary period, most of the accounts look at three different levels: lexicon, word formation, and style.[2] All agree that the most substantial changes had taken place in the area of lexicon, and each author identifies most, if not all, of the following features:

1) **words or phrases that had disappeared from everyday usage**, had been relegated to the realm of historicisms *(tsar', kniaz', graf, zemstvo, Senat, Sinod, gimnaziia)*, and, in some cases, had been forcibly replaced by Soviet alternatives *(gorodovoi —> militsioner, ministr —> komissar, chinovnik —> sovetskii sluzhashchii, soldat —> krasnoarmeiets, zhalovanie —> zarplata, prisluga —> domrabotnitsa, prazdnik —> den' otdykha)*;[3]

2) **words that had undergone semantic shifts over the course of the revolutionary period** *(gospodin, tovarishch, barin, partiinyi, burzhui, intelligent, shef, iacheika, chistka)*;[4]

3) **the sharp increase in words borrowed from foreign languages**— especially ones describing new phenomena in social, political, and economic spheres *(demonstratsiia, revoliutsiia, agitatsiia, miting, mandat, rezoliutsiia, deputat, delegat, kommuna, proletariat, burzhuaziia, boikot, diskussiia, platforma, privilegiia, repressiia, lozung, shtreikbrekher, deklassirovannyi, konstatirovat', fordizatsiia)*;[5]

4) **the militarization of everyday language**, through the use of military terminology in a metaphorical manner to describe nonmilitary notions *(front, bor'ba, liniia, armiia, orudie, mobilizatsiia, nastuplenie, udarnyi)*;[6]

5) **the onslaught of neologisms**, specifically in the form of **acronyms** ("literal": *ChK [Chrezvychainaia komissiia po bor'be s kontrrevoliutsiei, sabbotazhem i spekuliatsiei], RSFSR [Rossiiskaia Sovetskaia Federativnaia Sotsialisticheskaia Respublika], SR [sotsialist-revoliutsioner], SSSR [USSR], TsK [Tsentral'nyi komitet]*; "syllabic": *BUP [Biuro Ukrainskoi Pechati], GUVUZ [Glavnoe Upravlenie Voenno-Uchebnykh Zavedenii], GVIU [Glavnoe Voenno-Inzhenernoe Upravlenie], MONO [Moskovskii Otdel Narodnogo Obrazovaniia], NEP [Novaia ekonomicheskaia politika], STO [Sovet Truda i Oborony], TsIK [Tsentral'nyi Ispolnitel'nyi Komitet]*); and "**stump-compounds**": *(Glavbum [Glavnoe upravlenie bumazhnoi promyshlennosti], Ispolkom [Ispolnitel'nyi komitet], Gubprodkom [Gubernskaia prodovol'stvennaia komissiia], Komintern [Kommunisticheskii Internatsional], nachdiv [nachal'nik divizii], Narkompros [Narodnyi Kommissariat Prosveshcheniia], rabkor [rabochii korrespondent], Proletkul't, Sovnarkhoz [Sovet narodnogo khoziaistva])*.[7]

The last three features stand out most prominently in the discussions, with most of the scholars tracing their origins before October 1917. The French Revolution provided numerous political, social, and economic terms *(kommuna [Fr. commune], biurokrat [bureaucrate], revoliutsioner [révolutionnaire], ekspropriatsiia [expropriation], propaganda [propagande], massy [masse—in the meaning of human rather than material masses], soznatel'nyi i organizovanyi rabochii [ouvrier conscient et organisé])*, as did the

Russian revolutionary movements of the 1880s and 1890s (*krasnyi* [to refer to someone or something "revolutionary"]) and the reforms following 1905 *(agrarnyi, anarkhizm, biurokratiia, demokratiia, kvorum, kollektiv, lozung, komitet [partiinyi], mandat, orator).*[8] Several accounts trace the acronyms and stump-compounds back to telegraphic communication of the war years, when conservation of both time and space was of the utmost importance; others go back still further to the names of agencies and private organizations in prerevolutionary Russia *(Lenzoto [Lenskoe zoloto-promyshlennoe tovarishchestvo], Prodamet [Obshchestvo dlia prodazhi russkikh metallicheskikh izdelii]).*[9] All accounts point out that, although the models for these forms may not have been entirely new, their collective prominence in the language culture associated with the Bolshevik assumption of power certainly was.

The linguists make similar observations about word formation. None of the nominal suffixes identified as especially productive in the revolutionary language culture was entirely new (e.g., *-ets [krasnoarmeiets, leninets, kornilovets]*, *-ik [bol'shevik, massovik, shkol'nik, udarnik]*, *-shchina [kolchakovshchina, kerenshchina, belogvardeishchina]*, *-ka [kerenka, listovka, govorilka]*, *-tel' [soglashatel']).* Some were clearly of foreign origin *(-ist, -izm, -ant, -ator [aktivist, kommunist, trotskist, chekist, bol'shevizm, tsarizm, spekuliant, sabotant, agitator, likvidator])*, but all could be found in prerevolutionary Russian. The same went for verb formation. While forms with infixes in *-nu- (spekul'nut', mobiliznut', cheknut')*, and *-ova-/-izova-/-irova- (mitingovat', natsionalizovat', proletarizovat', agitirovat', sovetizirovat')* may have become more productive during the war and revolutionary period, the forms were certainly not new to the language.[10]

Most of the studies also refer to significant shifts in style and tone. Stylistic shifts stemmed primarily from an influx of words, phrases, and expressions previously located outside the bounds of the "standard" literary language—either in the coarse speech of the streets or the technical jargon of sociology, economics, and political philosophy. In accounting for this stylistic shift, some of the linguists describe it as the sort of verbal jolt that is inevitable whenever a new group or class takes control of the reins of power.[11] Others attribute it more specifically to the increased public participation of new, less trained and experienced speakers and writers.[12] Still others ascribe it to a certain vulgarity or general disdain on the part of Bolshevik culture for the traditional markers of "bourgeois" civility—a form of linguistic "leveling" akin to that which took place in other spheres of life.[13] Other factors contributing to the stylistic shift included the influence of local dialects on all levels of the literary language; the rise in prominence of certain class or professional jargon, such as the vocabulary of the factory, peasants, thieves, or youths; and the growth of the Soviet bureaucracy, notorious for its penchant for complex sentences and deverbal nouns.[14] In addition to this stylistic hybridization of public discourse, linguists also note its heightened emotional markedness—a feature they attribute to the increased import and prevalence of public oratory and agitation.[15]

Any one of the novel features described in isolation might have had little effect on the general contour of and attitude toward public discourse. Only Barannikov goes so far as to call the changes "revolutionary" from a linguistic standpoint. But the often chaotic combination of many or all of the features in the most prominent spheres of the printed and spoken word had an enormous impact on both the language and public perceptions of it. The large influx of neologisms and loanwords, for instance, when combined with bureaucratese and agitational slogans, gave rise to a stark new style of speaking and writing, which appeared in any number of permutations when it was employed by a growing number of newly empowered but inexperienced speakers and writers. Taken together, then, the massive shifts in the postrevolutionary language culture gave rise to a verbal cacophony in the main arenas of public communication, where incomprehension on the part of the intended audience was quite often the rule, rather than the exception.

GAUGING REACTIONS TO THE NEW LINGUISTIC (DIS)ORDER

The number of studies devoted to the popular reception of the new language phenomena alone attests to the degree of official and professional concern regarding effective communication with rank-and-file citizens. Most of these studies pointed to a distinct problem in comprehension, primarily on the part of the less educated members of the peasantry and, to a lesser degree, among the urban working class. Barannikov, for example, discovered problems with the new lexicon during field studies in Petrograd, Samara, and the Poltava province. Most troubling among them were mispronunciations that strongly suggested conscious subversion in the form of punning and word play. In the speech practices of some informants, for example, an "operational army" became a "virginal army" *(deistvuiushchaia armiia —> devstvuiushchaia armiia)*, a "militiaman" became a "hypocrite" *(militsioner —> litsimer)*, and key words such as "proletariat" and "revolution" were reduced to comical nonsense words—*pereletarii* and *levorutsiia*.[16] Too symbolically potent to be dismissed as accidental, this sort of folk etymology, like the gossip and rumors of Iakov Shafir's "oral literature," invited conjecture about popular verbal resistance.

Fieldwork conducted by Selishchev at three Moscow factories in 1925 showed mixed success on the part of urban workers at comprehending and correctly using the new language material.[17] On the one hand, he found signs of successful acquisition, especially among what he called "the intellectually developed and more economically well-off" and the "active participants in the social-political life of the plant and factory."[18] For these groups, it was a language of empowerment. On the other hand, traces of dialect and misuse were readily detectable, ranging from phonetic and lexical variants to alternative renditions of revolutionary terminology.[19] In some of the more disconcerting cases, younger factory workers had begun to use thieves' jargon in order to "distinguish themselves from the intelligentsia," referring to it as their own "proletarian language."[20]

Beyond the ideologically troubling equation of proletarians and thieves, this sort of innovation greatly contributed to grade-school teachers' concern about declining levels of literacy.[21] One instructor warned that the language of thieves and *besprizorniki* (homeless waifs) was undergoing a naturalization process, infiltrating the public sphere and becoming standard fare for the speaking and writing population at large. His sober account called it a "natural experiment" that could not be stopped.[22] In a somewhat less dire analysis, "On the Perversion and Coarsening of Student Speech," another pedagogue admitted that much of the street jargon brought into the classroom by contemporary youth was simply a product of age.[23] But she still saw ample cause for concern, noting that the coarseness had grown more intense under Soviet power and that students' language skills had fallen markedly.[24] Among the factors contributing to the decline were the growing prominence of *besprizorniki*, whose language was heavily laden with thieves' argot; the general pervasiveness of vulgar speech in public places (sites listed included schools, tramcars, theaters, and literature); the massive influx of foreign words; and the increasing prevalence in daily life of newspapers and oratory.[25] The overly complex and bureaucratic style of both newspapers and oratory forced students who dutifully listened and participated "to master all sorts of linguistic clichés" that only hindered their verbal development.[26] The new emphasis on public discourse, she concluded, was too much to handle for the student "of little culture," leading more often than not to grave and frequent perversions of standard literary Russian.

Studies of the reception and production of the emerging language of state among schoolchildren seemed to corroborate these concerns. As late as 1928, one report concluded that most seven- to twelve-year-olds had only a vague notion of such basic concepts as "Lenin," "Communists," and "Pioneers" and characterized the majority of definitions as either "clichéd" or "absurd." Its author lambasted the system for leading students into a verbal "fog" and "cacophony" that would more likely "deaden" than develop students' conscious and critical understanding of social relationships.[27] A 1929 report listed the three main difficulties faced by schoolchildren in their language skills as "improper use of foreign words," "use of dialectisms [and] vulgarisms," and "overly concrete perception of abstract concepts."[28] Overall, then, while cultural leaders could find some grounds for reassurance that the message was getting out to Soviet youth, the majority of studies and accounts of verbal reception (and reproduction) presented a troubling portrait of miscues—ranging from reappropriation by subgroups intent on establishing alternative identities (such as members of the Communist Youth League, or Komsomol) to vulgarization and complete lack of comprehension.

Perhaps even more distressing was the degree to which Red Army soldiers misunderstood the new language of the official public sphere. Despite the state's concerted efforts to provide them with both basic and political literacy, several studies pointed to a considerable gap in communication. The most extensive of these was the psychologist Isaak Shpil'rein's *Language of the Red Army Soldier*.[29] Working at military bases outside Moscow in 1924 and 1925, Shpil'rein investigated soldiers' active and passive knowledge of the language of contemporary sociopolitical affairs. The "great majority" of them were peasant youths from the countryside—one of the segments of the population most lagging in literacy, but one of the most important for the future of the country. Their term in the Red Army offered the best and perhaps only opportunity for the state to exert on them its educational and linguistic influence.[30] The importance of this particular demographic group did not escape Shpil'rein. His own language abounds with references to the soldiers as "objects" of the "assimilating" forces of the collective, forces that properly prepared them for life outside the army:

> [In this study] we always viewed the Red Army soldier as an object of systematic sociopolitical influence in the army. The collective of Red Army soldiers assimilates and reworks this influence in a certain manner, qualitatively reorganizing the experience of each separate individual, and preparing that individual for certain practical activity after departure from the army. The results of our experiments permit us to come closer, on the one hand, to characterizing the Red Army soldier as an object of influence and, on the other, to clarify the general principles of influence by means of the word.[31]

His results also clarified the stubbornness of the gap impeding this important means of "sociopolitical influence." Despite improvements in the "cultural preparation" of the new recruits, misunderstanding and total lack of comprehension of the new vocabulary and concepts still posed significant threats.[32] Some soldiers struggled just to make out the unfamiliar typescript on the surveys and often had trouble understanding the menu of definitions they were to choose among.[33] One complained that the abundance of foreign words in the newspaper prevented them from "understanding how and toward what . . . Socialism [was] aiming."[34] Shpil'rein elaborated on the potential dangers of such verbal confusion in his closing remarks, noting that misinterpretation was as much a foe of the state as total ignorance: "New words may be perceived not only truthfully *(verno)*, but with a distortion *(iskazhenie)* of meaning as well."[35]

If Red Army soldiers, who were under the direct instruction and supervision of central authorities, showed traces of verbal corruption, then their nonmilitary counterparts in the countryside could only have fared worse. The tenuous status of the emerging public discourse among rural populations became well documented by the mid-twenties, chiefly as a result of the much-publicized (and aforementioned) work of Iakov Shafir, who was commissioned by the Subdivision of the Press of the Communist Party Central Committee to spend two weeks during the summer of 1923 in the Voronezh *gubernia* collecting information on the distribution and reception of state newspapers.[36] In the published results of the study, *The Newspaper and the Village,* Shafir divided his subjects into three categories—peasants, workers, and Red Army soldiers (though all resided in rural locales)—and gave each a separate chapter in the book. He used both personal and group interviews to collect his data: the former he based on a twenty-six-item questionnaire, and the latter, on oral readings of newspaper articles.[37] The questionnaire began with general biographical questions (age, party status, size of estate) and then asked for respondents' opinions on different aspects of the newspapers in their current form. Issues ranged from the cost, format, and availability of papers to the relevance and quality of local coverage, antireligious agitation, and agricultural and legal advice. Shafir also included a list of words and phrases taken from familiar rural newspapers, for which definitions were to be supplied.[38] In addition to a number of loanwords, such as *sistema, ofitsial'no, element, konstatirovat', ul'timatum, avtoritet,* the list included acronyms *(RSFSR, SSSR),* stump-compounds *(prodfront* ["food front"], *gubprodkom),* and Russian words that had acquired altered or supplementary meanings *(pokazatel'noe khoziaistvo* ["demonstration farm"], *soglasovannye deistviia* ["coordinated actions"]).[39]

Readers' responses to the papers offered little consolation to the already perplexing problems of distribution and access. The majority of subjects polled fared poorly on the vocabulary test, quite frequently identifying fewer than half of the words and phrases presented to them. On numerous occasions they failed to find any suitable definitions for new Soviet terms such as *element, kategoricheski, gubzemupravlenie, sel'mash,* and *gossel'sklad.*[40] "Darned if you don't need a translation!" one peasant exclaimed after missing most of the words in the survey (34). Another echoed, "Ekh, all those different words. Our soul aches on account of them. You gotta have a dictionary. You chew them over and over, and still don't get it *(Zhuesh', zhuesh' i nichego ne poimesh')"* (43). Later in the interview, he expressed his dismay over the seemingly needless ambiguity of the new terminology, as exemplified by the word *nota* (in the meaning of "diplomatic note"): "Look at how they're spoiling and screwing up our thought! A note's the thing in church. Have them write 'letter', instead. You need to make it closer to our way of talking, or else it'll make the head spin" (47).

Even such apparently semantic misunderstandings pointed to signs of deeper cultural division between the peasantry and the emerging state. The lament over the foreignness of the language of the papers, the distinction between "us" (in *our* thought") and "them" (in *portiut . . . pishut*), and the implicit opposition between the Church and the state all indicate the peasants' self-perceived isolation or independence from the new order. The Soviet "culture boss" *(kul'tshef)* was likened to a Catholic priest. "Class enemy" was reduced to a conventional sign of little substantive significance ("They've split us up into classes now" [50]). The Soviet-imposed *Gubprodkom*, or *Gubernia* Food Committee, elicited derision through both language and gesture ("We're sick and tired of it . . . it sits right here [pointing to his neck]" [55]). And the exotic *ul'timatum* was diminished to a fancy term for 'bald threat' ("Either you pay the money, or you give me your horse, or I kill you" [55]).

Whether intentional or unintentional, such verbal distortions by consumers of official language redefine that language in a manner not only unexpected but highly detrimental to the authority of its central producers.[41] As with the rumors, gossip, and folk etymologies referred to earlier, they resemble forms of popular resistance on the part of culturally and politically marginal groups, a means of using the official language of the state toward alternative, often competing, ideological ends. Yet even the cases that appear less intentionally oppositional, and more a product of illiteracy, serve to undermine the linguistic order imposed from above by the state. For if Ernst Cassirer's observation on "the act of 'naming'" is accurate—that it "does not simply add a mere conventional sign to a ready-made thing . . . , it is rather a pre-requisite of the very conception of objects; of the idea of an objective empirical reality"—then it would follow that misrepresentations of those names (or *iskazheniia*, as they were often called by contemporary observers) corrupt that presupposed reality.[42] Regardless of whether those distortions were deliberate, they created the same problem of undermining implied models of authority and identity.[43]

Lest too much be made of the "art of resistance," one should remember the profound impact Bolshevik "namers" had on the institutional, geographical, and even personal landscape of early Soviet Russia.[44] The widespread use of *tovarishch'* ("comrade") and the informal *ty* ("thou") form of address, the renaming of most all branches and organs of the state apparatus, and the influx of new sovietized toponyms are only some of the more obvious. At the grassroots level, well-documented signs of civic enthusiasm came in the form of naming children after Soviet leaders, production terms, and agitational phrases.[45] The point is not so much that the above-mentioned semiotic acts were either pro- or anti-Bolshevik but that the language culture of the time was dominated by an atmosphere of transformation and change as well as a related sense of verbal empowerment. A less well-known study of registered name changes in the early Soviet years brings this point to bear, by showing that, apart from those taking on sur-names in the Soviet spirit *(Maiskaia, Oktiabr'skii, Leninskii, Mashininskii, Kombainov, Boitsov)*, hundreds of other citizens took advantage of the spirit of revolution to realize their own, personal transformation, which often had little or nothing to do with supporting or resisting the state.[46] Some took the opportunity to abandon derogatory "talking" surnames (a relatively common trait in Russian), such as *Sobachkin, Korovin, Krysov, Tarakanov, Dikarev, Negodiaev, Durakov, Zhirnyi, Sliun'kov, Pupkov, Pupkin, Kulibaba, Likhobaba,* and *Sorokobabkin*.[47] Others simply opted for more prestigious, poetic, or euphonic names—again, having little to do with the new Soviet order per se *(Pushkin, Tolstoy, Onegin, Nevskii, Gorskii, Amurskii, Uralov, Anis'ia Khliupina —> Galina Borovaia, Samodurov —> Poliarnyi, Kurochka —> Orlov)*.[48] It would be a far stretch to interpret the adoption of the surname "Pushkin" as an act of anti-Bolshevik resistance—at least in the language culture of the 1920s. At the same time, however, one can hardly see it as a popular means of advancing the Bolshevik cause.

It is this second type of communication problem, resulting more from conscious reappropriation of linguistic power and authority than from a basic lack of comprehension, that is so masterfully portrayed in Isaak Ba-bel's *Red Cavalry* narratives. The story "My First Goose," for instance, de-picts a web of overlapping, yet not always compatible, interpretive voices, all reacting to an agitational speech by Lenin from the central party news-paper, *Pravda*. The speech, whose status as utterance is already compli-cated—or "dialogized"—by its reproduction in newsprint, undergoes a sec-ond transformation through the narrator and party activist Liutov's almost mystical representation of the text and, then, finally, a third, through the reaction to it by his Cossack listeners:

> I gromko, kak torzhestvuiushchii glukhoi, ia prochital kazakam leninskuiu rech'.
>
> Vecher zavernul menia v zhivitel'nuiu vlagu sumerechnykh svoikh prostyn', vecher prilozhil materinskie ladoni k pylaiushchemu moemu lbu. Ia chital i likoval i podsteregal, likuia, tainstvennuiu krivuiu leninskoi priamoi.
>
> "Pravda vsiakuiu nozdriu shchekochet," skazal Surovkov, kogda ia konchil, "da kak ee iz kuchi vytashchit', a on b'et srazu, kak kuritsa po zernu . . ."[49]

[*"And loudly, like a triumphant deaf man, I read Lenin's speech out to the Cossacks.

"Evening wrapped me in the quickening moisture of its twilight sheets; evening laid a mother's hand upon my burning forehead. I read on and re-joiced, spying out exultingly the secret curve of Lenin's straight line.

"'Truth tickles everyone's nostrils,' said Surovkov, when I had come to the end. 'The question is, how's it to be pulled from the heap. But he goes and strikes at it straight off like a hen pecking at grain!'"*]

Babel's representation of Lenin's language nicely captures the nature of its appeal, at least as portrayed by contemporary observers. It is equally comprehensible and "sense-making" to three distinct audiences and levels of interpretation: the bureaucratic demands of the party-state newspaper, the multivalent mysticism of the modern intellectual, and the popular reverence of the Cossack warrior.[50] Yet even in the idealized case of Lenin's language, those multiple levels of interpretation rely on conflicting interpretations of power. While the newspaper seeks to transform Lenin's oratory into a printed canon of central state authority, Liutov's mystic reinterpretation celebrates its elusiveness (even to "dumb" party intellectuals such as himself), a magical quality whose force stems more from the secret of the Word than from some external bureaucratic structure. The Cossacks latch onto yet a different source of authority—the "Truth" of everyday common sense. Even though all three audiences agree on the power of Lenin's word, in other words, they hold starkly different images of the roots of that authority.

The impersonal voice of the state fares more poorly in the verbal reappropriations of Babel's heroes. In a manner akin to Shafir's peasants, the peripheral voices of Cossacks in *Red Cavalry* exhibit many of the features characteristic of the emerging language of state but do so in forms and contexts either unintended or unanticipated by that language's central producers. A Red Army soldier invokes the state discourse to justify murdering a peasant stowaway ("And having taken my trusty rifle off the wall, I washed that stain from the face of the laboring land and Republic" [126]). A peasant gets revenge on his former master for stealing and raping his wife by conjuring up a fictitious decree from Lenin: "In the name of the people and for the foundation of a future radiant life, I (Lenin) order Pavlichenko, Matthew son of Rodion, to deprive certain persons of life according to his discretion" (105). And a pair of aging war heroes employ the language of the central state to settle a dispute over the ownership of a much-sought-after stallion:

"A vam, tovarishch Savitskii, kak vsemirnomu geroiu, trudiashchaia massa Vitebshchiny, gde nakhozhus' predsedatelem urevkoma, shlet proletarskii klich—'Daesh' mirovuiu revoliutsiiu'—i zhelaet, chtoby tot belyi zherebets khodil pod vami dolgie gody po miagkim tropkam dlia pol'zy vsemi liubimoi svobody i bratskikh respublik, v kotorykh osobennyj glaz dolzhny my imet' za vlast'iu na mestakh i za volostnymi edinitsami v administrativnom otnoshenii." (202–3)

["And to you, Comrade Savitskii, as a worldwide hero, the laboring masses of Vitebsk, where I am now located as president of the Local Revolutionary Committee, send their proletarian cry: 'On with the World Revolution!' and wish that that white stallion may walk beneath you long years along soft paths for the good of the freedom that we all love and the fraternal Republics, in which we ought to keep a special eye on the local authorities and district units in administrative matters."]

Authority in all these cases is checked not only by the incongruity between language and context—the use of the essentially public language of state for the legitimation of personal actions or claims; it is also brought into question by the faulty use of that language by the fictional speaker or writer. Collectively, they reveal speakers cognizant of the power of the language, but who have not yet mastered it.

While recognized by many critics as a pathos-filled portrait of civil war, Babel's narrative vignettes were sufficiently evocative to attract the ire of those for whom the issue of state authority and heroism were paramount to depictions of the military effort. One of the more irate reactions came from General Budennyi himself, who accused "citizen Babel'" of offering petty insights worthy of a peasant "wench." Invoking the full rhetorical force of the language of state, he complained of Babel': "It is unimportant to him why and for what the First Red Cavalry Army, among the greatest weapons of the class struggle, fought. Despite the fact that the author was in the ranks of the glorious Red Cavalry, albeit at the rear, he did not notice—it passed by his ears, eyes and comprehension—either its heroic struggle, or its terrible inhuman sufferings and deprivations. Being by nature . . . ideologically alien to us, he did not notice its struggle of gigantic sweep."[51]

What for Budennyi constituted portraits of "alien ideology" was, for a significant portion of the mostly rural Soviet citizenry, the sign either of a total lack of comprehension or of alternative interpretations of the revolutionary language and ideas thrust upon them by newspapers, agitators, and educators. In both cases, however, the gap was tangible and worrisome. Terms such as "revolution," "class," "party," "proletariat," "purge," and "unions"—if understood at all—tended to carry different semantic markings in the vocabulary of the peasant than those assumed by the official lexicon of Bolshevism.[52] Shafir himself alludes to these fundamental differences in reception in the summary remarks to his study, specifically in reference to perceptions of "power" and competing discourses of identity:

> One of the main shortcomings of our papers was expressed by one peasant to me as follows:
> "All they write about is power [vlast']. . . ."
> Of course, there is a misunderstanding here, as Soviet power reflects the interests of the workers and peasants.
> For the time being, however, several layers of the peasantry still see "power" and "we" [i.e., the peasants] in opposition to one another. Under such conditions, the newspaper—in order to bring closer and link the peasantry with Soviet power—must speak to the peasant in his own language.[53]

Further on, he elaborates on what he means by "speak[ing] to the peasant in his own language":

> [The newspaper] cannot spend the whole time on agitation, slogans, and campaigns; instead, it should provide, first and foremost, informative material—of any type: local, international, domestic—from our perspective *[v nashem osveshchenii]*.
>
> This would not constitute, on our part, a rejection of the essence or content of our agitation, but rather an alteration of the form, the approach, the method. And it fully corresponds . . . to the wishes and questions of the wide layers of the poor, as well as of the middle peasantry.
>
> Up until now, our newspapers have devoted most of their attention to *what should be,* as we see it, in the countryside, and have said relatively little about *what is.* Such an approach is inaccessible and incomprehensible to the peasant. For this reason, it must be rejected.[54]

Aside from foreshadowing the "impossible aesthetic" later proposed as a solution to the problem in the form of "socialist realism," Shafir's assessment highlights the central dilemma faced by all those involved in transmitting the ideas and values of the state producers to the consumer population.[55] How could the producers of a radically new set of institutional values—replete with new visions of identity and authority—transmit their ideas to a populace ill equipped to process the language through which those values are expressed, and suspicious of the ideas themselves? How could the Bolshevik message be transmitted without altering the essential tones or integrity of its perspective?

FRAMING THE DEBATE: TO SIMPLIFY OR EDIFY?

Not long after the publication of Shafir's study, the problem of the communication gap dominated the agenda of the first conference of worker correspondents in November 1923.[56] The setting should not be surprising, as it was the worker correspondents *(rabkory),* along with the village correspondents *(sel'kory),* who were to be the verbal conduits between the state and the masses. They, more than any other group, embodied both the problem and its potential resolution. The main speakers at the conference framed the issue as a choice between two options: either raising the verbal skills of "the masses" up to the level of the Soviet newspapers, or adjusting the language of the papers to better reflect the language of the people. The published transcripts of the debate show the degree to which the differences between the two positions were grounded in divergent perceptions not only of the language but also of its real and ideal producers and consumers.[57] The comments of two keynote speakers, the editor-in-chief of the newspaper *Bednota,* Lev Sos-

novskii, and the prominent party leader Nikolai Bukharin, sufficiently illustrate the link between language and voice, on the one hand, and notions of identity and authority, on the other.[58]

In his reaction to Shafir's study, Sosnovskii presents himself as a
spokesperson for the people, calling for the simplification and popularization of newspaper language. Framing his argument in terms of a linguistic
clash of classes, he bemoans the fact that the *rabkory* have abandoned
their own popular dialects for a cliché-ridden newspaper language
adopted from the intelligentsia: "It is not tragic that we are inveterate intellectuals *(otpetye liudi-intelligenty)* and it is impossible to retrain us in a
new language; what is tragic is that you, worker correspondents, write like
us. Hence the tragedy of the worker agitator, the chief *(vozhd')*—he loses
his popular *(narodnyi)*, simple, succulent, clear, expressive language, and in
its place gets the stock language of our newspapers."[59] Once the worker
correspondents discard the language of the intelligentsia, rife with complexity and subordination, and begin writing in the "simple, succulent,
expressive language" spoken by their own cohorts in the factory and the
fields, Sosnovskii presumes, the message of the revolutionary party will be
clearly articulated and clearly understood. The difficulty lies not in the inaccessibility of the revolutionary words and ideas themselves but in the
lingering linguistic traces of the former ruling class. In their search for verbal authority and identity, the worker and rural correspondents should
look to their own roots.

In his address to the same conference, Nikolai Bukharin offers a
markedly different solution, in part out of concern for the issue of administration. "This sort of thing is completely unavoidable," he remarks, referring to the communication gap, "when a party of the working class is in
power. . . . You—the whole party, the working class—have a dual problem:
on the one hand, you have to run the government, on the other, [you
have to] maintain ties as much as possible with the last worker and peasant, with the most backward. All of our difficulties flow out of this dual
task."[60] For Bukharin, the problem lies not in the language, which is necessarily fulfilling the administrative tasks of the party.[61] Instead, it rests with
the "backward" *(otstalye)* masses, who are not yet capable of comprehending that administrative language. He advocates, then, temporarily diversi-
fying the newspaper language, adjusting the papers and sections within
them to better fit their probable readers.[62] He envisions the eventual "lifting up" of the masses, but, until conditions can permit that, he advocates
the maintenance of multiple discourses, corresponding to the various social categories that make up the reading and speaking population:

> We are going to have to live in conditions where we don't simply have masses,
> but heterogeneous masses, we have different layers: . . . among the peasants,
> different layers; . . . among the workers, different layers; we have cadres of

workers that are party members and nonparty members. Among the party members there are a number of layers. We have workers who need specific directives from the news, who have grown enormously in a cultural sense. Thus, we have a heterogeneous audience; one, therefore, requiring various types of newspapers.[63]

Restricting the various subclasses of the proletariat to the role of addressee in the communicative act, Bukharin reserves the role of addressor for the select group in control of both the channels and code of communication. No longer the agents of linguistic authority implied in Sosnovskii's vision, the Soviet masses must with time and attention acquire the language of the establishment rather than rely on their own, local sources of verbal identity and authority. In this sense, Bukharin's position more closely represents the administrative priorities of a centralized state in the process of formation than it does any effort to generate authority for the voice of the proletariat.

A perceptive worker correspondent attending the conference took issue with Bukharin's implied power relations precisely on the grounds of the resulting gap between power and voice. Criticizing Bukharin's proposal to differentiate, even temporarily, among the various voices of the reading and speaking citizens, he complained that *Pravda* had already done so, and it had led to the marginalization of the voice of the worker (and therefore the worker himself). "In the section 'Workers' Life'" (which appeared on the fourth page of each issue), the *rabkor* explained, "the articles are written in a worker's language *(rabochii iazyk)* and seem detached from the rest of the issue, which is written in a terribly smart language *(umnyi iazyk)*—not because things are more stupidly written in 'Workers' Life,' but because there is a difference in style." He proposed, instead, a means by which the linguistic gap between the people and the state could be bridged—but to the ultimate advantage of the working class: "If you were to situate a portion of the serious articles by worker correspondents on the front page, then it would smooth over the impression of division in the paper. The workerization *(orabochenie)* of the newspaper will [eventually] have its day."[64] Whether this was possible without compromising either language remained to be seen.

• • •

The two views of the communication gap expressed by Bukharin and Sosnovskii do not exhaust the assumptions about the ideal voice of the citizen and state articulated in the language debates of the 1920s and early 1930s. But they do illustrate several basic, recurring, and interrelated tensions underlying those discussions. One is the tension between administrative and ideological authority—the need to govern, but to somehow do so "in the name" (and voice) of the people, or proletariat.[65] A second tension is between essentially revolutionary models of language, writing, and speaking (such as rewriting the newspapers using the language of the worker) and those that are more rooted in some established authority or tradition (such as that of "inveterate intellectuals"). A final tension lies in the competition for authority between what are essentially oral and written modes of expression—here, the voice of the people versus the language of the press.

Through a combination of conscious and natural forces, the events of October 1917 brought into the domain of public speaking and writing a hodgepodge of linguistic features, ranging from a vocabulary peppered with acronyms, stump-compounds, and words with transformed meanings to a discursive style that displayed an often bizarre mix of bureaucratese, substandard slang, and high Marxist rhetoric. Though in many ways essential to articulating the substance of Bolshevik ideology, this language was not always received and reproduced in the manner intended by the citizens upon whom the party depended for legitimacy. For some, it was both alien and alienating, a restrictive rather than a universal tongue, a bureaucratic babble to those with no links to the emerging bureaucracy. For others, as with Babel's protagonists, it was recognized as a language of power and authority, but reappropriated toward ends unintended or anticipated by the state. Because of the breadth of the communication gap and its underlying social, cultural, and ideological fissures, debates over its origins and resolution dominated most every social and cultural sphere involved in some form of public language production. It is to these voices, and their proscriptions for the ideal language of state and the ideal speaking and writing citizen, that we now turn.

CHAPTER TWO

THE REVOLUTIONARY VOICE

AND THE RESURRECTION OF MEANING

Elbows, chests, heads were densely pressed around me and above me. I spoke as if from a warm cave of human bodies. . . . No weariness could resist the electric tension of this passionate human throng. It wanted to know, to understand, to find its way. At moments it seemed like your lips felt the demanding inquisitiveness of this crowd which had blended into one. At those times, the pre-designed arguments and words yielded, backed down to the peremptory pressure of sympathy, and out of latency there appeared, armed to the hilt, different words, different arguments, unanticipated by the orator, but necessary to the masses. And then it would seem as if you yourself were listening to the orator just a bit to the side, unable to keep up with his thoughts and alarmed that he might, like a sleep walker, fall off the box from the voice of your argumentation. Such was the Cirque Moderne.

—Lev Trotsky (1930)

Without independent production work on literary material (language, plot construction), without the experimental study of it, without a break with the canonized devices of art, it is impossible to use artistic works in the capacity of contemporary ideological influence. Form is not a mechanical means; form organizes the psyche in all directions, and forgetting about it means becoming its slave.

—Boris Arvatov (1923)

The language culture in the years following October 1917 was distinguished by the commonly held assumption that language could and had to be, in essence, reinvented in order to reflect aptly the ideas and the symbols of the revolutionary society. Journalists, educators, and cultural leaders encouraged citizens, first, to become literate in the language and ideas of the new Bolshevik order and, then, to speak out and express themselves in a variety of forums—from meeting halls and factory floors to newspapers, classrooms, and publishing venues for "proletarian" fiction. Many of the leading linguists of the day, themselves involved in academic institutions, editorial boards, and policy committees, gave their own disciplinary legitimacy to the belief that language could be "engineered" to more adequately articulate the revolutionary ideas of the emerging state and society. Writers and critics explored a variety of innovative narrative styles for doing the same in imaginative literature. In fact, the first two voices discussed in the following chapters—the revolutionary and the popular—both shared this utopian mentality toward language culture. In contrast to those that followed (the national and the party-state voice), both shared the fundamental belief that public discourse could be reinvented to better reflect the grander reinvention taking place in Soviet society.[1]

Two complementing drives lay at the core of that belief, already exemplified by the revival of the "living word" just after the revolution: a desire to shake off the shackles of old forms of linguistic authority, most graphically represented by the written political, religious, and literary canon of tsarist Russia, and a desire to empower common citizens—those in whose name the revolution was ostensibly carried out—to participate verbally in the process of revolution and construction. While the two aims carried quite different assumptions about where the balance of linguistic authority should lie, they shared a strong orientation toward oral models and genres of language production. Beyond their common challenge to traditional, text-based sources of authority, however, the revolutionary and the popular voices differed substantially in the particular models of speaking and writing they advanced as alternatives.

Despite obvious differences in institutional interests, the leading representatives of the revolutionary model of public discourse, whose views enjoyed greatest linguistic capital in the years surrounding and just following October 1917, shared three basic attitudes about the form and function of language in the new social order. First, like Bukharin, they recognized that the emerging Soviet society was by necessity a complex structure and that public language had to reflect this. Second, although they welcomed the impact of the Bolshevik revolution on public discourse, they also understood that the language culture was in the process of continual change, and they emphasized the need for public language to keep abreast of that change. Third, the representatives of the revolutionary model of discourse viewed language production—be it oral or written, by peasant or party leader—as a process of creative, innovative expression and an integral force in the legitimation and regeneration of the society under construction.[2]

Four of the more prominent sources of this revolutionary model of language culture were the philologist Grigorii Vinokur, the linguists and literary critics of the avant-garde journal *Lef* ("The Left Front of Art"), the Bolshevik party leader Lev Trotsky, and the poet Vladimir Maiakovskii. Although the contexts and practical agendas of their discussions of language differed, each reflected a conviction that the emerging social order would greatly benefit from a manner of speaking and writing sophisticated enough to express the complexities of the modern world, flexible enough to adapt to the continual changes occurring in that world, and creative enough to accommodate the alternative perspectives of statesmen and citizens of the new Soviet society.

VINOKUR AND THE BATTLE AGAINST VERBAL IMPOVERISHMENT

Given his belief that humans had the power to manipulate, if not engineer, the language of their social experience, Grigorii Vinokur was generally enthusiastic about the verbal shifts that had taken place largely as a result of the change in political and social orders. Yet, as a linguist with a keen interest in related fields of journalism and education, he was also well aware of the challenges that accompanied the change. The Bolsheviks faced a gargantuan task given the scope of their reforms and the massive breadth of their audience. In Vinokur's view, however, a stylistic simplification along the lines proposed by Sosnovskii and others was not the solution. In an essay on the language of the newspaper published shortly after the public exchange between Sosnovskii and Bukharin, Vinokur explained the rationale behind his opposition to any watering down of newspaper language: "The more complicated the cultural life, the more complicated, too, becomes the mechanism of language. It selects new modes of expression, specifies and perfects the means of transmitting the facts and ideas that make up the cultural content of a given epoch."[3]

The complexity of the language per se was not at all bad, as it appropriately reflected the corresponding complexity of modern society. More germane to the communication problem was the inappropriate manner in which the language of revolution was invoked by those who wrote and spoke in public. At one time, he explained elsewhere, the words and phrases of the revolution brimmed with meaning and necessity: "Outside of this phraseology it was impossible to think about the revolution in a revolutionary manner. The phraseological shift *[sdvig]* corresponded to a political one."[4] As a result of its singularly revolutionary force—that is, its perfect articulation of the needs of the moment—the language served as a flawless transformer of words into actions: "the transition from perception . . . to action was not complicated by any collateral associations: you read it—you acted!"[5]

Because that historical moment had passed, though, so too must the phrases used to express it. Through overuse, they were no longer perceived, but rather "slip[ped] . . . past the hearing of the masses." Vinokur invokes Viktor Shklovskii's notion of "automatization" to make his point: "When the form of a word ceases to be felt as such, [when it] does not strike the perception, then the sense ceases to be felt as well."[6] Slogans such as "Down with imperialism!" and "Long live the international solidarity of the working class!" had lost all real meaning through repeated use.[7] Their continued presence in public discourse, therefore, especially in the context of social construction, could only have a pernicious effect on language culture. Not only did they fail to reflect the realities and needs of the present moment, they trapped the community of writers and readers in a state of thoughtlessness:

> Behind all of this verbal impoverishment, behind all of this catastrophic decline of our linguistic hard currency . . . an enormous **social danger** is concealed.
>
> In truth, it is not difficult . . . to see that, insofar as in our sociopolitical daily life *[byt]* we use slogans and expressions that do not mean anything (for their form is no longer perceptible), our thought also becomes senseless, void of meaning. . . . We do not know what, in reality, "capital offensive" means when we use the expression for the hundredth, thousandth, millionth time. It is only a cliché, a convenient cover used by us in order not to think.[8]

The threat of linguistic devaluation demanded that a speech community be capable of rejecting the "convenient covers" of worn-out, meaningless phrases. For Vinokur, the "first gleams of language culture" began to appear in the act of linguistic revitalization and selection, in "a speech community striving to realize and organize its language experience."[9] So, although he expresses some reservation about the rapid growth of stump-compounds and deverbal nouns, he recognizes on a deeper level a healthy process in which speakers are attempting "to construct their speech consciously," "to master the speech environment."[10] They simply had not yet perfected the process. To do so, according to Vinokur, they needed help from the "achievement" end of the language-culture spectrum—the writers who produced stylistic models for emulation, and the linguists and critics who served as intermediaries—able to make "sense" and "organize" rationally the elemental impulses of each extreme.[11]

Particularly in his earlier writings on the issue, Vinokur placed greatest hope for closing the communication gap in the language production of the Russian futurists, where he saw the beginnings of an effort to "create a language of the streets" in order to "overcome the tongue-tiedness of the masses."[12] But he also recognized the scale of the task, given the extent of illiteracy among the targeted community of speakers and writers. "Here in Russia, there are not even the basic technical, not to mention social, preconditions for such a broad culture: an enormous majority of the Russian people are plainly and simply illiterate." While he harbored no illusions of a total revolution of the language of the masses, he nevertheless saw cause for optimism: "A mass scale here is patently impossible. But the Russian futurists have shown us that the scale of the poem, of the *poema,* is possible. And that is already a lot. It is a **beginning.**"[13]

Though his enthusiasm toward the transformative capabilities of the futurists dampened over the 1920s, Vinokur retained his belief that the language of poetry, through the application of "practical stylistics," could lend support and life to a struggling public discourse.[14] The futurist experiment had failed, he argued, because, in the name of "transrational language," or *zaum,* it had abandoned completely all familiar language models and had created as a result a discourse that was entirely incomprehensible, or "nihilistic." Only poetic models solidly based on the conventional Russian vocabulary could serve as models for practical language. Rather than something to be feared, the "poeticality" of such writers, by virtue of their status as exemplars of the finest achievements of language culture, should be used to articulate the new language policy of the emerging society.[15] Almost equal to poets in importance were linguists, as they were most qualified to formulate a language policy based on the models provided by writers: "The leadership of this policy, seeing as it would be senseless without strict linguistic knowledge, it, of course, should belong to linguists—the language technologists. Any other kind of leadership would smack of the policy of tsarist bureaucrats and contemporary outlying states."[16]

AVANT-GARDE EULOGIES TO LENIN'S LANGUAGE

No less self-serving than Vinokur's utopian vision of a street language created by poets and managed by philologists was the collection of theoretical articles dedicated to Lenin's language in the first 1924 issue of the avant-garde journal *Lef (The Left Front of Art),* appearing shortly after the Bolshevik leader's death. The collection of articles is important for this discussion for a number of reasons. First, it demonstrates how some of the more fundamental ideas of the leading "Formalist" critics were applied to the study of public discourse.[17] Second, the articles address the language issue in the context of political oratory—a genre critical for the articulation and development of the language of state in Soviet Russia. Finally, they do so by examining the verbal production of Bolshevism's founding father. In the sphere of language, as in a wide variety of other social, cultural, and political domains, the speeches and writings of Lenin quickly assumed the status of gospel. Interpretations of that gospel, however, differed widely, particularly in the earliest readings.[18]

For the literary scholar Boris Tomashevskii, the popular study and practice of rhetoric—witnessed in the growing enrollments in courses on public speaking, journalism, and debate—constituted nothing short of the "democratization of art" in Soviet society. As a form of highly artistic language based in concrete, everyday life, oratory linked the poetic and practical worlds, thereby making a society's "spiritual life" (and its public forums) accessible to a broader cross section of its citizens.[19] For the rhetorician, the logical point of departure was the eloquence of Lenin, "the most prominent world figure in contemporary social-political literature."[20] Lev Iakubinskii's justification of the focus was more to the point: Lenin's "verbal behavior . . . forcefully and inevitably . . . achieved its goal."[21] His concrete demonstration of language's power in bringing about radical change provided ample evidence for more broad-based linguistic "organization" and training, to be conducted, naturally, by the linguistic and literary specialists.

In their celebration of Lenin's language, the *Lef* critics highlighted three exemplary features: its resistance to cliché, its perpetuation of meaning through multivalent shifts, and its use of colloquial and even vulgar speech as a means of lowering (and thereby invigorating) the lofty language of traditional rhetoric. Shklovskii's characterization of Lenin as a "decanonizer" stems primarily from his view of the evolutionary relationship between a word and the object it signifies. Words and expressions are created to designate not so much objects, as the "place which they occupy in space." The borders of such space change rapidly with time, and the original words and expressions, if left unmodified, cease to adequately reflect the reality contained within. Instead, they become "a false shadow of the object," or "incantations." Lenin, Shklovskii claims, was a master at avoiding incantation: "Every speech or article almost seems to start again from the beginning. There are no terms, they appear already in the middle of a given thing, as the concrete result of disjunctive *(razdelitel'naia)* work."[22] Shklovskii's notion of the dangers of incantation contains the same idea as Vinokur's: the language of the past is static, if not entropic, and by virtue of its disassociation from the phenomena it purports to express it actually devalues or falsifies speech.[23] Lenin's ability to avoid such detached phraseology made him an innovator oriented toward the continual change, rather than the standardization, of language.[24]

Iurii Tynianov also describes the problem of the revolutionary phrase in terms of a static-dynamic opposition, identifying the complexity of a word or phrase's semantic potential as the factor that keeps it meaningful. An image is "alive" when it still contains a "discrepancy" *(neviazka)* of two or more levels of meaning.[25] A word or phrase's complexity, or dynamism, allows it to evolve together with that which it signifies. Once a word fails to "keep up" with the evolution of an object, it loses meaning, and itself becomes a mere "object of *byt*."[26] To demonstrate the important social and political implications of this process, Tynianov offers a historical case in point by describing how the shortened acronyms of the prerevolutionary oppositional parties gave rise to purely emotive, and negative, connotations, and how these emotive phrases were used as ideological weapons by communist newspapers. In order to deprive the opposition of a similar weapon, Lenin fought to change the name of his own party, from "Social-Democrat Bolsheviks" to "Communists." For Lenin, political and linguistic routinization went hand in hand:

> Lenin conceived of the change in name as a **shift**, as a struggle with language routine; the habituation of the old name was not an argument for preserving it, but for changing it:
> [quoting Lenin] **"The masses have grown accustomed, the workers have 'become enamored' with their Social Democratic Party."**
> . . . This is an argument for routine, an argument for lethargy, an argument for stagnancy. And we want to reconstruct the world.
> . . . And we are afraid of ourselves.
> **We are hanging onto a "habitual," "dear," filthy shirt.**
> **It is time to cast off the filthy shirt, it is time to put on clean underwear.**[27]

The changing of the semiotic underwear constituted, for Lenin, the revitalization of the party—for Tynianov, the revitalization of language. Both levels of interpretation recognized that only through the continual shift of symbolic garments could the inevitable routinization of objects be avoided and the perpetuation of meaning secured.

Nearly all of the contributors to the *Lef* issue noted Lenin's sensitivity to language—particularly to its ability to conceal or altogether annihilate meaning. Two aspects of his oratory reflected this consciousness: his polemical attacks against the "lofty phrases" of his opponents' language, and his own adeptness at lowering the high style of traditional rhetoric through the infusion of colloquial and nonstandard speech. Both techniques represented a kind of "laying bare" of concrete meaning.[28] Attacks on the lofty phraseology of opponents exposed untruths and the absence of sense. Tynianov quotes as an example Lenin's criticism of the opposition's use of the term "equality": "'Equality is an empty phrase, if by equality the elimination of classes is not understood. We want to eliminate the classes. In this respect, we stand for equality. But to presume that we will make all people equal to one another—this is the emptiest of phrases and the invention of the intellectual who sometimes conscientiously behaves in an affected manner [and] twists around words with no content.'"[29]

Lenin's coarsening of the conventionally lofty style of political rhetoric had the similar effect of revitalizing meaning.[30] For Iakubinskii, the injection of nonstandard language disrupted the fluidity and solemnity of traditional rhetoric and thereby gave oratory an ironic bite.[31] For Tynianov, inserted vulgarisms functioned to "heighten the activity *[deistvie]* of speech" and "attract attention, . . . 'beat,' [and] 'offend.'"[32]

Although the *Lef* essays on Lenin's language were not as overtly pro-grammatic as some of Vinokur's discussions of public discourse, their revo-lutionary orientation is equally manifest. It appears in their collective be-lief that, as one of the major weapons in the effort to transform reality (or "reconstruct the world"), verbal expression had to be meaningful. Because relationships between the signifier and signified were continually chang-ing, they believed, language had to be instilled with the capacity to change—a quality ensured both by the semantic multivalence central to the notions of discrepancy and shift and by the rejection of formulaic words and expressions whose meanings had become reduced to incanta-tion or *byt*. The implications for the emerging state and its citizens also re-semble Vinokur's. As public discourse was rescued from the narrow do-main of the intellectual elite through the process of stylistic decanonization, rank-and-file members of the speech community faced a new opportunity—if not obligation—to participate verbally in the con-struction of the new social order, the new Soviet identity. To do so, how-ever, they were also obligated to acquire the skills necessary for producing meaningful public discourse. Forums for such language training included classes on writing, journalism, public speaking, and debate. For living models of language production, they were to look to the new authorities of speaking and writing, the prominent voices of social politics. Lenin, as the most successful and renowned orator and rhetorician, presented the ideal linguistic model of the new state. Finally, also like Vinokur, the *Lef* writers assigned great social authority to linguists and literary critics, who were most qualified to act as interpretive intermediaries between the heights and depths of verbal production.[33]

TROTSKY'S CHARISMATIC BOLSHEVISM

Lev Trotsky brought a unique portfolio to the language debates. A pow-erful orator himself, he was also one of the more vocal Bolshevik partici-pants in the ongoing debate over public discourse and an astute critic of contemporary literature. Given that he was, at best, skeptical of the stylis-tic experiments of the formalists and futurists, it is something of a surprise that his views on language were quite akin to theirs. One clear difference lay in the object of focus: whereas the *Lef* critics concentrated on the "achievement" end of Vinokur's language-culture spectrum, Trotsky fo-cused on the "baseline." His most relevant speeches and essays from the mid-1920s, collected in the volumes *Issues in Cultural Work* (1924) and *Is-sues in Everyday Life* (1925), address the social role and writing of the worker correspondents *(rabkory)* and the speech habits and living styles of rank-and-file Soviet citizens.[34]

Like both Vinokur and the *Lef* essayists, however, Trotsky advocates the

"enlightenment" of the people, rather than some form of linguistic "proletarianization"—an attitude plainly evident in, and justified by, his un-
compromising view of the ideological role of the newspaper.[35] He states
outright that the newspaper is "the main instrument for the political and
cultural education of the broad masses" and refers to it as "an authentic
weapon of daily . . . influence, an instrument for concerted educational efforts."[36] He similarly views the librarian as a "cultural warrior, the Red
Army soldier of socialist culture."[37] In response to complaints that his own
newspaper commentaries were packed with loanwords and abstract terms
that made the worker's head spin (e.g., *kriterii, metafizika, dialektika, ab-
straktsiia*, and *antagonizm*), Trotsky defends complexity in a manner similar to Vinokur and Maiakovskii: Though unnecessary foreign terms should
be eliminated when possible, it would be wrong to think that translating a
discussion of Marx's *Capital* into popular Russian would make it that
much easier to understand. "The exposition must correspond to the subject, to the level of its complexity or simplicity. . . . The difficulty is not in
the words, nor in the exposition, but in the issue itself."[38] Any attempt to
rephrase such issues in simpler terms would sacrifice precision and compromise meaning.[39] The only way for the worker to "rise up to *Capital*"
was by starting simply, acquiring practice and knowledge, and gradually
progressing to more difficult material.

Trotsky's defense of meaningfulness stemmed more from social pragmatism than from the aesthetic concerns held by the *Lef* critics. More
like Vinokur in his justification of deverbal nouns, he saw in the growing
complexity of public discourse an effort on the part of a speech community to come to terms with the intricacies of the modern world. In all
three formulations, however, the underlying assumption was the same:
once the language was subjected to simplification, so too was thought.
In a speech to the *voenkory*, or military correspondents, Trotsky described
the pernicious effect of revolutionary cliché on the minds of both writers
and readers:

> The *voenkor* immediately begins with clichés: it seems better to him, more ap-
> propriate, more worthy . . . "The Heroic Red Army" and so on. Is it true? It is
> true that [the Red Army] is heroic. But he has not shown it, he simply repeats
> clichéd phrases that kill thought. Everything he writes is smeared with the
> same conventional color. He does not have the capacity to individualize, to
> evaluate concretely the situation at hand, to capture the particularities of the
> place and time. He does not even have the need to ask himself, "And what
> about my unit, does it differ from the others, and, if so, how?" Once there is a
> ready-made cliché and that cliché is accepted by the newspaper, he goes and
> writes in bureaucratese *[pokazennomu]*. Meanwhile, little by little, the cliché
> kills awakened thought. A crust of routine immediately forms on it, and the
> crust deadens independent thought.[40]

His image of thought-killing phrases recalls the notion of routine and automatization put forth by Shklovskii and others as well as the "social danger" articulated by Vinokur in his treatment of the revolutionary phrase.[41] In Trotsky's case, the concern was closely connected to his view of the newspaper as the most important political and cultural weapon in the construction of socialist society—and of the citizen's role in that process. The active consciousness of the masses was instrumental in the implementation of the Bolshevik master plan and therefore demanded that worn-out, revolutionary phrases be abandoned for the promulgation of fresher, more immediate thoughts: "Like a habitual, tiresome autumn rain, tens and hundreds of abstract articles repeating the 'bureaucratic' commonplaces about the bourgeois-ness of the bourgeoisie, or the stupidity of the petit-bourgeois family structure, do not even graze the consciousness of the reader. But a competently narrated article highlighting a court trial stemming from a family drama can capture thousands of readers and awaken in them new, fresher, and broader thoughts and feelings."[42]

Trotsky repeatedly stresses the need to provide material that is first and foremost interesting and relevant to the needs of the readers and only covertly didactic.[43] When addressing the issue of writing, he encourages the writer to begin from personal experiences; the appropriate form would then work itself out. Underlying this formula, again, is the image of a "thinking," "active" individual and a notion of "style" that expresses "the character of the person, their development, their will, their conscientiousness *(dobrosovest'nost')*."[44] Only the thinking citizen could provide the necessary antidote to what in his mind was the greatest threat to socialist construction—an entrenched and ever-growing bureaucratic leviathan. The connection appears in his reference to the bureaucratic jargon in the passage quoted above and in numerous other attacks on the clichéd language of officialdom. In an essay on "The Newspaper and Its Reader," Trotsky offers his most pointed attack on bureaucratic language, denouncing the overuse of obscure acronyms such as *OKKh*: "You have to be a hardened Soviet bureaucrat to guess that it is the Division of Communal Economy that is being talked about. The mass reader will never figure this out, of course, and, with vexation, will toss out the article, if not the whole paper."[45] In the process, he leaves no doubt that the phenomenon is a mark of party-based elitism: "The danger of a split of the party from the nonparty masses in the area of agitation is manifested in the exclusiveness *(zamknutost')* of the agitational content and its form, in the formation of an almost conventional party language *(uslovnyi partiinyi iazyk)*, inaccessible nearly always to nine-tenths of not only peasants but workers as well."[46]

To prevent the rise of a party officialese that was inaccessible to the uninitiated and not only killed thought but prevented it altogether, Trotsky rigorously promotes individual reflection and expression among the reading and writing population. Deploring a practice that would later become one of the hallmarks of Soviet language culture, he warns the military correspondents that, "To take from Lenin universal teachings, to cut them out with scissors so that they may be useful every day for the teacher, for the artillerist, and for the economic planner—that is not right, that contradicts Leninism. Lenin does not provide recipes, but rather teaches one to figure out a situation."[47] With rhetorical deftness he notes how such creative interpretation on the part of the general population is, in fact, the only way to fight back against the routinizing forces of bureaucracy in a society that demands a monopoly on education: "A monopoly on education in an improper arrangement is capable of engendering bureaucratism, routine. What is the sign of bureaucratism? That there is form without content. What is its danger? That life is directed into its sphere. How is bureaucratism to be paralyzed? Through the organized and always live pressure of the consumer of education, that is, the lower classes."[48] Trotsky advises citizen-writers to resist the freeze-dried, routinized language of the entrenched party bureaucracy, because it threatens to bring about the degeneration of the country's verbal production.[49] Only through the creative and thoughtful reproduction of language in meaningful contexts can the speaking and writing population contain the forces of bureaucratic routine.

Trotsky's inclusion of the additional notion of "organized" pressure, however, suggests that individually inspired verbal resistance was insufficient for the battle against language routine. As with Leninist thinking in general, he at least leaves the potential for a third element at work in the revolutionary process, independent from the party bureaucracy and "conscious" enough to organize the masses in their struggle. For Vinokur and the *Lef* critics, we recall, this figure was the poet, polemicist or linguist. For Trotsky it was also a poet of sorts, but one dressed in the leather jacket of the charismatic Bolshevik leader, as in the orator described in his recollection of his own speeches on the steps of the "Cirque Moderne," quoted in the epigraph to this chapter. Speaking from within a "warm cave of human bodies"—followers who pay no mind to the physical blows of his gestures—he becomes one with the crowd, or *becomes* the crowd, articulating its concerns purely and immediately.[50] In his act of abandoning his preordained, written words and articulating spontaneously the crowd's immediate, inner concerns, Trotsky's orator emanates what Max Weber called "charismatic authority," where "formally concrete judgments are newly created from case to case and are originally regarded as divine judgments and revelations. From a substantive point of view," Weber writes, "every charismatic authority would have to subscribe to the proposition, 'It is written . . . but I say unto you. . . .'"[51]

Trotsky's charismatic Bolshevik commands authority not by virtue of his own ideas or thoughts as much as by his ability to generate language that expresses the concrete and living needs of the people. It is precisely the *loss* of this ability, according to Weber, that characterizes the process of routinization: "When the tide that lifted a charismatically led group out of everyday life flows back into the channels of workaday routines, at least the 'pure' form of charismatic domination will wane and turn into an 'institution'; it is then either mechanized, as it were, or imperceptibly displaced by other structures, or fused with them in the most diverse forms, so that it becomes a mere component of a concrete historical structure. In this case it is often transformed beyond recognition, and identifiable only on an analytical level."[52]

As soon as the words and ideas of the charismatic leader begin to lose their freshness, their immediacy, their meaning, the power of charisma gives way to routine. It is just such bureaucratic routinization of public discourse that Trotsky saw as the main threat to the construction of the new socialist society. For in the bureaucratization of the party, as evidenced by its exclusive language, he saw the stagnation of ideas and absence of meaning. Only the perpetuation of a charismatic Bolshevism could guarantee the realization of the new order, and for this the continual revitalization of discursive meaning was required—a kind of a permanent linguistic revolution to reflect the political one he advocated elsewhere in his writings.[53] That is why Trotsky implored librarians, Red Army soldiers, and worker correspondents to follow, thoughtfully, their personal linguistic impulses instead of repeating clichéd phrases, to concentrate on expressing their immediate interests and concerns rather than praising the lofty achievements of the Soviet state. They were to serve as evangelical intermediaries and rabble-rousers in the construction of the new order.[54] He viewed the *rabkor* in particular as "an organ of public conscience, who follows, who exposes, who demands, who forces," whose criticism of the bureaucracy "encourages newspaper readers to verify state operations and gradually prepare them for participation in the direction itself." In this sense, Trotsky continues, "The *rabkor* is not just a newspaper worker: he is a new and important element of the Soviet constitution, he supplements the activity of governmental organs, counteracting their bureaucracy."[55]

THE POETIC AGITATION OF VLADIMIR MAIAKOVSKII

In the context of this discussion of the oral and charismatic orientation of the revolutionary model, we can now more fully appreciate Proletcult evocations of thundering orators engulfing entire factories with their verbal magic and of the penetrating force of initially strange speech. While hardly models of formal innovation, they nevertheless capture the vitality and spirit of the revolutionary voice and attest to the breadth of its linguistic capital. The image of the charismatic orator was one that enjoyed power and authority from a range of perspectives within the early Soviet language culture—from the "talk"-hungry crowds of the Putilovskii

Factory, to the avant-garde literary critics of *Lef,* to Bolshevik propagandists like Lev Trotsky. This final section turns to a voice that, more successfully than others, articulated the revolutionary mentality in a manner that found resonance on all three of these levels—the streets, the critical circles, and the state. More concertedly and effectively than most other contemporary writers, Vladimir Maiakovskii fused the pragmatic aims of transforming public language to reflect the new order of things with the aesthetic principles of modernism, enthusiastically accepting the mantle of revolutionary poet, orator, and agitator.

Aesthetically, Maiakovskii embraced the futurist aim of expanding the boundaries of poetry by abandoning the preestablished models passed down by the "classics" of previous generations and introducing innovation on virtually all levels of poetic structure. On the level of voice, his verse featured speech registers previously foreign to the poetic realm—the colloquial, often vulgar, language of everyday street life, on the one hand, and the language of revolution, on the other. This blend of what Arvatov, Vinokur, and others referred to as "poetic" and "practical" languages managed to articulate a new verbal identity for all the voices involved, and Maiakovskii thereby established for each of them new sources of authority.[56] He addressed the issue thematically as early as his 1914–1915 narrative poem, *A Cloud in Trousers,* in which the poet's own voice, "thundering the world with its might" *(Mir ogromiv moshch'iu* [1:175]), serves as an imposing (and decidedly oral) calling card in the opening stanzas.[57] The poem's second section addresses the issue of poetry and the poet in greater depth, setting up a contrast between the flowery language of the poets of old and the "tongueless" voice of the streets:

> poka vykipiachivaiut, rifmami pilikaia,
> iz liubvei i solov'ev kakoe-to varevo,
> ulitsa korchitsia bez"iazykaia—
> ei nechem krichat' i razgovarivat'.

> Gorodov vavilonskie bashni,
> vozgordias', voznosim snova,
> a bog
> goroda na pashni
> rushit,
> meshaia slovo.

> Ulitsa muku molcha perla.
> Krik torchkom stoial iz glotki.
> Toporshchilis', zastriavshie poperek gorla,
> pukhlye taxi i kostliavye proletki.
> Grud' ispeshekhodili.
> Chakhotki ploshche. (181–82)

[While refined poets, harping on their rhymes, are busy boiling, concocting some slop of nightingales and romance, the tongueless street contorts—it has nothing with which to yell or talk.

We raise anew the Babylonian towers of the cities, becoming proud, while God pulls down the cities for fallow lands, confusing the word.

Silently the street pushed through the torment. A scream stood up on end from the gullet. Plump taxis and bony droshkies bristled, stuck in the throat. And the chest was trampled down by pedestrians, flatter than a consumptive's.]

Garbled in a series of decidedly unflowery consonant clusters (particularly in the last stanza quoted) and grotesque images of stifled shrieks, plump taxis, and consumption, the tongueless streets clearly have no place for the love, nightingales, and strumming rhythms of romantic verse. The city and its pedestrians have shut down the road, trampling on the chest of the poet in the process. Any hope for divine vengeance on behalf of tradition is, in the following lines, dashed by the vernacular of the streets "coughing out the mob to the square," its voice howling, "Let's go chow down!" *(Idemte zhrat'!)*. The only words to emanate from the "dead little corpses in the mouth" are the "fatty" and profane "bastard" and "borshch"—not the sort of utterances one would expect from the gilded tongues of the classical or romantic poets, who can only stand by in disbelief, wondering how, in such vulgar tones, songs "can be sung of ladies, love, and a flower in the morning dew" (182–83).

Maiakovskii's poet sympathizes with the common hordes of "students, prostitutes, and contractors," and urges them not to fawn in wonder and obedience before the traditionalists, but rather to recognize their own creative potential to generate "burning hymns from the noise of the labs and the factories" (183). Continuing the destruction of old standards of sacred and profane by "spitting" on the memories of the Homers and Ovids, he declares that "tendons and muscles are truer than prayers . . . We—each one of us—hold in our five fingers the drive belts of the worlds!" (184).

Although revolution appears in *A Cloud in Trousers* only as a "thorny-crowned" specter "at the head of the hungry hordes" in the year 1916, the tenor of the verses already expresses the demands of the revolutionary voice: an innovative, complex, even chaotic form of expression that rejects existing canons of language and authority in order to more accurately and meaningfully express the power relations of a new state of affairs. Although the authority of the traditional poet is likewise challenged, that of the modern poet, who revels in his trampled state and, like a dog, "licks the hand that has beaten him," is nevertheless the sole harbinger of revolution. In the name of revolution, we read in the section's closing stanzas, the poet tears out his soul and pounds it into a bloody banner, a gift for the tongueless streets (185). Sacrificial gestures aside, Maiakovskii leaves little doubt as to the dynamics of verbal authority in the city of the future: it is the consumptive screams of the charismatic poet that open the eyes of the masses to the power of their own voice.

If symbolist poets before him elevated the vulgar language and images of prostitutes and drunks to the status of what Iurii Tynianov called "literary fact," Maiakovskii melded the additional voice of the Bolshevik revolution (which itself had a penchant for profanity and brashness) into the mix—and in so doing not only further shocked the literary language but also injected a new dimension of authority into the marginal language of the profane.[58] He penned "odes" to the revolution and its heroes that irreverently fused the language of Bolshevism with that of the streets.[59] At times the amalgam bordered on the sort of transrational language, or *zaum*, for which poets such as Velimir Khlebnikov and Aleksei Kruchenykh had become notorious:

> Mimo
> > barov i ban'.
> Bei, baraban!
> > Baraban, Baraban'!
> Byli raby!
> > Net raba!
> Baarbei!
> > Baarbei!
> > Baaraban! (2:127)

[Past the barons and bathhouses. Beat, drum! Drum, drum! Once there were slaves! The slave is no longer! Drum-beat-barons! Them-bathhouse-barons! Drum-beat-them-bathhouse-barons!]

"It is a new language environment," he declared in his 1926 essay on "How to Make Poems": "How do you make it poetic? The old rules with 'storms, roses,' *(grozy, rozy)* and alexandrine lines are insufficient. How do you introduce colloquial language into poetry and extract poetry from colloquial language? [You must] immediately give all rights of citizenship to the new language: the shriek, instead of the melody, the crash of the drum, instead of the lullaby" (12:84–85). As brazen as that language was, it quickly acquired (in contrast to the less politically oriented *zaum*) "the right to citizenship" in a variety of spheres of public discourse where Maiakovskii's verse appeared: declaimed at public rallies, printed on the front pages of newspapers, plastered in storefront windows, and even mimicked in language textbooks. One of the more popular of the adult literacy readers of the day abandoned the Christian themes and the bucolic nature and domestic motifs that dominated pre-revolutionary primers and instead adopted lines that strongly evoked Maiakovskii's voice of revolutionary protest:

Ty ros bos, rabotal na bar, bary ne bosy,
ty vyros, ty bos, bary bosy, no ty rad sovetam, a bary ne rady
sovety baram ne dar, a udar, u bar dosada na sovety.[60]

[You grew up barefoot, worked for the barons, the barons are not barefoot, you're a grown man now, you are barefoot, barons are barefoot, but you are glad for the soviets, while the barons are not glad—the soviets are no gift for them, but a blow, the barons are vexed by the soviets.]

Particularly in his postrevolutionary work, Maiakovskii took very seriously and literally the dual mission of "revolutionizing" the languages of poetry and the streets. The effort assumed its most graphic form in the plethora of agitational verse that Maiakovskii generated during his feverish, two-year stint designing illustrations and text for the Russian Telegraph Agency *(Rosta)*. There, Maiakovskii generated hundreds of illustrated texts that merged the language of poetry, the streets, and the state in perhaps the most direct and public contexts possible: verse plastered across telegraph office and storefront windows all across the country. The short messages most frequently addressed themes relating to the ongoing civil war, and while certainly not some of the most dazzling verse of the volumes of lines he generated in his lifetime, they nicely exemplify the creative merger—toward practical ends—of the cacophonous voices of the modern day.[61]

As Viktor Shklovskii explained in his book on Maiakovskii, the *Rosta* windows filled a verbal and emotional void created by a public sphere marred by wartime anxiety, shortages, and store closures: "It was important that the street did not remain silent. The magazine windows were blind and empty. It was necessary to open up thought *[vytarashchit' mysl']* in them."[62] Shklovskii likewise recalled Tynianov's observations that the *Rosta* verses represented a modern-day version of "poems in an album."[63] Maiakovskii himself saw his work at *Rosta* as an important stage in his general campaign to "clean the poetic peel from [the Russian] language on themes that did not allow for wordiness" (12:208).[64]

While Maiakovskii no doubt made aesthetic compromises in these endeavors, subordinating complexity and innovation to the practical demands of coherently transmitting important facts, he continued to defend himself against accusations by some of his avant-gardist contemporaries (and many critics to this day) that he "sold out" to the state. In a published analysis of one of the many poems submitted to the journal *Novyi Lev* by beginning writers, Maiakovskii enumerates those features that are desirable, or "pro-*Lef*": among them, "a sense of topical interest" *(zlobodnevnost')*, unanticipated thematic development (including the displacement of familiar words with unfamiliar ones), the rejection of "generally accepted poetic language," and the introduction of "the speech of everyday life, the conversation of the street, words of the newspaper," and the optimistic engagement of approaching alarm and the possibility of struggle.[65] "We do not want to know the differences between poetry, prose, and practical language," declared a collective statement appearing in *Lef*. "This entire work for us is not an aesthetic goal in and of itself, but a laboratory for the best possible expression of the facts of modernity" (12:449).

Maiakovskii's revolutionary orientation can also be found in his persistent attacks on the growth of an emerging Soviet bureaucracy. Like Trotsky, he considered it most threatening to the cause and fought it in every form (linguistic and institutional) at every turn. Published in the central newspaper, *Izvestiia TsIK*, and earning rare praise from Lenin himself, his poem "Meeting-mongers" *(Prozasedavshiesia* [1922]) exposed the creeping state of bureaucratic routinization in part by performing a satirical dissection of the various components of the neologistic Soviet institutional names:

> Chut' noch' prevratitsia v rassvet,
> vizhu kazhdyi den' ia:
> kto v glav,
> kto v kom,
> kto v polit,
> kto v prosvet,
> raskhoditsia narod v uchrezhden'ia.
> . . . .
> Snova vzbiraius', gliadia na noch',
> na verkhnii etazh semietazhnogo doma.
> "Prishel tovarishch Ivan Vanych?"
> "Na zasedanii
> A-be-ve-ge-de-e-zhe-ze-koma." (4:7–8)

["Just as night turns to dawn, I witness every day the people going off to their offices—some to the *glav*, some to the *kom*, some to the *polit*, some to the *prosvet*.
. . . .
Again I climb, now as day turns to night, to the upper floor of the seven-story building. 'Has Comrade Ivan 'Vanich returned?' 'He's at the meeting of the A-b-c-d-e-f-g-com.'"]

Maiakovskii complemented his hatred for routinized language and bureaucracy with a widely recognized charismatic flair in both his verse and his public persona. By most accounts, he transfixed audiences in a manner similar to that described by Trotsky, where the spell of the orator and his words takes hold of listeners and both captivates and transforms them. Themes of poetic novelty, charismatic, superhuman power, captivation, and transformation reappear in numerous recollections of Maiakovskii's public performances. One contemporary recalled how Maiakovskii stood on the stage during a reading, "brilliantly highlighted against the white background of the screen, with burning, fiery eyes, enormous, tall, reading his poems. Everything in him was stunning. Everything was new and unusual—the might of his voice, the beauty of its timbre, the temperament, the new words, and the novel mode of delivery."[66] As another put it, "By his one thousandth public reading, Maiakovskii was no longer simply a poet reading his poems. He had become a natural phenomenon, somewhat like thunder or an earthquake—that is how his audience responded to him, with its breath held in silent tension and a sudden explosion of voices, literally, not figuratively, with the thunder of applause. To the elements familiar from childhood—fire, wind, water—a new one was added, given the conventional name of 'poetry.'"[67] A third highlighted the uniqueness of his powerfully macaronic oratorical style:

> The manner and style of Maiakovskii's readings were themselves unrepeatable, where the inner strength and might of his poems combined with the might and strength of his voice; where tranquility and confidence combined with the special conviction of his poetic pathos, which would thunder and steam regally, then suddenly shift into simple, at times harsh, almost mundane intonations. . . . The impression left by it was not only enormous, it lay the foundation for me of that new model of *the greatest poet of our times*, a certain magnificent model of *the person of the new age*.[68]

Maiakovskii himself stressed the oral orientation of contemporary verse, dictated by an intertwining of aesthetic and sociopolitical principles. The "love whispers of samovar-laden verandas" were no longer appropriate for poetic expression; instead, he explains in a 1918 introduction to a collection of futurist poems, "We frightened the cloudless sky of manors with the roars of factory glows. . . . These are our meters—the cacophony of wars and revolutions" (12:12–13). The need to expand the linguistic base likewise meant for Maiakovskii the utilization not only of alternative modes of poetic expression, such as agitational slogans and advertisements, but also new media. Given its ability to transmit the spoken word immediately to thousands across the country, radio had particular appeal. "Herein lies the further advancement of the word, the slogan, poetry," he wrote in a 1927 essay. "[With the advent of the radio,] poetry has ceased to be only that which is seen by the eyes. The revolution has given us the audible word, audible poetry" (12:162). The "audibility" of the poetic word manifests itself in the other genres that regularly figured into Maiakovskii's envisioned and enacted expansion of the poetic language—"the orator's speech at a public rally, the frontline *chastushki*, the daily agitational headlines, the live voice of the radio and slogans glimmering by on the sides of buses—are all equal to, and sometimes more valuable than, the models of poetry" (12:211).[69]

Throughout his critical and theoretical writings, the importance of novelty and creative capacity remained central. At the same time he promoted the verbal empowerment of the working-class masses, he lambasted the mediocre poetic output of "proletarian" writers, dismissing them for their generally facile representation of revolutionary themes and their overreliance on worn-out poetic movements and tropes.[70] Despite the verbal authority and identity he granted both the "streets" and the "state," Maiakovskii maintained a privileged view of the authority of the poet and orator similar to that seen in the writings of Vinokur, Trotsky, and the *Lef* critics. When forced to defend the relative complexity of his verse, he likewise placed the burden of comprehensibility largely on the shoulders of the audiences, arguing that a "mass-orientation was the result of a long struggle, not a shirt in which the lucky books of some literary genius were born" (12:166). Just as "comprehensible" literature was not produced out of thin air, readers (and upstart writers) had to cultivate, appreciate, reproduce, and further generate new, accessible forms of art. Rather than literature that provided the reader with an entertaining, but unchallenging, story to the tired worker, the Soviet people needed a new type of poetry that, even though difficult to understand, would "enrich their brain, their imagination, [and] also sharpen their will in the struggle for Communism, in the struggle for Socialism" (12:424–25). In this same 1930 speech Maiakovskii names the two greatest difficulties facing the modern poet: rejecting, on the one hand, "a language thought up by the intelligentsia, which is disconnected from the language of the streets, from the language of the masses, and is called a literary language," and raising, on the other hand, the cultural level of the working class so that it can make sense of the poet's revolutionary amalgam (12:425).

• • •

While speaking in different contexts and toward different ends, advocates of a revolutionary voice all emphasized that the language of public discourse should be capable of expressing the complex realities of the contemporary world in a meaningful way, dynamic enough to accommodate the constant shifts in those realities. They likewise stressed the creative, innovative potential of language in the revolutionary society and its power to transform thought and expression. As the antithesis of such language, they pointed to the words, slogans, phrases, and abbreviations that had carried meaning during the early revolutionary period but, through overuse and immobility, had acquired the status of "empty," "meaningless," "thought-killing," "incantation." To reestablish meaning, to revitalize a truly revolutionary language, representatives of the revolutionary model invoked the authority of those whose domain was defined by the creative articulation of the word: the poet, the linguist, the polemicist, the orator. As these voices were most adept at articulating the changing complexities of the modern state, it was they that were to serve as models for the speechless citizens of that state. The process of enlightenment, however, involved not mindless repetition and mimicry but rather the conscious application of the styles of their mentors to aid them in their own personal articulation. The result depended on the specific orientation of the vision: for some, it was the creation of a citizen capable of engineering language to serve his revolutionary needs; for others, it was the nurturing of the citizen-polemicist, able to employ thoughtful and innovative language in public writing and speech, with the end goal of swaying public opinion; for still others, it was the formation and inspiration of a citizen-apostle, capable of interpreting and spreading the gospel of Bolshevism in a manner that spoke to the collective needs of the immediate speech community. In all cases, the language they spoke and wrote earned and maintained authority by virtue of its dynamic, meaningful, and multivalent form—three elements essential for putting into words the permanently revolving circus of the modern world.

CHAPTER THREE

AWKWARD AMBIGUITIES OF

THE SOVIET VOX POPULI

Gleb's fist got itchy, but he just spit. In his head, though, he marveled at the sharp language of the youth. The foreign words were like pepper in their savory Russian.

—Lidiia Seifullina, *Humus* (1922)

The popular model of public discourse shared the revolutionary voice's preference for the spoken, or at least orally oriented, word. And both models envisioned a dramatic shift in the distribution of linguistic capital in the new Soviet society. Where they differed was in their vision of the ideal speaker (and writer) of that society. Rather than regarding the population at large as a mass of unenlightened citizens in need of social and verbal edification from the cultural elite, advocates of the popular model looked precisely to the voice of the peasantry and working class for a source of inspiration and authority. Like Lev Sosnovskii, they saw in the unpolished speech of the newly empowered classes an appropriate model for verbal expression in Soviet society, set distinctly apart from the bourgeois language established and perpetuated by the creative intelligentsia before October 1917. In this respect, their answer to the "simplify versus edify" debate was quite the opposite, putting the onus on the language of the press to better reflect the speech patterns of the people *(narod)*, rather than on the people to accommodate the language of the press.

A variety of reasons account for this difference in orientation, some pragmatic, some more historical and philosophical. On the historical and philosophical side, lingering affinities with the populist movements of pre-revolutionary Russia combined with literal interpretations of the Marxist-Leninist pronouncements (about a dictatorship of the proletariat and a worker-peasant state in which even the common cook would be able to run the government) to generate considerable authority for the voice of the people. On the pragmatic side, it became quickly apparent to those with a keen eye on the language culture that not all citizens enjoyed the charismatic authority afforded by a gilded tongue or caustic pen. In fact, it was clear that much of the population was still too inexperienced in, confused by, or adversely disposed toward the language of Bolshevism.

That combination of factors largely accounts for the popular voice's particular abundance of linguistic capital during the mid-1920s. Its dual sources of authority, however, presented an entirely different set of problems from the elitism and inaccessibility that afflicted the revolutionary voice. Depending on one's understanding of the more specific demographic and ideological identity of the vox populi (people or proletariat?), two very different models of speaking and writing emerged, neither of which was compatible with the other. For a state concerned with establishing symbolic power and authority, that ambiguity of identity was a serious problem.

EMPOWERING THE VOICE OF THE PEOPLE

Sosnovskii attributed the communication gap to both a stylistic and ideological rift between "inveterate intellectuals" and the new writers from the working class and peasantry—the rabkory and sel'kory. The latter two groups, by virtue of their direct connection to the people *(narod),* had the ability to instill the newspapers with a new, fresh, and even "succulent" language, based on the colloquial speech of the factory and the farm. In contrast to the hackneyed journalistic discourse of the old newspaper intelligentsia, the worker and village correspondents, if they had not been infected by the bourgeois virus, wrote "simply," "clearly," and "precisely," making no effort to embellish or engage in abstraction. Their style may have been a little rough around the edges, but it was direct and to the point.

Advocates of a more popular language advised aspiring writers and journalists from the people accordingly, urging them to write "simply and clearly," in the colloquial language they used when speaking to friends or writing a letter home. Theirs was the "language of the people," or "the masses," "fresh" and "closer to life" than the "intricate" *(zamyslovatyi)* "language of *literati.*" This traditional intellectual language, in contrast, consisted of "wise words," "foreign words," and "encyclopedic words" that created a mystifying fog of ambiguity or abstraction. As tempting as it may have been to the beginning writer, this language was "a capitalist lie," to be avoided at all costs, and even "spat on."[1] Iakov Shafir characterized the bookish language of bourgeois journalists as a "tendency toward the construction of illusion, the concealment, the obscuring of actually existing social ties"—which was why they did not like "sharp words" and "'vulgar' popular speech that 'cut to the truth,'" calling things by their own names.[2] That was why, wrote Shafir in his own discussion of Lenin's

language, the great Bolshevik thinker had been so preoccupied with breaking down and tearing apart the language of his opponents: "Lenin's
thought, clear and precise to the end, shunned all those foggy veils with
which the ideologues of the ruling classes clouded their light-sensitive
ideas."[3] A 1924 instructional circular to worker correspondents of the
Tver' newspaper *On Watch* reiterated the positive contrast of oral and colloquial speech—in all its unorthodoxy—to that of the traditional journalistic pen, when it recommended that they write the way they spoke, without fearing the colorfulness and distinctiveness *(svoeobraznost')* of their
language, and without thinking that journalistic writing requires some
special sort of boring "officialese" *(kazennyi iazyk)*.[4]

Russian intellectual infatuation with the voice of the *narod* has its roots
in the romantic search for an authentic national culture and identity
(looking to folklore in particular) in the late eighteenth and early nineteenth centuries, in the literary portraits of Turgenev, Nekrasov, and
Leskov (among others), and in the more politicized populist movements
surrounding the emancipation of the serfs in 1861. The populist monu-
ment to the organic authenticity of the people had a strong linguistic
foundation, beginning with the fundamental notion of *zhivoe slovo,* or the
"living word." Vladimir Dal's *Tolkovyi slovar' zhivogo velikorusskogo iazyka*
(1863–1866) described the "living language," first, as "the language spoken currently by the people" and, then, when employed in fiction, as "a
language full of life, warm, boiling, and natural." The *narod,* according to
Dal', was more than simply those united under a common language or nation; it was the "mob" *(chern'),* the "common folk" *(prostoliud'e),* the "impoverished" *(nishchie),* in particular. It was, in other words, the idealized
conglomerate of social, cultural, and political "have-nots." And the voice
of this *narod,* as the adage went (noted by Dal' as well), was the voice of
God *(Glas naroda—glas bozhii)*.[5]

Despite the prominence of the working class and proletariat in Bolshevik discourse, the *glas naroda* was still a voice to be reckoned with in early
Soviet Russia. Terms such as "the people" *(narod)* and "the masses" became
even more plastic than in populist and romantic discourse, in some cases,
referring specifically to the rural peasantry (in the more traditional notion
of *narod*), in other cases, implying the inclusion of some or all of the urban working class.[6] In fact, a large part of the symbolic power this category retained lay in the ease with which the *narod*—together with its language—could be recruited to serve the ideas and visions for a new society
held by the political and cultural elite. Beyond its demographic and economic import, the "people," however narrowly or broadly defined, served
as a powerful symbolic "black hole," as Aleksandr Etkind aptly puts it,
"into which discourse spilled and to which any meaning could be ascribed."[7] It should be of little surprise, then, that, particularly in the years
just following the onset of Bolshevik rule, writers, scholars, and cultural

leaders directed their attention to this portion of the population in an effort to record its attitudes toward contemporary social, economic, and political changes. The contents of the earliest issues of the journal *Red Virgin Soil (Krasnaia nov')*, the first state-supported "thick journal" to appear after 1917, offer a case in point. In addition to featuring the stylized colloquial narrative voices of Aleksandr Arosev, Vsevolod Ivanov, Boris Pil'niak, Pantelemon Romanov, Artem Veslyi, and Mikhail Zoshchenko, the journal gives prominent space to political, economic, and popular discussions of agriculture, land reform, and the peasant way of life.[8] The journal also included a considerable amount of folklore and pseudofolklore, in some cases documenting elements of traditional folk culture and, in others, featuring material that somehow spoke to more "contemporary" issues.[9]

ETHNOGRAPHIC FICTIONS OF A PEOPLE AT WAR

Folklore and ethnography presented a particularly powerful medium for advancing the popular modes of speaking and writing because of their widely perceived status as direct, unfiltered channels to the mentality of the people. Unlike post-structuralist practices of more recent times, which thrust the role of the ethnographer and folklorist as reality-shaper into plain and problematic view, early Soviet folklorists and ethnographers made no qualms about presenting their material as the authentic living word. The potency of this illusion in establishing (and calling to question) symbolic power and authority becomes apparent at nearly every turn when one looks more closely at the institutions most directly responsible for documenting the voice of the people.

Sof'ia Fedorchenko's *People at War (Narod na voine)*, a folkloric representations of the *glas naroda* published in various forms between 1917 and 1927, offers one of the more curious cases in point, in part because of the way the wartime field nurse presented her work, in part because of the ideologically charged scandal that surrounded it several years after its first printing. The most direct authorial presence comes in the form of methodological introductions appearing in prefaces to the separately published editions of the first volume and a journal excerpt from the third and final volume.[10] According to the most detailed description of her collection methods, Fedorchenko copied down conversations with, and overheard among, soldiers at the front during World War I and, later, during the civil war, doing so "without being shy, often on the job and during every free minute."[11] The 1917 volume gives the same impression in its subtitle, "Frontline Notes." Along with attempting to establish the authenticity of her texts, Fedorchenko's introduction reveals her own bias as to what constituted the legitimate voice of the people: "Less interesting was that which was said directly to me, especially by the younger soldiers. They all tried to adapt themselves to my level [of speech], they all thought that 'I wouldn't understand the simple stuff,' but when they began to talk in what in their opinion was an appropriate language, it was boring and not worth writing down."[12]

Added to this stylistic bias was the fact, which became public only a decade after publication, that there was considerable delay between her experiences at war and the actual composition of *The People at War*. In a 1928 interview that gave rise to accusations that the material was little more than a hoax, Fedorchenko admitted that she actually "did not record the conversations," "was not an ethnographer or stenographer," and only compiled the material after the war and her return from the front—an admission that essentially ruined her writing career.[13] Whether she was in fact guilty of "falsification," or simply failed to make sufficiently blatant the "device" she was using to counter existing narratives that were either too dry or too romanticized, is irrelevant to the present discussion. More important is that, regardless of the source of inspiration, hers was essentially a fictional work posing as folklore, constructed to take full advantage of the authority of the vox populi and highlight that collective voice in a period of chaos and suffering. The quick and wide praise it received for the manner in which it captured that voice attests to the power of the device.[14]

Aside from the short prefaces, the texts lack all traces of a narrative voice, consisting entirely of direct quotes from unidentified sources, ranging in length from a single sentence to a short paragraph. The only additional sign of overt authorial manipulation appears in the division of the soldiers' comments into thematic sections (a device used in all editions except for the first). Section headings to the civil war volume include those more obviously related to the title theme, such as "White Officers," "The Enemy," "Workers," and "Lenin," but also address topics less commonly associated with war: "Women," "Nature," "Dances," and "Dreams."

Despite their apparent differences in speaker, setting, and origin, the utterances, in their formal groupings, often give rise to a distinct sense of artistic coherence. The following observations, for example, appear in the section "On the War Itself":

> Zhzh . . . zhzhzhzh . . . —puli. Azhno dyshut oni na tebia, azhno volosy poshevelivaiut, azhno laskovyi ot nikh veterok.
>
> U nas sgovor budet: svoiu voinu dovoiuem, na chuzhuiu ne idti.
>
> Da "dumali li", da "gadali li"? Nikto ne gadal, da bog ugadal. Kaku nadobno voinu, tu i terpim.
>
> Byvalo, na kulachki vyidesh'—veselo, serdtse igraet. Byla nemetskaia voina—kak vo sne voevalosia. Kuda povernut, tuda i tychesh', glaz ne prodiraia. A vot teper' i zriachi, i zzhelch' kipit, i serdtse igraet.

Komdiry u nas—bosiachnia bosiachnei. Ni u nego loshadki, ni u nego korki lishnei. Odin binokl s nami v razlichie, a tak vse my—kak odin. Nichego eta voina na tu nepokhozha. Idesh' cherez golod, cherez silu. Doshel—krik strel'ba, khovaiutsia ot nas v panike. Tut vorvalis', vse ponashemu, i plachut, i krichat. Kakoi ty est', takoi i predstavliaesh'sia. Vse poniatno—i kto, i za chto. Eto tebe ne zagranitsa, da po chuzhoi vole.

Na toi voine nas bili, na etoi—my b'em. Mozhet, mne tol'ko tak sdaetsia, a dumaiu, potomu tol'ko my i b'emsia, chto my vsekh spravedlivei i sami za sebia. (160)

[Zing . . . zin-n-ng . . . —bullets. They breathe on you, they do; ruffle up the hair on your head; it's a tender little breeze they make alright.

We'll make a deal: our own war we'll fight; others' . . . —no go.

"Who woulda thought it?" "Who woulda guessed?" No one guessed, just God guessed. Whatever war's necessary, we put up with it.

It used to be, you got into a fight—it was fun, got your heart going. There was the German war—that was like fighting in a dream. Whichever way they turned, that's where you jabbed, without opening your eyes. Now in this one you can see, the bile seethes, and the heart gets going.

Our commanders are out-and-out tramps. Haven't got a horse, haven't got an extra crust of bread. Only their binoculars set them apart from us, otherwise, we're all like one.

This war isn't anything like that one. You put up with hunger, with exhaustion. You get there—screams, shooting, they bury themselves from us in a panic. They're the same way we are here: they burst in, they cry, they scream. You are what you appear to be. Everything's clear—who and why. This isn't your overseas, where you're there because somebody else made you.

In that war, we were the beaten ones: in this one, we do the beating. Maybe it just seems this way to me, but I think the only reason we're fighting is because we're more just than everyone else and (fighting) for ourselves.]

The collective pronouncements mark a voice colloquial, substandard, or regional in tone *(azhno, vyidesh' na kulachki, tykat', glaz ne prodiraia, zriachi, bosiachnia, xovat'sia)*, but not adverse to basic poetic devices such as anaphora *(azhno . . . , azhno . . . , azhno . . .)*, metonymy *(idesh' cherez golod, cherez silu . . . Doshel—krik, strel'ba . . .)*, word play, rhythm, and rhyme *(Da "dumali li", da "gadali li"? Nikto ne gadal, da bog ugadal)*. It is likewise a discourse prone to aphorism *([S]voiu voinu dovoiuem, na chuzhuiu ne idti. . . . Kakoi ty est', takoi i predstavliaesh'sia)* and emblematic of a certain folk justice in which "right" and "wrong" depend not on social, class, or historical considerations, but rather on who is beating whom.

In fact, signs of the language and ideas of the emerging Soviet state are few and far between, and even in their more positive manifestations carry an air of the exotic about them—such as in one soldier's declaration regarding his own political transformation: "I'm a state man now, I don't just think about my own hut; I'm new, I am" (*"Ia teper' chelovek gosudarstvennyi, ne o svoei tol'ko khate mysl' imeiu, novyi ia"* [156]). More often, statements evoking the language and ideas of the new order assume a more ambivalent tone—similar to Shafir's peasant respondents—permeated with a sense of estrangement and, on occasion, trepidation:

> Ia partiinykh kak-to ne liubliu, strashus'. Vot kak kon' neob"ezzhennyi, drozhu dazhe, ei-bogu. Mne kuda trudnee vsiakoi ustali po chuzhoi ukazke zhit', xot' by po spravedlivoi. Menia eshche oblamyvat' nuzhno, esli by u partiinogo vremia nashlos'. (154)

> [I don't really like party members—they scare me. I tremble even, by God, just like an unbroken horse. It's far harder than any sort of fatigue for me to live under someone else's edict, even a just one. I still need to be broken in, if the party member were to find the time.]

Particularly mixed are the peasant-soldiers' comments about workers. While some show admiration, most convey a sense of puzzlement, resentment, or disdain:

> S otsov na etoi fabrike iz nikh krov' tochili, a oni etu fabriku luchshe pashni liubiat, pushche glaza beregut. Chudaki! (355)
> [Their fathers were bled white at this factory, and they love it more than the fields they plow, cherish it more than the apple of their eye. Kooks!]

> Razve nasha bednost' s fabrichnoi v sravnenie? U nas net-net da otkolupnesh' kusok. Letom iagoda, grib, ryba byvaet. U nikh zhe—khot' gaiku sosi, do togo nichego net, odni mashiny maslo p'iut. (357)
> [Can our poverty really be compared to the factory workers'? We'll scrounge something up every once in a while—berries, mushrooms, fish in the summertime. As for them, they might as well suck on a wing nut, they've got so little; they can't drink oil like machines.]

> U nego sam-piat', mal mala men'she, a on, sukin syn, za chto zabastovku delaet? (356)
> [He has a brood of five kids, one smaller than the other, so what's he striking for, the son of a bitch?]

> Azhno smekh. Rabochie u nas vse zabratye veshchi pootnimali. "Ne

khorosho, mol, tovarishchi, eto narodnoe dostoianie." Tiu! A ia ne narod? Da eshche i sam dobyval. (358)
[What a laugh. Our workers have taken away all the appropriated goods. "Not good, comrades," they say, "it's the people's property." Phooey! And who am I, if not the "people"? What's more, I was the one who got it in the first place.]

In addition to this class-based ambivalence, the collective memory of the war projects a profound sense of trauma and confusion. In a manner reminiscent of Babel's civil war prose, the most gruesome images are articulated in startlingly matter-of-fact tones:

Zhena rozhala, kak prishli oni. Zashli v khatu, glianuli—griaz', vonishcha, ne ponravilos', da i baba vopit. Odnako vsiu sned' zabrali, molchki. Tak ia ni s chem i stal ditiati dozhidat'. Da razve v ispuge dorodish'? Pomerla zhena. (168–69)
[The wife was giving birth when they arrived. They stopped into the hut, looked around—filth, stench, and the woman howling to boot. But they took all the grub anyway, without a word. So I waited empty-handed for the kid to arrive. But how can you finish labor in such fright? The wife died.]

Po vsem khatam bureiu, ston stoit. K uchitel'nitse staroi: "Ty skol'ko," sprashivaiut, "godov zdes' uchitel'stvovala?" A ona bol'she tridtsati godov zdesia. Skazala. "Znachit," govoriat, "ty i kommunistov zdeshnikh obuchila, na zh tebe pensiiu za to," i cherez litso ee nagaikoi. (182)
[They stormed through all the huts, groans filled the air. "How long you been teaching here?" they asked the schoolteacher. And she's been around here more than thirty years. She told them. "So," they tell her, "you taught the local communists, too—here's your pension for that,"—and let her have it across the face with a whip.]

The brevity of the utterances also recalls Babel, offering little in the way of extended (or coherent) plot development, as is the narrative focus—directed as much to the margins of battle as to the "heroic" effort itself. Compounded by the frequent use of the present historical verb tense, they convey a sense of confusion and tumult, whose meaning remains largely unfathomed.[15] This collective anxiety is perhaps most vividly transmitted by the section titled "Dreams," in which Fedorchenko strings together a series of nightmares retold by her soldier-informants. One captures the sense of horror and brokenness in barely a line:

Ia tozhe teper' ne ves' tselyi. Son u menia vsegda s odnim nachalom do

edinogo kontsa: nachalo—budto padaiu, oru togda; konets zhe—budto
dushit menia verevochka, i togda oru tozhe. (240)

[I'm not all together now either. My dreams all have the same beginning
leading to the same end: in the beginning, it's as if I'm falling, and screaming
also. In the end, it's as if the ol' rope is strangling me, and I'm screaming
then, too.]

More pronounced than any overarching story of battle, struggle, and
ultimate triumph, is the polyphonic portrait of a non-Bolshevik Russian
rural population in the throes of war, sickness, starvation, and death. Too
immediate for any intelligible plot, meaning, or message to emerge from
the rubble, experiences appear in a disjointed, confused, even horrific
manner. They are narrated in a voice that is without question simple and
fresh (though simplicity is not always an accurate gauge of authenticity),
but the stories they tell generate little coherence or sense out the elemental chaos and violence of the war-torn world of the civil war front, and
only faint, infrequent, and often faulty understanding of the new Bolshevik language and order.

FROM BARBARIAN TO PROLETARIAN LANGUAGE

A variation of the popular model of language attempted to avoid the
demographic bind and ideological shortcoming it entailed by focusing
more specifically on the language of "the proletariat" as the desired model
of writing. Like the broader popular model, it embraced as its ideal a language that was colloquial, concrete, and unembellished; it went further,
though, by identifying the labor conditions and life experience of the *politically conscious* worker as the source for such a discourse. According to
Lev Kleinbort, a prolific historian of proletarian letters of the time: "The
worker struggles for the right to write. He writes after work, physically, often morally broken: this is no writer-nobleman, who rewrites manuscripts
five times."[16] Nor is he prone to fits of lofty abstraction. The worker's writing was deed-oriented *(delovityi)*, direct, to the point, and based in the
concrete experiences of everyday life rather than on some obscure "ideal-
ism and mysticism."[17] In fact, for the beginning writer there was an inverse relationship between the expression of class consciousness and the
ornateness of form: the finer the aesthetic value of a work, the further it
was from a "conscious creation"; conversely, the more consciously dependent it was on the spirit of the collective, the less concern it reflected for
form, the less value it brought as art.[18]

The vision of a language that was concrete, deed oriented, and integrally connected to experiences relating to the factory and the work
collective reappeared in the opinions of other contemporary cultural

commentators. G. Seryi, an advocate of the "gray" masses and of a strong proletarian literature, urged contemporary writers to turn away from the classics and contemporary intellectuals, to look instead for stylistic inspiration to the living language of the factory: "Study the language of the factory. Become familiar not only with all the words of the factory language, study the style of that language—new turns-of-phrase, similes, comparisons, allegories, symbols. Pay attention to the development of plot in the colloquial narratives of workers. That is where the work on form is for proletarian writers."[19]

The key feature that set the "proletarian" voice apart from the more general "popular" one was its focus on political consciousness. Compared to the cosmic orientation of the "Smithy" group *(Kuznitsa)* and other self-proclaimed poet-proletarians during the years leading up to and just following October 1917, the formulations of Kleinbort and others represented a more ideologically grounded model of proletarian discourse. Rather than advocating the use of complex machine metaphors to create an art that deified production, they highlighted the concrete connection to the factory and production relations that the enlightened worker brought to art.[20] This notion of "consciousness" or "awareness" *(soznatel'nost')* was equally if not more important than mere demographic affiliation. In his book *The Russian Reader-Worker,* for instance, Kleinbort distinguished between "worker-masses" and "worker-intellectuals."[21] The latter differed from the former not so much by their socioeconomic status as by their frame of mind: "The lower layers of the proletariat think in a peasant manner, feel in a peasant manner, and these layers are more numerous than the industrial cadres of the proletariat. This disrupts both the order *(stroinost')* of material and the integrity *(tsel'nost')* of conclusions which are, of course, evident a priori: in the worker who lives by means of the sale of labor power and is tied to the factory for a lifetime, a half-tradesman, half-peasant still attached to land allotment shows through."[22] The "mass-worker" and the "intellectual-worker" may have shared the same apartment or workbench, but the latter was nonetheless more "proletarian" than the former—or at least had a higher level of awareness. To the "proletariat," in the sense discussed here, belonged all those, rural and urban inhabitants alike, who exhibited in their language an understanding of the issues and goals embodied and articulated by the ideological vanguard of the new society. To the *narod* or "masses" belonged the less politically enlightened peasants and workers, who may have fit the proletarian profile demographically but who were not quite "up to snuff" ideologically.

By Kleinbort's own account, the mass-oriented citizens far outnumbered the proletarian-oriented ones, a fact that lay at the heart of the tension within the popular model of public discourse, reflecting in miniature the problematic status of the "leading class" of the proletariat in a largely peasant country.[23] While the proletarian voice more closely reflected the *ideal* of the new Soviet citizen as dictated by Bolshevik ideology, the popular one more accurately mirrored reality. The underlying linguistic likeness of the working class and peasantry and rural populations is well illustrated in a textbook for beginning writers, where the author advocates the use of "provincialisms" in fiction:

> Barbarisms are in general undesirable. But it is essential to introduce provincialisms. . . . Popular (peasant) words and workers' words, as the language of social groups, are our words, our language, and it would be ridiculous to brush them off. It is essential to introduce such words into literature—to introduce them not only into dialogue, but also into the author's text, taking care only to put them in phrases that are comprehensible without explanation.[24]

More than two discrete socioeconomic groups, "the people" and "the masses" constituted a linguistic bloc united by their political and social peripheralization in bourgeois capitalist society. Bringing this periphery closer to the center of power was the ostensible task of the new Soviet society; one important method for doing so was to transform the barbaric language of the masses (peasant and working class) into the more enlightened discourse of an empowered proletariat. The question remained, however, whether the fresh language of the people could be blended with the ideologically conscious voice of the proletariat, without the stylistic and conceptual compromise of either one.

THE ELUSIVE PROLETARIAN VOICE IN LITERATURE

A similar confusion of, and tension between, these two voices can be found in the debates over a state policy on literature in the mid-1920s. The advocates of a "proletarian literature," centered around the "October" group, its literary journals *October* and *On Guard (Na postu)*, and the umbrella organization of the All-Union Association of Proletarian Writers (VAPP), learned well the lesson of power provided by the unsuccessful struggle for independence by the maverick Proletarian Culture (Proletcult) movement, whose efforts to wrap itself and its art in the mantle of Marxism while still claiming autonomy from the party and state were squelched by Lenin, Trotsky, and other Bolshevik leaders in 1920. In their 1924 demands for a clearly articulated party policy on literature, Leopold Averbakh, Aleksandr Bezymenskii, Georgii Lelevich, Illarion Vardin, and other leaders of the group took great care in describing literature as an ideological weapon of the party rather than some independent sphere into which any writer or literary movement could freely wander.[25]

Such a regrouping also brought adjustments to the valence of the key terms of the debate. The notion of "proletariat" remained at the center of their ideological plan, but with a semantic ambiguity that effectively narrowed its demographic scope to refer to individuals qualified to organize the urban working class. It was first and foremost a marker of ideological identity. The proletariat, according to the platform declaration published by the October group in the first issue of On Guard, oversees the working class, attending to the "organization of its awareness," and "proletarian literature is literature that organizes the psyche and consciousness of the working class and the broad laboring masses toward the end goals of the proletariat, as the rebuilder of the world and creator of communist society."[26] It may, more often than not, presume urban laborers, but, more important, it implied citizens conscious of their political lot. At the same time, they used the terms "people" and "masses" most often to refer to a body of citizens that was politically uneducated, "unconscious," and "elemental," a population open to and in great need of enlightenment.

If the proletarian writers privileged ideology in their use of such keywords as "proletarian," "masses," and "people," their opponents in the literary debates—Lunacharskii, Trotsky, Voronskii, and others—brought the demographic reality into full light. Although the proletariat and the masses were still separated by significant ideological differences, the real demographic similarities between workers and peasants precluded any attempt to advocate a purely proletarian discourse in literature. Lunacharskii, for instance, maintained the same basic semantic distinction between "proletariat" and "masses," and he argued that the state of proletarian art was so "embryonic" precisely because of the prominence and cultural backwardness of the "dark masses."[27] Ia. Iakovlev drew a closer parallel between the working class and the peasantry, describing the former as "still remaining half illiterate because of the enormous percentage of peasant elements at the factories who have not yet been recooked in the factory cauldron."[28] The proletariat retained its status as a "working vanguard" and "Soviet power in the village," remaining above the fray of the "dirt, illiteracy, and ignorance" of the majority of the Soviet people, but that position was offset by the further recognition that "the masses" comprised a large majority of the Russian population—not only of the peasantry, but of the working class itself.[29]

Although Voronskii, as editor of Red Virgin Soil, published numerous works by "proletarian" authors promoted by the advocates of a proletarian literature, he was clear in his opposition to a policy that recognized and promoted only this literature.[30] He went one step further than Lunacharskii and Iakovlev by denying that the notion of the "proletarian writer" had any meaning based in concrete reality: "The proletarian writer, viewed from a historical perspective, is not simply a writer-communist, nor a proletarian by origin; rather, it is a specific literary type that has taken shape over the course of recent years. Meanwhile, its living social and literary identity is time and again replaced by an abstract image, estranged from reality and constructed in an exclusively rational manner."[31] Trotsky, in his own well-known critique of the idea of a proletarian literature, argued that, by the time the working masses reached the stage of cultural literacy needed to produce the next Shakespeare or Goethe, the "proletariat" would no longer exist as a class, making the new culture "socialist," not "proletarian." He further claimed that the few manifestations of proletarian literature that had appeared did so in the form of anonymous writings in factory newspapers—not in the collections of the more professional "Smithy" group. But even these were of the "molecular" sort, because of the "cultural immaturity of the working class."[32]

Just as in the earlier discussions of proletarian language, debates over the viability of a proletarian literature faltered in the face of the demographic reality of a country dominated by semiliterate peasants and a working class of questionable consciousness. The block of peasant citizens that dominated both the village and the factory needed to be taken into account—linguistically and ideologically—in the construction of the new society and in the development of a new literary language. Peasants, it was believed, spoke, thought, and reacted differently and therefore required a language and themes that would both reflect their interests and gradually bring them into the proletarian fold.

THE "FELLOW-TRAVELERS" AND THE LITERARY SMYCHKA

Part of the literary solution to this problem lay in the figure of the "fellow-traveler" *(poputchik)*, a term introduced by Trotsky in his articles on literature in *Pravda*. He defined fellow-travelers as writers who did not come from the proletariat or openly espouse communist principles, writers who wrote fiction that was "more or less organically connected with the Revolution, but . . . at the same time not the art of the Revolution." Their separation from—and potential threat to—the revolutionary cause arose primarily from their closer affiliation to the peasantry than to the working class and communism: "They do not grasp the Revolution as a whole and the communist ideal is foreign to them. They are all more or less inclined to look hopefully at the peasant over the head of the worker."[33]

The group of prose writers most frequently labeled "fellow-travelers" by Trotsky and others included Boris Pil'niak, Isaak Babel', Lidiia Seifullina, and members of the "Serapion Brothers" (including Vsevolod Ivanov and Mikhail Zoshchenko).[34] All were published in the leading literary journals of the day and widely recognized as talented writers. Most of them wrote fiction set in the countryside and made ample use of the colloquial speech of the village. Pil'niak's *Naked Year*, for example, documented the chaos of the countryside in the wake of revolution and the chaotic mix resulting from the infusion of revolutionary discourse into local peasant dialect.[35]

In "Armored Train No. 14-69," Ivanov depicted the heroic civil war efforts of Red partisans in the Soviet Far East, using extensive wordplay to explore the exotic form Bolshevik language and ideas assume on the margins of the new state.[36] Seifullina wrote almost exclusively about life in the countryside during the revolution and civil war—most prominently in her works "Humus" and *Virineia*—and was widely praised for the rich language she used to depict her rural characters.[37] In his widely read and published short stories, Zoshchenko used satire and *skaz* narrative to highlight the multiple layers of often contradictory registers that influenced the speech practices of new Soviet citizens.[38] Although most of these authors came from bourgeois intellectual backgrounds, they also came to be identified with a brand of literary populism that, in mildly polemic language, was referred to as *narodnichestvo* ("populism"—from the idealist social movement of the late nineteenth century) and, in stronger polemic language, was called *muzhikovshchina* ("peasantifying," or "playing the redneck").[39]

The popularity and prominence of the "peasantifying" fellow-travelers underscored the challenges of establishing a hegemonic proletarian voice in a literature dominated by the voices of the periphery of the new cultural order—bourgeois writers writing about unenlightened peasants. The list of established proletarian writers was slim, even by the account of their own advocates. Judging by the discussions at a 1924 conference on literary policy, Dem'ian Bednyi, Iurii Libedinskii, and Aleksandr Serafimovich were the only stars of the group by the middle part of the decade (none of whom was from a working-class background). In his address to the participants, Trotsky chided his opponents for lacking the literary firepower to back up their hegemonic claims: "Just look at the baggage we bring to the issue of literature: . . . we boast that we've found, in the thick of the proletariat, *literati* and poets, while upon verification Dem'ian Bednyi alone answers for that entire 'thick.'"[40] He offered a simple explanation of the peasantifying tendency, linking it, in the process, directly to the fellow-travelers: "What is it with the peasantifying 'fellow-travelers' *(muzhikovstvuiushchie 'poputchiki')*? It is not at all an accidental phenomenon, nor is it small, or fleeting. We have, I beg you not to forget, a dictatorship of the proletariat in a country populated primarily by *muzhiks*."[41]

Voronskii echoed Trotsky's explanation when he defended his journal's record of publishing the work of the fellow-travelers, which was being broadened to include the proletarian writers themselves: "[The workers] are tied to the peasantry either by their milieu, or by origin. For this reason it is natural that, as soon as literary activity began to come to life, as soon as young writers appeared on the scene, a peasant, *muzhik* tendency took shape absolutely clearly and distinctly. I'm not only talking of the 'fellow-travelers.' I'm also talking about the proletarian writers, because that which has been said about the tendency must also be applied to the proletarian writer."[42]

None of the participants of the conference embraced this *muzhik* tendency as ideologically desirable; the comments by Voronskii, Trotsky, and others were more aimed at convincing the proletarian group that demographic and linguistic reality belied their attempts to acquire immediate and full cultural hegemony. To bring about reconciliation without compromising the central pillar of the state's ideology—the dictatorship of the proletariat—they recruited the metaphor of the *smychka*, which by then had gained common currency in the social sphere. The *smychka* (literally, "union" or "linking") was a plan of social engineering whereby the more "enlightened" urban proletariat (particularly political activists from the factories and the Komsomol) would link up with their peasant comrades in the villages and "take them in tow" socially, culturally, and politically. With the proletarians in the lead, the "dark masses" would gradually make their way into the daylight of consciousness, thereby allowing them to participate actively in the construction of the state.[43]

In literature, the notion of *smychka* provided the ideological justification for the proletarian writers to adopt a more conciliatory role not only toward the so-called "peasant writers" but toward the fellow-travelers as well.[44] It was entirely natural, argued Trotsky and Voronskii, that the new generation of writers displayed these "peasantifying tendencies" given the fact that the country was dominated by peasants and that the writers themselves, in many cases, came from rural backgrounds.[45] In fact, because they were "organically connected with the revolution," they offered a link to the countryside that the state could not afford to ignore. With some time and enlightenment into Marxist ways, it was hoped that the bourgeois fellow-travelers would begin to introduce into their well-crafted popular discourse a more conscious, *proletarian* voice.

Under that rationale, Voronskii offered a new criterion by which to judge artists: "Do they work to the advantage of a union between workers and peasants? . . . If we see that in the end the work of a given artist has such significance, that it promotes the union between the city and village, that it is directed toward a *smychka* between the proletariat and the peasantry, then we will forgive such an artist of a considerable amount. I believe that such work is helpful from the point of view of the proletariat, [and] submit that it is conducive for the creation of a proletarian literature."[46] I. Vareikis emphasized the need for the eventual ideological conversion of the peasantry and their verbal representatives, the *poputchiki:* "In a peasant country such as the USSR, a comparatively prolonged period marked by the presence of the 'fellow-travelers' in literature is absolutely unavoidable. . . . For in our peasant country we must in every way possible succeed in winning the 'fellow-travelers' over to our side. In the construction of socialism, the peasantry constitutes our 'fellow-travelers,' a block without which advancement forward would be unthinkable and impossible."[47]

With some range in modality, the language of the *smychka* figured prominently in the official policy statements on literature from the mid-1920s, appearing in the resolution to the above-mentioned conference itself, in the resolution to the Thirteenth Party Congress later that same month, and then, again, in the resolution to the June 1925 Central Committee meeting. All three documents called for a more conciliatory relationship with bourgeois and peasant elements (with the ultimate goal of "conquering" them) and identified guarded reconciliation with the *poputchiki* as one of the best means of doing so.[48] Regardless of the probability of such a union actually taking place in the manner suggested by the metaphor (i.e., along proletarian lines), the discourse of *smychka* at least gave the proletarian writers the ideological cover they needed to justify the rapprochement necessitated by the demographic, literary, and political climate of the day. Whether the policy would lead to stylistic and ideological "enlightenment" on the part of the fellow-travelers remained to be seen.

LOCAL POWER AND VERBAL CORRUPTION

One of the obstacles impeding a *smychka* of discourses was the sort of alienation and confusion displayed so palpably in Fedorchenko's fictional wartime fieldnotes. Another obstacle came in the form of the corrupt reappropriation of the new language of power—an equally common practice that likewise received considerable attention in the literature of the day. In a 1921 story entitled "The Ailing One" ("Boliashchii"), the peasant writer Semion Pod"iachev, one of the few published writers who could actually boast coming from peasant stock, portrays Foma Kirsanych, a rural official of limited education, but keenly aware of—if not plagued by—the power of public speech.[49] Any sense of the orator as a charismatic "welder" of mass minds disappears in the face of anxiety and self-importance. In either manifestation (as a source of local authority or of public humiliation) oratory is stripped of its awe-inspiring force and reduced to a basic instrument of power, to be used or abused according to the abilities and intentions of the individual speaker. That the struggle for power is primarily a verbal one based in the construction and articulation of ideas is clear from the prominence Pod"iachev gives Kirsanych's premeeting practice oration, performed in earnest (and isolation) before his bedroom mirror. Though obsessed with his self-presentation, all he can muster are half-baked phrases and broken clichés of new Soviet rhetoric:

Foma Kirsanych, uvlechennyi rech'iu i svoim sobstvennym vidom v zerkale, prisel kak-to po-chudnomu na kortochki i, protianuv vpered ruki so szhatymi kulakami, krichal, nabliudaia svoe otrazhenie:

"Tovarishche, grazhdane! Ia, kak mestnaia vlast', sovmestno s otdelom narodnogo obrazovaniia, prizyvaiu vas na bor'bu s temnotoiu . . . My dolzhny borot'sia . . . my, narod-titan, smetem vse, a svoe voz'mem . . . My . . . my . . . Ia i sovmestno otdel narodnogo obrazovaniia dolzhny pobedit' . . . My prosim vas . . . Ia khochu skazat', prizyvaem vas soedinit'sia i splotit'sia voedino i udarit', kak molotom, po golove gidru nevezhestva!(5)

[Foma Kirsanych, carried away by his speech and his own image in the mirror, assumed an odd, squatting position and, stretching out his arms with clenched fists, yelled, following his own reflection:
   "Comrade citizens! I, as local power, together with the division of people's education, summon you to the struggle with darkness. . . . We must struggle . . . we, the people-titan, will wipe out everything, and take what is ours. . . . We . . . we . . . I—and together the division of people's education—must be victorious. . . . We ask you—I want to say—summon you to unite and rally together to strike, like with a hammer, at the head of the hydra of ignorance!"]

The "oration" extends over two pages, marred by broken sentences, fractured syntax, and constant clearings of the throat. Kirsanych's God-fearing wife, eavesdropping at the door, pleads with him to come to his senses before the "satanic force of the commune" completely takes control, but he curses her defiantly for belittling the import of his speeches: "Each of my words, each of my looks and gestures must be not in vain, but well considered, because I am local power and everything emanates from me" (7). The author-narrator believes otherwise, however, and never even lets his hero before a live audience—reducing him, instead, to a state of near insanity.

Pod"iachev's was by no means the only contemporary portrait of inept and ill-motivated appropriations of the language of Bolshevism, though it is among the more telling owing to his own rural origins. Lidiia Seifullina, who herself lived and worked as a schoolteacher in the provinces, also thematized this sort of verbal corruption. Her novella, *Humus* (*Peregnoi*, 1922), offers one of the more vivid depictions of this nonliterary language and the more general problem of competing languages of authority.[50] It describes a small village of the Tambov region during the years just following the revolution and civil war, which its self-appointed chairman, Sofron Artamonovich, attempts to transform from a village of sectarians into a model of the Soviet commune. Sofron, however, is a petty tyrant. Instead of coaxing the local citizenry and economy through the necessary transformations, he tries to force it on them verbally and physically. In a story dominated by peasant language, the language of the nascent Soviet state appears infrequently and, when it does, is usually met with suspicion: "in the morning some guy with a thorn in his flesh came 'with a mandate' and read baffling words at the assembly: 'The *Sovnarkom*—to the *ispolkom*'s of all the *sovdep*'s.' Lenin hasn't disappeared. He speaks in that language."⁵¹ Sofron himself shows a basic understanding of the language, but the coarse, rudimentary nature of the interpretation becomes a convenient license for exercising his thirst for personal power and control. In addition to imposing dictatorial rule over the peace-loving sectarians, he beats his wife and son, rapes the librarian who was recently sent from the city, and murders a local doctor who refuses to report to him at municipal headquarters until he has completed an operation.

In the course of her tale about rural tyranny, violence, and excess, Seifullina offers two positive models of reception of Soviet power, each marked linguistically. The first is Kocherov, the mentor of the sectarians, who offers a populist solution to the communication gap and an antidote to the demagoguery practiced by the legions of Sofrons of the day. He suggests, essentially, that all that is needed is a good translation for the "trusting" Russian people to come around to the teachings of Marx:

> Byl on chelovek ne russkii, zapisal po inostrannomu svoe uchen'e. Vot uznat'-by doskonal'no podlinnost' Karlom Marksovym propisannogo. Russkii narod, on u nas skoro uveriaiushchii. Kak nam podali, tak my i glotaem. Razboru netu u nas v privychke. Naschet obrazovan'ia, kasatel'no inostrannykh iazykov, slab. Esli k inostrannomu nesumnitel'no dopustit'—Lenin chego pripisal, kak uznat'? Nado inostrannye iazyki urazumet' i Karlo Marksovo pisanie s russkimi sverit'. Vot togda mozhno: proletarii vsekh stran! (6)

> [He was a man who wasn't Russian, he wrote his teaching in a foreign language. Now if we could thoroughly find out the authenticity of Karlo Marxov's prescriptions. . . . Our Russian people are a quickly persuaded lot. We gulp it down however it's served up to us. Investigation is not a habit of ours. As for education concerning foreign languages, it's weak. If you indubitably tolerate foreign, how are you to know what Lenin ascribed to? You have to comprehend foreign languages and check Karlo Marxov's writing with Russians. Then it's okay—proletarians of all countries!]

Beyond his call for the translation of Bolshevism into a language comprehensible to the Russian people, Kocherov's own language serves as a positive model of a commonsense colloquial discourse void of any naturalized use of language of state, which, when complemented by the uncritical support of the narrator, enjoys a degree of authority lacking in the mutilated discourse of Sofron. It is a discourse potentially sympathetic to the new state, but its authority lies entirely outside of the language of the center.

Seifullina's other positive model offers quite a different solution—the voice of the urban center and political activism. The stranger who appears toward the middle of the story, referred to after his arrival simply as "the instructor," is fluent in the language of the party activist, of the "conscious proletariat" as described earlier in this chapter. The first lines attributed to him read like a primer in proper Bolshevik speech:

> "Gde zdes' ispolkom! Eto kakoe sobranie? Iacheika v sele imeetsia?"
> Sofron ni na odin vopros otvetit' ne uspel, a on uzh opiat' skoro, skoro sypal slovami.
> "Zdravstvuite, tovarishch! Ia vas v gorode videl, srazu zh uznal. Vy kazhetsia zdes' predvolispolkom? Aga, otlichno! Poedemte v biblioteku seichas. Vot moi mandat. Eto sobranie iacheiki? Slyshal, slyshal, vam udalos' srazu mnogochislennuiu organizovat'. Zdravstvuite, tovarishchi, gotovites' k vyboram v sovety? Kakie plany u vas zemel'nogo raspredeleniia? Da, da, znaiu, razbilis' na kommuny! A gde zdes' menia chaem napoiat?" (23)

> ["Where's the *ispolkom* here! Which meeting is this? Is there a (party) cell in the village?"
> Sofron didn't have a chance to respond to a single one of his questions before the words poured out again.
> "Greetings, comrades! I saw you in the town and immediately recognized you. And you would be the *predvolispolkom*[52] here? Um-hm, excellent! Let us now go to the library. Here's my mandate. Is the cell meeting? I heard, I heard, you've succeeded in organizing numerous ones. Greetings, comrades; are you making preparations for the *sovet* elections? What plans do have for land distribution? Yes, yes, I know, they've been divided into communes! And where might I get a drink of tea around here?"]

As diametrically opposed to the language of Kocherov as it is, the instructor's speech shares in common a linguistic integrity that prevents him from even attempting to communicate in a language foreign to him. His speech is void of the colloquial discourse that defines the speech of Kocherov and most of the other peasants portrayed in the story. Yet he not only makes himself understood to the initially perplexed villagers ("After a half hour . . . he had already taught them to understand his patter" [24]), he performs organizational miracles in the village in a short three days, including the political enlightenment of Sofron's previously derelict son. In Seifullina's view, either the language of the seasoned peasant or that of the conscious party activist has the most potential for making sense and communicating the language and symbols of the state to the people, and both are far preferable to the obviously corrupt tongue that results from the barbarous admixture of conflicting voices concocted by Safron. While Seifullina leaves her reader with an ambivalent feeling about the likely success of even these positive models (by the end of the story, the mentor Kocherov still awaits his popular translation of Marx, and the "instructor" has disappeared back to the city), she, like Pod"iachev, makes it perfectly clear that the primitive, half-mangled understanding of the language of Bolshevism poses a serious threat to the state and the peasantry alike. Clearly, a more reliable and concerted effort at language proletarianization was needed.

■ ■ ■

Like the revolutionary model of public speaking and writing, the popular one drew on ideas and sentiments that had taken root in Russia well before October 1917. And, while the prerevolutionary populist and modernist visions of cultural authority were nearly diametrically opposed, each proposed a dramatic, if not utopian, shift in balance of linguistic authority—the first in favor of the charismatic innovators, poets, and priests, the second, for the unrefined speech practices of the people. For each, the revolutionary language culture created an environment that gave new authority and momentum to ideas of social transformation, infusing them at the same time with a heightened sense of pragmatic urgency. Gone were the restraints of the old regime; new models of authority were desperately needed. Yet this same urgency underscored the shortcomings of each as language models on a broader scale. For advocates of the revolutionary voice, the challenge lay in reconciling the competing demands for verbal innovation and mass comprehension, a challenge that even more pragmatically oriented poets such as Maiakovskii had difficulty meeting. For proponents of the popular voice, it lay instead in coming to terms with the awkward ambiguities of a proletarian revolution in a peasant state, scripting a language that would allow the people to speak and write as politically conscious proletarians without forsaking their verbal roots in the village and factory.

CHAPTER FOUR

MODELS OF PROLETARIAN

LANGUAGE ACQUISITION

I continued to write. Writing is hard: the metalworker's job is so much easier. You have to write in a "comprehensible" language. There's the rub. There are two types of language: comprehensible and incomprehensible. It must be here that the class division of society is reflected.

—Aleksandr Arosev, "Toil. The Notes of T. A. Zabytyi" (1921)

The word is the most sensitive *index of social changes* and, what is more, of changes still in the process of growth, still without definitive shape and not as yet accommodated into already regularized and fully defined ideological systems. The word is the medium in which occur the slow quantitative accretions of those changes that have not yet achieved the status of a new ideological quality, not yet produced a new and fully fledged ideological form. The word has the capacity to register all the transitory, delicate, momentary phrases of social change.

—Valentin Voloshinov, *Marxism and the Philosophy of Language* (1929)

For all its traditional appeal and authority in Russian culture, the voice of the people was by most standards too raw to register the phrases of social change in the new Soviet state. Somehow this fresh source of verbal power needed a heavy dose of "proletarianization"—be it through the nurturing of more "conscious" writers from among their own ranks, through the deft pens of the fellow-travelers, or through a shift in emphasis away from the word altogether. The problem of how to ensure that the newly empowered citizens from the factories and villages acquire at least the basic vocabulary of the emerging state structure without abandoning their own linguistic roots and becoming either overly intellectualized or bureaucratized took on particular importance as the days of charismatic revolution gave way, in the mid-1920s, to the more mundane and daunting task of organizing and enlisting an enormous population in the reconstruction of the socialist state.

THE TONGUE-TIED VOICE OF THE "NEW INTELLIGENTSIA"

A second aspect of the literary debates and resolutions that reflected a general readjustment in orientation toward public discourse was the new emphasis placed on nurturing the worker and village correspondents *(rabkory* and *sel'kory)*—the leading representatives of the "new intelligentsia."[1] Although their original purpose had been to represent the voice of the workers and peasants in state-run newspapers, the *rabkory* and *sel'kory* also came to be viewed by some as the most promising proletarian fiction writers. In middecade discussions about literary policy, advocates of a proletarian literature, despite their tenuous rapprochement with the fellow-travelers, also demanded greater monetary and educational support for the worker and village correspondents. Citing the correspondents' "organic ties to the worker-peasant masses" and their ability to "participate actively in the political and economic construction of the Soviet state," a resolution from a 1924 writers' conference concluded that, beyond being mere journalists, the correspondents should be seen as "the reserves whence the new worker and peasant writers [would] arise."[2] Dem'ian Bednyi envisioned the dying off of the literature of "refined tastes" and the influx of "new, quick-sighted, real writers from among the *rabkory* and *sel'kory*."[3] Averbakh declared that the *rabkory* and *sel'kory* were just as important in the construction of a new literature as such stars of the proletarian camp as Libedinskii and Bezymenskii.[4]

The combination of their ties to the masses and their relative political consciousness made this body of amateur journalists prime targets for realizing the ideal profile of the proletarian writer.[5] But, as has been noted earlier, this combination also gave rise to its own set of ambiguities. If the correspondents were, on the one hand, to serve as the "voice of the people" with whom they lived and worked and, on the other, to bring the party and its ideas closer to the *narod*, in which language were they to communicate: the colloquial language of the people, or the ideologically "conscious" language of the state?[6] Discussions dedicated to the style of these new writers promoted almost exclusively a language model based on the colloquial speech patterns of the village and working-class communities—a popular, anti-intellectual voice from the "new intelligentsia" (an oxymoron that nicely illustrates the dilemma). Fedor Raskol'nikov, a Bolshevik critic and regular contributor to the literary journal *On Guard*, advised that "the worker correspondents who come to literature should least of all attempt to write in an intellectual language. Let them write just as they are accustomed to speaking. Let them write in the language that the working masses gave to them. Let them write in their own way, in the ordinary language of everyday practice. It is sufficiently expressive and attractive that it can bring to the Russian language more novelty than any one of the bourgeois writers could dream of."[7]

Little mention was made of any need to adopt the language features brought about by the revolution and the emerging state bureaucracy. It was precisely the nonbureaucratic freshness of the "language of everyday practice" that made the upstart authors so attractive. But they were expected to write not only as organic links to the people but as politically active representatives of the Soviet state, which meant that their language had somehow to reflect that authority verbally. And this meant adopting at least some of the new linguistic markers of the emerging state.

In point of fact, the flood of correspondence from peasants and workers that appeared in newspapers and separate collections over the course of the 1920s revealed a range of registers, a collective heteroglossia that reflected stylistically the ambiguous tasks of the new writers. At one end of the range was a colloquial, often nonliterary, language that was stylistically rough on the edges—traits that contributed to the ambience of freshness and novelty touted by the mentors of the worker and peasant writers. At the other end was a language strongly influenced by the vocabulary and phraseology of the new Bolshevik ideology. Rather than complementing one another, however, the two languages more frequently appeared in inverse proportions. The more colloquial a tone the language assumed, the less it showcased political consciousness; the more political awareness the *rabkor*'s writing exhibited, the less evident were the conversational features of popular discourse.

One of the first separately published collections of *rabkor* writings, the *Anthology of the Worker Correspondent*, offers ample illustrations of the range.[8] A brief, page-long entry in the collection, bearing the title "Between Workbenches" and written by a certain *"Rabkorrespondent* A. K.,"* provides a good example of the more colloquial style used in the reports:

> Ozhivliaet zavod. Serdtse uzhe zabilos'. Golova i ruka s perom iaviatsia pozzhe: "posle chaiu" . . . A poka pristupaiut k rabote. Ot stanka k stanku letit metkoe slovo. Sem'ia rabochaia druzhnaia, "kompaneiskaia." Vdrug udarilsia v steny raskatistyi smekh: vspominaiut komsomol'skie sviatki.
>
> "Zdorovo eto rebiata ustroili!"
>
> "N-da . . . lovko. Basniam popovskim, vidno, konets prishel . . .
>
> V zavkome nasushchnyi vopros ne daet pokoiu. Kogda stanet izvestnym, chto dumaiut khoziaeva s zavodom delat'? Skoro li skazhut, kakie mery k rasshireniiu prinimaiutsia? Pravdu govoril odin krasnyi director, chto na trest nadeisia, da i sam ne ploshai.

Sami-to, mozhet, i ne ploshali, da na trest nadeialis'—i naprasno: podvel. Odno zhelanie—uznat', chto budet s zavodom, da raskinut'sia, zarabotat' vo vsiu, "s dymom," kak govoritsia.[9]

[The factory comes to life. Its heart has already begun to beat. The head and hand with pen appear later, "after tea." . . . In the meantime, they set to work. The pointed word flies from workbench to workbench. The family of workers is friendly, "good-companied." Suddenly, peeling laughter strikes the walls: they're recalling the Komsomol Christmas.
"The boys threw an excellent one!"
"You said it—real pros. Seems that's the end of priests' fables."
In the zavkom a vital issue leaves no peace. When will it become known what the owners are thinking of doing with the factory? Will they soon say what measures are being taken toward expansion? One red director said it right: count on the trust, and don't slip up yourself.
Even when we didn't slip up, and counted on the trust, it was in vain—it let us down. There is one desire—to find out what will become of the factory, then to spread out, earn all we can, "smoking," as they say.]

The narrative voice reflects the colloquiality praised by those advocates of proletarian writing, with "organic" factory metaphors (its animation replete with the synecdochic "heart," "head," and "hand"), phrases such as *kompaneiskaia, sami-to, mozhet, ne ploshali, zarabotat' vo vsiu,* and *s dymom,* and a general comfort with the innocuous banter of the workers during their shift. Yet it is also comfortable with the state-originated aspects of this new life: the opposition between "Komsomol Christmas" and "priests' fables"; the new bureaucratic hierarchy of Soviet production, including the *zavkom* and the "red director"; and the idea that the workers have a stake in the future of their factory. The use of language and images of the state is neither abundant nor suggests direct affiliation with the source of power (here, the "red director"). It does, however, suggest considerably more sympathy for the new order on the part of the budding intellectual than was the case in Fedorchenko's pseudoethnographic narratives of the war.[10]

In other texts, the language of the revolutionary epoch occupies a more prominent position. The report "G.P.U. on a Visit to the Workers of the Arsenal" offers a lengthy description of a rally held in honor of a visit by the Soviet secret police, written by a *rabkor* entirely comfortable with, and immersed in, the language of the state:

Miting byl otkryt rech'iu tov. Gaitsana, ukazavshego na tiazhest' raboty GPU po bor'be s vragami rabochego klassa.
Tovarishch Evdokimov kratkim otchetom o rabote GPU pokazal arsenal'tsam,

chto GPU stoit na strazhe zavoevanii rabochikh i diktatury proletariata.
Vystupaet bespartiinyi kuznets tov. Kravtsov. Iarko i obrazno kleimit es-
erov.

"Pust' brodiashchie vokrug Arsenala esery zakleiat svoimi gazetami vse
steny Arsenala, arsenal'tsy za nimi nikogda ne poidut! Arsenalets vsegda stoit
za Sovetskuiu vlast' i kompartiiu! Arsenal'tsy privetstvuiut GPU v den' pi-
atiletiia raboty po bor'be s vragami rabochego klassa, otmechaia, chto vsia
rabota kontrrevoliutsii na Kievshchine razbita karaiushchim mechom proletariata—GPU . . ."

Tov. Evdokimov daet kliatvu arsenal'tsam, chto sotrudniki GPU vsiu svoiu
energiiu prilozhat k zakrepleniiu vlasti rabochikh. Gromkoe ura, grom
muzyki i applodismentov. Desiatkami rabochikh ruk tov. Evdokimov pod-
khvatyvaetsia i vzletaet na vozdukh. Komsomol'skaia molodezh' zaiavliaet,
chto ona budet uchit'sia po podvigam GPU, kak nuzhno zakrepliat' diktaturu
proletariata.

Torzhestvo zakoncheno. Dlia vsekh vragov rabochego klassa dolzhno byt'
iasno, chto GPU dorogo, i blizko rabochim, i oni vpolne solidarny s ego rabotoi.

Rabochie veriat, chto i na shestom godu proletarskoi revoliutsii sotrudniki
GPU takzhe stoiko i samootverzhenno budut rabotat' na pol'zu Sovetskoi
vlasti i zakrepliat' diktaturu proletariata.

Rabochie mogut spokoino vosstanavlivat' krupnuiu promyshlennost'.
GPU okhraniaet ikh tyl.[11]

[The meeting was opened with a speech by comrade Gaitsan, which
pointed out the difficulty of the GPU's work in the struggle against the enemies of the working class. . . .

In a brief report on the work of the GPU, Comrade Evdokimov demonstrated to the arsenalists that the GPU was on guard for the workers' conquest and the dictatorship of the proletariat.

Then, the blacksmith Kravtsov, a nonparty member, speaks. He brands the
S-R's vividly and expressively.

"Let the S-R's roaming around the arsenal stick their newspapers on all the
walls of the arsenal—the arsenalists will never follow them! The arsenalist always stands behind Soviet power and the Communist Party! Arsenalists greet
the GPU on the fifth anniversary of its work in the struggle with the enemies
of the working class, noting that all the work of the counterrevolutionaries
on the citizens of Kiev has been smashed by the punishing sword of the proletariat—the GPU. . . ."

Comrade Evdokimov vows to the arsenalists that the GPU employees will
invest all their energy into the strengthening of the workers' power. A loud
hurrah, the thunder of music and applause. Tens of workers' hands take up
comrade Evdokimov and hurl him into the air. The Komsomol youth announces that it will learn from the feats of the GPU how to strengthen the
dictatorship of the proletariat.

The celebration has ended. It should be clear to all enemies of the working class that the GPU is near and dear to the workers, and that they are in complete solidarity with its work.

The workers believe that in the sixth year of the proletarian revolution the employees of the GPU will work just as persistently and selflessly to the advantage of Soviet power and strengthen the dictatorship of the proletariat.

Workers may restore large-scale industry in peace.

The GPU is guarding their rear.]

From the commentary on the GPU's "struggle against the enemies of the working class" to the depiction of the thunderous applause and total commitment of the worker and Komsomol audience, the narrative reads like a model primer on how the population is to behave in the context of the new Soviet order—culminating with the final moralizing passages reassuring workers that "the GPU is dear and near" to them, so that they "may restore large-scale industry in peace." Missing from the narrative voice, however, are any signs of the "fresh," colloquial speech of the people. Instead, it represents the ideologically charged, eyewitness account of an insider party bureaucrat. Colloquialisms have given way to markers of Bolshevik rhetoric and officialese, including convoluted nominal and participial phrases (*ukazavshego na tiazhest'* . . . ; *stoit na strazhe zavoevanii* . . . ; *vsiu svoiu energiiu prilozhat k zakrepleniiu* . . .), propagandistic and militaristic clichés (*bor'ba s vragami rabochego klassa; diktatura proletariata; pol'za Sovetskoi vlasti, okhraniaet tyl*), and crisp, concrete, action-oriented modifiers (*iarko i obrazno; stoiko i samootverzhenno*).

The two examples offer a stylistic parallel to the demographic and ideological dilemma discussed earlier. The first text presents the "fresh" and "living" language of a worker correspondent organically tied to "the common folk," a voice that is receptive to the new order, but not entirely a part of it. The second marks the voice of a more politically conscious worker-activist, entirely at home with the language, symbols, and message of the state, but also lacking the colloquial freshness so valued by the advocates of a "new intelligentsia." To a certain degree, the two languages, like the two roles envisioned for the worker and rural correspondent, were incompatible. The voice of the *narod*, by virtue of its simplicity, was incapable of transmitting naturally the abstract ideas, language, and symbols of the central state; and once it had successfully adopted that language, it no longer reflected its organic link to the people. The choice of language represented a choice between two different sources of authority.

This is not to say that the two registers were simply incapable of appearing in the same narrative voice. The problem, instead, was that when they did they more often than not caused a transformation that in all likelihood compromised, or even deformed, its original strength. One of the more convoluted examples of the mix of state and colloquial language came from a "Komsomol Member K. A. Papoviants," who wrote an angry letter responding to a satirical feuilleton in which the author (Sosnovskii) ironically condoned drinking and wife beating for party members. In his letter, reprinted in the trade magazine *The Journalist*, Papoviants lectured editors and readers about the proper behavior of the conscious young communist:

> Vo-pervykh, kommunist, da voobshche kazhdyi soznatel'nyi chelovek, v lichnoi semeinoi zhizni a takzhe i v obshchestvennoi dolzhen byt' kommunistom, a, vo-pervykh, my kak komsomol'tsy, svoei smene (pionery) pripodnesem uchen'e deistvitel'no revoliutsionno-leninskoe, t.-e. pioner, buduchi na postu staroi gvardii, na vopros ugnetennykh narodov—svernut' sheiu kapitala i zabit' poslednii gvozd' v grob kapitala dlia togo, chtoby zavoevannyi tsennyi Oktiabr' prevratit' v Velikii "bud' gotov" i nesomnenno, chtoby otvet byl leninskii: "vsegda gotov."[12]

> [First of all, a communist—in fact, each conscious person—should be a communist in personal family life as well as in social life; and, secondly, as Komsomol members, we present to our replacements (the Pioneers) a truly revolutionary-Leninist teaching, that is, the Pioneer, being at the post of the old guard, to the question of the oppressed peoples—is to twist the neck of capital and beat the last nail into the coffin of capital in order to transform the conquered, precious October into a Great "be prepared," and so that, undoubtedly, the answer will be a Leninist "always prepared."]

What is intended as a testimony to the proper attitude and behavior of the young communist becomes an eruption of catch phrases and keywords of the central state ideology. In an apparent effort to instill the comment with the spirit of the party, all lexical and syntactic cohesion is destroyed. Hyperbolic and nonstandard use of high Bolshevik rhetoric, carved into colloquial syntax and run-on afterthoughts, invade the main flow of the discourse to the point of steering it off into a different direction altogether. This is made even more glaring by the writer's clear misunderstanding of the text about which he is complaining. More than relaying any concrete message, he draws attention to the contorted construction of his discourse. The author tries to communicate his ideological stance (that communists must set a good example and practice at home what they do in public), but the words get in the way. In the terminology of Bakhtin, it might be seen as an example of an accidental "hybrid" on the part of a learning author-narrator, the product of two language (and belief) systems mixing within the same utterance.[13] In sociological terms, it resembles what Pierre Bourdieu has called the "tongue-tied" efforts of the petite bourgeoisie, who, stigmatized by their status as dominated speakers, "strive desperately for correctness" or remain "'speechless' . . . 'at a loss for words,' as if they were suddenly dispossessed of their own language."[14]

THE NEW SOVIET NARRATOR AND THE POLITICS OF *SKAZ*

This element of "tongue-tiedness" is a hallmark feature of the fiction of the early 1920s—particularly of the fellow-travelers. Despite its perceived potential for bringing about a literary *smychka*, as Trotsky and Voronskii had hoped, the majority of the fiction produced by this loosely linked group of writers highlighted the verbal struggles of the predominantly peasant population attempting to come to terms (literally) with the emerging language of state. More often than not, as in Seifullina's story analyzed above, the fiction of the fellow-travelers "laid bare" the problem of translating the discourse of the central state into the peripheral language of the *muzhik*, tending to stress reappropriation rather than unadulterated acquisition.[15] Perhaps the most striking fiction of the day went so far as to thematize the popular permutations and distortions of central discursive authority. The peripheral voices of Cossacks and peasants in Babel's *Red Cavalry*, as seen in chapter 1, exhibit many of the features characteristic of the language of state, but they do so in forms and contexts either unintended or unanticipated by that language's central producers.

Still more notorious for his satirization of the new Soviet writer, Mikhail Zoshchenko likewise makes light of the tongue-tied perversions of would-be new intellectuals, depicting in his feuilletons from the mid-twenties what the author described as "the contemporary intellectual writer who may not exist now, but who ought to exist, if he were to fulfill precisely the social demand . . . of that sphere and that society that has now been thrust into the spotlight."[16] His 1924 sketch, "Monkey Language," offers a spoken version of the new sociolinguistic profile in a "very smart and intelligent conversation" between two delegates to a local party conference—an exchange utterly contorted by their misuse of the jargon of the emerging Soviet bureaucracy:

> "Vot vy, tovarishch, nebos' ne odobriaete eti plenarnye zasedaniia . . . A mne kak-to oni blizhe. Vse kak-to, znaete li, vykhodit v nikh minimal'no po sushchestvu dnia . . . Khotia ia, priamo skazhu, poslednee vremia otnoshus' dovol'no permanentno k etim sobraniiam. Tak, znaete li, industriia iz pustogo v porozhnee."
>
> "Ne vsegda eto," vozrazil pervyi. "Esli, konechno, posmotret' s tochki zreniia. Vstupit', tak skazat', na tochku zreniia i ottuda, s tochki zreniia, to—da, industriia konkretno."
>
> "Konkretno fakticheski," strogo popravil vtoroi . . .[17]

["Now you, comrade, I dare say, do not approve of these plenary sessions. . . . To me they are somehow closer. Everything in them, you know, comes out minimally, in the essence of the day. . . . Although, I'll say it directly, lately I've regarded these sessions relatively permanently. You know—an industry from the idle to the empty."

"Not always," objected the first. "If, of course, you look at it from a point of view. Assuming, that is, a point of view, and from there, from the point of view, then—sure, an industry concretely."

"Factually concretely," the second strictly corrected.]

A 1923 Zoshchenko feuilleton specifically highlights the difficulty of writing for one newly bestowed with the title of *rabkor*. Entitled "The Writer," it portrays the rural clerk Nikolai Drovishkin ("distinguished by his eloquence," according to the narrator) who, immediately upon appointment as *rabkor* for the paper *Red Miracle*, becomes dumbstruck by the demands of his new calling. His final product—an exposé about the moral decay of local residents who hang their wet underwear in public to dry—exhibits a convoluted mix of substandard and revolutionary discourse similar to the hybridized text of Komsomol member Papoviants (though Zoshchenko's writer adds a dimension of poetic language lacking in the earlier excerpt):

"I vmesto togo, chtoby videt' pered oknami landshaft prirody, trudi-ashchiesia poroi litsezreiut pered glazami mokroe bel'e, kotoroe povesheno dlia prosushki. Za primerom khodit' nedaleko. Ne dalee kak segodnia, vernu-vshis' posle trudovogo dnia, ia uvidel vysheukazannoe bel'e, sredi kotorogo byli i damskie prinadlezhnosti, i muzhskoe ispodnee, chto, konechno, ne otvechaet esteticheskim zaprosam dushi.

"Pora polozhit' etomu predel. To, chto pri starom rezhime bylo obychnym iavleniem, togo ne dolzhno byt' teper'."[18]

["And rather than seeing before the windows a landscape of nature, laborers at times behold before their eyes wet underwear hung out to dry. One does not have to search far for an example. No further than today, returning home after the work day, I saw the aforementioned underwear, among which were included both ladies' accessories and men's undergarments, which, of course, do not answer the aesthetic needs of the soul.

"It is time to put an end to this. That which under the old regime was an ordinary occurrence, now must not be."]

The main difference is that the hybrid here is deliberate on the part of the implied author—it appears by design, rather than by accident—and is directed at making fun of the struggling scribe. It occurs through a combination of ungainly lexical and syntactic constructions *(landshaft prirody;*

trudiashchiesia . . . litsezreiut . . . mokroe bel'e; vernuvshis' posle trudovogo dnia; vysheukazannoe bel'e), the incompatibility of the trivial topic with the gravity of tone, and the *rabkor*'s eventual realization that the underwear in question is in fact his own.

It is not accidental that many of the more problematic verbal portraits involve *skaz* narrators. In its narrower meaning, *skaz* is a parodic device that depends precisely on the undermining of narrative authority, mainly by creating discursive distance between narrator and implied author. It does so in part by invoking the speech of the "other" *(chuzhaia rech')*, the "not-author."[19] Generally identified as colloquial in tone, this voice exhibits an additional feature in the *skaz* texts of Babel', Zoshchenko, and other writers from the 1920s—namely, the irregular and seemingly unconscious infiltration of the emerging language of state. This specifically sociolinguistic component of *skaz* depicts a new Soviet writer-intellectual struggling to establish authority but caught up in a tongue-tied hybrid. "True" authority remains outside the margins of the perverted text with the implied author, who is usually sharing a chuckle with the implied reader at the narrator's expense.[20] Although these hybrid narratives may acknowledge the language of state as a discourse of power (by virtue of the writer's impulse to invoke it), they are unlikely candidates for a viable *smychka*, or union, because they either deprive the *narod* of the authority to exercise or articulate that power altogether, or grant it, but in a manner entirely unintended by the state.

Curiously enough, the *rabsel'kor* texts bear a strong resemblance to *skaz* narratives in this sense of deferred authority. Viewing them in their broader context—be it a newspaper or a collection edited by a central publishing house—it is quite possible to perceive their "narrators" as voices introduced, if not entirely created, by outside "authors" (in the guise of editors).[21] In the case of the papers, the distancing comes also by the fact that *rabkor* contributions were most often restricted to a special section toward the back of the paper entitled "Worker's Life" (giving rise, as seen in chapter 1, to objections from the worker correspondents themselves). In the case of the separate anthologies, most were presented in the same manner as the *skaz* narratives of Babel', Zoshchenko, and others—with a preface by an editor or literary figure accounting for their origin and significance. In the *Anthology of the Worker Correspondent*, the editor praises the texts within as models of the direct participation of the "new intelligentsia" in the construction of the new state and the transformation of the "worker and peasant masses."

But such descriptions reduced the authority of any one text to the mechanical act of penning the piece: the fact of its existence overshadows any authorial message contained within. At best, it is a kind of display narrative, presented as documented proof that the *narod* is actively doing its part.[22] In contrast to the fictional *skaz* narratives, the *rabkor* collections lack the open discord between narrator and implied author, the parodic rift that calls into question the credibility of the narrative itself. More pa-tronizing than parodic, they stand out simply as an objectified measure of the discursive influence of the central state on its cultural peripheries.

This appropriation of the *rabkor* literary output was perhaps most prominently practiced by Maxim Gorky, who devoted considerable atten-tion to what he termed "self-made writers" *(pisateli-samouchki)* and made little effort to conceal his doubts about their literary potential. His preface to a 1931 collection of stories by a *rabkor* "Gudok-Eremeev" illustrates the patronizing tone that such state appropriations frequently assumed:

> In the language of Eremeev speaks not the *literator*, but rather the ad-vanced individual of the working masses; it is the shout of their revolution-ary reason and heart. It is the raw material from which, with time, splendid dramas and novels will be manufactured; it is an authentic document of his-tory, which the masses themselves create. . . . With every year the working masses ever-more-loudly, ever-more-directly, ever-more-mightily announce themselves, their understanding of the tasks of the battle day and goals of the universal revolutionary epoch. And it could be, that soon there will not be a single workbench at which a conscious revolutionary, a communist, does not work—it is precisely to this which the mass surge of workers into the party testifies.[23]

Here, as in other prefatory remarks, the editor depersonalizes the voice of the *rabkor* into the voice of the "masses," reduces it to the level of "shouts" and "raw material," and limits its strength to the realm of *poten-tial*. Rather than the primeval stirring of the masses, it is the pronounce-ment of the writer Gorky that stands out as the authoritative point of view. And, in this distance between "authority" and "authorship," the *rabkor* collections differ little from the parodic *skaz* texts. Only the end goal is different. Rather than problematizing the hybrid discourse of the "new intelligentsia," the editors of the *rabsel'kor* collections hold them up as proof of an emerging cultural hegemony, which is a hegemony decid-edly *of* the state *over* the people, rather than the other way around.

By this reading, then, the efforts to promote some sort of popular voice in which the state could communicate with peripheral citizens were fraught with ambiguities of identity and authority. The early writ-ings of the *rabkor* themselves suggested the coexistence of two distinct discourses—the language of "ordinary everyday practice" and the lan-guage of the emerging Soviet state—which, in their most innocuous form, functioned in inverse proportions to one another. When they were mixed, an unpredictable and potentially threatening hybrid resulted. It was just this hybrid that the "peasantifying fellow-travelers" so incisively explored. In their narrative representations, popular reappropriations of the state discourse at best signaled a primitive, if not cruel, interpretation of the central value system; at worst, they marked its total perversion. In most all cases, they fell short of a credible model of authority. Occasionally, however, a *skaz* narrator would emerge from the cacophony of voices in the language culture of the 1920s who would manage to make use of the emerging language of state without undermining the authority of the state and, perhaps, even furthering its cause in the process. And these exceptions often prove as informative as the rules. Instructive to the present discussion is Nikolai Ognev's *Diary of Kostia Riabtsev* (*Dnevnik Kosti Riabtseva,* 1926), a widely published (but now largely forgotten) *skaz* narrative that, in its depiction of the new writing citizen in the process of acquiring the language of state, managed to defang the satirical bite of the genre by making its narrator a twelve-year-old working-class schoolboy. Because of this twist, the story can be read as something other than subversion—as a kind of allegory of linguistic adolescence for the budding proletarian.

THE DIARY OF A PROLETARIAN HOOLIGAN

First appearing in *Krasnaia nov'*, Ognev's *Diary* portrayed the reflections of a grade-school boy who decides to keep a diary after buying a notebook one day for "three bills" *(tri limona).*[24] The diary begins with the opening of the 1923 academic year and extends through the following fall (1924) term. As one would expect from a fictional diary, it is organized in chronological entries and lacks any real overarching plot. The young diarist focuses much of his attention on school life, but he also writes about such fashionable political and social issues as the homeless orphans *(bezprizorniki),* communist youth ethics, the organization of young "pioneers," educational reform, *shefstvo,* and *smychka.* He likewise addresses more taboo topics, including child abuse, teen suicide, masturbation, pregnancy, abortion, and even pedophilia. All this is done in a *skaz* narrative voice that had at least one critic wondering whether Ognev had not simply compiled the material from "authentic documents."[25]

As in other *skaz* narratives of the time, Ognev's diary makes ample use of the emerging language of state, often intermixed with the colloquial voice of the streets. In Kostia's case, the latter is further colored by his rough childhood, which, we are led to believe, was spent largely among the thieves and *besprizorniki*—the very groups labeled by pedagogues as the main source of discursive "perversion."[26] Among the nonstandard speech, school slang, and *besprizornik* argot peppering the diary's pages: *zanuda* (bore), *merzavets* (scoundrel), *skotina* (swine), *idiot, chort* (devil), *podléts* (scoundrel), and *svoloch'* (bastard); *shit'sia* (hang out), *zasypat'* (fail), *zadryga* (jerk), *guboshlep* (lip wagger); *buzá* (nonsense), *buzit'sia, mil'ton* (cop), *pilit'* (to nag), *dralka* (scuffle), *chistit' na vse korki* (to tear into), and *dat' krasnoarmeiskii paek* (to give a Red Army ration—the approximate

Russian equivalent of the American "flipping the bird," though with a slightly different gesture).

Language of state figures into the *Diary* on a variety of levels. Kostia and friends take pleasure, for instance, in generating stump-compounds— syllabic blends of multiple words, such as *Narkompros, Sovnarkom,* and *Goelro*—forms that constituted perhaps the most prominent sign of early Soviet language reconstruction. In addition to employing neologisms such as komsomol, *uchkom* (school committee), and the infamous *shkrab* (school teacher, from *shkolnyi rabotnik*), they use the same principle to create their own "telegraph language," a secret argot in which they utter entire phrases in stumped form (e.g., *Doto—Dovolen toboi* [Pleased with you], *Verzavok—Veren zavetam Oktiabria* [True to the testaments of October], 199–200). They likewise revolutionize the names of all of their teachers. The math teacher Aleksei Maksimych Fisher becomes *Almakfish;* the social studies teacher Nikolai Petrovich Ozhigov, *Nikpetozh;* the science teacher Elena Nikitichna Kaurova, *Elinikitka.* In the diary's opening entry, Kostia himself yearns for a revolutionary change in identity:

> Mne ochen' khochetsia peremenit' imia "Konstantin" na "Vladlen," a to "Kostiami" ochen' mnogikh zovut. Potom Konstantin—eto byl takoi turetskii tsar', kotoryi zavoeval gorod Konstantinopl', a ia plevat' na nego khotel s shestnadtsatogo etazha, kak vyrazhaetsia Serezhka Blinov." (5)

> [I really want to change my name 'Konstantin' to 'Vladlen' (from Vladimir Lenin—MSG), because many people are named 'Kostia.' Besides, Konstantin was some Turkish tsar who conquered the city of Constantinople, and I'd like to spit on him from the sixteenth floor, as Serezhka Blinov puts it.]

Much of Kostia's language reflects this sort of mix of basically sound (and brazen) revolutionary reason and the playful experimentation characteristic of youth slang. On other occasions, his use of the language of state hints at more problematic and potentially pernicious reappropriation of central state ideology. One school-related subplot finds him rallying a faction of his mates to oppose the monopolistic practices of the teachers' committee and forming a separate union (complete with a *komissar inostrannykh del* [commissar of foreign affairs] to negotiate with the teachers) to battle the injustices in the name of "self-governance" *(samoupravlenie).* Their primary aims—to eliminate obligatory greetings and standing for teachers *(obiazatel'noe zdorovan'e i vstavan'e)* and to win the right to wear hats in the classroom—initially resemble the symbolic struggles exercised by Bolsheviks soon after their assumption of power. But their proletarian goals soon devolve into ganglike warfare between the *soiuznik* (unionists) and their rival students, the *shkolniki* (pupilists), along with the enjoyment of less ideologically honorable activities such as playing soccer during recess.[27] Kostia's reaction to one teacher's description of Pushkin's untimely death suggests that much of his "revolutionary spirit" has at least some connection to the hooligan street ethics of his difficult childhood:

A ia by etogo Dantesa ne stal by na meste Pushkina vyzyvyat' na duel', a prosto otozval by ego v storonu i nabil by emu mordu v krov', a esli by on ne perestal pristavat', dal by emu odin raz datskim po-futbol'nomu, ponizhe zhivota: nebos' togda by perestal. Dantes etot byl, kak vidno, svoloch' poriadochnaia, vrode nashego Volod'ki Shmertsa, kotoryi pod-riad so vsemi devchatami sh'etsia i kotorogo vse kolotiat. (189)

[I would not have challenged that Dantes to a duel if I had been in Pushkin's place. I would have just called him over to the side and beaten his face bloody, and if he didn't stop flirting I'd have given him a single Dutch soccer chop below the belt: then he'd probably stop. It's obvious that this Dantes character was a complete bastard, like our own Volod'ka Shmertz, who hangs out with girl after girl and gets thrashed by everyone.]

On other occasions, his language and behavior pose more open and anarchistic threats to all forms of order and authority, be they bourgeois or Bolshevik.[28] In a supplement to the diary Kostia relates an episode in which he incites a group of young pioneers to rob a local apple orchard, justifying his actions by invoking the Bolshevik slogan of "expropriating the expropriators."[29] Recalling his own justification of the act, he writes:

Seichas—diktatura proletariata. Poniatno? Politicheski—eta diktatura oznachaet perekhodnuiu epokhu k kommunisticheskomu gosudarstvu. Chastnik—vrag takogo gosudarstva, a my—chast' proletariata. Poniatno? Poetomu—ideologicheski vpolne pravil'no, esli my otnimem u chastnika v svoiu pol'zu tridtsat' vosem' iablok. (252)

[We now have a dictatorship of the proletariat—clear? Politically, this dictatorship signifies a transitional epoch to a communist state. The private landowner is the enemy of such a state, and we are part of the proletariat. Clear? Therefore it is entirely proper ideologically if we take thirty-eight apples away from the private landowner to our own advantage.]

His articulate reasoning delights a majority of the hungry pioneers, who proceed to rob the orchard, but proves embarrassingly misapplied when they discover that the landowner is at least sympathetic to the new order and already hands over a substantial portion of his earnings to the state. Other episodes feature similarly misguided, excessive, and even anarchistic applications of the language of the state, such as picking fights with kids smaller than him, ostensibly because of their bourgeois origins (274–76), and alienating peasants by asking them, in the condescending tone emblematic of the *shefstvo* movement, whether they really believed in devils (150–52; 166–69).

The parallels to actual social and political issues are direct—and not always favorable to the emerging state. Nevertheless, although Ognev himself never quite made it into the pantheon of "proletarian writers," his *Diary* was widely praised soon after its appearance, at least through his death in 1938.[30] One critic, using Ognev to support his claim that contemporary literature had finally begun to offer positive role models for Soviet youth, praised the *Diary* as one of the more lasting representations of the revolutionary epoch.[31] Another referred to Kostia Riabtsev as a "typical model," a "fighter, builder, [and] activist," and even hailed the *Diary* as an example of the "path from idealistic romanticism to socialist realism."[32] When considered together with the accolades attributed to Maxim Gorky himself (who supposedly cited the *Diary* as one of the first serious and effective treatments of the "youth issue"), such comments give rise to a question central to the issue of voice, writing, and representation in the emerging Soviet state: given the degree of linguistic mix, reappropriation, and at least implicit anarchy, why did the fictional diary of this borderline hooligan remain a popular and positive model not only of proletarian youth but of what one critic called "living construction" itself?[33]

In contrast to the *skaz* narratives noted earlier, which produced critical portraits of the reception and reproduction of language of state among the predominantly rural and less educated population of Soviet Russia, Ognev's *skaz* is largely inoculated ideologically by the additional fact that the language rift can more easily be attributed to Kostia's youth and difficult upbringing than to some antagonistic class-based sentiment. Beneath the language confusion, the boy is basically a decent, budding proletarian. And it is in this sense that Kostia's *skaz* is relatively unique—a "proletarian *skaz*," if you will—that affords the reader a less threatening view of the potentially disruptive discourse due to the possibility of at least imagining that, with the proper nurturing of his proletarian instincts, Kostia would, in effect, "get over" his more problematic tendencies.[34]

THE LINGUISTIC ADOLESCENCE OF THE NEW SOVIET CITIZEN

Contemporary specialists in child psychology and language acquisition—most prominent among them Lev Vygotskii—lent credibility to the idea that only over time and through social contact did young speakers become responsible speaking and writing subjects. Challenging what he perceived to be an overdependence by previous psychologists on either physiological or personal development, Vygotskii argued that language developed primarily through meaningful interpersonal communication, or "mediation," from the surrounding social environment.[35] It was through such mediation, for example, that schoolchildren such as Kostia Riabtsev developed more accurate command of the often abstract language of state.

In research from the early 1930s, Vygotskii and his student Zhozefina Shif examined how children acquired "scientific concepts" *(nauchnye poniatiia)*, examples of which they took directly from the curriculum for fourth-grade social studies courses—words like "slavery," "exploitation," "bourgeoisie," and "revolution."[36] One such study asked children to complete logical statements using the conjunctions "although" and "because," providing prompts containing either "scientific concepts" or what they called "everyday concepts." Prompts for the latter included such phrases as "The girl reads badly, although . . ." and "The boy fell off his bicycle because . . ."; those for scientific concepts—"The police shot the revolutionaries because . . . ," "The capitalists prepare for a war against the USSR because . . . ," and *"Kulaks* and priests do not have the right to be voted into the Soviets because. . . ."[37]

Children responded correctly more often for the scientific concepts than for the everyday ones, but their interpretations of the former were more schematic in nature.[38] The further along in their schooling they were, the more accurate was their understanding. Both Shif and Vygotskii concluded that with proper mediation students' comprehension of scientific terms grew more sophisticated over time and even led to a more profound understanding of everyday concepts.[39] The abstract terms had something of a transformational or enriching power over the concrete.[40] Primitive or otherwise misguided use of scientific concepts, in other words, such as that found in Kostia Riabtsev's diary, was a natural part of the acquisition process and, when subjected to proper mediation, served as a framework for advanced cognitive development.[41]

Ognev "comes to terms" with the rift between popular reality and the proletarian ideal by couching the problem in the *skaz* narrative of a young Soviet citizen who carries the social and ideological credentials of a budding communist, and whose occasional deviations can be attributed to his youth and inexperience. The *Diary* can thus be understood as an apt metaphor for the developing language culture of the society as a whole. By virtue of their inexperience with the new "scientific concepts" that largely constituted the language of state, as well as the relative lack of social mediation, Soviet citizens—particularly those with no other verbal ground to fall back on—found themselves in a state of linguistic adolescence when operating in the official public sphere, a state in which the (often inadvertent) mixing of registers and language play was not at all uncommon.[42] Indeed, as Voloshinov suggested (in the second epigraph to this chapter), the language itself could be understood to have been in a state of adolescence, given its status as "the most sensitive index of social changes . . . changes still in the process of growth, still without definitive shape and not as yet accommodated into already regularized and fully defined ideological systems."[43]

This metaphorical link appears in contemporary discussions of Ognev's work. Aleksandr Voronskii viewed Riabtsev as a model citizen of the future generation who was sensitive toward injustices and demonstrated "rich social instincts." Another critic declared the *Diary* a testimony to the fact that youth had been "nullified" by recent social and political transformations and that Kostia's identity crisis embodied the predicament of the state and every other citizen within it. A third called Kostia a "little Bolshevik," who "was forcing his way through the wire entanglement of a difficult, transitional everyday life and through a series of impediments of personal character borne out of that everyday life."[44] In earlier comments on the contemporary language culture, Ognev himself suggested that the widespread and popular experimentation with language—similar to that re-created in his *Diary*—was actually a sign of growing democratization. The masses had finally understood that they now had "the right to create discourse *[slovo]*—and [had] thrown themselves into the source of that creativity with a passion."[45] Using language similar to that Vygotskii would later employ, he denied that such verbal creation constituted some sort of "deformation," referring to it instead as "an elemental process that is so important to our capacity for invention *[izmyshlenie],*" a sign of broader revolutionary impulses.[46]

A closing look at excerpts from a literacy primer for Red Army soldiers from 1922 suggests how this process of mediation, or proletarianization, was designed to take place in the case of adult learners. As noteworthy as the modernist innovation of some of the rhymes used to teach literacy were the explanatory notes that went along with them—a centrally proposed Socratic dialogue for instilling the language and ideas of the state:

> **2nd day. Slogan: "We will build a new world without tyrants and slaves." "p", "j".**[47]
>
> It is essential in the discussion to clarify the following: How is Soviet Russia now to be built? Who runs the country? How is it to be run and what have the Soviets done with the bourgeoisie, with the former tyrants and exploiters?
>
> In the fundamental law on the governmental structure of the RSFSR—the Constitution ratified by the fifth All-Russian Congress of Soviets on 10 July 1918—it says: . . .

A page-long discourse on the state governance laws ensues, only then followed by a transition into the actual reading exercise:

> After a brief discussion familiarizing [students] with the aforementioned order of elections to the Soviets, the teacher may turn to the isolation of the

sounds "j" and "p" if only in the following manner. Are those who exploited, oppressed, tyrannized the laborers permitted to take part in the construction of Soviet Russia? No. And how was it earlier? Who had the right to select and be selected to the State Duma, the zemstvo, the city dumas? The ones who were rich, those who lived on the labor of others, who enslaved the workers and peasants. And from this the conclusion can be drawn that we are building our world anew. Enslavers and exploiters are not taking part in this. "We will build a new world without tyrants and slaves."

Then [the teacher] can turn to a reading of the phrase, "We will build a new world without tyrants and slaves," and isolate in it the letters "i" and "j," in a parallel manner acquainting them with the orthography.[48]

Whether the actual literacy training followed neatly according to script is questionable at best. Studies of early Soviet schools suggest that education officials were hard pressed to convince teachers to follow the programs in the first place. In many cases, they simply ignored the new and often utopian methods thrown at them and fell back on tried and true methods of the prerevolutionary days.[49] Adult education instructors—even among Red Army soldiers—while perhaps less entrenched in traditional methods, ran up against a wall of still more basic problems, such as materials acquisition and the availability of qualified instructors.[50] Regardless of the impact of these efforts at state language acquisition and the likelihood of their giving rise to a viable proletarian hybrid, however, it was equally clear, first, that the process was meant to serve as a form of mediation between basic language skills and more abstract ideas and, second, that it would take considerable time to carry out. In the meantime, reliable sources of verbal authority were desperately needed. The refrain of the charismatic orator was growing stale, outdated, and corrupt.

MUTING THE ROUTINIZED REVOLUTIONARY WORD

Just as the overuse of terms, according to the *Lef* critics, leads to their deadening, so too, for Weber, does charismatic authority become "weakened by everyday life"—especially when adopted and redeployed by less eloquent and less admired followers.[51] This natural process of routinization, in language as well as other spheres, gives rise to unanticipated, and often undesirable, transformations, and it was these verbally suspect portraits —exemplified by Pod"iachev and Seifullina in the previous chapter—that dominated the fiction of the fellow-travelers in the years just following the civil war. In conjunction, one finds a curious related trend in the fiction of the more orthodox "proletarian" Soviet writers: a similar suspicion toward words (especially when disconnected from deeds) accompanied by a muting of the charismatic voice.

Interestingly enough, it is another *skaz* narrator who best articulates the general disillusionment over the fate of the charismatic word in the mouths of less able revolutionary disciples. The twist that allows such an authoritative statement about the corruptibility of the revolutionary word is that Aleksandr Arosev's "Toil: The Notes of T. A. Zabytyi" is written from the pen of a budding writer and first-generation Bolshevik activist of working-class origins.[52] Published on the pages of *Krasnaia nov'*, the notes convey the ambivalence toward language through one of the rare *skaz* narratives that does *not* encourage the reader to take the narrator's words with a grain of salt. This struggling storyteller clearly has something serious to say.

To set up his *skaz* narrative, Arosev employs the time-honored technique of editorial framing to introduce the collection of stories, explaining in an "editorial preface" how they had been found written out in pencil on crumpled scraps of paper stuffed under the mattress of the deceased author.[53] Eight stories then follow, each narrated in the first person by Zabytyi, whose straight-talking, no-nonsense narrative voice is as proficient in the "conscious" language of the emerging state as it is in the clear and simple style touted by advocates of a proletarian language. In contrast to the legions of either mediocre or subversive attempts at writing in such a style, Arosev's narrator would seem to present us with a voice that is at once popular and politically correct. The only problem is, in all his exemplary articulateness, Terentyi stands out as a dying linguistic breed, a *skaz* narrator whose "otherness" is constituted not by his own lack of credibility, but by his verbal isolation in a degraded language culture. Terentyi displays his profound ambivalence toward language in a variety of metalinguistic comments. He elaborates on his own struggles as an upstart writer, the difficulty of the writing process itself, the challenge posed by an unresponsive audience, and the humiliation of having manuscripts rejected (27, 47). He bemoans the inadequacy of language in expressing the depression and dismay conveyed by a disillusioned comrade ("He sought a means of expressing himself, but found none. All that came out were words, and words were not enough" [47]). He complains about an emerging class of party dilettantes who turn orators into a crude sort of commodity ("'I'm not a great admirer of the orators in these parts . . . but those Moscow orators . . . ,'" opines one of his characters, as she "fans her red, sweaty face with a paper fan" [44]). Offering a striking contrast to Trotsky's charismatic self-portrait of the orator communing with the crowd, Arosev's storyteller describes the great Bolshevik orator in a manner much more suspicious of the power of language:

> Trotskii zagovoril.
> V obshchem, nichego osobennogo. Tol'ko golos metallicheskii i liubit slova, narochito ikh vybiraet. V chem zhe magneticheskaia sila ego? Net, sila ne v slovakh, a v muzyke golosa. V umenii vo-vremia perevesti dukh,

vovremia peredokhnut'. Gde nado,—skazat' gromche. Gde nado,—spauzit'. A gde nado,—pustit' slovo s iazyka tak, kak strelu s tetivy, pustit' i chtoby vidno bylo, kak slovo-strela vonzaetsia v serdtse slushatelia. I eshche sila ego v figure. Shirokie plechi i kakie-to ob"emliushchie ruki. Kogda on govorit, da eshche tak osobenno pridykhaet, to kazhetsia, chto on neset i menia, i vsekh nas. Upiraetsia lbom vpered, nakloniaet i vskidyvaet golovu, rukami khvataet to vozdukh, to opiraetsia o piupitr, perevodit dykhanie, ustaet nesti. I snova i snova neset.

Bud' ia khudozhnik-futurist, ia izobrazil by Trotskogo dvumia treugol'nikami s osnovaniiami vverkh, a vershinami vniz: treugol'nik malen'kii—eto litso—na treugol'nike bol'shom—eto tulovishche. Vot ves' Trotskii. . . .

Na samom zhe dele na menia Trotskii proizvel bol'shoe vpechatlenie. On slovno vorvalsia v moiu golovu, i otdel'nye kusochki mysli, kotorye, kak razorvannye oblaka besporiadochno brodili v mozgu stal privodit' v poriadok. Eti razroznennye mysli on kak v vikhre zakrutil vokrug sterzhnia svoei rechi i povlek za soboi. (31–32)

[Trotsky began to speak.

Not bad, on the whole. Only his voice is metallic and he loves words, selecting them deliberately. So where does his magnetic force come from? No, the force is not in his words, but in the music of his voice. From the ability to take a timely breath, to pause for breath on time. Where necessary, to speak louder. Where necessary, to pause. And, where necessary, to release a word from his tongue, like an arrow from a bow, release it so that people can see how, like a verbal arrow, it penetrates the heart of the listener.

The force also comes from his figure. Wide shoulders and voluminating arms. When he speaks, and especially when he inhales, it seems as though he is sustaining me, all of us. He rests with his forehead forward, bends and throws up his head, his arms first grasping for air, then leaning on the pulpit, he takes a breath, tired from sustaining. Then again and again he sustains.

Were I a futurist artist, I would depict Trotsky as two inverted triangles—a small triangle, the face, on top of a big one, the torso. That's the whole Trotsky. . . .

In point of fact, Trotsky impressed me greatly. It was as if he had burst into my head and begun to put into order separate bits of thought that had been wandering confusedly in my brain like broken up clouds. As in a vortex, he twisted these uncoordinated thoughts around the core of his speech and pulled them after him.]

Terentyi clearly acknowledges the "magnetic strength" of Trotsky's oratory and its extraordinary ability to take hold of the crowd and transport it to another dimension of comprehension, but not without severely undercutting the charismatic pretensions of language that were characteristic of the revolutionary model of public discourse. The subversion takes place through a two-staged process of "defamiliarization"—first, in the reduction of Trotsky's magical speaking powers to such mechanical factors as breathing, tenor, timing, and intonation and, then, by offering a parodic "futurist" rendition of the Bolshevik that reduces him to a pair of inverted triangles. While the force of Trotsky's words still stands out, it becomes substantially weakened by the sense of irony and distance assumed by the first-person recollection. The orator is more a manipulator of words and gestures than an inspiring force, capable of capturing and articulating the thoughts and mood of the crowd (as Trotsky himself portrayed it). He is a caricature of modernist invention, a conjurer more than a three-dimensional leader with ideas. The revolutionary genre of oratory fares far worse in the mouths of inept rank-and-file speakers participating in a public rally, where Terentyi observes with dismay inarticulate party representatives blathering on and "getting mixed up in foreign words" (44).

This growing ambivalence toward language and public speaking likewise became a regular theme in the early classics of "proletarian" literature, which tellingly made little attempt to replicate the colloquial voice of the worker or peasant in the authoritative position of storyteller. Iurii Libedinskii's *The Week* (1922), for instance, a book that was embraced early on as one of the best guideposts for the proletarian cause, not only promoted a clearer, more measured manner of speaking and writing; it also conveyed marked ambivalence toward public language displays themselves. As such, it mapped out the historical and social logic that justified the transition from revolutionary words to proletarian deeds.[54]

As in many of the officially praised narratives of the day, the story is framed by public gatherings. The opening party meeting, in contrast to the animation and psychic energy of Trotsky's modern circus, is a model of organization and control. The audience appears as "a huge, gray, docile beast, lying at the feet of the chairman" (64). The first speaker, a leading party official, outlines the problem at hand (chopping enough wood to fuel the locomotives that will haul the seed to the village in time to ensure a successful sowing campaign) in the language of cold, hard facts ("inaudibly and deafly *[glukho]* raising his voice to the figures . . ."); he fails, however, to offer a concrete solution to the dilemma—a rift between word and deed that gives rise to minor chaos. Scores of working-class orators take to the podium in an attempt to articulate the solution, but their speeches, characterized by the narrator as "agitated," "awkward," and "disconnected," prove as incomprehensible to the audience as they are blind to the ultimate solution (provoking from one observer the angry accusation of "demagoguery, *mitingovshchina*" [65]).

It takes the old Bolshevik Robeiko to stop the cacophony, but even he is largely devoiced. Suffering from tuberculosis of the throat, so violent an illness that "the sounds tear his throat into shaggy, blood-red pieces," Robeiko is forced to "speak little, only several words, [so that] the issue would be clear, [and] everyone would . . . know how to speak of . . . the solution, that many saw only vaguely" (66). Though punctuated by excruciating pain and uncontrollable coughing, his speech does succeed in articulating—concisely and directly—the task at hand. The reduced emphasis on some charismatic link between orator and audience is further accentuated by the author's decision to convey the speech through the voice of the narrator, using quasi-direct discourse, rather than Robeiko himself:

> Ne nuzhno tol'ko teriat'sia, nuzhno oglianut'sia krugom, i gde-nibud' vyxod budet naiden. Nuzhno spokoino, khladnokrovno oglianut'sia. Razve partiia ne nakhodila poroiu dverei iz khudshikh zastenkov? V spokoinom izuchenii i v reshitel'nom deistvii nasha sila i mudrost'. . . .
>
> Nuzhno delat' vse skoro i reshitel'no, vziat' samim topory i pily, vstat' vperedi, prinudit' lodyrei i burzhuaziiu, privlech' Krasnuiu armiiu i vsekh trudiashchikhsia. Tol'ko ne medlit'; esli cherez dve nedeli semena budut zdes', to cherez mesiats pashni budut zaseiany. (66–67)

> [We must not get lost, we need to look around and somewhere a way out will be found. We need to look around calmly, coolly. Hasn't the party found doors out of the worst torture-chambers in the past? Our strength and wisdom lie in calm study and decisive action. . . .
>
> We must do everything decisively and soon, take up the axes and saws ourselves, stand in front, constrain the idlers and bourgeoisie, and draw in the Red Army and all laborers. We just can't delay; if the seeds are here in two weeks, the crops will be sown in a month.]

From action-oriented constructions built off of modal expressions of necessity (*nuzhno* appears five times) to repeated emphasis on calmness *(Ne nuzhno tol'ko teriat'sia . . . Nuzhno spokoino, khladnokrovno oglianut'sia . . . V spokoinom izuchenii)*, clarity *(iasno . . . iasno)* and decisiveness *(reshitel'noe deistvie . . . delat' vse skoro i reshitel'no . . . Tol'ko ne medlit')*, the address offers the perfect organizational alternative to a charismatic voice mutilated over the years by destruction and disease. Instead of rabble-rousing, it is at once straightforward and deed governed.

The ultimate confirmation of the shift comes in the story's closing scene—another party meeting held after Robeiko and most of the other leaders have been killed off in the successful defense of the town against a band of white terrorists. The survivors appoint as meeting chair the younger worker Gornykh, a "deed-oriented lad" *(delovoi paren')* so confident that the results of his work would speak for themselves that "he never spoke at rallies and did so very rarely at party cell meetings" (73, 144). His speech, we are told, emerges not from some charismatic gift but from the "reason and will" borne out of concrete tasks and experiences of the preceding week (144).[55] His final message to the crowd of rank-and-file party members—calling upon them to assume positions of responsibility for which they are less qualified than their former Bolshevik compatriots—underscores the challenge of the growing postrevolutionary, postwar state. Hundreds and thousands of young, inarticulate, and often poorly trained party members must fill the public-speaking roles of first-generation revolutionaries.[56] But doing so, given their backgrounds, their audiences, and the reconstructive tasks before them, would require a new way of speaking—a more simple and direct mode of expression, well-informed, and uncomplicated by the stale phrases of revolutionary rhetoric.[57]

BACK-TO-BASIC INSTRUCTIONS FOR THE NEW PROLETARIAN ORATOR

As in many of the post–civil war fictional portraits, professional and instructional manuals on public speaking likewise reveal a transition from a charismatic ideal to a more routinized reality. *Agitprop* journals and new manuals for public speaking began, toward the middle of the 1920s, to alter the focus of the discussion from the emotional, psychological, and transformational powers of the spoken word to more mundane issues: speaking in clear, comprehensible, and straightforward sentences, obtaining and mastering information about the issues, and refraining from speaking out on unfamiliar topics. According to the *Agitator's Guide*, a journal put out by the Central Committee's Division of Agitation and Propaganda, public communication was impeded by basic inadequacies—"the inability to formulate thoughts clearly and precisely, to concentrate them . . . in a united, orderly plan; the absence of habits relating to the oral exposition of ones thoughts, the inability to command speech sufficiently. . . ."[58]

Beyond oratorical incompetence, though, the times themselves had changed. Orators could no longer rely on "revolutionary pathos" to persuade their audiences, even if they had the power and authority to invoke it, according to the 1923 book, *Public Addresses: A Guide for Beginners*. It had disappeared.[59] Gone, likewise, were the days when short slogans and rallies were sufficient for conceptualizing new realities and spreading the word.[60] Slogans had become "naked"; rallies had become "hackneyed" and morphologically mocked by terms such as *mitingovanie* and—still worse—*mitingovshchina*.[61] Central organizers advised agitators to use the format only rarely and, then, with careful delineation of concrete issues.[62] The more complex educational and training tasks of the reconstruction period required more substantive forms of communication. In place of the ungainly mass rally, critics recommended the more focused "meeting" *(sobranie)* or the "discussion" *(beseda)*.[63] The shift in preferred context reflected a changing attitude toward audiences as well—in particular, a growing suspicion of the crowd's destructive potential under the spell of a charismatic orator. The crowd *(tolpa)*, according to *The Ability to Speak in*

Public (one of the more widely circulated manuals of the 1920s), was a pernicious and primitive force that could easily get out of hand. The orator's first priority was therefore to "organize" it.[64]

Finally, the growing emphasis on organization showed up in altered attitudes toward the spoken word itself. In addition to encouraging more simple and straightforward forms of expression, even those reflecting the colloquial speech of the factory and farm, commentaries shifted the balance of power between the word *(slovo)* and the deed *(delo)*, describing the former as an inferior appendage to the latter, rather than an essential, if not divine, conduit.[65] Even in the lofty context of the eulogy, as one author remarked, the "tedious, overchewed gum" and "contentless phrases" of "eloquence" should be abandoned for more deed-oriented praise: "Give a sober, deed-oriented evaluation of what the person has actually done, or a survey of what the person still stands to do. If he has not done anything useful, then there is no value in talking about him."[66]

. . .

Though invoked across a variety of institutional spheres and toward often differing ends, all these images of misappropriated, subversive, corrupt, simplified, muted, and toned down public language address a common problem—the transfer of power and authority from charismatic heights to the imperfect babble of everyday routine. A broad range of writers, from lesser known figures such as Fedorchenko, Seifullina, Ognev, and Arosev, to those such as Babel', Zoshchenko, and Libedinskii who help define various twentieth-century canons, used the medium of narrative fiction to explore the possibilities of the voice of the people. And, although their ideological range was wide, many of the more prominent experiments attested to the incompatibility between a popular and a proletarian model of public discourse—a fact supported by the verbal production of the worker and village correspondents themselves. The incompatibility lay in the tension between the ideological prototypes of the "proletariat" and "masses" and the demographic realities behind them. The ideologically charged debates over the language and policies of a proletarian literature demonstrated that the distinction between the two, though based to some degree in class, really lay in the degree of political consciousness and enlightenment. More than just the language of the village or the factory, the language of the people came to represent a discourse that was colloquial and fresh—or "elemental," to use another term common to this context—but also a discourse that remained ideologically dark, politically unenlightened.

The worker and village correspondents showed greatest promise for the beginnings of a new intelligentsia precisely because they were more likely to have received some political education and to write along ideologically prescribed lines. To ask or expect of these new model writers to then write in the colloquial language of the factory and village was to ask them to regress to the unconscious discourse of the laboring masses. And, in doing so, the politically enlightened proletarian discourse at best assumed a state of dormancy; at worst, it became transformed into an object of parody.

Paradoxically enough, the comment by Arosev's fictional writer, cited in the epigraph to this chapter, was right: language determined class, not the other way around. You either spoke or wrote in the "incomprehensible" language of the party activist, and remained isolated from the peasant masses, or you adopted a language "comprehensible" to them, in which case your ability to transmit the message of the party became doubtful. In Vygotskian terms, once the verbal mediation has been successful, it is hard going back. A verbal *smychka*, or link, was possible, but gave rise, more often than not, to a tongue-tied hybrid of questionable narrative authority. In light of this dilemma, the best that one could do was to deflect attention away from the revolutionary powers of the word in general—so as to avoid its subversive and corrupting potential in the mouths of lesser orators—and focus on the clarity of the message and deeds of the messenger instead. And the more fitting models for such clarity, as it turned out, were more readily found in the language inscribed by national tradition than in the fleeting harangues of revolutionary zeal.

CHAPTER FIVE

THE CLEANSING AUTHORITY
OF THE RUSSIAN NATIONAL VOICE

The question about the relationship to the literature of the classics amounts to a question of mastery.

—Maxim Gorky,
"The Working Class Must Raise Its Own Cultural Masters" (1929)

A whole disorder flows through speech and gives it this self-devouring momentum which keeps it in a perpetually suspended state. Conversely, writing is a hardened language which is self-contained and is in no way meant to deliver to its own duration a mobile series of approximations. It is on the contrary meant to impose, thanks to the shadow cast by its system of signs, the image of a speech which had a structure even before it came into existence.

—Roland Barthes, *Writing Degree Zero* (1953)

The Russian national view of language shared the culturist attitude of the revolutionary voice—that the burden of communication lay with the less literate citizens of the state, not with the language.[1] The colloquial, nonstandard language of the semieducated peasant or worker, instead of a fresh, new source of power for the new state, represented a hindrance to real power and legitimacy. To have any clout in the new society, the people would have to rise up to meet the standards of the Russian literary language.

The details of those standards, however, set the national model of language apart from the revolutionary view. For, unlike those formalists and modernists sympathetic to the transformations brought about by October 1917, who viewed language innovation as a means of perpetuating the revolutionary state, the proponents of the national model of public discourse sought to ground it solidly in the authority of the prerevolutionary Russian literary tradition—more specifically, in the realist "classics" from Pushkin, Turgenev, Tolstoy, and Chekhov up through Bunin and Gorky.

As the following discussion will show, this outlook was essentially a reaction against the discursive babble resulting from the barrage of revolutionary and popular voices in the realm of public language during the early years of Bolshevik rule. And, although its proponents ranged from anti-Soviet Russian émigrés to Maxim Gorky, the national voice found coherence in its desire to restore Russian to its rightful status, in the oft-cited words of Ivan Turgenev, as "a great and mighty language."[2] To this extent, efforts to promote the national model of language also represented a turn from the charismatic and chaotic strains of a revolutionary, orally oriented discourse to the more established voice of a written and canonical literary language.

LANGUAGE PURISTS, HOME AND ABROAD

Protests against the infiltration of foreign words into the Russian language and the "spoiling" of Russian by poorly educated speakers and writers sounded early on in the revolutionary years.[3] Perhaps the most significant of these was a note supposedly written by Lenin to Bukharin while listening to speeches at a party meeting in 1919 or 1920, in which the Bolshevik leader commented: "We are spoiling [portim] the Russian language. . . . Is it not time to declare war against the mangling [koverkan'e] of the Russian language?"[4] More than any other pronouncement, this note by Lenin served as a battle cry for those who took issue with the tumultuous state of public discourse during the early Soviet period. It reappeared throughout the debate on language to justify a broad variety of positions on the issue. But no group made such a worn aphorism out of Lenin's words than the one that advocated a return to the Russian literary classics for a positive model of public discourse. Less canonized in the lore of the Russian literary language, but equally as significant, were Lenin's efforts to assemble a committee of leading linguists and philologists to compose a dictionary that would replace Vladimir Dal''s *Interpretive Dictionary of the Living Great-Russian Language,* known for its abundance of dialectisms and other forms of nonliterary language. Lenin explained his rationale for the replacement in a letter to Lunacharskii:

> Comrade Lunacharskii!
>
> Not long ago (unfortunately and shamefully for the first time), I had the opportunity to acquaint myself with the famous dictionary of Dal'.
>
> It's a fantastic thing, but it is a *regional* dictionary and has become obsolete. Is it not time to create a dictionary of the *real* Russian language, say, a dictionary of words used *now* and by the *classics,* from Pushkin to Gorky?
>
> What if we were to set 30 scholars to this task, providing them with Red Army rations? How would you regard this idea—a dictionary of the classical Russian language?[5]

We may be tempted to attribute Lenin's inquiries to the "culturist" concerns of an old guard intelligent, and leave it at that. His skeptical attitude toward Maiakovskii, modernist experimentation, and even the so-called proletarian writers are well enough known.[6] But the discourse of purification suggests there is more to it than that. Notions of *purification, spoiling, mangling, regional, obsolete, real,* and *classical*—when used in conjunction with language—all function as broader moral and ideological signifiers, indications of a certain dynamic of power and authority. If a language is "spoiled," "impure," "defiled," "marginal," and "outdated," someone, or some group, is most likely perceived as the source of the spoiling, contamination, marginalization, and thereby the target of "cleansing" or "purification." Similarly, someone must serve as the linguistic "purifier," the creator and perpetuator of the "real" Russian language. Language "purism," as it is commonly termed, more often than not indicates an underlying struggle for power and authority and is closely linked to the issue of national identity.[7]

Particularly in times of radical change, when the language of the public sphere is most subjected to broad-based experiment and fluctuation, the purification process seeks to reestablish boundaries between self and other, stable sources of identity and difference, through the imposition of "standards" or "norms."[8] The underlying power play is built into the notions themselves: a language norm or standard is declared such (not always overtly) by those in positions of cultural power; they are most often recognized precisely when "violated."[9] In the context of early Soviet state building, the attitude spelled trouble for those workers and peasants who did not have command of the standard literary language: in the eyes of the national culturists, they were destined for the periphery of linguistic taste. They were tongue-tied foreigners in their own land.

However ironic, it is not surprising that some of the earliest echoes of Lenin's calls for purification (independent in origin though they were) came from Russian émigrés antagonistically disposed toward the Soviet state. Their pronouncements regarding the "defilement" of the Russian language under Soviet rule most vividly reflect the nationalist strains of language purism. Protests against the emerging language of the Soviet state flooded émigré newspapers and journals, often assuming parodic form. Words and phrases of the revolutionary epoch were more often than not qualified by quotation marks, or twisted around in form or context to serve as discursive weapons against their very source. In a 1922 editorial, "Hackwork" (the Russian *khaltura* mockingly evokes *kul'tura,* or "culture"), the linguist Sergei Kartsevskii claimed that the new language symbolized the "slovenliness" and "debauchery" that had taken control of the Soviet state and its citizens.[10] The émigré writer Vladislav Khodasevich dismissively mocked the *Lef* critics' celebration of Lenin's language, attributing the Bolshevik leader's coarse, anti-aesthetic, and polemical style not to a penchant for verbal innovation but rather to Lenin's own coarse and crude intellect.[11]

In letters and diary entries from the years just following the revolution, Ivan Bunin wrote of a general "vulgarization" of Russian speech practice as a result of Bolshevik bad manners. The crudity not only emanated from So- viet newspapers ("The papers are full of swearing. The word 'bastard' has become a technical term. . . ."); it infected the speech of the people them- selves ("the language is breaking up, it is sick even among the people"). The *muzhiki*—peasants who served as the focal point of so much of Bunin's fiction—"had begun to speak in a language that they themselves did not understand, twisting around urban words *[gorodskie slovechki]* making no sense at all."[12] Bunin's attitude toward contemporary fiction reflected a similar distaste for the events transpiring in the great Russian nation. In lit- erature, the demise had begun with the decadent writers at the turn of the century and continued through the contemporary plagiarisms of the Rus sian folk tradition by "self-satisfied insolent dupes, pretending to be elder experts of the word," the verbal and behavioral antics of Maiakovskii, and the excess experimentation of the majority of writers from Soviet Russia.[13]

In contrast, Bunin's praise for masters such as Tolstoy, Chekhov, and Kuprin most frequently rested on those authors' ability to create and pre- serve "the special storehouse *[sklad]* and character of *Russian* literature."[14] Even the reforms to the Cyrillic alphabet, which were enacted before the Bolshevik takeover and discussed by credible linguists still earlier, become a politically charged symbolic field. Bolsheviks embraced the reform as a sign of revolution and soon refused the import of books published in the old orthography (mostly by the Russian émigré press). Russian émigrés, for their part, lay blame for the reforms squarely on the new regime, calling them a "diabolic invention of Bolshevism."[15]

A pair of émigré Russian linguists, brothers Aleksandr and Sergei Volkonskii, elaborated on the vulgarity of the contemporary language and its link to the decay of the Russian national character. In a 1928 collection of coauthored essays bearing the mildly purist title, *In Defense of the Rus- sian Language,* Aleksandr wrote, "One needs to recognize that the *language* of a people, just like the *name* of a people, is an inalienable condition of its being, and that if we want the Russian people to continue to exist, then we must hold onto these two beginnings, as other peoples hold onto them—with frenzy, tooth, and nail."[16] Although they too traced the source of the problem back before 1917, they saw the Bolsheviks as being particularly egregious "vulgarizers" by virtue of their internationalist ide- ology, which rejected national identity and gave rise to a "perversion of patriotic consciousness."[17] "Class," for the Volkonskiis, was something that showed only when language was used improperly, as in the case of incorrect word stress: "[Incorrect word stress] imparts a certain classness *[klassovost']*, a familiar provincialism that is incompatible with real, absolute correctness of speech."[18] This latter type of language was a product of "cultivation" *(kul'turnost')*, not class.[19]

Only those with the purest and noblest of cultural blood lines—the Pushkins, Lermontovs, Turgenevs, and Tolstoys—were the rightful dictators of language standards, of "absolute correctness."[20] And it was their heirs who were to be the contemporary "guardians" *(okhraniteli)* of the great Russian language, and through it, Russian national identity: "They preserve . . . the literary language, a mighty force that unites all tribes of Russian roots, and a weapon for the cultural unification of all the peoples of the Russian world; they preserve at its very trunk not only the status of its people as a great power, not only its independence, but its very existence."[21]

For the Volkonskiis, the contemporary suffering of the Russian nation went hand in hand with the chaotic state of the national language; the downfall in its authority, in turn, stemmed directly (though not entirely) from a combination of the modernist rejection of the literary canon and the Bolshevik vulgarization of the literary language. Language was the ultimate guarantor of national strength and spirit: the greatest "authorities" in language, in turn, were the literary greats of the Russian Empire. The restoration of this language, through the revitalization of the realist tradition of its greatest authors, was tantamount to "the preservation and rebirth of the suffering Russian Land."[22] And the only hope for such preservation lay outside the borders of Soviet Russia, in the hands of the "free Russians" and their offspring (to whom the essays were dedicated).[23] Only there, where cultivation reigned over class, could there be a conscious respect for the purity of the discursive heritage and an effort to pass it on through the generations.[24]

Though they had in some cases antithetical origins, the views on language expressed by Lenin, Bunin, and the Volkonskiis shared three common features. First, they were in essence purist reactions against some combination of poor education, modernist experimentation, and intentional Bolshevik bad manners. Second, they envisioned as the antidote to the problem the standard literary language as codified by the Russian realist authors of the nineteenth century. Finally, implicit in all three views was the notion that the Russian language manifested its full power, authority, and legitimacy only in this standard literary form. Where at least the Volkonskiis, and most likely Bunin as well, differed from Lenin, was in their image of the logical perpetuation, or extended "genealogy," of that authority. The Volkonskiis saw it in the next generation of free Russian émigrés; Lenin saw it in the Russian acculturation of new Soviet citizens. Only in the writings of Maxim Gorky, the "founder of socialist realism and originator of Soviet literature," did this second idea receive full expression.[25]

MAXIM GORKY AND THE LANGUAGE OF MASTERY

The émigré discussions make blatant the strong nationalist undercurrents only hinted at in Lenin's comments on language. The fight for a clean, authoritative language was a matter of national legitimacy, identity, pride, and even survival. In the wake of the verbal chaos of the early 1920s, it was precisely that sort of semiotic stability that Soviet cultural leaders sought to reinstate—in the literary language among other spheres. It was Maxim Gorky, more than anyone, who managed to rearticulate these nationalist and elitist ideas in a language more palatable for a Soviet audience. His writings reflected a staunchly culturist attitude, but did so with a socialist twist that became more prominent over time. Gorky shared with the anti-Soviet Russian expatriates, in addition to the distance and dislocation from events in Russia (he lived outside of Soviet Russia from 1921 to 1931, mostly in Italy), the conviction that the future health of Russian culture rested in the preservation of the authority of the Russian language, which in turn meant the restoration of the classics of prerevolutionary Russian realism. He differed, however, in the ultimate goal of such preservation: far from an anti-Soviet national renaissance, he viewed in language preservation a means of ensuring the survival of the Soviet state as a legitimate and respected power. Through this amalgam, aided by Gorky's own voice of authority, the features of a Soviet Russian language of state began to emerge from the confused language culture of the day.[26]

Gorky recognized that the "writers from the people" had great potential due to the everyday experiences they brought to their work, but he was highly critical of the language and style they used to convey those experiences. The mix of colloquial speech and hackneyed phrases was a vestige of oppressed rural backwardness.[27] His responses to the scores of upstart writers seeking his advice continually returned to their language deficiencies, generally attributing them to an overall lack of cultural tools and training—in particular, to a poor knowledge of the national heritage. He likewise criticized their overdependence on contemporary newspapers for style and themes and their unrealistic expectations about the ease with which one became a successful writer.[28] Writing clearly and concisely came through education, diligence, and practice. Too often beginning writers rushed to produce works of literature and proclaim themselves successful literati. Too often they were "deafened by the dry crackle of newspaper language, [and] absolutely failed to hear the acoustic caprices [zvukovye kaprizy] of the language of living speech."[29]

The alternative to a language hastily forged from the "burning issues of the day" was one shaped slowly and authoritatively by the great writers of the prerevolutionary intelligentsia, from Pushkin to Bunin (and, presumably, Gorky himself).[30] Gorky repeatedly implored beginning writers to read the Russian classics for the best models of the literary language—an exemplary breadth and richness that did not exaggerate or falsify the speech of the people.[31] In response to criticism that the classics were ideologically unsound, he countered that the people were sufficiently strong in "class consciousness" to avoid falling prey to alien world views. While political training was best left to the specialists (and not literary critics), literary technique and language were best studied from "Tolstoy, Gogol', Leskov, Turgenev . . . Bunin, Chekhov, [and] Prishvin." "To fear ideological infection," he wrote, "is to doubt the strength of class consciousness."[32] Besides, he argued in a deft rhetorical twist, some of the more influential party activists were from nonproletarian roots: "The founder and genius of the party is not a worker. Beyond 'class consciousness' there is still the *consciousness of truth and of the creative force of class consciousness,* a consciousness of its historical necessity to be a creator of the new state, the new culture. It is this consciousness that has entered into the life of workers—people of other classes gave them the strength to organize the party."[33]

By arguing that the intelligentsia (in Gorky's vocabulary, the "nonworker") played a crucial role in generating language models and creatively realizing class consciousness (and, by extension, the new Soviet order itself), Gorky greatly furthered the cause for reinstating the classics (and the intelligentsia as a whole) in the struggle for language authority in the Soviet state.[34] The strength and purity of their voice far overpowered the potential for ideological contamination. "The question about the relationship to the literature of the classics," he wrote in another essay, "amounts to a question of mastery."[35] Young writers could either follow the "secrets" of mastery already provided by Pushkin, Tolstoy, and others, or they could wallow in the "verbal chaos" and "anarchical motion" of some yet-to-be-discovered notion of perfection.[36]

In form, Gorky's effort to reestablish the authority and stability of the Russian language closely resembled similar campaigns by the Volkonskiis, Kartsevskii, and other Russian émigrés; ideologically, however, Gorky saw the campaign as the only hope for preserving and maintaining the Soviet state. Whereas Kartsevskii and company dismissed the whole of Soviet discourse as "hackwork," Gorky sought to debunk the association between vulgar, nonliterary language, on the one hand, and "revolutionary" language, on the other. On the contrary, he complained in a 1926 letter to I. A. Gruzdev, such practices smacked of bourgeois philistinism: "This pursuit of new words, this fornication with language and excessive use of regional lexicons, I personally find most depressing. You must excuse me, but in this desire to decorate fiction with *nonliterary* words one senses— apart from the littering of language with rubbish—a bourgeois aesthetic at work: the desire to decorate an icon with foil, paper flowers, and 'grapes.'"[37] Such philistinism, or *poshlost'*, bore no relationship to anything even faintly resembling true revolution and only impeded the task of establishing verbal authority, or mastery, in the Soviet state. Prose writers' vulgarization of "the most splendid, aphoristic Russian speech, the expressive and pointed *[metkoe]* Russian word" may have been natural during times of chaotic social change, but it did not serve the interests of the language and citizens of the new republic.[38] Instead, they bore the responsibility of educating and unifying an enormous, multiethnic population, and the only way such education could take place was through the creation and maintenance of a single, national language.[39] Perpetuating the current state of verbal mediocrity, in addition to threatening multiethnic unity, would create an enormous burden on the state itself, compromising its authority at home and abroad. "The sickly condition of grammar reflects upon the health of ideology," he wrote in a 1927 letter to Voronskii.[40] If the hundreds of hack writers did not get any better, Gorky warned elsewhere, "the working class, Soviet power might inherit in their name tens and even hundreds of unrecognized geniuses, . . . grumblers, . . . spiteful critics and, in general, useless people."[41]

Gorky's stance on the power of the classics came to find support behind the literary scenes, where legions of "consultants," from proletarian groups such as the Russian Association of Proletarian Writers (RAPP) and the "Smithy" poets, were assigned the task of reading and responding to manuscripts submitted from beginning writers. Despite the nominal and declared allegiances of these groups to the burgeoning population of writers among the new intelligentsia, the tone and substance of their recommendations are, for the most part, dismissive and condescending.[42] One characteristic critique from 1928 likened the fiction of a village correspondent writer from Novgorod to "undeveloped raw material" completely lacking in "general grammar, to say nothing of literary grammar," and mocked it for "imitating the lisping speech of populist epigones." A second described a beginning poet's work as "illiterate in all respects" and recommended reading "the Classics."[43] A third consultant's summary of literary material submitted offered similarly damning critiques, dismissively suggesting that the consulting work be understood primarily as a means of nurturing "qualified readers" with some vestige of "literary taste."[44] In some cases, the consultants crossed the line from mere patronizing tutelage to verbal abuse—such as the RAPP representative who wrote to a Kagan telegraph operator: "It is difficult, in the nonsense . . . that you sent us, to find any sort of meaning. . . . It is all expressed in an almost tongue-tied manner. . . . It is bad, comrade. So bad, that worse is rarely encountered."[45]

The condescension echoes themes encountered in earlier discussions of a proletarian literature and proletarian voice. Despite what was no doubt sincere interest in nurturing writers from the expanding class of new intellectuals, it was quite clear that most viewed these efforts as, at best, a kind of literary training ground, a verbal adolescence for young working class and rural writers. Any hope of developing out of this literature some authoritative voice was thwarted not only by the imperfect articulations of the writers themselves but also by the manner in which these literary efforts were represented—often under the paternalistic editorial care of mentors such as Gorky, and often through condescending critiques that treated them like the products of well-meaning children, and no more. The overtly patronizing tone comes out in metaphors like "primitive," and "creative immaturity," and in comments such as the following critique of a collection of prose written by a group of Leningrad worker correspondents: "In it there is much that is unripe, naive, sometimes helpless and childlike, but, in addition to this, [there is also that which is] joyful, promising, smelling of the 'sticky leaves' of youth."[46] It is telling in this regard that, beginning in 1927 at the State Academy for the Arts, the study of the literary production of the worker correspondents was assigned to the "Committee for the study of the language and literary work of children and adolescents."[47]

CLEANSING THE LANGUAGE OF THE SCHOOLS

Those whose primary business it was to educate the younger citizens of the state offered resounding support for the views of Gorky and others. By the latter half of the decade, after a period of pedagogical courting of the revolutionary and popular experiments of contemporary writers, schoolteachers and other leading spokespersons for education turned back in favor of the more comprehensible classics.[48] This refocus in attention can be seen in the later issues of one of the leading pedagogical journals, *Native Language in School*, which, in contrast to earlier promotions of postrevolutionary literature, expressed by 1927 the predominant opinion that the majority of contemporary writers were too difficult—and often pernicious—for beginning readers. Moscow librarians echoed Gorky's concern over the dangers of the pseudopopulist style of contemporary writers ("The new literature perverts popular speech . . .") and demanded that writers who "created new grammar" or offered "false imitations of the language of the worker or peasant" be subjected to beatings.[49] Just because workers and peasants spoke in such a manner did not authorize writers to write that way. By the account of the *narod* itself, if we are to believe the librarians, such colloquial experiments were not only inappropriate but also an affront to the authentic language of the people. Much preferred was the "smooth, clear, pretty language of classic literature," presumably, as Gorky argued, because it attempted to convey the "spirit" of popular discourse without trying to reproduce its sometimes mangled letter.

That same issue featured "Seven Lessons in Politeness for Russian Language Classes," whose author strongly discouraged reading Zoshchenko, because, by the accounts of students themselves, his style negatively influenced their speech habits.[50] Similar attacks were aimed at the language of the newspaper. In a speech on the language of oratory, the party leader Mikhail Kalinin rejected the press as a positive model, noting that "Not a single orator, not a single agitator will be an agitator, orator or propagandist, if he studies Russian only from the newspapers. You don't learn Russian from the newspapers, you forget it. . . ."[51] Mikhail Peterson echoed those sentiments, deeming both Soviet newspapers and contemporary works of fiction that "injudiciously employ dialectisms and thieves' jargon . . . completely impermissible as material for the study of language." Only the classics and more contemporary writers who follow the tradition of the classics were appropriate models for language instruction.[52]

Perhaps by virtue of their location of the front lines of language instruction, teachers assumed a more conservative position in general with regard to language change. If other groups were more open to the neologisms, dialectisms, vulgarisms, and foreign loanwords that flooded the language of the public sphere in the years following October 1917, those connected to the world of pedagogy were far less willing to bend the norms and accept the idea of a changing balance of power in discourse.[53] Traditional biases manifested themselves in the dismissive manner in which they discussed the speech practices and influences of their clientele, which included adult learners as well as children. Bemoaning the general decline in students' speaking and writing abilities, one pedagogue explained that "today's pupil of the secondary school level, and especially of adult schools, who comes from a proletarian or peasant family is located in a surrounding outside of school that does not ease, but rather complicates the matter of mastering the literary language. It is for this reason that the school becomes the basic source for contemporary pupils to pick up the life-essential practical skills."[54] Another one warned that "measures need to be taken immediately to somehow fight for the purity and correctness of speech," because "the everyday language of the home and, to some extent, the social life of the student has sharply diverged from the language of classical literature, which has up until now been the criterion for the correctness of speech."[55] "Life votes for the classics," categorically stated a third: "The literary models of the past manifest themselves in language and consciousness; they are the resources for language, they have transformed into metaphors, into symbols. This is also culture, which should be critically mastered; the recognition of this necessity must be soberly taken into account by the masses."[56] The verbal power relations in all instances were clear: only within the controlled setting of the classroom and under the careful guidance of the teacher could students hope to function effectively in life. Responsible citizenship required (at least) the rejection and purification of insidious class-based linguistic influences and the "mastery" of the literary language—as embodied by "classical literature" (as defined, no doubt, by the teachers and curriculum designers).

The educational establishment's concern for maintaining the integrity of the spoken and written literary language was also reflected in the curricular recommendations for grade-school language and literature classes, published annually by the *Narkompros* and regional educational boards.[57] The changes in the literature programs from 1926 to 1927 are particularly instructive. The reading lists for grades five through seven in 1926, for instance, strongly favored contemporary writers, outnumbering prerevolutionary works nearly three-to-one. Of these, the vast majority highlighted thematically, if not stylistically, the life and language of the village and factory—the "peasantry" and the "proletariat." Readings were grouped together under such headings as "Poetry and Labor," "The Village and October," "Pictures of the Life of the Laboring Population of the City," "Workers' Struggle for the Liberation of Labor," and "Images of Fighters for the World Revolution: Lenin." The prerevolutionary fiction that did appear seemed equally driven by these sociopolitical topics (e.g., Turgenev's "Bailiff," Tolstoy's "Morning of a Landowner," Gogol's *Inspector General*, Chekhov's "Van'ka," and Lermontov's "Song of the Merchant").[58]

The program's explanatory notes that were dedicated to formal issues focused on the language of the proletarian and peasant masses and writers. Sixth-grade students were required to study "the *rabkor* and *sel'kor* movement and its role in the introduction of the worker and peasant masses to literature," and seventh graders considered such topics as "the socially subservient role of poetry," "the concept of the class ideology of the artist (the dependence upon it of images, *siuzhet*, language)," and "the distinctions in content and form of proletarian and peasant writers."[59] The notes likewise made liberal use of the discourse of the *smychka*, promoting themes about workers and city life and encouraging comparative studies of proletarian and peasant fiction as well as fiction of the *rabkory* and *sel'kory*.[60] Finally, the 1926 program included ample discussion of contemporary language phenomena and the need for students to master them—"archaisms and neologisms, in which the art of contemporary writers is so rich, words common to the peasant and worker environment, the language of the wall newspapers in the village, the factory and plant, the correspondence of the *sel'kor* and *rabkor*, [and] finally, foreign words."[61]

The 1927 program, in contrast, reflects a shift back to the classics, emphasizing proper usage as much as political ideology and remaining entirely mute over the issue of contemporary language change.[62] Of the thirty-five reading assignments listed for these grades, twenty-six involved authors and works that predated October 1917 (including early Gorky). Of these, titles from Pushkin, Tolstoy, and Turgenev dominated. No text from any of the early modernist movements (decadence, symbolism, futurism) was included, and only nine postrevolutionary authors made the list: Seifullina *(Lawbreakers)*, Libedinskii *(The Week)*, Serafimovich *(Iron Flood)*, Bezymenskii (selected poems), Bednyi (selected poems and fables), Vsevolod Ivanov *(Armored Train No. 14-69)*, Aleksandr Zharov ("Ice Flow"), and Aleksandr Neverov *(Tashkent—City of Bread)*. Of the prose works, only Seifullina, Ivanov, and Neverov presented narratives that posed alternatives to the literary language of the nineteenth-century romantic and realist classics, and they were strongly oriented toward the voice of the village or non-Russian ethnic groups. Beyond these two "sympathetic" fellow-travelers, the group included only two younger "proletarian" poets (Bezymenskii and Zharov) and works by two pseudo-"proletarian" writers (Libedinskii and Serafimovich), whose prose closely resembled the classics in language and narrative style.

To safeguard against the negative influence of the prerevolutionary roots of the classics, the 1927 program gave detailed instructions for appropriate ideological interpretation, using "the principle of Marxist-sociological study."[63] The note to the sixth-grade reading list, for instance, which included no postrevolutionary works, declared that "the sociological course . . . orients students in the economic and historical development of the nineteenth century, which in Russia was characterized by the development of urban culture and, in the second half of the century, the transfer of the class struggle's center of gravity from the peasants and the landowners in the village to the struggle between the workers and the capitalists in the city."[64]

Yet the 1927 curriculum placed at least equal emphasis on fostering basic language skills in reading, speaking, and writing. The main goals for fifth graders were "to establish a firm foundation of skills for independent work, develop the ability to interact with oral and written speech, . . . [and] enrich significantly the literary language of participants."[65] The bulk of the notes were dedicated to "reading culture," "speaking culture," and "written work" as well as discussing ways to enhance readings skills and foster self-expression.[66] The more pragmatic reorientation is corroborated by one of the more widely published language methodology guides of the late 1920s, whose author states outright that "to create cadres of writers and orators—an innumerable production of novelists, feuilletonists, etc.— would be a great misfortune for our country." What were needed, instead, he continued, were "people who, when asked, would be able to speak and write correctly, sensibly, convincingly, [and] sometimes expressively and strongly. . . ."[67] For models of such discourse, they depend largely on the literature of the Russian classics, with only minimal reference to the contemporary language culture.

LANGUAGE AND VOICE IN THE NEW SOVIET CLASSIC

A similar shift in orientation can be found, surprisingly enough, in the backward glance of the proletarian writers themselves. By the latter part of the decade it had become painfully clear that the new proletarian prose was not likely to come from the upstart writers among the new intelligentsia. Nor did the fellow-travelers prove useful in bringing about a proletarian-forming *smychka*. These sober acknowledgements, along with the awkwardly mediocre results from among their own ranks, brought their discourse on language more in line with Gorky's. We have already seen this new focus in the advice from literary consultants to novice writers in the late 1920s, and a similar focus appears in their policy statements, as exemplified by the 1927 editorial declaration that read: "The classics are the bygone days! Yes, the classics are a great day-before-yesterday. But it is through Tolstoy, and not through Babel', that our tomorrow will fly!"[68]

The main stylistic appeal of this "classic" voice was that the language did not "get in the way." In contrast to the prose style of Babel' (and Babel' was a popular negative contrast in this aspect of the language debates)—which, according to one critic, gave off a distinct sense of "constructedness" *(sdelannost')*, a self-consciousness that it was a "work of art"—the narrative style of the classics permitted the reader more direct and easy access to the content of the work: "The reader *forgets about the word* and sees only the movement of the heroes, their travails, the psychological shifts taking place within those living people whom the writer creates into life. And the more perfected the word in the understanding of the classics, the less it is noticed. . . . Not for a minute does the word become for them an end in itself."[69]

While earlier examples of this more "transparent" narrative style can be found (in Libedinskii's *The Week,* for instance), the landmark work for this realist model was Aleksandr Fadeev's *Rout* (*Razgrom*, 1927). As one proletarian critic wrote of Fadeev's "Tolstoyan simplicity" (again, using Babel' as foil), "In contrast to Babel', Fadeev does not stylize at all. His discourse does not pursue the tasks of linguistic connoisseurship. He builds his images not according to the principle of repulsing verbal material, he does not startle with an unusual attribute. His image is organically tied to the material; it is so transparent that the words disappear during reading and give way to reality."[70]

This impression of transparency, of course, is arguably as "constructed" a facade as the more word-conscious prose of Babel', "loaded," as Barthes put it, "with the most spectacular signs of fabrication." What it merely strives for—and achieves, if executed well—is the establishment of "an ideal intelligibility of things."[71] But it was this impression of transparent intelligibility that appealed to contemporary critics, who immediately welcomed the novel as a pivotal event in proletarian letters. The novel quickly became obligatory reading for schoolchildren, and it remained central in the literary canon throughout the Soviet era. More than anything else written at the time, *The Rout* invoked comparisons to the one "classic" writer who really mattered, Lev Tolstoy—a comparison not entirely unsought by Fadeev, who, by his own admission, modeled the book after the prose style of *War and Peace.*[72]

Like so many of the important works from this first decade of Soviet literature, the novel is set during the civil war, probably the seminal event in the Bolshevik quest for postrevolutionary legitimacy. And like so many of the narratives dealing with that topic, it features a largely unsuccessful effort by partisans, in this case, in the White Army controlled regions of Siberia.[73] The group, whose principal members include its leader, Iosef Levinson, his young adjutant Baklanov, the orderly Morozka and his wife, Varia (a nurse), the intellectual Mechik, and the miner Dubov, finds itself encircled by Japanese troops sympathetic to the Whites. Their only chance of escape is by fleeing through an overgrown swamp, where they are ambushed by Cossacks and subjected to great losses. Despite subplots involving class tensions, local pillaging, cowardice, and infidelity, the story line is straightforward.

What it lacks in complicated plot twists, *The Rout* makes up for in narrative clarity and character development—particularly on the psychological level. Edward Brown has already pointed out the symmetry of Fadeev's characterization, featuring few figures, but each of whom represents a different key social group.[74] In the direct speech replicas one finds similarly differentiated speech styles, ranging from the blatant use of nonstandard language by the local peasants (who play a relatively minor role in the book) and the brazen, vulgar speech of the seasoned rebel and foulmouthed Morozka (who, at the ripe age of twelve, "was speaking unnecessary, mostly swear, words and drinking vodka" [8]) to the naive, starry-eyed urban intellectual, Mechik, who, in contrast, is chastised for his "correct speech" (17). The language of the model proletarian platoon commander, Timofei Dubov, contains few regional or other nonstandard markers and stands out as one of the more authoritative, if aggressive, voices in the book, described by the narrator at first encounter as "brazen and thick," "buzzing," and "cutting" (38).

It is Dubov who, in the central scene of the novel's first part, steps forth at the town meeting over Morozko's act of petty thievery and brings verbal authority to a situation that is fast becoming incomprehensible owing to the "foggy and indecisive" and "scattered" speeches of the local peasants. He breaks in "with a muffled and restrained strength" to recommend throwing the criminal out of town ("There was something in Dubov's voice that made all heads, flinching, turn in his direction" [39, 41]). Morozko, in contrast, when asked for his own judgment as to the appropriate punishment for his crime (stealing melons), is unable to utter a coherent line, his speech reduced to babble out of shame:

> "Da razve b ia . . . sdelal takoe . . ." on opiat' ne nashel nuzhnogo slova i kivnul na Riabtsa . . . "nu, dyni eti samye . . . sdelal by, ezheli b podumal . . . so zla ili kak? . . . A to ved' syzmal'stva eto u nas—vse znaiut, tak vot i ia . . . A kak skazal Dubov, chto vsekh ia rebiat nashikh . . . da razve zh ia, brattsy! . . ."

vdrug vyrvalos' u nego iznutri, i ves' on podalsia vpered, skvativshis' za grud', i
glaza ego bryznuli svetom, teplym i vlazhnym . . . "Da ia krov' otdam po
zhilke za kazhnogo, a ne to, chtoby pozor, ili kak! . . ." (43–44)

["Could it really have been me... gone and done such a thing..." again he
could not find the right word and nodded at Riabets... "you know, them melons... D'ya think I'd have done it if I'd a thought...out of malice, or what?..
Everyone knows we used to do it as kids—same with me, too... And just like
Dubov said, that all of our guys I...could it really have been me, brothers!..."
he suddenly wrenched out from the gut, and he moved forward clutching at
his chest, with his eyes spurting out a warm and humid light... "I'd give my
last drop of blood for those guys, to avoid any shame, you know what I'm
sayin'?"]

For his own part, the main protagonist, Levinson, in keeping with the
trend noted in the closing chapters of Libedinskii's *The Week*, maintains
a low linguistic profile throughout the book, preferring action over
words. When he is linked to the issue of language, he is depicted as an
"attentive and patient" listener as often as he is a contributor to the
arena of public speech (27, 36, 39). When he speaks, he does so "calmly
and convincingly" (27), "quietly but distinctly," "amazingly quietly, but
audible to all" (41), "trying not to raise his voice" (109). As with Libedinskii's new proletarian leaders, his speech replicas are short, clear, to the
point, and deed-oriented to the end (47, 78–79); he exercises his authority not so much by dictate as by subtle manipulation of the course of a
meeting or conversation (54). The handful of metalinguistic thoughts attributed to him reflect a general suspicion toward language and its role
in "masking reality" (52) and a frustration of its inadequacy to express
inner thoughts and feelings (118, 149–50). This general ambivalence becomes particularly glaring in the closing scene of the book, when, in the
wake of a terrible decimation of their ranks, Levinson and company are
overcome by a mute silence: the only words of hope—laconic in comparison with other past and future Soviet novels' penchant for closing with
a didactic harangue meant as much for reader as fictional audience—are
confined to the main hero's inner thoughts ("they needed to live and
fulfill their obligations" [217–19]).

It was not the differentiated speech profiles that struck contemporary
readers, however, so much as the relative fluidity and unobtrusiveness of
the narrative voice—especially in contrast to the modernist *skaz* and simply mediocre narratives that had dominated Soviet literary production up
until that point. Compared to the oratorical cries of Maiakovskii; the confused, scattered impressions of Fedorchenko's peasants; and the misappropriated, subversive, and at times disillusioned articulations of the *skaz* narrators in Seifullina, Babel', Ognev, and Arosev, the boundaries of verbal

authority in Fadeev are as unmistakable as they are unproblematic. Fadeev's storyteller, like the Tolstoyan narrator that served as its model, avoids any language or stylistic devices that would draw attention to itself as being "constructed," unreliable, or associated with any social milieu or class. Through its lucid transmission it establishes a stable authorial voice that encourages the reader to take it at its word.

Fadeev's narrator also enjoys a degree of omniscience unmatched by the dominant voices of earlier Soviet prose. With access to the unspoken thoughts and reactions of nearly all the main characters, the narrator has the power to guide the reader through a range of social and class issues without appearing heavy-handed. Internal confrontations with fear, cowardice, love, resigned indifference, rape, lost hope, euthanasia, and death add a psychological dimension that distinguishes the book from earlier Soviet civil war narratives. Most noticeable to contemporary critics was the narrator's insights into the main hero's inner frailties, making Levinson the model of the "living man" so critical to the realization of the "Red Lev Tolstoy."[75]

The issue of language is also the object of the narrator's quasi-direct musings, mostly reiterating the dual themes of its inadequacy and abuse, such as the proliferation of verbose bureaucratic documents (49, 51) and the tendency of people from all social backgrounds to use language to veil the truth (52, 122). By way of contrast, we learn that deeds speak louder than words (110–11) and that our sixth sense about human nature makes us more powerful leaders than do exceptional rhetorical skills (55). The combination of these levels of voicing helps create a narrative that is short on verbal games and long on content and character—the very sort of storytelling envisioned by Gorky and other advocates of learning from the classics—and offers a three-dimensional, psychologically enriching tale of revolutionaries who more closely resemble living human beings.

Critics welcomed this more subtle form of "infection" (to borrow a term from Tolstoy). In contrast to earlier proletarian literary endeavors, wrote one, "Fadeev in no way agitates; he divulges people in all their complicatedness—in both their good and bad, strong and weak sides. There is no masking at work in events—relentless truth and only that!"[76] And yet there was room for improvement. As another critic explained, Fadeev's book was among the best available for beginning writers to mimic, but it still stopped short of the manner in which Russia's classics were able to impose their ideology—by "developing certain images, invoking certain 'party' words that signal a certain attitude, a certain quality, and a certain way the reader is to react."[77] In fact, Fadeev is startlingly spare in his invocation of "party words," a feature that would become a rarity in the tumultuous years following the book's debut.

. . .

For all who advocated a return to the language of the classics, the embrace constituted a rejection of the turmoil, experimentation, and mediocrity that characterized the language culture of the postrevolutionary years in exchange for a more stable verbal power and order. Be it to preserve the purity of the Russian nation or to strengthen the integrity of the Soviet state, Lenin, Bunin, the Volkonskiis, and Gorky all viewed the key to transformation in the reestablishment of a language of authority, as epitomized by the "mastery" of the great books of Russian realist fiction. In the language culture of early Soviet Russia, their approach marked a break with the oral orientation of the revolutionary and popular models, operating under the assumption that a text-based national identity and cultural tradition held greater promise for ensuring the integrity and legitimacy of the new symbolic authority.[78] In contrast to oral modes of communication, such as oratory, and of orally oriented genres such as the *skaz* narrative, the realist mode of writing, according to Barthes, "meant to impose, thanks to the shadow cast by its system of signs, the image of a speech that had a structure even before it came into existence."[79]

Such a reinvestment in the past thus marked a decline in the linguistic currency of the voice of the charismatic revolutionary (deeds were now more potent and trustworthy than words) and of the voices supposedly destined to inherit the "Worker-Peasant State." And it did so to the benefit of that class purportedly destined for destruction. In this sense, the national model brought the language debate well along the road from the charismatic, but chaotic, babble of revolution to a stable and sacredly inscribed language of state. Yet it still retained one highly problematic ideological gap.

CHAPTER SIX

CANONIZATION OF THE
PARTY-STATE VOICE

If we study the development of human speech we find that in the history of civilization the word fulfills two entirely different functions. To put it briefly we may term these functions the semantic and the magical use of the word. Even among the so-called primitive languages the semantic function of the word is never missing; without it there could be no human speech. But in primitive societies the magic word has a predominant and overwhelming influence. It does not describe things or relations of things; it tries to produce effects and to change the course of nature. This cannot be done without an elaborate magical art. The magician, or sorcerer is alone able to govern the magic word. But in his hands it becomes a most powerful weapon. Nothing can resist its force.

—**Ernst Cassirer,** *The Myth of the State*

Of the ideal-typical models discussed thus far—the revolutionary, the popular, and the national—the first two shared one common belief: that the construction of the new society required a fundamental transformation of the existing language culture. The combined force of political and social revolution, on the one hand, and the rapid influx of new language material into the realm of public discourse, on the other, created both the belief in and the need for new sources of authority for speaking and writing. The revolutionary voice best articulated the views of those who envisioned a society of perpetual development and change and of citizens who were full-fledged participants in that profoundly creative process. The popular voice expressed the belief that, as the new "dictators," the working class and peasantry should redefine the substance of the bourgeois literary language to make it more an expression of their own colloquial discourse—simple, fresh, based on the concrete everyday experiences of the workplace, and, for the same reason, a bit rough around the edges. Essentially innovative in orientation, both likewise privileged oral over written modes of expression, be it through the fiery rhetoric of the orator, the declamatory verse of the revolutionary poet, or the everyday speech practice of the people.

The national model marked a departure from this trend in two ways. First, its gaze was more retrospective than revolutionary, envisioning as its source of verbal authority in the new Soviet society a reconstitution of the language of the Russian literary classics, which would serve as an antidote to the experimental excess of the first decade of Soviet rule and thereby restore to the language the authority and respect it once commanded. Second, and directly related to the first, it marked a shift in priorities from charismatic and oral to established, written modes of verbal expression. In this sense, its design for language in the social, cultural, and political arenas was more one of state building than revolution.

The model discussed in the remaining two chapters, the party-state voice, resembles the national voice in its underlying concern for state building and its reliance on a written canon.[1] But it is a canon shaped not so much around the narrative prose of Tolstoy and Gorky as it is on the "patristic texts" of the Communist Party and revolutionary movement, first among which are the sacred writings of the founding fathers of "the Union of Soviets"—Lenin and Stalin.[2] Much of the growth of the voice's influence stemmed from institutional changes experienced in Soviet Russia during the late twenties and early thirties, a period roughly corresponding to the First Five-Year Plan. As in other spheres of social and political life during this time, the party-state leadership played a more active—and regulatory—role in those institutions most directly involved in the nurturing and production of public discourse, resulting in the gradual homogenization of the language debate and, gradually, of the language models themselves.

What is often overlooked, however, is the degree to which the language of the party-state borrowed heavily from all three of the other voices that enjoyed linguistic currency through the first decade and a half of Bolshevik rule. It was largely the appropriation and assimilation of key rhetorical elements of these other models that helped transform the often mystifying babble of Bolshevism into a sacred tongue of the Soviet party-state, bestowing power and authority upon those members willing to espouse the state's central value system and relegating those less willing to a discredited and largely muted realm of verbal outcasts.

INSTITUTIONALIZING THE ORATOR

The routinization of successful charismatic movements, according to Max Weber, quite often leads to the creation of stable institutions, which is fundamental to the transfer and preservation of a movement's accumulated power.[3] Although for Weber that power was primarily economic, more recent thinkers such as Claus Mueller and Pierre Bourdieu have demonstrated that it comes in other forms as well—including linguistic. Bourdieu, for example, describes "linguistic capital" as a critical means by which one group dominates another. People enjoying positions of power over linguistic capital regulate not only the channels of communication and flow of information but also the very medium, or code, in which meaningful communication can take place.[4] They help define what constitutes appropriate and inappropriate linguistic practice (in the public arena, at least); they determine what will be the "standard," the "norm." Weber likens them to "apostles," who in the emerging institutions become "privileged table companions . . . priests, state officials, party officials, officers, secretaries, editors and publishers . . . employees, teachers and others with a vested occupational interest [in the charismatic movement]." He goes on to note that, "even though the apostle admonishes the followers to maintain the purity of the spirit, the charismatic message inevitably becomes dogma, doctrine, theory . . . law or petrified tradition."[5] In other words, the maxim "It is written . . . , but I say unto you" becomes null and void by the resurgence of the written word.[6]

The church metaphors are apt in the case of the language culture of early Stalinism—particularly to the changing role of the agitator. The authority of priests comes not from their ability to create new, revolutionary language but from their skills at preserving, disseminating, and interpreting preexisting texts. This canonical discourse becomes the chief gauge and guarantor of all subsequent communicative acts. It functions both as a cue to membership and a kind of incantation, whose evocation secures truth, and whose disregard or misuse spells falsehood and corruption.[7]

Public speaking and *agitprop* literature from the period corresponding to the First Five-Year Plan clearly reflects these various levels of language institutionalization. If previous models privileged either speakers (by virtue of their charismatic authority) or audiences (because of their "backwardness"), here the code of party doctrine becomes the driving communicative force. A 1928 textbook, *How to Deliver Reports and Speeches at Meetings*, reduces the "art of oratory" to the practical day-to-day operation of the party, and it restricts the pool of would-be orators to "rank-and-file party members."[8] Public speaking was no longer an obligation of "every Soviet citizen," as earlier manuals had contended: it had become, instead, a medium of communication reserved strictly for "the realization of *internal* party democracy."[9]

The primacy of the "party line" shifted emphasis away from oral and creative modes of public expression, toward written and rehearsed texts. Greater authority went to the growing canon of party documents as represented in centrally controlled newspapers, books, and pamphlets. As the same manual put it, "It is essential not only to know the party line, but to be able to link it to the general foundations of the party world view provided in Lenin's collected works. . . . It is [also] essential to survey the collections put out by the party, which combine the most important articles illuminating current issues of party life."[10] Even the models of spoken language that were offered, such as the speeches of Lenin and Stalin, were themselves derivative—transcribed from their original oral status into a lifeless printed and polished form.

The task of "enlightenment" so critical in earlier revolutionary models of oratory was largely assumed by these canonical texts. It was they, more than the orators themselves, who were the "illuminators"; the public speaker's task was more that of an intermediary, a kind of secular priest. As one writer put it, "It is by no means essential that one express something absolutely original, exceptional, never-before conceived of": more important, instead, was that the speaker "know and understand the party line in its application to personal experience."[11]

Dogma reigned over clarity and originality in the domain of style as well, shifting the burden of comprehension from the language to its users—speakers and listeners alike. The "language of the party" *(partiinyi iazyk)* was the only appropriate form in which to articulate its ideas: "Over ten years our party has been able to create its own language—simple, strong, and expressive. Each orator must meditate on the party language, study it and develop it further. Nearly all the leaders of the Communist Party speak a comparatively uniform *[odnoobraznyi]* language, using generally accepted expressions, without striving for flowery phrases."[12]

The formulation borrows from revolutionary and popular models in its nod to expressiveness and simplicity: but the party language was "living" and "revolutionary" only to the extent that it had its roots in the language of revolution and once-living revolutionaries—adding a distinctly linguistic dimension to Maiakovskii's infamous slogan declaring Lenin "more alive than the living" *(zhivee zhivykh)*.[13] Nevertheless, in a deft rhetorical twist of their own, commentators such as the Marxist critic Viktor Gofman, in his 1932 book *Speech of the Orator,* saw in the impending domination of a single "party language" nothing short of a "liberation of oratory from rhetoric." The "objective" and "scientific" language of the proletariat would tear away the deceitful veils of traditional bourgeois rhetoric and replace them with a "more perfect and precise method of perceiving reality."[14] And this, in turn, would lead to a most remarkable synthesis—through the falling away of the "principal distinctions between written and oral language, private and public speech, the language of science and the language of agitation."[15]

The dialectical synthesis of these opposing spheres harks back to formalist notions of the dissolution of differences between poetic and practical languages. Although the earlier utopian formulations may well have contributed conceptually and lexically to the later party-state synthesis, however, the implied model of communication was quite different.[16] The synthesis would come about not by poets giving the tongue-tied masses expression through a charismatic "language of the streets" (as Maiakovskii had envisioned) or, for that matter, by realigning public discourse to better approximate the simple, straightforward structures of everyday speech. It would occur, rather, through the complete naturalization of the party language in all spheres—written and oral, public and private, scientific and agitational—as canonized in the decrees, resolutions, speeches, and writings of the founding and reigning party leaders.[17]

RECASTING THE CURRICULA IN THE IMAGE OF THE PARTY-STATE

The concern for the general cultural competence of Soviet schoolchildren in the late 1920s gave way at the decade's turn to the more immediate economic and ideological concerns of the party-state. If the earlier purpose of language and literature instruction had been largely to develop in young citizens a level of linguistic competence that would allow them to participate actively in the construction of the new society, it now bore a more pressing and tangible responsibility: to facilitate the realization of the dual campaigns of industrialization and collectivization.[18] Toward this end, state educational planning programs advocated increasing the number of vocational grade schools, particularly in rural and industrial regions.[19] The success of the schools was to be measured not so much according to progress made in reading, writing, and speaking skills but rather by the extent to which students had been prepared, in the countryside, to become "organizers and workers of collective forms of economy" and "help in the practical implementation of the policy of the liquidation of the kulaks as a class," and, in the city, to meet production goals and "help the socialist reconstruction of the village by means of *shefstvo* . . . [and] socialist competition."[20]

The Russian language curricula from the period reflect the nearly complete reduction of educational principles to fulfilling the tasks of the party-state. In contrast to earlier recommendations that expressed a stylistic preference for the classics, the primary models for emulation became the writings and speeches of Lenin and Stalin, and the genre of preference became the newspaper. As a 1932 program put it, "It is absolutely essential to include the speeches and articles of Lenin and Stalin in the lessons in stylistics. An analysis of these speeches—their construction and linguistic shape—must demonstrate to students the model toward which they must strive in their oral and written speech."[21] Once praised by leading formalist linguists as the great revolutionary decanonizer, Lenin was now presented to teachers (in however convoluted a manner) as the ultimate canon builder:

> The first goal is decanonization, but the *decanonization of the decanonized* (the trivialized, the distorted *[oposhlennoe, iskazhennoe]*), in other words, the

reestablishment of the true strength of the word. Such a decanonization thus leads through its end goal to the canon, just as analogously the polemics of Lenin cleared the foundation for Leninism. In connection with the aforementioned one can suggest a most interesting assignment for students—to select the *contentious words* in the works of Lenin, establish their semantics in [the discourse of] Lenin's enemies and, in turn, establish that path of Leninist irony and logic by which the word is returned to its norm.[22]

Classroom assignments from the fifth through seventh grades centered on three basic tasks: "working with newspapers," "working with books," and "conducting meetings." Others included "selecting slogans from articles and speeches of Lenin and Stalin," "the social contract" *(sotsdogovor)*, and "deeds of investigation into the activity of a school, organization, enterprise, etc."[23] At every step along the way, language instruction engaged students directly and exclusively with the discourse and machinery of the party-state.

Though it departed from the models of language that preceded it, the party-state model, as manifested in the school curricula, nevertheless bore their legacy in varying degrees of distortion. It invoked the negative notion of "phrasemongering" *(frazerstvo)* so vilified by advocates of the revolutionary model, but rather than referring to old, worn-out revolutionary phrases and slogans (which had become the stock of the party-state voice) equated it with language that was lexically or syntactically complicated.[24] It celebrated as its own the "tumultuous language creation *[rechetvorchestvo]* that characterize[d] the coming into being of the language of the proletariat" but implied that it was a phase in the development of the language culture whose time had passed.[25]

The later school programs likewise addressed the issue of "popular language," resolving the tension between positive and negative manifestations by distinguishing between the colloquial language of the "authentic proletariat," on the one hand, and the bogus representation of that language by populist intellectuals, on the other. One of the topics to be discussed in seventh-grade Russian language class captured the contrast nicely: "Framing of the issue of the popular language of the bourgeoisie and the proletariat. Oversimplification *[uproshchenchestvo]*, vulgarization, lisping as the basic features of the 'popular' language of the bourgeoisie. The maximal correspondence of objective reality, class expediency, clarity, concreteness as the distinguishing features of the language of the proletariat."[26]

By distinguishing between the popular language of the proletariat and the popularizing tendency of the bourgeoisie, the program avoided the formally problematic implications of the popular model and the ideologically problematic implications of the national model.[27] The "language of the proletariat," by this account, did not reflect the fresh, colloquial speech of the farm or factory. Rather, it was marked by the more abstract characteristics of "maximum correspondence to objective reality, class purposefulness, clarity, and concreteness." The first two features provided the sound, class-based authority of the popular model, and the last two invoked the authority of both these and the realist tradition of the national classics. The "literary language," in turn, lost its awkward association with the prerevolutionary bourgeoisie by being recast as "the language of the dominating class" and through the gradual "formation of a literary language of the proletariat."[28]

With this semantic shift, the phrase "language of the proletariat" came to be identified with an established literary language, concealing (at least superficially) the fact that those changes came about not from the rank-and-file worker but from the party-state leadership (or "revolutionary vanguard"). They were to a large extent introduced by that leadership, institutionalized by it, and now maintained by it—all through the sacred texts of primarily Lenin and Stalin, and institutions such as the classroom, the newspaper, the academy, and the literary establishment.[29] Emblematic of this linguistic canonization was the 1932 commentary, which for the first time gave detailed suggestions on how to decorate the language classroom, recommending that portraits of the four "founders of Marxism" be hung, accompanied by language-related quotes from their writings—a form of iconic deification of the party-state's language genealogy. Constructing a new, unified language culture in the schools under Stalin thus required that young citizens engage in simultaneous acts of forgetting and remembering—forgetting the linguistic and ideological differences reflected in regional and class-based dialects, and remembering the newly codified Soviet literary and linguistic heritage.[30]

STYLISTIC AND INSTITUTIONAL REFORMS IN JOURNALISM

Later discussions about the press—in particular, the worker and village correspondents—displayed a similar resolution of earlier tensions and contradictions. As discussed in preceding chapters, the worker *(rabkor)* and village *(sel'kor)* correspondent movement throughout its early years wavered between social and political roles that proved to be, more often than not, mutually exclusive. On the one hand, its participants were expected to serve as mouthpieces of the central state in the countryside; on the other, they were touted as the leading voices of the workers and peasants, reporting spontaneously and voluntarily, in the language of the people, about the state of affairs in the factories and farms. Later policies concerning the language and the function of these corps, however, show increasing concern with political organization and control—at the expense of verbal popularity, spontaneity, and volunteerism. Calls for the formal organization of these cadres began as early as 1923, but were denounced as a move that would cut their organic ties to the masses and turn them into a body "with a narrowly agitational-propagandistic point of view."[31]

Toward the end of the decade, that concern became largely overshadowed by the need for the political education of the corps. A Central Committee resolution from 1926 called for greater party control over the *rabkory* and *sel'kory* and promised rapid responses to their exposés of corruption and mismanagement as well as financial support and physical protection—a solid indication that the correspondents were not only dependent on the state but were *perceived* as such (and endangered as a result) by unsympathetic elements.[32] This unofficial relationship of protector and representative became official with a reform of the movement in 1931, which stated outright that the correspondents were to become, in the words of Stalin, "the commanders of proletarian popular opinion, trying to direct the inexhaustible forces of this mightiest of factors to the aid of the party and Soviet power."[33] The restructuring called for an elaborate oversight mechanism made up of representatives from no less than nine different political and professional bodies.[34] In turn, the more "advanced" correspondents were for the first time offered the incentive of promotion into the permanent ranks of the press corps.[35]

The 1931 restructuring essentially institutionalized a process that had been occurring for a major part of the state-building period. Although early discussions made much of the voluntary and spontaneous nature of the movement, it even then served the purpose of maintaining forms of surveillance in peripheral regions and of recruiting able-minded workers and peasants into the party-state apparatus.[36] And if, in the earlier years, the guise of volunteerism had likewise provided legitimation to claims of successful, "organic" acquisition of the language of state among workers and peasants, such a guise, by the early 1930s, was no longer deemed necessary. By then, the *sel'kor* was simply held up as the "most advanced Soviet peasant-citizen" by virtue of his or her mastery of the language, which, by definition, was the language of progress in the new social order. As one 1930 chronicler of the movement put it, "The *sel'kor* is no kvass-brewing lad pouring forth in a devil-may-care way flowery Old-Russian words: he is a vanguard Soviet peasant—a social activist, mixing the language of books, newspapers, the city, the factory, [and] the proletarian Revolution with the oncoming wave of not-nearly-exhausted discursive possibilities hidden in the flexible language of the reforming village."[37]

But even the most progressive peasants could not be expected to submit ideologically flawless reports. Earlier warnings not to turn party-state oversight into "cheap censorship" gave way by the mid-thirties to demands that the material submitted by the *rabkor* be subjected to careful scrutiny by "literary correctors" in order to achieve "an increase in the political significance of the report." This placed an increased burden on editors, one observer noted, but could not be helped: "[The editor] must be able to understand the fact communicated by the *rabkor*, draw from it conclusions, and give it a political evaluation. The literary corrector *[pravshchik]* under no circumstances may be an apolitical, neutral journalist, a specialist *[spets]* who approaches a note only from the point of view of language, grammar."[38]

At the same time, the burden of comprehension shifted from the writers and the language itself to the consumers of a discourse deemed most ideologically useful for their enlightenment. As the *sel'kor* language analyst put it, "The city, the factory, proclamations, brochures, political discussions, the abundance of new technological terms edging their way into the language in accordance with the general industrial growth—all this is the yeast on which the relatively beggarly village lexicon quickly rose, grew, and swelled."[39] If the "backward" peasant failed to react to the discursive "yeast" of the party-state language, he or she would simply remain a backward peasant and fail to reap the rewards of the new social order.

The Party Congresses also noted the shift in burden from the writer to the reader. If, in the early 1920s, focus had been on the need to simplify the language of the press, by as early as 1924 it had switched to strategies for expanding readership. The press-related resolution to the Thirteenth Party Congress, for example, demanded a situation in which *"every single party member [was] a subscriber to a party newspaper; every single working man and woman, and every Red Army soldier [read] a paper; that two million papers were distributed to the countryside—amounting to no less than one newspaper per every ten peasant households."*[40] A year earlier at the Twelfth Party Congress, Stalin offered a spirited characterization of the press as "the strongest weapon with which the party—daily, hourly—[spoke] to the working class in a language that [was] its own, and necessary to it ['it' referring in both cases to 'the party']".[41]

Not until the early 1930s, however, did the notion of a "party language" assume full status as a positive linguistic model—in sharp contrast to the negative connotations given to it by Trotsky in his earlier warnings about alienating readers (that "the danger of a split of the party from the nonparty masses in the area of agitation is manifested in the exclusiveness of the agitational content and its form, in the formation of an almost conventional party language, inaccessible nearly always to nine-tenths of not only peasants but workers as well").[42] In addition to the agitational discourse discussed above, the model was also common in discussions of the language of the Soviet press and—like the descriptions of language in the school curricula—was characterized as an ideological construct more than a conglomeration of discrete linguistic features. As one language maven declared, language was not simply a matter of style, of putting all the punctuation in the right place: "Bolshevik language" was first and foremost a language that reflected a sense of "party responsibility." Without this sensibility, an unhealthy "literature-ism" *(literaturshchina)* resulted.[43] A study of the language of *The Peasant Newspaper* spoke about the "Communist word," identifying its distinctive feature in no less grandiose terms than "life's truth": "The strength of the Communist word lies in truth *[pravda]*. Life's truth is on the side of the party, on the side of the workers and collective farmers, on the side of the builders of socialism, *on our side*. The distortion of truth is advantageous to the enemies of the Revolution alone."[44] The notion of "truth" recalls the revolutionary model's privileging of the poet, orator, and philologist as creators of the word. Here, however, the party-state assumes the role of sage, and meaning itself is monopolistically seized.[45]

Qualities of alternative voices are invoked—clarity, simplicity, or the ability to influence—but they are done so in a manner that makes clear their subordinate status to language's function as a cue to membership: "The language that works as the best agitation, propaganda and organization of the masses, is not simply living, engaging, clear, etc., but first and foremost *our own, party* language."[46] Rather than an alienating quality, the *partiinost'*, or "party spirit," of discourse was, at minimum, an essential form of identity, and, in its most perfected form, a "gift of tongues" prophesying the Truth. No longer was the language of the party-state battling to win over converts from the villages and factories. It made its case, instead, as an established, even sacred language of power, which, when obtained, would lift the masses out of their backward, disenfranchised state and deliver to them the modern benefits of the new society.

SOCIOLINGUISTIC FOUNDATIONS FOR THE VOICE OF THE PARTY-STATE

One of the more interesting indicators of the shift in the burden of communication, and of the newly empowered language of the party-state, can be found in a 1932 study by Afanasii Selishchev, the same linguist who wrote *The Language of the Revolutionary Epoch* just four years earlier. Entitled "On the Language of the Contemporary Village," the article presents a much different picture of rural language reception than Selishchev's earlier book.[47] The first significant change is in the narrative voice of the linguist himself. No doubt in partial response to the intense methodological attacks he had been subjected to by the followers of Nikolai Marr—the comparative linguist whose "new theory of language," despite its outlandish logic and lack of empirical grounding, came to hold ideological sway in Soviet linguistics by the early 1930s—Selishchev replaced the relatively neutral, scholarly tone of his earlier work with a more politically correct mode of expression.[48] He remarks in his conclusion, for example, that "the collective farm, the poor and middle peasant *[bedniak i seredniak]*, are setting off on the path of collective labor, on the path of the construction of the socialist economy, erasing the borders between the city and the village. They must break off with the traditional way of life of the petty commodity producer and owner, with the traditional striving for privately managed accumulation."[49]

For the Selishchev of 1932, questions of origins and features were no longer of interest: the language material was assumed as an established fact in the fabric of Soviet public discourse. Instead, he focuses on the degree to which the new language of power had made its way into the lives of rural citizens of the Soviet state. In sharp contrast to the confusion, alienation, and distrust revealed in the studies conducted by Shafir and others nearly ten years earlier, Selishchev sketches a portrait of enthusiasm and linguistic empowerment. The main difference, he argues, lay in the sense shared by most peasants that the new language was "their" language:

> The striving toward mastery of the urban, literary language during the revolutionary epoch, especially in recent years, has intensified to a high level and has acquired a different class significance in comparison with the process of the emergence of a literary language among the broad masses during prerevolutionary times. Not only do the economic, sociopolitical, and everyday-cultural demands motivate such mastery, but also . . . the elements of the urban, literary language are no longer linked to alien classes—the landowners and the bourgeoisie. This language in its modern appearance is now the language of the broad proletarian community.[50]

Throughout the discussion he refers to the new public discourse as the "language of the proletariat." Lexically, its defining features differed little from that language he had described in his 1928 work as the new, relatively unstable lexicon of the revolutionary movement and civil war. The only difference was that the collectivization campaign had "enriched" the vocabulary even more.[51] Phonetically and syntactically, the language of the proletariat featured a transition from the dialectal particularities and simple sentence structure characteristic of rural speech to the more standardized conventions of the urban literary language. Combined, the components provided mutual legitimation: the language (mainly, lexicon) of the party-state acquired the formal status of a literary language while the literary language obtained the ideological status of the language of state.

Selishchev is careful to show that the improvement resulted from more than the normal acquisition to be expected from a literacy campaign. Beyond cultural literacy, there was a direct correlation between language acquisition and political activity. He ascribes the greatest degree of language acquisition to the "activists," who exhibited, according to the linguist, "extraordinarily significant language innovation." The advances included not only lexical and syntactic features but also "several stylistic features of contemporary oratorical discourse."[52] He describes "nonactivists," in contrast, as "archaists" and "backward, conservative individuals" who showed little signs of language "innovation," relying instead on the dialectal, nonstandard, and Old Church Slavonic structures traditional to peasant discourse.[53]

According to Selishchev's study, then, those who participated most actively in the construction of the new Soviet village, the administration of the collective farm, and the implementation and legitimation of party-state ideas in general exhibited the greatest degree of verbal "progressiveness." Those least involved and interested in the current social transformations showed the least degree of competence. The conclusion was as self-serving as it was circular. With a "literary language" newly defined to include the ideological discourse of the party-state bureaucracy, it is not surprising that those peasants who had participated most in that bureaucracy had made the most gains in "literacy."

Another aspect of Selishchev's study offers a somewhat more substantial confirmation of the power of the party-state language in the village. The observed patterns of public language use suggested that, regardless of the level of village members' acquisition of the new language of state, they appeared strongly inclined—if not obligated—to employ the discourse in those contexts where community membership, power, and authority were most at stake:

> In general, the new conditions of life in the collective farm motivate the intensified use of the new words and constructions. One is particularly driven to use them under specific collective-farm circumstances—for instance, in expressing the desire to join the collective farm organization . . . , or, from the opposite perspective, discussing the class profile of candidates. At these moments, the oral and written speech can be particularly saturated with sociopolitical terminology. The degree of use of this terminology differs among various individuals. But everyone, not excluding the backward and semiliterate inhabitants, considers it essential to use it.[54]

That the language of the party-state had acquired a state of verbal hegemony in the public power relations of the village is not to say that the traditional local dialect had assumed a status of complete disfavor. The party-state language had simply come to dominate the realm of *official* public discourse and interaction. Citizens may well have maintained their old speech habits in personal conversations or the confines of the household. If and when it came time to petition for membership into the local collective farm, however, they were compelled to employ the discourse of the party-state.[55] Whatever one makes of this spread of a party-state language, the demonstrated skill of code switching undeniably served to empower those who mastered the party language, either by giving them access to the verbal controls of power or by supplying the tools for verbal resistance. The precise manner in which it constituted either a "language of the proletariat" or a "literary language," as Selishchev claimed, however, still remains to be seen.

In contrast to the language of the countryside, which had been the focus of a number of serious sociolinguistic studies in the 1920s, the "language of the proletariat" remained largely undocumented until the end of that decade.[56] Only in the early 1930s, with the First Five-Year Plan and cultural revolution in full swing, was this embarrassing dearth of linguistic fuel for the party-state cause remedied. One of the more productive forums for such discussions was the journal *Literary Study* (*Literaturnaia ucheba*), which began publication under the editorship of Gorky in 1931 and targeted an audience of beginning writers. The journal became one of the leading forums for the articulation of the party-state model of language, taking up the culturist task set by Gorky by offering writing tips, discussing the appropriate language for prose fiction, and addressing issues of style and production of local (amateur) newspapers. Emblematic of its attempt to legitimate a literary model that fused old and new was the journal's regular rubric, "Studying under the Classics," which contained articles discussing the classics as positive *national* models for writing and reading while at the same time providing the correct *socialist* interpretation of their contents.[57]

Similar efforts to bridge past language cultures with the present appeared in the five-part series on the origin of language, written by the former *Lef* critic Lev Iakubinskii who, by this time, had become a proponent of the ideas of Nikolai Marr. Intended as a primer for the study of language and its social origins, the series provided a theoretical resolution to the ideological tension among the voices examined in the present discussion—all three of which presented only partial and problematic solutions to the quandary of creating a new model of public discourse that reflected at once the revolutionary nature of the new society, the social transformation that defined it, and the authority and legitimacy it was to command. To resolve the tension, Iakubinskii concentrates on the broader role of language in the new society, rather than on discrete linguistic features.[58]

More important to Iakubinskii than innovation of form was the manner, or spirit, in which citizens used the language at their disposal. Herein lay the distinctiveness of what he, like Selishchev, called the "language of the proletariat." To demonstrate the functional difference, Iakubinskii traces the various uses of language through the history of human civilization, concentrating, not surprisingly, on the development of the language of the peasantry. He begins with a sociolinguistic portrait of feudal society, where what little state language there was remained within the elite circles of feudal lords, thus permitting the language of the countryside to retain its colloquial, unregulated form.[59] The ensuing capitalist period saw the creation and broad dissemination of a "public discourse" (*publichnaia rech'*), due to the need to bring economic and legal order to the peripheries of the state.[60] Even under this social order, however, the "normalization" of the peasant language was imperfect, as the capitalist influence in the village was (and always would be) selective and spotty.[61] Only under a truly democratic "dictatorship of the proletariat" would the language of the countryside match the same cultural standards as the "literary language" that had emerged in urban cultural centers.

The notion of a "literary language" (or what he also calls a "national language" and "Russian national language") rooted in the public discourse of capitalist society remains the positive standard throughout Iakubinskii's discussion—even in his excursus on the "language of the proletariat."[62] He envisions the gradual weaning of the urban working class from the peasant discourse brought from the countryside to the city through the increased exposure to the Russian national language (which was both dominated and defined by urban centers).[63] Although the language of the proletariat exhibited certain lexical features specific to working-class culture and experience, it assumed the basic intonational, morphological, lexical, and syntactic form of the existing national language. The key difference between this new language and the language established under bourgeois capitalism was not so much formal as it was ideological:

> The proletariat sets itself apart as a class from the bourgeoisie not in pronunciation, grammar, [or] the lexical composition of its language, but rather in the *means of utilizing* the national language material, in the *treatment* of this material, in the *means of selecting* from it the facts necessary for a concrete goal, in its *relationship* to these facts and their evaluation, that is, in the *method of discourse [rechevoi metod]*. The proletariat works out *its own specific proletarian method* to the extent that it works out in the unfolding battles with the bourgeoisie its *own proletarian psychology and ideology.*[64]

As in the formulations settled on in propagandistic, pedagogical, journalistic, and ethnographic discussions, this specific proletarian language ideology had more to do with a certain psyche, or style, than with discrete linguistic features. Iakubinskii writes not of lexical or syntactic elements but rather in terms of an "elemental process" linked to specific genres and communicative contexts: "The proletarian discursive method . . . is formed by the vanguard language worker-ideologists of the proletariat (literati and orators) in various genres of oral and written public speech; for entirely understandable reasons, the formation process of the proletarian method of discourse encompasses first of all the political, philosophical, [and] scientific genre[s] of public speech."[65]

His description of the context of the "proletarian discursive method" differs markedly from that posited in the popular working-class model discussed in chapter 4. Instead of the rough, colloquial language of the workbench glorified by Kleinbort, Bezymenskii, and Bednyi, among others, the model depicted by Iakubinskii is based specifically on the language of "the political, philosophical, [and] scholarly genre of public discourse," as articulated by "the advanced language worker-ideologists of the proletariat." And it is the key phrase "worker-ideologists of the proletariat" that distinguishes the view from earlier visions of a "language of the factory": implied in it is not the language of the working class (or of modernist poets or the literary vanguard, for that matter), but that of the "revolutionary intelligentsia" and its figurehead, Lenin.[66]

By reducing the model of public discourse to the language of the revolutionary intelligentsia, and that of Lenin in particular, Iakubinskii essentially transposes Lenin's own justification for a "revolutionary avant-garde" into the domain of language.[67] The working class had neither the organizational capacity nor the political consciousness to realize the language of the proletariat on its own; it needed the skills of a small group of full-time language revolutionaries to organize, educate, direct, and mobilize it. The ideal-typical model for this vision of language was the intellectual both fluent in the Russian national language and committed to the work of the Communist Party. In the absence of a truly universal, proletarian language (which both Iakubinskii and Marr envisioned as a feature of world communism), the Soviet state would rely on the ready-made authority of the Russian national tongue (in Russia, at least) to coherently articulate the "will of the proletariat," essentially adopting for linguistic policy the same slogan of "national in form, socialist in content" that Stalin invoked with regard to the broader nationalities question.[68]

THE CONVERGING AUTHORITY
OF THE LANGUAGES OF LITERATURE AND STATE

For writers who still had questions about the status of the organic *glas naroda* in this equation, Gorky alleviated all doubt. As suggested in his comments about "rural backwardness," the unfiltered voice of the Russian peasantry, in particular, fell well outside the boundaries of the legitimate language of state. Gorky's critical view of the rural population is perhaps most well known from his 1922 essay, "On the Russian Peasantry," in which he argued for the need to transform the "terrifying," "half-wild, stupid, slow-witted people of Russian villages and towns" into "a new tribe of literate, reasonable, hearty people."[69] In the early 1930s, he concentrated his opinion against the fictional representation of dialectal and other nonstandard forms of speech.

Gorky's most visible attempt to purify the language by condemning fictional misrepresentations of rural speech appeared in the beginning of 1934 in his criticism of the multivolume novel by Fedor Panferov, *Bruski* (1928–1937). Set in rural Russia during the First Five-Year Plan, Panferov's story had been widely praised in the official press as an "epic of collectivization" in all its various strengths and complications.[70] Criticism of the work was sparse between the publication of the first and third volumes, but Gorky's critique of the novel's language, in particular, changed the tone of its reception dramatically.[71] His comments, appearing in *The Literary Gazette (Literaturnaia gazeta)* in January 1934, admonished Panferov for his verbiage and carelessness, citing in particular his overuse (and misuse) of dialect and his graphic distortion of words in an attempt to capture nonstandard pronunciations. Gorky questioned the author's apparent belief that "Dal"'s dictionary still hangs over the Russian literary language," and, in closing, he condemned Panferov's claim that "if, out of 100 words, you wind up with five good ones and ninety five bad ones, then that's pretty good." It was this sort of language ideology and practice, Gorky warned, that led to the "fabrication of literary waste."[72]

Though clearly enough marking the boundaries between pure and perverse, Gorky's critique set off a yearlong debate in the writing community that quickly assumed an even more politically and socially charged tone. One of Panferov's more prominent allies, the writer Aleksandr Serafimovich, countered Gorky's remarks by defending *Bruski* for its authentic depiction of everyday life in the countryside and its raw portrait of *muzhik* strength.[73] Gorky responded in kind, criticizing the book again for littering the Russian language with words that did not exist and chiding the reviewer for glorifying the "strength of the *muzhik*." "Permit me to remind you," he wrote, "that the strength of the *muzhik* is a socially unhealthy force and that the consistent cultural and political work of the party of Lenin and Stalin is aimed precisely at exterminating from the consciousness of the *muzhik* that 'strength' that you are praising."[74] As in earlier writings on the topic, Gorky's critical frame directly linked style and politics —authority in language with the authority of the state. And here, as in most previous formulations, it was the Russian peasantry in particular that was the main source of poisoning—in both realms. Invoking the antirural discourse of Marx and Lenin to complement his own vocabulary of "extermination," Gorky went on to wonder how it could be possible "to express the heroism and romanticism of the reality created in the Union of Socialist Soviets" using an "idiotic language?" Echoing the same idea, he reminded Serafimovich and his broader reading audience that there was a direct correlation between literacy in language and ideological literacy.[75]

With the exception of some of Panferov's allies from the disbanded Association of Proletarian Writers, participants in the debate generally sided with Gorky, including writers such as Mikhail Sholokhov and Lidiia Seifullina, renowned for their own heavy use of dialect and vulgarisms in fiction.[76] Seifullina justified her earlier narratives by arguing that the "primitive" state of the village at that time left no other option: "We were unable to depict the Russian *muzhik* in the first period of the October Revolution with speech that was pure of primitive crudeness. . . . Grief, elation, gaiety—all emotional manifestations of identity in the old village were usually expressed in very rude words."[77] Another critic carried on where Seifullina left off, offering a more precise description of the verbal identity of the new village: "The language of the old village is withdrawing into the past. The beginning of the destruction of the contrast between the city and the country finds its reflection in the language of the collective farm peasants. The lexicon of the modern village has been enriched by new words, terms, and concepts. In general, the village has ceased being a village, and the linguistic differences will with each year decrease more and more."[78]

Less out of Gorky's culturist concerns for a basic level of literacy than in an effort to solidify the stature of the party-state, lower-level critics writing on literary policy eagerly latched on to the patriarch's arguments and used his rhetoric about national authority and identity. In the process, all three of the models discussed earlier—the revolutionary, the popular, and the national—underwent considerable refinement, if not total transformation. The battle against the use of colloquialisms most directly engaged the popular model. As recalled from chapter 4, it advocated a language that reflected the speech practices of the *narod*—be they members of the peasantry or the urban working class. The criticism of fictional portraits of this language in the early 1930s turned the underlying argument on its head: instead of promoting the people to the center of verbal power, such a mode of expression only distanced them further from its controls. One commentator wrote that a writer's graphic differentiation of speech differences constituted a form of "social alienation."[79] Another attributed such practices to misguided populism that linguistically isolated the peasantry from the more advanced proletariat: "The populists, who mourned the unlucky fate of the Russian *muzhik* . . . [and] sought to fence off the village from the noxious influence of the city and strengthen the patriarchal commune *[obshchina]*, fixed into literature those language features that constituted inalienable membership to the village, its narrow-mindedness, its dullness, its closedness—[features] that distinguished the language of the peasantry from the language of the proletariat."[80]

Gorky's supporters were likewise careful to invoke the voice of the people themselves in their defense, citing reactions of working-class and collective-farm readers who criticized Panferov's books for being "difficult to read" owing to his use of "verbal waste" and "parasites of speech."[81] This voice found additional, if not ultimate, codification in the 1935 *Interpretive Dictionary of the Russian Language*, the linguist Dmitrii Ushakov's realization of Lenin's wish to replace Dal''s nineteenth-century lexicon with a "real" dictionary of the Russian language.[82] Echoing the discourse of party-state purism inspired by Gorky and his followers, Ushakov's introduction dismissed Dal''s work for its focus on "bourgeois vernacular and peasant language," praised the new lexicon's inclusion of postrevolutionary "innovations" to Russian, and finally invoked the authority of both Lenin and Gorky in staking its claim as "a weapon in the struggle 'for the quality of the language spoken every day by literature, the press, and millions of laborers,' 'for the purification of a language that is good, clean, accessible to millions, [and] truly of the people *[narodnyi]*.'"[83]

Such interpretations defused once and for all the hopes of those who advocated that the spoken language of the people be raised to the status of a language of power, advocating instead a return to the already established Russian literary language, newly refined with ideological grounding in Bolshevik authority. Like Iakubinskii, Khavin invoked Lenin to justify the educated revolutionary as the model for public discourse:

> Simplicity and popularity—in the Bolshevik sense of these words—have nothing in common with oversimplification *[uproshchenstvo]* and petty popularizing *[populiarnichan'e]*.
>
> Lenin wrote: "Primary attention must be directed toward raising the workers up to the revolutionaries, and not by any means lowering [the revolutionaries] to the 'working masses.'" . . .
>
> Petty popularizing serves as a means for the bourgeoisie to drag an alien ideology into the ranks of the proletariat. That is why Lenin tirelessly exposed "lisping" literati.[84]

As terms such as "simplicity" and "popularity" emerged at the center of the debate as positive banners for nearly all of the models of language of state, so too did the need for further refinement. And the refining so commonly practiced in the articulation of the party-state model assumed ideological proportions more than formal ones. Bourgeois simplicity may have shared many of the formal features of Bolshevik simplicity, but, when cut ideologically, they suggested two entirely different models of reality.

Like the catchalls "simple" and "popular," the notion of "revolution," so central to the advocates of the revolutionary model of language, also underwent considerable transformation in the literary debates of the early 1930s. Whereas the revolutionary model viewed the language of state as a dynamic force, constantly changing to reflect the changing times, innovative and charismatic in form, content, and execution, the party-state model used "revolution" to describe achievements in political literacy in the village. Kovarskii raised the same specter of idiocy evoked by Gorky to emphasize this point: "Revolution in language manifests itself in the fact that the words that reflect the narrow-mindedness and crookedness of village life, its eternal idiocy, are now dying. Revolution in language manifests itself in the growth of the vocabulary of the collective farmer, in the fact that international political terms and new production terms are appearing in large numbers in that vocabulary, in the fact that, entering into the richest of ties of our public life, the peasantry in all its mass is mastering all kinds of forms of public discourse, written as well as oral, . . . the syntactic and the stylistic literary language."[85]

Rather than placing the onus on the literary language to better reflect the speech practices of the factory and farm, as advocates of the popular voice had recommended, the Soviet purists spoke of the social and cultural transformation of those who did not measure up to the standards of an old "literary" language fortified by new "revolutionary" terminology (here, the language of collectivization). Revolution in language was no longer a matter of formal innovation. Invoking Stalin's by then well-known slogan, Gofman declared that the new literary language was "national in form and socialist in content."[86] And the model for such revolutionary fusion? "The Soviet writer will find the key to understanding the new, socialist content in language in the decisions of the Party, in the pronouncements of comrade Stalin."[87] And herein lay the difference between this and the revolutionary and national models, which also placed the burden of comprehension on the "consumers" of language. If for them the positive models were the charismatic poets, orators, and philologists, or the "classics" of prerevolutionary literature, the party-state model identified its model more narrowly in the linguistic mold formed by the party-state elite.

That sort of infusion of socialism into an essentially national ideology provided the formula needed to ensure a nonthreatening means of talking about state authority and identity through language. If Gorky, by virtue of his own status as a "classic," could afford to talk simply in terms of culture and nation, it was the literary critics and party operatives after him who recast this essentially purist stance into less reactionary and more ideologically correct terms. One amended Gorky's own notion of "mastery," in fact, to "Bolshevik mastery," in order to distinguish the new Soviet literary language from those models perceived to be to subservient to the bourgeois West.[88] Another refined the notion of "purism" to set it apart from reactionary, anti-Soviet attitudes by modifying it with the epithet "revolutionary": "It is also possible to talk about a *revolutionary purism*, which reflects the moods, tastes, and drives of those classes victorious in the October Revolution, about the linguistic policy of the proletariat. The history of revolutionary purism, in the tightest manner linked to the name of Lenin, begins almost from the first years of the existence of Soviet power."[89]

Instead of a policy of restructuring, or even reinventing language, the party-state model embraced a position that called for the maintenance and broader dissemination of the established literary language, as constituted formally by the Russian classics, but infused with the new Soviet ideology. The positive features most frequently identified with this new discourse reflect the general transposition of the issue of form into one of content. Proponents of the party-state model spoke most about a language that was "truthful" (*pravdivyi*)—a term that, in Andrei Zhdanov's infamous formula for Soviet literature, came to mean depicting reality "not in a deadening manner, not simply as 'objective reality,' but . . . in its revolutionary development."[90] They emphasized also a language that was "efficacious" *(deistvennyi)*, one that never breached the unity of word and deed.[91] And the primary models for such language were the language of the press and the speeches and writings of the major leaders of the party-state.[92] Notions of "revolution," *narod*, and "mastery" all found a place in the formula, but they were disassociated from issues of form and were transformed into ideological incantations for a different deity. Revolutionary, popular, and masterful language became, in effect, discursive fodder for the language of the party-state.

. . .

Taken together, the changing verbal landscape in journalism, pedagogy, linguistics, and literature reflected, by the early 1930s, a language culture in which primary emphasis was on state maintenance, not state building. Central to that culture was an already established model of speaking and writing founded on the principles of membership and *partiinost'* and based on a canon that included, most importantly, the language production of Lenin, Stalin, and the central party press. Certainly much of this success was afforded by centralized control and greater efficiency of the channels of communication and flow of information. The language of the party came to dominate the school curricula, textbooks, and classrooms; the central press; the professional discourse of linguistics; and contemporary literature and folklore. But no less important was a process of linguistic routinization that, through years of innovation, simplification, and purification, made the language of Bolshevism both more accessible and authoritative to the speaking and writing population. Whether by verbal force, greater exposure, or willful adoption for whatever the reason, the language of the party came to assume the status of a language of power, a cue to membership; those who recognized this and sought to advance their standing in Stalin's Soviet Russia *at least* embraced the language as "their own" *(svoi)* for practical purposes. The worker and village correspondents saw in it the key to institutional advancement and professionalization; villagers and workers recognized it as the best language in which to petition or influence local factory and kolkhoz administration and politics; and linguists, ethnographers, and writers saw in it the key to their own survival and professional empowerment.

In the descriptions of the now-dominant language of state, the legacy of the three earlier models could certainly be felt. Critics and commentators knew well the importance of invoking notions of revolution, *narod*, proletariat, and classics in conjunction with the language of Stalinist Russia. But descriptions of the language as such carried significantly different implications for state and citizenship than they did in their original forms. More than charismatic orators, peasants, workers, or Russians, Soviet citizens had to be active supporters—if not members—of the party. In order to advance in the new society, they had to acquire the gift of tongues by emulating the language practice of the revolutionary vanguard—starting with its two sacred embodiments, Lenin and Stalin.[93]

NARRATING THE PARTY-STATE

The supreme danger for our art is the transformation of labor-creation *[trud-tvorchestvo]* into a song about labor.

—Andrei Platonov, "Proletarian Poetry" (1922)

I would sometimes hear reproaches for the fact that my novel did not show the *narod*, just the leading heads of the party organization. This reproach, it seems, is not serious. . . . party spirit *[partiinost']* is the highest manifestation of national character *[narodnost']*. It is so clear, that there is no place here for idle philosophizing.

—Iurii Libedinskii, on reactions to his 1922 novella, *The Week* (1956)

In each epoch certain speech genres set the tone for the development of literary language. . . . Any expansion of the literary language that results from drawing on various extraliterary strata of the national language inevitably entails some degree of penetration into all genres of written language (literary, scientific, commentarial, conversational, and so forth) to a greater or lesser degree. . . .

—Mikhail Bakhtin, "The Problem of Speech Genres" (1953)

The relationship between literature and the language culture of the social and political sphere was one of awkward interdependence. In some cases, literature helped reinforce models of speaking and writing advocated in other spheres, using the strength of its narrative authority and imagination to do so in ways that agitators, textbooks, and political pamphlets simply could not. In other cases, literature brought to the forefront of the language debates embarrassing realities of miscommunication, reappropriation, and verbal distortion. Yet there is no denying the influence in the other direction—of the nonliterary language culture on the voice, tone, and form of literature. Although a study of this sort by necessity privileges narratives that speak to the issue of language, and the emerging language of state in particular, the broad range of authors and works that did somehow address the issue attests to the degree to which language was problematized. Few writers living and producing inside of Soviet Russia wrote prose entirely impervious to the profound crisis in voice constituting the language culture of the day. (And, after a certain point, the few that did were, by their very omission, making a charged statement about language and voice.) It was an issue that virtually could not be ignored.

Only by the early 1930s did this acute linguistic self-consciousness begin to give way to a dominant manner of writing and speaking that exhibited at least a veneer of unproblematic authority and legitimacy. The preceding chapter traced some of the key metalinguistic shifts that helped establish the voice of the party-state as that authoritative model in a variety of nonliterary spheres—the newspaper, the classroom, linguistics, and literary criticism—showing how competing models of language were not so much rejected as they were assimilated and, frequently, reappropriated. This chapter examines how the voice of the party-state came to assume authority and legitimacy in a variety of narrative genres central to the imaginative representation of that new language of state. Those domains include prose fiction, which was the dominant voice of "big" literature and arguably the main source of verbal authority; folklore, the most potent domain for playing out vocal tensions within the mythic vox populi and taming the verbal threat that it posed; and the sketch, which came to be recognized as the most accessible and useful outlet for new intellectual writers. As in the case of the nonliterary language institutions, these literary genres reflect substantial adaptation and reappropriation that highlight the synthetic nature of the new Soviet language of state. Even some of the more notorious literary distortions of the 1930s attest, in an albeit twisted manner, to the hegemony of this party-state voice and the degree to which the roots of their narrative transgressions are linguistic.

BRIDLING CHAPAEV:

A FICTIONAL PROTOTYPE OF THE PARTY-STATE NARRATIVE

Although Maxim Gorky's *Mother* (1906) often earns the status of the "original" socialist-realist novel, Dmitrii Furmanov's *Chapaev* (1923) was one of the first narratives to feature the party-state voice in the role of authoritative and "transparent" narrator. As with Babel's *Red Cavalry*, Fedorchenko's *The People at War,* and Fadeev's *Rout,* Furmanov's *Chapaev* is set at the civil war front—in this case, with the partisan regiments of the legendary peasant Divisional Commander Vasilii Chapaev. The popularity of this setting and theme is no accident: beyond its military significance, the civil war was an important symbolic victory for the Bolshevik party, strengthening its legitimacy to the controls of power not only over the White Army and tsarist Russia but also over the less organized peripheries of the new state.[1] Because service in the Red Army, for most of the predominantly peasant soldiers, marked the first direct encounter with the new Soviet ideology, the civil war provided fertile ground for establishing a common language between the state and its citizens.[2]

Like Babel's collection of stories, Furmanov's book is narrated from the perspective of an educated and trained representative of the central state—Fedor Klychkov—a political commissar sent to coordinate the agitational campaign among Chapaev's spirited, though somewhat anarchistic, regiments.[3] Each narrative describes an encounter between the politically "organized" center and the "elemental" chaos of the periphery, but their focus is quite different. Babel's highlights the unintended consequences of verbal distortion; Furmanov's, the mobilizing force and didactic clarity of political enlightenment. His poetics of mobilization begins promptly with the opening scene—a public rally at the Ivanovo train station, where local textile workers have gathered to bid farewell to their comrades who have volunteered to fight against Kolchak and the White Army in the Volga-Urals region. In ideologically charged speeches, Communist Party activists spell out for the crowd (and the implied reader) the tasks of the mobilization effort. This theme carries the story forward, following the newly transformed worker-soldiers on their journey to the front. At local train depots along the way, agitators from the geographical and ideological center organize instructional meetings for the unenlightened masses of the periphery: "No matter the stop, the echelon had new work. The entire route was filled with numerous meetings, gatherings, conferences, lectures, a variety of separate discussions in circles of enthusiast-participants."[4] Narrative events fall into two kinds of conflicts: between the Red Army and its enemy, and between the politically enlightened representatives of the central state and the peasant masses of the outlying regions. The spheres in which these conflicts are played out—the battlefield, the demonstration, the meeting of military and political strategists—define the central space of the novel. They are for the most part *public* arenas, constituting the legitimate domain of the party-state, and in turn help define public life for readers. As they are drawn into the plot of *Chapaev*, they themselves become the *objects* of mobilization and the addressees of political education.

Furmanov grounds his didacticism linguistically by employing the language and symbols of state generously and transparently throughout the novel. Klychkov's is the voice of a seasoned party activist keen on organization and results:

> Klychkov . . . ne stal dal'she rassprashivat' i chut'em organizatora ponial, chto emu nado delat'.
>
> Vo-pervykh, on reshil oznakomit'sia fakticheski, po dokumentam i otchetam, s rabotoi v brigade, esli ne cherez Ezhikova, to cherez ego pomoshchnikov i sotrudnikov, dobyvaia ot nikh ofitsial'nye otchety i vsiakie svedeniia.
>
> Vo vtoruiu ochered' on reshil nastoiat' na sozyve nebol'shikh soveshchanii-konferentsii partiinykh iacheek, kul'tkomissii, kontrkhozkomissii, sobranii voenkomov i t.d. Eto pomozhet emu srazu mnogoe uvidet' i poniat'.
>
> Dal'she on sobralsia ob"ekhat' chasti i posmotret' tam dopodlinnuiu postanovku raboty i, nakonets, v predstoiashchikh boiakh khotel uchastvovat' lichno v kachestve riadovogo boitsa i tem zasluzhit' sebe imia khoroshego tovarishcha i khrabrogo cheloveka. Eto obstoiatel'stvo moglo imet' vliianie na uspekh ili neuspekh vsei ego dal'neishei politicheskoi raboty.
>
> Blizhaishie neskol'ko dnei, vplot' do nastupleniia, Fedor osushchestvlial nastoichevo postavlennye pered soboiu zadachi. (61)

[With the feel of an organizer, Klychkov understood what he needed to do.

In the first place, he decided to familiarize himself factually, through documents and reports, with the work in the brigade. . . . In the second place, he decided to insist on the convocation of small meeting-conferences of the party cells, cultural commissions, committees for economic control, meetings of the military commanders, etc. That would help him immediately see and understand a great amount.

Further, he planned to travel around to the units and observe the actual status of the political work there; and, finally, in the upcoming battles he wanted to participate personally in the capacity of a rank-and-file fighter, and in so doing earn himself the name of a good comrade and brave man. This condition could influence the successes or failures of his future political work.

Over the next several days, right up to the offensive, Fedor persistently carried out the tasks set before him.]

The passage does more than reflect a mastery of language of state, from the numerous stump-compounds to the employment of such classic Soviet turns-of-phrase as *fakticheski, riadovoi boets,* and the bureaucratic *osushchestvlial nastoichivo postavlennye pered soboiu zadachi*. It also shows a manner of thinking characteristic of the model activist of the day: ideologically conscious *(chutiem organizatora)*, organized (in both life and language), and oriented toward overachievement *(srazu mnogoe uvidet' i poniat')*. Quasi-direct speech creates an echoing of voices between Klychkov and the narrator around issues of political organization (a domain Fadeev's Tolstoyan narrator avoided altogether), giving rise to a doubly authoritative narrative voice. This model is further "authorized" by the close ideological proximity of the implied author himself. It was common knowledge that Furmanov himself had served as political commissar in Chapaev's division; in fact, his diaries show that he had seriously considered retaining in the book the same first-person narrative he used in his wartime diaries.[5] Neither the legitimacy of the activist's work nor the need to organize the masses through such work is questioned by the "insider"-narrator: they are a given. And so they are meant to be understood by the implied readers of the novel. The question posed by the narrative on agitation and propaganda is not whether to organize and control, but by which means to do so.

The same didacticism Furmanov displays in plot structure and narration can be seen in his orchestration of direct speech and, in particular, in his wholesale muting of the voices of the periphery. Aside from Chapaev himself, none of the peasants, Cossacks, or other nonparty, nonofficial characters is given a direct voice. Instead, they assume the collective portrait of a dehumanized mass, whose verbal production is limited to animalistic sounds—as in the scene of the mobilized workers' departure for the front: "The crowd fixed itself closer, it poured out of the windows of the train in a completely faceless mass. The mass grumbled, buzzed, grew agitated, like an enormous woolly beast—one-thousand-pawed, one-thousand-eyed, complacent, like a fur-covered bear" (30).

Chapaev provides an exception to this gag rule, but he still suffers at the editorial hands of the narrator. More often than not, his speeches to the soldiers are reduced to isolated phrases and sentences, the rest being filtered through a combination of indirect discourse and critical commentary from the storyteller. On one such occasion, the narrator offers a revealing critique of Chapaev's oratory: "He began without any introduction or explanation of the reason for which he summoned the fighters. . . . He then proceeded to latch on incidentally to an enormous mass of the most unnecessary details, he kept latching onto anything that accidentally popped into his head. . . . There weren't even any signs of order, unity, or the emergence of any one general idea in Chapaev's speech: he said whatever came to mind" (96).

The opposition here, between "accidental" and "orderly" *(sluchainyi* and *stroinyi)* language, is clearly intended as an ideological contrast between political chaos and cohesion. The possibility of alternative ideological views and forms for expressing them is ostensibly denied by the tag of "accidental" to all that fails to conform to the "order" as defined by the language of state. Furmanov's narrator underscores this denial of content when he later refers to Chapaev's "speeches" (the narrator uses this word in quotations) as "contentless," "meaningless," and, in the tenor of Gorky (and Marx and Engels before him), "idiotic" (85–86). Contrasted to Chapaev's "empty", "childlike," and elemental language is the substantive, mature, "conscious" language of the Soviet state, displayed by Klychkov and his activist colleagues at key junctures throughout the novel. This second language stands without commentary as truly direct and authoritative speech; it is the language of power, the model for all those aspiring to become citizens and spokespersons themselves.

SOVIET FOLKLORE AND THE "SONG TO THE PROLETARIAT"

If Furmanov, in his relatively early fictional narrative, could simply opt to ignore, chastise, or dismiss the disturbing perversions of official language common among the voices of the ideological and geographic periphery, those whose profession dealt directly with these voices—folklorists and ethnographers—were faced with a more delicate task. Traditionally, the sources for their material came from the rural peasantry, precisely that faction of the population most likely to exhibit distorted linguistic perceptions and practices. Under increased pressure in the late 1920s to justify what increasingly came to be seen as a profession buried in the antiquated past, leading folklorists adopted two lines of defense.

The first defense was to increase attention toward contemporary, and particularly "urban," folklore.[6] The second, not unrelated to the first and particularly ironic in light of the attacks on Sof'ia Fedorchenko's "falsification" of the mythic *glas naroda,* was to reconfigure their object of study as imaginative literature. Reading contemporary folklore and oral narratives like fiction would show that the *narod* still had much to offer of cultural value. Another benefit was more generic in nature: recasting the voice of the people into pseudoliterary creations allowed for freer representation of that voice and made it more ideologically potent. By the early 1930s, prominent ethnographers such as Iurii Sokolov were openly calling for the use of folklore toward specifically didactic ends, for stricter control over less "conscious," "elemental" manifestations of "oral creation of the masses," and for folklorists' active intervention against "all that was hostile to socialist construction."[7] It was precisely that sort of pronouncement coming from one of the leading scholars in folklore studies that led, eventually, to the wholesale invention of new folkloric genres, such as the *noviny,* dedicated to the glorification of Soviet leaders.[8]

For traditional genres of folklore, this aesthetic component was neither new nor difficult to justify. Dating at least back to the mid-nineteenth century, writers and collectors alike touted songs, tales, and *byliny* primarily for their artistic merits. Adding to this list the more recent folk genre of the *chastushka* was both natural and unproblematic.[9] But as instrumental to the new efforts to capture the voice of the people and recast it as a didactic model for new art forms were collections of oral narratives of a more documentary and autobiographical nature—genres that, by virtue of both form and content, were more historically charged and therefore open to factual (and narrative) contestation.

One such aestheticized collection of a more "proletarianized" vox populi appeared in 1931 under the title, *Revolution: Oral Stories of Urals Workers about the Civil War*, edited by Semen Mirer and Vasilii Borovik.[10] It is significant not only because of its notoriety among contemporary folklorists and ethnographers but also because of the claims *about* the people's voice made in introductory remarks by the collection editor, the compilers, and Sokolov himself. As with Fedorchenko, all three highlight the authenticity of the texts—especially Sokolov, who contrasts the effort directly to Fedorchenko's "falsification" and draws the reader's attention to the detailed biographical information about each of the storytellers appended to their narratives. The chief editor, Mikhail Morozov, links the issue of authenticity directly to that of voice:

> It is not just what a man said, but how he said it that is important. All of these stories are of value not so much because of the total sense that can be gleaned from them, as much as for how, by whom exactly, and in what kind of linkage with reality the narrative of events and experiences (already familiar to some by personal experience, to others by memoirs) is conducted. The main point is not in the bestial brutality of the Whites, about which we all know sufficiently well, but rather in how these evil acts were perceived by the masses and the narrators who are the mouthpieces of those masses. (9)

In other words, the facts themselves are familiar to everyone; more important is the narrative voice behind the recollections. In contrast to the concocted populist narratives of Fedorchenko and others, what the reader gets here is the authentic "narrative mouthpiece" for the masses. Mirer in his own introduction goes one step further by adding an aesthetic dimension to the collective voice and linking it directly to the language of state. The stories in the collection, he writes, represent "the birth of a new epic, which feels the influence of the newspaper article and the revolutionary agitational speech" (38).[11] This aestheticization of the language of state, prominent in the literary and linguistic debates described in the previous chapter, assumes even more pronounced status in Mirer's bold claim regarding the very "tellability" of tales involving the state:

> The new culture has so taken root in the consciousness of the working masses that thoughts going against our [Soviet] construction are unable to find eloquent expression. If the storyteller feels any sort of unbelief, he tells the story with a limpness and lack of confidence, whereas the story about victory and construction sounds with the voice of a storm. When the storyteller begins to speak about construction, he feels an expanse *[prostor]* for his thoughts, he feels an expanse for their expression. This is why we often witness how a storyteller, caught up in the process of his story, begins to speak like an orator. (37)

The eloquence of the *narod* has less to do with some innate quality or "purely" artistic gift or skill as it does with the conscious mastery of a certain way of talking based in the language, ideas, and dominant genres of the state. In this formulation, the aestheticization of the popular voice becomes so by virtue of its politicization. Only once this ideological foundation is in place can one find the verbal "expanse" needed for inspired expression.

On closer look, the contours of that expanse differ markedly from those invoked by Fedorchenko. At the center of attention throughout the collection is the war effort itself. Storyteller after storyteller relates memories of specific battles, commanders, and comrades-in-arms. They devote little attention to the more private spheres explored and described by Fedorchenko's peasant soldiers. A second distinctive feature, related to the first, is the length and structure of each narrative. In contrast to Fedorchenko's laconic, capsule articulations, the texts here are rarely less than a page and are often five pages and more. (The entire collection fills 454 pages.) When considered along with the conscious attempt by most of the narrators to introduce and conclude their stories, and to highlight one or two climactic moments, the narratives give more "coherence" to the memories, more sense to the stories.

The final distinctive feature has to do with voice itself—more specifically, with the prominence of the language of the state. Words, phrases, and styles evoking the image of the Soviet state and its official voice (most clearly articulated in the press, but also prominent in key fictional works of the period) inform the stories of the workers in a manner that is, for the most part, fluid and unproblematic. This language of state is more a mark of membership than alienation or estrangement. Its prominence varies across narratives, but when it is invoked it is done so with a distinct singularity of purpose: to affirm that language, to recognize it as a language of power and a cue to membership. In a like manner, the level of colloquialness varies, but rarely does it appear as aestheticized as it does in Fedorchenko's texts. The *glas naroda* here is more of a hybrid of colloquial speech, military jargon, and Soviet bureaucratese. The following examples offer a sense of the range in styles, beginning with the strongly colloquial voice:

> A chto zhe ia tebe skazhu istoricheskoe-to? Ia tebe pro svoiu zhizn', dorogoi tovarishch, rasskazhu ochen' dlinnuiu istoriiu.
> Ia tebe skazhu prosto opredelenno. U nas tovarishchi vse organizovannye byli, kak odin. Poshli, poshli, da i tol'ko. Burovili pochem zria! Bili nas, i my bili. I my ne shchadili! Ne shchadili! Nazukinskii otriad prokliatyi byl. Kolchak ego proklial. Pod puliami byli. Ne boialis' my! U menia vse bylo prostreleno, ia—i to nichut' ne boialsia, raz ia reshitel'no poshel. Kuda poshel, to poshel—i tol'ko.
> Dorogoi tovarishch, vernulis' kogda, nas prisoedinili k dvadtsat' vtoromu

Kizelovskomu polku. Eto naznachalasia voobshche deviataia letuchaia rota. Samaia boevaia. U nas nazvanie bylo "Chernykh orlov." Kak tebe teper' ob"iasnit'? Chort znaet kuda my proshli! (54)[12]

[What's there for me to tell you, historically, so to speak? I'll tell you about my life, dear comrade, I'll tell you a very long story.

I'll tell it to you straight. All of our comrades were organized like one. We'd go and go, and that was that. We would kick ass something mean. True, we were beaten. But we beat, too. And we showed no mercy! Showed no mercy! The Nazukin detachment was cursed, it was. Kolchak cursed it. We were under fire. But we weren't afraid! I was all shot through, and even then I wasn't afraid, since I had made up my mind to go. Wherever I went, I went—and that was that.

When we returned, dear comrade, we were attached to the twenty-second Kizelov regiment. In all, it was designated the ninth mobile company. The most militant. We called ourselves the "Black Eagles." How do I explain it to you now? The devil only knows where we went! . . .]

For all its colloquial markers (*-to, proklel, —i tol'ko, Chort znaet kuda . . .*), the narrator displays a solid understanding of the emerging language of state, employing the textbook Soviet use of *opredelenno, organizovannyi,* and *dorogoi tovarishch*. As significant is the narrator's conscious recognition, stated directly in the second paragraph, of the broader, social import of his narrative: through his recollections, he is participating in the verbal construction of history.[13] More direct efforts to contextualize narratives in party-related activity—a strategy employed by many of the contributors—assume a more official, bureaucratic voice, such as in the following passage from a narrative entitled "For Bolshevism":

Pri organizovannosti partii bol'shevikov, sostavliaiushchei shest'-sem' chelovek, razbili agitatsionnuiu propagandu men'shevizma burzhuaznuiu, spisok nomer vtoroi, znachit, na vybornom sobranii pri byvshem volostnom pravlenii. Rabochie gorniaki kak podzemnye, tak i poverkhnostnye, uchityvaia ugnetenie burzhuaznym klassom . . . , poshli ruka ob ruku s nashim bratom, znachit, s ranenymi byvshimi soldatami na pozitsii, za spisok tovarishchei-bol'shevikov. (85)[14]

[Under the organized nature of the party of Bolsheviks, consisting of six–seven individuals, we destroyed the bourgeois agitational propaganda of Menshevism—the second list (of candidates), that is—at the election meeting at the former *volost'* government headquarters. The mine workers, both underground and surface, on account of being oppressed by the bourgeois class, went hand in hand with our folk, that is, the ex-soldiers wounded at the front, in support of the list of comrade Bolsheviks.]

Nearly void of slang, dialect, or other forms of nonstandard speech, the remembrance reads more like an official protocol, dominated by complex sentences, verbal adverbs and participles, nominal phrases, and a rich and fluid, ideologically marked lexicon. If the oral origins are suspect in such officially steeped narratives, they become even more problematic in those displaying a strongly poeticized voice—fewer proportionally, but nevertheless numerous enough to make a lasting impression:

> Po doroge ot stantsii v gorod, za mostom, est' gorodskoi sad. Zimoi, skloniv nizko svoi kurchavye golovy, osypannye snegom, derev'ia grustno smotriat na mogily pokhoronennykh tam pavshikh v boiu pod Mertvymi Soliami tovarishchei. Na odnoi iz nikh otdel'no stoiala podbitaia batareia nepriiatelia, podniav svoi khoboty kverkhu, slovno khotela krichat', chto eto mogila zasluzhennogo deviatnadtsatiletnogo iunoshi-krasnoarmeitsa, nazvannogo synom slavnogo krasnogo komandira, starogo ofitsera artillerii tovarishcha Trizny,—mogila Kanareikina, prozvannogo batareei i polkom klichkoi Kanareika. (198)[15]

[Along the roadway from the station to the town, behind the bridge, there is a city garden. In the wintertime, the trees, lowly bending their curly snowladen heads, looked sadly at the graves of the buried comrades who had fallen in the battle of Dead Salts. At one of them were some knocked out enemy artillery pieces with their elephant-trunk-like barrels raised up as if it wanted to cry out that this was the grave of the honorable nineteen-year-old Red Army youth, known as the son of the renowned Red Army commander and old artillery officer comrade Trizna—the grave of Kanareikin, whom the battery and regiment nicknamed "Canary."]

If the central narrative can be seen as a kind of a control—a model of that standard narrative voice of the Bolshevik operative—it is the other two that are perhaps more revealing in terms of the representation of the *glas naroda*. The first suggests that, even in the most colloquial of narratives, the language of state is not "misused," as is often the case in the Fedorchenko collections, the *skaz* fiction of Babel' and Zoshchenko, or the tongue-tied efforts of the early worker correspondents, for that matter. It bears the mark of a voice of authority. The last and arguably most striking (for a collection of "oral" narratives) exemplifies the "high style" of new Soviet narrative, which couches the language, images, and pathos of the new state in a narrative "space" that is highly aestheticized and far from oral in inspiration and execution.

The effort to elevate the stories to the level of "art," as boasted by the editor in his introduction, can also be seen in the collection's section and chapter headings, which evoke more traditional folklore genres: "Military Epics *(poemy)* and Recollections," "Garrulous *Byliny,*" "The Individual and the Mass in the Revolution (novellas, stories and tales)." A closer look at the style and content of these sections shows little generic differentiation. All assume the form of prose narratives told in the first person, and all, as mentioned before, focus on narrow episodes of war.

The Soviet mythologization of the *glas naroda* can be detected with increasing frequency through the first decade of Bolshevik rule, in the growing number of collections of politically correct *chastushki*, public testimonies, autobiographies, and as shown here, oral narratives.[16] Yet, despite the temptation to interpret Mirer's idea of a widened narrative "expanse" as a euphemism for stricter editorial censorship (external or internal), the dynamic is more complicated. First, by no means were all the folklorists and ethnographers producing their representations of the *glas naroda* out of thin air; there is ample evidence in both cases discussed here of some degree of ethnographic accuracy. Similarly, regardless of the context, it would be wrong for this same reason to assume a completely passive, manipulated, and amorphous *narod*. It is as likely that the language of state represented for certain peasants and workers a means of empowerment as it did either a source of repression or target for subversion.[17] Finally, one cannot overlook the importance of time itself in the process of finding the appropriate voice, or "getting the story straight." The articulateness of the 1931 collection was made possible in part by the simple fact that a number of prominent and effective fictional and nonfictional works dedicated to recounting and narrating the civil war had preceded it (Furmanov's and Fadeev's among them). The generic model for the civil war recollection had become more firmly established and, in the process, smoother, more formulaic, and less problematic than the fractured and largely marginal confusion featured in Fedorchenko's book.[18]

As important for this study of voice, however, is the striking symmetry in representational strategy between Fedorchenko's earlier collection and Mirer and Borovik. Beyond any evidence of resistance, oppression, or manipulation, both collections represent a common attempt to establish dual sources of authority: factual and aesthetic, ethnographic and narrative. Aside from the clear differences, each tries in essence to have it both ways—in the first case, passing off an essentially fictional collection as a nearly transcribed text and, in the second, presenting the recollections of Urals workers as a new literary "epic." The order in which they privileged these genres was exactly reverse. But the fact that each settled on some weave of the two voices and disciplines is itself instructive. It demonstrates, first, the power of narrative in imposing a particular order on events still very much under symbolic negotiation. Second, it suggests the need for some semblance of authenticity to legitimate that order (particularly when it is the *glas naroda* in question). Finally, it suggests that in the state-building period of Soviet Russia the "voice of the people"—be it reproduced in the context of fiction, folklore, or ethnography—was a particularly sensitive and important object of documentation, reconstruction, and imagination. Precisely for that reason, it was subjected to a new version of the centuries-old practice of verbal mythologization.

THE PRODUCTION SKETCH:
A BEGINNER'S GUIDE TO NARRATING THE STATE

Bringing greater aesthetic (and ideological) coherence to the imperfect and unpredictable written language practices of the people proved a still more challenging task, given the greater complexity of the medium and the closer link between authorship and authority. We have already seen two of the more common methods of controlling this voice on the part of literary institutions. Editorial framing kept the imperfect texts of worker or rural correspondents in check by transforming them into "display narratives" of a proletarian voice in the making; and patronizing recommendations from "literary consultants" directed the bulk of aspiring writers back to the drawing board with instructions to bone up on the classics before taking pen in hand again. By the end of the 1920s and the onset of the First Five-Year Plan, a third and more useful channel for these creative energies was found in the genre of the sketch *(ocherk)* and, in particular, the "production sketch."

If, at its very etymological core, the *skaz* narrative evokes an essentially oral notion, the sketch, or *ocherk* in Russia, elicits the basic act of writing, or graphic portrayal.[19] From its inception in Russia in the satirical journals of the late eighteenth century, the genre constituted a generic mix of journalistic documentation (freely borrowing from the language of the press, science, and statistics) and prose, most often employing a realist style and an eyewitness first-person narrator loosely associated with the sketch writer. Quite often, the subject of the sketch lay outside the immediate cultural, social, or economic purview of the sketch writer and implied audience—a practice evident in the plethora of physiological sketches written in the genre's heyday of the 1830s and 1840s. Frequently, the object of study was located on the geographical periphery, be it rural Russia or non-Russian ethnic territories.

A rural focus stands out in the literary production of the 1920s. Most of the leading "thick" journals regularly featured sketches, often under rubrics that made clear their rural orientation: "The Soviet Land," "Village Sketches," "Rural Sketches," "Provincial Sketches," and "From the Village Notepad."[20] They also exhibit a similar trend as witnessed in the evolution of folklore studies in the previous section—a gradual shift during the later part of the decade from populist celebrations of the countryside to studies of how rural populations were coming to embrace the language and ideas of the Soviet state. Andrei Bely's 1933 characterization of the genre as a means of bringing "distant" cultures out of the "museums" and into the fold of modern civilization just as easily could have applied to the Russian peasantry under Soviet rule, even more so on the eve of the First Five-Year Plan, when the sketch was most directly and forcefully recast as a mechanism for promoting the ideas, goals, and language of the party-state.[21]

The most pressing need was to document the successes and setbacks of the dual campaigns for industrialization and collectivization in a voice that not only underscored the legitimacy and authority of those efforts but also engaged the writing and reading populace in the process. Though odd when viewed in isolation, the well-oiled "Calling of Shockworkers to Literature" campaign marked, in the tradition of the various amateur correspondent movements and the formation of a "new intelligentsia" in "big" literature, a continued belief that one of the critical means of engaging the population in the task of revolution and state building was to involve them in some narrative, or documentary, mode.

That the sketch became the primary generic vehicle for this and similar campaigns was no accident. As reinvented by Soviet writers and critics, it met the demands of the changing language culture of early Stalinist Russia for a number of reasons, all on prominent display in the intensified discussion of the genre in literary periodicals beginning in 1929 and continuing well into the 1930s. In its ability to "combin[e] a brilliant display of important and typical facts and their competent and effective verbal-iconic [slovesno-obrazovaia] transmission with the precision of journalistic analysis and political conclusions," as one sketch writer put it, the hybrid nature of the sketch served all concerned parties well—aspiring writer, reading audience, and state.[22] In contrast to the high literary genres with which the upstart writers from the factory and village struggled, the sketch emphasized the centrality of facts and the need for their clear transmission, shunning the efforts to overembellish with literary devices that were so common (and commonly mediocre) in the manuscripts that crossed the desks of the RAPP consultants.[23] There was no room in the sketch for "fantasy" or "fabrication." Its advocates even went so far as to encourage the incorporation of nonliterary texts that aided the process of factual transmission—everything from production data and scientific formulas to political slogans and quoted speeches—a practice that both simplified the direct transmission of the voice of the party-state and encouraged the sketch writers (and their readers) to master it.[24] Its factual orientation also made the genre more accessible, according to commentators, as witnessed in one's characteristically condescending remarks about an aspiring poet's potential as a writer: "While a poet may not emerge from him, there is no question that a sketch-writer will."[25]

The sketch's proponents by no means dismissed the importance of the aesthetic component. On the contrary, recalling the aesthetics of Gorky and Tolstoy, they saw in its artistic dimension the genre's great potential for infecting its readers with the urgency of socialist construction, for "raising their spirits and strengthening their will for future struggle."[26] The sketch, insisted one advocate, was "a literary-imaginative work built entirely on documentary material."[27] It was this aesthetic feature, along with the persistently encouraged short, clear, simple, and "action-oriented" *(deistvennyi)* style, that would make the genre most accessible to mass readers, whose involvement in the process of production and collectivization was so instrumental to the state's success.[28] But they were equally as adamant about the need for a strong and unmistakable ideological component. In the early Stalinist reinvention of the genre, the sketch was to offer vivid, concrete, and fact-based contexts for understanding broader, more abstract notions of "socialist construction, "socialist competition," "tempos," and other concepts critical to the implementation of the Five-Year Plan. Sketches that fell short of the mark in this regard drew criticism for being too concrete and documentary, for offering little guidance or indication as to how the portrayed facts should be received and interpreted by readers, and for lacking sufficient "social purposefulness" and "party spirit" *(partiinost')*. The sketch writer was to function as an "operative" or "spy" in the name of "our common interests," in the "struggle for the general line of the party," issuing reports that sounded "like a blow."[29] The most successful newspaper sketches, according to several commentators, were those that provided an ideological complement to the reports, editorials, and slogans appearing on the very same page.[30]

The combined demands regarding form (brief, clear, and simple), content (industrialization and collectivization), ideology (Marxist-Leninist), context (newspaper or multiauthored collection), authorship (the new intellectual writer-worker), and audience (mass readers) made the sketch an excellent vehicle for promoting the party-state voice and enhancing its linguistic capital. But the actual production of the genre often fell short of the ideal, for several reasons already seen in preceding analyses. One major problem lay in the interference of alternative models of sketch writing. More revolutionary minded proponents of "factography" *(literatura fakta),* for instance, who viewed the sketch and the newspaper in general as the "new Soviet epos" that would eventually replace the cumbersome novel itself, were derided by more conservative proletarian critics for their overly formalistic and ideologically naive approach to writing.[31] Sketches that too strongly evoked the voice of the people were dismissed as fawningly romanticized, anachronistic populism.[32] Even sketches too attentive to the voice of the worker were criticized, in this party-state discourse, for their "shop-floor narrow-mindedness" *(tsekhovaia ogranichennost')*—a problem common to the worker correspondent sketches, in particular.[33] And when sketch writers let their narrative voices get too transparent in the spirit of the realist classics, they were castigated for being too objective, for their "crudely empirical orientation," for playing down the role of the party, and for failing to provide sufficient ideological signposts for its readers.[34] The new advocates of the sketch spoke of mastery, but now just as important as "crystal-pure language," "high literary mastery," and "mastery of the deepest clarity" was the "mastery of Marxist thinking."[35]

A second problem had to do with perceived mediocrity. As with the earlier journalistic and literary forays of the amateur correspondents and the "new intelligentsia," the efforts of the shockworkers and other novice sketch writers frequently elicited mild but distinctly patronizing reactions from the institutional professionals. This was in part because their literary production rarely met up to the lofty, multilayered, and largely utopian standards outlined above. Reviewed sketches were frequently lambasted for their "primitive," shoddy construction, their impoverished cultural level, or their excesses in any one of the alternative voices to that of the party-state. According to one damning assessment of the genre, "laziness has become habit, and the sketches . . . are all too often written poorly, carelessly, dully, illiterately; it's still worse when the exposed poverty of language is covered with the pretentious rags of flowery ornamentation."[36] Another critic went so far as to dismiss the entire shockworker-writer campaign as a doomed second attempt at recruiting writers from the working class in the aftermath of the failed worker correspondent movement: "First the RAPP-ists preached that the worker and rural correspondents would make literature. This came to naught. Now the RAPPists say that it is the shockworkers called to literature who will make the weather. But the shockworkers, don't you see, are those same worker correspondents."[37]

A final problem rested in the genre's own inferiority complex with regard to its literary worth.[38] While commonly invoking precedents for sketch writing among the literary canon of the classics, the sketch's defenders clearly assumed a defensive posture against critics who dismissed the genre as, at best, an easy way for real writers to put bread on the table and, at worse, below them altogether.[39] Too many writers, professional and amateur, held the attitude that, "If it turns out well, it's a short story; if it turns out poorly, it's a sketch."[40]

While riddled with problems of low esteem, inferior production, and the persistence of competing voices, the sketch nevertheless served an important function in the language culture of early Stalinism—not only for its further contribution to the ongoing process of proletarian language acquisition but also for its role as a basic primer for constructing ideologically sound and verbally authoritative models of state narration. One of the more notorious adaptations on a grander scale (of big-name writers) can be found in the collectively authored *History of the Construction of the Stalin White Sea–Baltic Canal*.[41] Spearheaded again by the ubiquitous publisher Gorky, the *History* documented the massive 1931–1933 construction project linking the White Sea to the Baltic and boasted three editors and twenty-six coauthors.[42] While the story of its production and its generic boundary crossing have already been laid out in detail by Cynthia Ruder, the book is worth brief mention in this study of the politics of voice for at least two reasons.[43]

First, it represents the most prominent attempt by the leading writers of the day to use the sketch to document socialist construction in a voice that brought it both authority and legitimacy. This mission is underscored by the collaborative nature of the effort: each chapter of the book (with the glaring exception of one by Zoshchenko) is ascribed to a group of writers who, according to Gorky in his introduction (where he once again assumes the role of metanarrator), shared equally in the tasks of composing and editing. Such collective fusion of the "author function," by virtue of the notoriety of the individual contributors, compounds the narrative authority of the language of the party-state by ascribing to it the voice of the Soviet Writer. That the only single-author chapter was given to the *skaz* narrative voice of Mikhail Zoshchenko demonstrates the dynamic of this parallel deferral of authorship and authority: the only narrative voice that could not be blended into the more potent, super-narrator of the party-state is precisely that which insists on retaining its individual (albeit contrived) linguistic identity.[44]

The second reason the collection represents an important landmark in the evolution of the politics of voice is in the manner in which it manages to incorporate elements of the other competing voices while not only maintaining, but arguably strengthening, the voice of the party-state. Its domination is made abundantly clear by the framing of the work: equal editorial billing given to the head of the White Sea prison camp, Semen Firin; the portrait of Stalin facing the title page; the collection's dedication to the Seventeenth Party Congress; Gorky's introductory and concluding chapters; and the quoted directives from Central Executive Committee of the USSR contained therein (both dated 4 August 1933—one announcing the awarding of the Medal of the USSR to the "workers, engineers, and leaders of the construction" of the canal [13], the other announcing special privileges awarded to the participants of the canal's construction [16]). It is in the chapters in between where the more creative appropriations of revolutionary, popular, and national voices occur. Ruder has demonstrated how they make ample use of the modernist device of montage, but in a manner largely beholden to the voice of the party-state.[45] The same sort of vocal reappropriation can be seen in the collection's use of ethnographic documents from various voices from the people—ranging from political and common prisoners who were used as slave labor on the project (themselves of varying degrees of ideological re-education) to the more enlightened workers, party enthusiasts, and GPU members whose "authentic texts" were integrated into the collective narrative.[46] But with the possible exception of Zoshchenko's lone chapter featuring his characteristic *skaz* narrator (here, a reformed prisoner), all of these voices wind up safely under the linguistic control of the grander narrative of socialist construction. A clear hierarchy of voice emerges, beginning with the "raw material" of the vox populi and ending with the supreme authority of the metanarrator, the party-state Writer.

SOCIALIST-REALIST CODIFICATION OF SACRED STATE DISCOURSE

Despite its widely perceived inferior status, the sketch featured several devices that became central, if not mandatory, components of the socialist-realist novel: a narrative voice that enjoyed a mastery of the language and ideas of the state; a clearly delineated top-down hierarchy of vocal authority as a means of incorporating, while still controlling, alternative models of speaking and writing; and a generous array of quoted, nonliterary texts from the political, economic, and technical spheres. The first two of these features became apparent in the discussion of Furmanov's *Chapaev*. The third component, non-literary quotation, was arguably one of the most distinctive speech genres of the language culture of Stalinist Russia.

Although earlier fictional works such as *The Week, Chapaev,* and Fedor Gladkov's *Cement* contained elements of this party-state voice, they still privileged oral modes of communication to represent symbolic power and authority. Public gatherings frequently framed and propelled the narratives, and oratory served as the central means of articulating problems, identifying solutions, and interpreting failures and successes in terms meaningful to targeted audiences. In the official literature of the early 1930s, these events are either overshadowed or permeated by heavy reliance on derivative and canonical (and primarily written) texts. In his 1932 novel *Time, Forward!* Valentin Kataev used written or quoted official texts, not local oratory, to mark the critical junctures of the story. The tasks of production are fully illuminated only by the quoted newspaper report from Stalin's legendary "backwardness" speech of February 1931 to a conference of industrial workers.[47] The solution to the problem of surpassing the norm for cement-mixture production is revealed not in a public address but in a six-page scientific article reprinted from the newspaper *For Industrialization,* replete with technical jargon, tables, indicators, and statistics (126–32). With the scientific "facts" clearly set forth, there is little need for oratory. The objective truth is already at hand. The superfluous nature of "mere rhetoric" is accentuated by the muteness that overcomes characters at moments when one would expect oration (a muteness foreshadowed by Robeiko's consumptive coughing fits in *The Week*). When addressing his workers before their record-breaking shift, the brigade foreman, Mosia, finds himself at a loss for words. The only language he is capable of generating consists of "snatches of inappropriate newspaper slogans":

"'Strana zhdet deshevykh ovoshchei. . . .' Net, net! 'Sistema Gosbanka—moguchii rychag khozrascheta. . . .' Ne to! 'Glavnoe seichas—eto . . . krol'chatnik. . . .' Net, net! . . .'" (180)[48]

["'The country awaits cheap vegetables . . .' No, no! 'The system of *Gosbank* is the mighty linchpin for self-financing . . .' That's not right! 'The main thing now is . . . the rabbit hutch . . .' No, no! . . .'"]

In a final, flustered attempt at a closing declaration, he turns to official institutions and incantatory phrases for authority:

"Tovarishchi," pochti zhalobno kriknul Mosia. "Dorogie tovarishchi! My vse—kak riadovye boitsy, udarniki-entuziasty vtoroi khozraschetnoi nashego avtoritetnogo shestogo uchastka. . . . I puskai budut svideteliami tovarishchi iz tsentral'nykh gazet. . . . Daem tverdoe, nerushimoe, stalinskoe slovo." (181)

["Comrades!", Mosia cried almost plaintively, "Dear comrades! All of us—as rank-and-file warriors, shockworker enthusiasts of the second self-financing brigade of our authoritative sixth section. . . . And let the comrades from the central newspapers be our witnesses—give our firm, invincible, Stalinist word.'"]

The mere mention of the "Stalinist word" serves as a sufficient, metonymic representation of oratory far more eloquent and authoritative than the foreman himself can muster. The 1934 production novel *Big Conveyer* by Iakov Il'in gives even greater prominence to the language of Stalin by re-creating and contextualizing, at the pivotal juncture of the book, the same speech on backwardness. Il'in's portrait is instructive in its portrayal of Stalin as a highly charismatic orator whose speech is nonetheless sacred:

Stalin govoril medlenno i negromko. Zhesty ego byli skupy. Izredka on podymal sognutuiu v lokte pravuiu ruku do urovnia plecha i opuskal ee, sgibaia kist' krotkim dvizheniem, zakanchivaia, zakrepliaia mysl', kak by vkolachivaia ee etim zhestom v soznanie slushatelei. Stavia voprosy, on otvechal na nikh, i samaia povtoriaemost' etogo priema, iasnoe, chetkoe razvitie mysli sodeistvovali tomu, chto kazhdyi mog povtorit' za nim ego slozhnye obobshcheniia, itog gigantskoi myslitel'noi raboty.

[Stalin spoke slowly and quietly. His gestures were sparing. From time to time he would raise his right arm, bent at the elbow, to the level of his shoulder and let it down, bending his wrist in a short motion, completing, reinforcing his thought, as if hammering it with this gesture into the consciousness of the audience. As he posed questions, he would answer them, and the very repetitiveness of this device, the clear, precise development of the thought helped make it possible for each person to repeat after him his complex generalizations, the result of his gigantic intellectual work.][49]

The features of charismatic authority are there (less the satirical undertone with which Arosev earlier recalled the oratorical skills of Trotsky), but the roles of "producer" and "consumer" are now strictly delineated. Stalin alone is capable of generating such "gigantic intellectual work" and translating it into a language accessible to all; it is up to the others simply to repeat that which has been so persuasively hammered into their consciousness. In a similar manner, Kataev's narrative finds closure only in the refrain from the Stalin speech and its resounding conclusion "Never again!"[50]

As in the cases of folklore and sketch writing, however, it is the aestheticization of this voice that brings it much of its power and authority. Inscribing the data, documents, and speeches into a realist narrative in the tradition of the classics helps elevate that voice to the level of literary language, makes of it a "literary fact," bestowing upon it the legitimacy that comes with that status. If the voice of the party-state becomes routinized doctrine when transcribed from oral to written media, it achieves the full status of "canon" only when aestheticized by the authoritative domain of prose fiction. It is not accidental, then, that Pavel Korchagin, the poorly educated and often brash proletarian hero of Nikolai Ostrovskii's *How the Steel Was Tempered* (1934), spends the final years of his life not only reading mounds of newspapers and party literature and leading *agitprop* circles for party activists but also inscribing his revolutionary experiences into the more codified form of a novella.[51]

MODELS OF VOCAL DISTORTION (I):
BORIS PIL'NIAK'S SOCIALIST-REALIST REMAKE

As has been the case throughout this discussion, some of the more instructive literary representations of various aspects of the politics of voice are those that for some reason—intentional or unintentional—"fail" at creating the verbal web of meaning dictated by the generic or institutional context. Babel's civil war narratives highlight discursive fissures far more than they celebrate the heroes of Budennyi's First Cavalry Division. For all his effort to give voice to the "tongue-tied streets," Maiakovskii remained tormented by accusations, largely substantiated, that the working class simply did not understand his revolutionary verse. And the literary production of the new intelligentsia understandably fell short of the proscribed ideals of their proletarian mentors.

In the language culture of early Stalinism, the "failure rate" decreased precipitously for at least two important reasons. The first and most obvious was that the stakes became much higher, the repercussions for narrative perversion far more severe. The second, less obvious reason was that, as suggested in chapter 6, time and experience afforded firmer codification of appropriate voices of authority and of a more coherent sense of what constituted authoritative narratives. Beyond any forces of censorship and coercion within the various institutions most centrally involved in language production and legitimation, readers, writers, and speakers simply had had, by the early 1930s, far greater exposure to effective models of speaking, writing, and storytelling. The dust of revolutionary language upheaval had had sufficient time to settle, allowing for accessible and coherent ways of articulating experiences of the recent past and ongoing efforts at the "construction of socialism." Verbal distortions continued to make their way into the public sphere, of course, but did so with decreasing frequency and a sharp rise in the shrillness of the response with which they were met.

Both the failure and the shrillness of critical response were particularly acute in the attempt by Boris Pil'niak to convert a modernist novella, *Mahogany* (*Krasnoe derevo*, 1929), into a novel about socialist construction entitled *The Volga Flows into the Caspian Sea* (*Volga vpadaet v kaspiiskoe more*, 1929).[52] He does so by incorporating the shorter piece, featuring bourgeois entrepreneurs from the New Economic Policy (NEP) period and their travels to a backwoods town on an antique buying spree, into a full-length novel set at the building site of a massive dam, the construction of which would enable the creation of a canal reaching from the Volga River to the Caspian Sea. Aside from the problem of Pil'niak's own suspect reputation and widespread vilification (by the late 1920s he had become notorious for his unorthodox interpretation of the Bolshevik revolution, his complicated, modernist prose style, and his cavalier views of art's independence from politics)—compounded by the scandal that arose in response to *Mahogany's* initial publication in a Berlin publishing house—the novel remake fails as an exemplar of socialist realism on linguistic grounds.[53] First of all, it features a narrative voice that displays the strong penchant for wordplay, archaisms, and structural experimentation (repetition, abrupt shifts in time and setting, etc.) characteristic of Pil'niak's earlier prose. Second, like Babel's *Red Cavalry* narrator with regard to the civil war and its heroes, the storyteller shows far less interest in documenting the motivations, goals, feats, and setbacks of socialist construction than he does in the marginal characters, plot lines, and themes. A far greater proportion of the novel's pages feature the multiple romantic liaisons among the main characters and their former, current, and future spouses than describe the building of the dam and its consequences for the future state. In fact, as one contemporary critic observed, we pick up on the construction plot quite belatedly, only during the final days of its completion.[54]

A third cause for the linguistic failure is the ambiguous, if not questionable, status of the language of state in the speech practices of the novel's three main protagonists. One of these is professor Pimen' Poletika, an old

Bolshevik (circa 1903) and chief designer of the dam project, who relies on none of the revolutionary symbols (language included) to prove his revolutionary credentials and spends his moments away from the construction project reading ancient Church texts. A second model comes in the figure of Ivan Ozhogov, a civil war hero and "true Communist until 1921," when he was expelled from the party owing to his opposition to NEP. Still passionately dedicated to the revolutionary cause, he lives with a band of fellow outcast revolutionaries—the "holy fools of Soviet Rus'" (120)—in a makeshift camp in the bowels of the construction site's factory furnace and wanders around town delivering "fiery speeches about communism, insane words that would cause many people to cry" (227). These revolutionary holdovers, referred to by Pil'niak as *okhlomony,* or "outcasts," are largely satirical in their presentation—exemplified most blatantly by their incendiary pseudonyms (Ozhogov [Burnman], Pozharov [Fireman], Podzhogov [Arsonist], and Plamia [Flame]). But Ozhogov's frequent associations to the truth-telling holy fools *(iurodivye)* of ancient Rus' make it difficult to dismiss his character as simply a misguided and somewhat comical figure.[55] On the contrary, readers aware of the ancient Russian (and Christian) tradition that attributes to the local village "idiot" the gift and authority of speaking the truth no matter how awkward it may be for earthly tsars are encouraged to take seriously the moral standard with which Ivan doggedly shadows the novel's other heroes, rooting out the evil and embracing the good. Although he supports the construction project as the true continuation of the revolutionary cause, however, that cause for him has more to do with fundamental principles of human decency than the sort of celebration of "party spirit" that normally assumed the moral focal point ("he insisted that communism was the rejection of material goods, that the first and most important issue for the true communist had to be trust, concentrated attention, respect for man, and people" [226]). That this only true spokesman of the original revolution should become the sacrificial lamb of the construction project, perishing in the floodwater released by the dam, does not help Pil'niak's symbolic cause.

The final positive model appears in the figure of Fedor Sadykov, the engineer and head of construction at the dam site and clearly the closest to the stereotype of the "new Soviet man" of all the book's heroes. His work is all-consuming, and he brings a businesslike demeanor into the workplace that spills into his personal life, where he tolerates no game playing or romantic intrigue. When he realizes that the affair between his wife and closest engineer-colleague has become more than a fleeting fancy, he calls the two to his office, announces that he is leaving her and expects them to marry, and marches off to a production meeting without missing a beat. But even this character failed to satisfy Pil'niak's critics, who dismissed Sadykov for being introduced as an afterthought and coming from dubious working-class origins.[56]

As dubious was the means by which Pil'niak introduced the language of the party-state into his construction novel, its final and perhaps most glaring failure. Other than the revolutionary voice of Ivan Ozhogov, discourse remotely resembling the party language appears at only two notable junctures. In the first, it is featured primarily in its capacity to mystify and perplex the uninitiated—in this case, the story's main antagonist, the "wrecker" engineer, Evgenii Poltorak. Already compromised by his sordid liaisons with a syphilitic actress and the dying sister of his lawful wife, Poltorak is further diminished by his inability to crack the code of an official protocol he struggles over after a night of sleepless cavorting (94–96). His linguistic impotence is reinforced later that morning at a production meeting with local worker crews, whose deed-oriented language, laden with the vocabulary of party and production, bury him into a helpless verbal stupor (96–99).

As with the proletarian credentials of Sadykov, however, the episode fails to convince Pil'niak's critics, who dismiss it as a gratuitous nod to revolutionary consciousness, the only appearance of anything resembling the language or issue of socialist construction in the entire book. That same sense of belated, halfhearted invocation of the voice of the state dominates reviewers' reactions to perhaps the most modernist of Pil'niak's invocations of the official state discourse—the insertion into the closing pages of the book a foldout facsimile of the 13 July 1929 (no. 28) issue of a weekly newspaper entitled *New River (Novaia reka)*, described in the paper's subheading as a production of the Kolomna construction project (Kolomstroi).[57] In contrast to the language of the surrounding narrative, the voice on display in this original newspaper page trumpets the cause of socialist construction with fluent and frequent references to the buzzwords of the cultural revolution and First Five-Year Plan. Article titles from the first two columns alone include: "Participate actively in socialist construction"; "Struggling with the deterioration of living strength"; and "They've begun with a five-horsepower dynamo."

Despite what may have been a well-intended and innovative effort at realizing the dual rhetorical force of the Soviet newspaper and novel (rather than a formalist rouse to "lay bare the device"), it was the very starkness of the linguistic contrast that drew the ire of Pil'niak's reviewers. Taking care to defend the right to incorporate the language of the newspaper and statistics into artistic prose, one critic criticized Pil'niak for trivializing this language by not integrating it into the authorial voice of the novel:

> We are not against newspaper words—on the contrary, we are against the contempt for them; these newspaper words must sound like themselves, like they are organically fused into the entire narrative. We are against the forcible shoving of newspaper words into a work when it is clear that they

have been fallen back on out of necessity owing to a lack of any other suitable artistic means. In such instances we are offended not on behalf of our art but on behalf of our newspaper words, which, in such circumstances, are better and higher than art.[58]

The problem, in other words, is not the newspaper language itself (which in certain instances is far superior to art) but the complete absence of a voice, intonation, and motivation that would serve as contextual and authoritative support. Pil'niak's crime rests in the manner in which he unceremoniously spliced the language of state into a narrative that, until this point, spoke in a completely foreign tongue.[59]

MODELS OF VOCAL DISTORTION (II):

ANDREI PLATONOV'S SKETCH WRITER AS HOLY FOOL

In contrast to Pil'niak's *Volga* storyteller, the narrative voice of Andrei Platonov's controversial sketches from 1928–1931 displayed ample command of the language of the party-state. His problem was that it did so only after filtering it through the convoluted ruminations of a truth-seeking proletarian, giving rise to a discourse that was not only so innovative that it could not but call attention to itself but that also seriously called into question the presumed integrity and legitimacy of the canonical party language under Stalin.

Few other writers from the early Soviet period could match Platonov's credentials as a sketch writer. His technical training in electrical and hydraulic engineering and early involvement in efforts to bring these sources of energy to the more remote regions of Soviet Russia uniquely qualified him to document the daunting task of rural modernization. As an accomplished journalist and writer with early allegiances with the proletarian culture movement, he had the skills to do so in a manner that was at once coherent, compelling, and ideologically grounded. Early sketches on issues ranging from electrification to the legacy of Lenin adequately demonstrate this rare combination of talents.[60] Yet two published sketchlike portraits written during the First Five-Year Plan, "Che-Che-O" (1928) and "For Future Use (A Poor Peasant's Chronicle)" ("Vprok [Bedniatskaia khronika]," 1931) stand out as much for their verbal distortions of the genre as for the degree to which they attempt to play by the rules of the established party-state voice.

The perversions of the first begin with its very title, a phonetic distortion of the acronym given to the newly created government region that served as its subject matter, the Central Black-earth Oblast' *(Tsentral'naia Chernozemniaia Oblast')* or *Tse-Che-O,* when pronounced correctly (which was evidently difficult by the region's inhabitants).[61] On the surface, the story carries all of the main features of the sketch advocated by contemporary critics: it was a fact-based narrative largely free of aesthetic adornment that describes, in an ideologically charged way, life under Soviet rule in an outlying geographic region. While there are some descriptions of modern technology—such as the complexity of modern railway technology and the increased demands it makes on a new generation of highly skilled engineers (77)—the sketch writer's main focus of attention, already hinted at in the story's subtitle ("Regional Organizational-Philosophical Sketches"), is the trenchant Soviet bureaucracy that has come to define these newly contrived administrative entities. And it is in his exposé of the expanding institution of paper pushers that the sketch writer oversteps his linguistic (and ideological) bounds.

The product of a centralized plan to unify two historically separate geographical regions (Tambov and Voronezh) into a single administrative entity, *TsChO* has become a bureaucratic black hole rife with "bureaucratic activists" perpetually on leave and legions of administrators and administrative committees with polysyllabic and largely unpronounceable titles (e.g., *predsedatel' raisoiuza potrebilovok, zamnarkomtorg, oblispolkom, oblprofsovet,* and *oblgorod*).[62] Trying to imagine a "general map of the organizational artifice of the USSR, so that any traveler could freely find out under whose immediate influence he was located at any given minute of his living state," the sketch writer names but a few of the various overlapping domains, the next more absurd than the last:

> Pod kolesami poezda proskakivali granitsy gubernii, uezdov, raivikov, rasprostraneniia vlasti sel'sovetov, raiony tiagoteniia k ssyppunktam i elevatoram, sfery upolnomochennykh po rasshireniiu ploshchadi posevov sakharnoi svekly, nakonets, razlichnye profsoiuznye raikomov, raiupolnomochennykh, raz"ezdnykh instruktorov i prochikh deiatelei, organizuiushchikh trud. (77–78)

> [Beneath the wheels of the train rolled away the borders of provinces, *uyezds,* areas under the jurisdiction of regional *volost'* executive committees and village soviets, regions focusing on grain-collecting points and elevators, the bailiwicks of authorized government officials in charge of expanding the area of sugar-beet planting, and, finally, districts accountable to different labor-union committees, plenipotentiaries, circuit instructors, and various and sundry other agents engaged in organizing labor.]

His list is interrupted only by the realization that completing the task would require a map the size of the entire territory of the USSR. Anything smaller would run the risk of blurring the boundaries of administrative authority. The result—"a completely continuous expanse of darkness, in which one would be unable to see who was leading whom—who was the brightest of activists and who was the backward masses liable to immediate cultural revolution" (78).

With imaginative digressions and distortions such as these, Platonov goes beyond the realist bounds recommended by advocates of the sketch within official literary circles, producing something more akin to a Gogolian satire. Similarly divergent is his comical portrait of the bureaucrats themselves, with uniformly long sideburns that are so common, the narrator conjectures, they must have been the result of some larger policy decision handed down through a series of agitational slogans—imagined perversions of official discourse that also fly in the face of the recommended voice of the party: "'For Soviet sideburns!'," "'Tidiness in physiognomy is a symbol of ideological stability: athlete—grow out your burns, be at the forefront! For the new physiognomy, for the new person!'" (85).

In contrast to this monstrous voice of party-state bureaucracy, Platonov's narrator offers a parallel portrait of the world of the local proletariat, which welcomes him as one of its own (having himself once worked in the town as an electrician). Among the workers, the narrator finds a world largely bereft of the trappings of the new bureaucracy, where the incessantly squawking radio is likened first to a deacon and then to a devil (88), where it is music and song, rather than any formal, state-run organization, that "bring people closer to one another" (88), and where the barrage of newspapers, books, radio broadcasts, culture, and criticism generated by the central organs of propaganda and agitation are likened to flying bricks that make "the body begin to hurt" (91). Handicapped by their inability to comprehend the organizational mazes, these lifelong laborers, much like Babel's Jews, can only sit back in wonder at the reality gap between the current state of affairs and the original contours of the promised world revolution.

While attacks on excess bureaucracy per se were relatively common, if not encouraged, in the late 1920s, "Che-Che-O" quickly became the object of attack from the proletarian corners of the contemporary language culture. Aside from the story's damning association with Pil'niak, who was listed as coauthor, it was labeled the work of an "anarchical philistine" who was "reactionary to the core" and denounced in particular for portraying collectivization as a bureaucratic concoction, rather than what it really is—a movement led by the party.[63] Within the context of the politics of voice, however, it is clear that Platonov's main crime lay not only in his failure to offer any positive model of party activity in combating this bureaucratic epidemic but also in the awkwardly close linguistic alliance the sketch creates between the discourse of bureaucracy and that of the party. Rather than a catalyst for empowering the proletariat, this verbal portrait suggests, the party is the invisible force behind the growing penchant for unthinking organizational structure and control.

A far more damning critique of the party voice—seen and treated as such by Stalin himself promptly after its publication in 1931—was Platonov's "For Future Use (A Poor Peasant's Chronicle)."[64] Also written as a series of sketches, this longer piece features the same sort of wandering proletarian truth-seeker featured in Platonov's novels, *Chevengur* and *Kotlovan*. True to the form of the sketch, the chronicle details the process and progress of "socialist construction," in this case, of life under collectivization in the Voronezh region during the spring of 1930. Platonov's narrator documents a wide range of facts, including the implementation of new technologies, levels of productivity for various crops and livestock, and the progress being made in attracting peasants to the collective farms and away from such antiquated practices as religion. At times, his writing style approaches that of a technical report—precisely the sort of scientific descriptive language encouraged by advocates of the sketch:

> V chem zakliuchaetsia reshenie zadachi? V tom, chtoby selit' kolkhozy i osnovyvat' sovkhoznye usad'by priamo na vodorazdelakh, v tsentre plodorodiia pochv. Dobavochnoe znachenie tut budet eshche v rezkom ozdorovlenii derevni. Ta zaraznaia zhizha otkrytykh vodoemov, kotoroi utoliaiut svoiu zhazhdu mnogie derevenskie raiony SSSR, poteriaet togda svoi smysl kak istochnik vodosnabzheniia. Artezianskaia zhe glubokaia voda trubchatykh kolodtsev bezvrednei, vkusnee i chishche, chem khlorirovannaia vodoprovodnaia. (109)[65]

> [Wherein lies the solution to the problem? In establishing the collective farms and basing the state-farm estates directly on the watersheds in the centers of fertile soil areas. Additional significance here will also be in the sharp rehabilitation of the village. The infectious swill of the open reservoirs on which many rural areas of the USSR have quenched their thirst will thus lose their importance as a source of water supply. The artesian-type deep water of tubular wells is tastier, cleaner, and less pernicious than that of a chlorinated water supply.]

The chronicle even has a clearly distinguishable subtext from the canonical voice of the party—Stalin's "Dizziness from Success" article (30 March 1931), a document in which the leader admits to certain "excesses" in the implementation of collectivization (in particular, the brutal and often arbitrary elimination of rural dwellers perceived to be ill disposed toward the socialist cause) and which marked a period of easing off from the head-spinning pace the campaign had up to that time assumed. With considerable attention devoted to instances of excess, Platonov's story could, on the surface, be intended as an imaginative complement to the Stalin speech. At closer examination, however, the episodes depicted by Platonov suggest far more profound distortions of the language and idea of the party in the countryside, with next to no visible means of organizational or ideological oversight.

At the root of the problem is the revolutionary means by which Platonov reinvents language in general through the voice of his proletarian truth-seeking narrator.[66] Common words and phrases sound slightly "off," in a manner that brings them a jolt of new meaning. The simple act of walking is rendered as "ambulatory work" (*peshekhodnaia rabota,* 96). The innocent acknowledgment of occasional passers-by becomes a more profound statement about the collective condition of the kolkhoz workers: "*Navstrechu nam chasto popadalis' kakie-to odinokie i gruppovye liudi—vidno, v kolkhoznoe vremia i pustoe pole imeet svoiu plotnost' naseleniia*" (108) ["We would often run into lone and group people coming our way; apparently, even the empty field has its own density of population in collective-farm times"]. It is this sort of abstracted pseudophilosophical manner of description that makes it far less possible to dismiss the linguistic shifts as an awkward or amusing quirk of a *skaz* narrator. Instead, the reader is somehow implored to take this storyteller at his word—however strange it may be. The result is an authoritative narrative voice that is anything but transparent. The language "gets in the way" at every turn. Instead of chuckling knowingly at the obvious unreliability of a *skaz*-like narrator, we are left wondering to what strange linguistic creature this language culture has given birth.[67]

Platonov's fictional author, who introduces the narrator of the chronicles in the opening pages, provides a somewhat enigmatic clue into the ideological foundation of this voice, describing him, first off, as a "poor peasant in spirit, tormented by the concerns of universal reality" ("*dushevnyi bedniak, izmuchennyi zabotoi za vseobshchuiu deistvitel'nost'. . .*" [92]). We later learn that he is a journeyman electrician and hydrologist, which, combined with his status as a "poor peasant in spirit," earns him a privileged class identity regardless of his actual genetic link to the poor peasantry. (The ambiguity is the first of many plays on the identity crisis brought about by collectivization, where the real consequences of being labeled a rich peasant *[kulak]* or a poor peasant were enormous while any rules for applying the labels were tenuous at best.) He is also a character with close, though not unproblematic, affiliation to the party and the revolutionary cause: "There were moments in the time and existence of this man," the author tells us, "when his heart would suddenly shudder inside him and, with tears in his eyes and sincerity and weakness of character, he would act in defense of the party and the revolution in the remote villages of the republic, where the *kulak* still lived and obliquely ate the poor" (92). But the author is also careful to draw attention to his human and ideological failings:

> U takogo strannika po kolkhoznoi zemle bylo odno dragotsennoe svoistvo, radi kotorogo my vybrali ego glaza dlia nabliudeniia, imenno: on sposoben byl oshibit'sia, no ne mog solgat' i ko vsemu gromadnomu obstoiatel'stvu sotsialisticheskoi revoliutsii otnosilsia na stol'ko berezhno i tselomudrenno, chto vsiu zhizn' ne umel naiti slov dlia iz"iasneniia kommunizma v sobstvennom ume. (93)

[Such a wanderer across the collective-farm land had one precious feature on account of which we selected his eyes for observation—namely, he was capable of erring, but incapable of lying, and regarded the immensity of the socialist revolution with such care and chastity that all his life he was unable to find the words for elucidating communism in his own mind.]

The storyteller is thus presented as a man of working-class and peasant stock, whose imperfect mastery of the language of communism comes more than anything from his acute sensitivity toward the socialist revolution. He is an adult Kostya Riabstev who has abandoned his youthful hooliganism, has set out on a spiritual search for the ultimate meaning and articulation of revolution and socialist construction, and has vowed to tell the world the absolute truth about what he finds, in whatever imperfect language he can muster. By setting up his narrative in this manner, Platonov attempts to put distance between the ideological voice of the implied author and that of his fallible storyteller—a kind of linguistic and ideological buffer zone (a strategy his critics accused him of employing in a manner that was as calculated as it was unsuccessful).

On a broader level, however, Platonov actually increases the stakes. The storyteller's primary redeeming trait was the combination of his proletarian roots and his inability to lie, and therefore his documentation of the state of affairs in the countryside in the midst of collectivization and cultural revolution becomes an entirely independent and authoritative measuring stick of the success of party policy and its fidelity to the revolutionary cause. Precisely because of his perception of socialist reality through a truth-seeking proletarian, Platonov's narrator assumes the status of a modern-day holy fool (less satirical and more philosophical than Pil'niak's Ozhogov) whose strange ranting must be taken in all seriousness given the authority bestowed on it from a source distinct from the bureaucratic, canonical authority of the party-state.[68]

With this elaborate demographic, psychological, and ideological introduction, the reader is little surprised to find the narrative voice strongly affected by the language culture of the late 1920s and early 1930s. The language of the party-state, in fact, peppers his speech at every turn, often with the same semantic twists noted above and in contexts one would least expect to see it appear. Animals are imbued with emerging proletarian consciousness (*"A loshad' zhila i zhila, tochno v nei byla kakaia-to ideinaia ustoichivost'"* ["And the horse lived on and on, as if in it there were some kind of ideological stability"] [104]). The simple act of going to bed for the night acquires profound socialist meaning (*"S davno ischeznuvshim soznaniem svoei obshchestvennoi poleznosti, ia leg v krovat' i predalsia otdykhu avansom za budushchii trud po vodosnabzheniiu"* ["With the long-disappeared consciousness of my social usefulness, I lay down on the bed and gave myself up to rest as an advance reward for my future labor in water supply activities."] [140]). The narrator's most explicit invocation of party consciousness is inspired by one of the chronicle's most violent acts—the beating of an ex-kolkhoz chairman who was "kicked out because of his excesses"—punctuated by an ambiguous collection of mental and physical states: *"Posle etogo akta Kuchum vnov' priobrel unyloe vyrazhenie svoego litsa, ia zhe pochuvstvoval znachenie partii dlia serdtsa etikh ugriumykh nepobedimykh liudei, sposobnykh godami tomit' v sebe bezmolvnuiu liubov' i raskhodovat' ee tol'ko v izmozhdaiushchii, schastlivyi trud sotsializma"* ["After this act, Kuchum once again assumed a despondent facial expression, and I felt the significance of the party for the heart of these sullen, invincible people, who were capable of smothering the silent love within them for years and expending it solely on the emaciating, happy labor of socialism"] (128–29). The central ideological keyword, "kulak," is subjected to multiple lexical transformations and invoked to justify as many different forms, most of them corrupt, of local power (e.g., *"Raskulachu za khuliganstvo, stervets!"* ["I'll de-*kulak*-ize you for your hooliganism, you shithead"] [134]). Stalin's own canonical speeches are transformed into a maze of party buzzwords that too quickly become a justification for persecution: *("Peregibshchik il' golovokruzhenets est' podkulachnik: kogo zhe ty slushaesh'?"* ["A person of excess or a head-spinner is a de-*kulak*-izer: who do you listen to?"] [135]).

If the narrative articulation of the party voice offers little solace for the seeker of state legitimation, neither do the metalinguistic episodes scattered through the chronicle. In one small encampment along the wanderer's way, a local mechanic has built an automatic applause machine to replicate the "spontaneous" affection shown by the mass audiences for political orators—a metaphor for the automatization of charismatic authority more fantastic than the printed speeches appearing in the party newspapers (replete with parenthetic editorial cues signaling the reactions of the listeners):

> Edva tol'ko my uglubilis' v prokhladu sna na svezhem vozdukhe, kak nas razbudil grom aplodismentov i dlitel'nye ovatsii. Vokrug nichego ne sushchestvovalo, krome tikhoi i porozhnei stepi, a v odnom stroenii khutora gremel vostorg mass i trezvo drebezzhalo steklo otkrytogo okna. Ia vstal v razdrazhenii isporchennogo sna, no so schast'em liubopytstva.
>
> "Neopredelennykh vozglasov ne khvataet!" uslyshal ia rassuzhdenie Grigoriia v tishine konchivsheisia ovatsii. "Liudi vsegda rabotaiut srazu, i v ladoshi i v golos krika! Inache nebyvaet. Kogda rad, to vse chleny organizma nachinaiut peredachu." (113)

[Hardly had we sunk into the coolness of sleep out in the fresh air when we were awakened by thunderous applause and extended ovations. Nothing existed around us apart from the quiet and desolate steppe, but one building in the hamlet resounded with the rapture of the masses, punctuated by the sobering jingle of a windowpane. I got up in irritation on account of ruined sleep, but with the happiness of curiosity.

"Not enough indeterminate exclamations," I heard Grigorii's assessment in the silence of the completed ovation. "People always work immediately—both in the clap and in the voice of the yell! That's the only way it happens. When you're glad, then all parts of the organism begin the transmission."]

The few remaining inhabitants of the same locale partake in a nightly after-dinner ritual of an oral newspaper reading during which a similarly absurd effort is made at resurrecting the spontaneity of the original utterance:

Chital Grigorii, a ostal'nye ser'ezno slushali i otvechali iskrennimi chuvstvami.

"'Nashei pogranokhranoi zaderzhan pol'skii shpion Zluchkovskii!'" chital Grigorii.

"K nogtiu!" reshali slushateli pro togo shpiona.

"'V Baku otkryt novyi moshchnyi zavod smazochnykh masel.'"

"Mashinam neobkhodimy zhiry. Eto perveishaia nuzhda," odobriali takoe delo masterovye, sochuvstvuia mashinam.

"'Kamchatskaia pushnaia ekspeditsiia Gostorga shlet privetstvie proletariatu Sovetskogo Soiuza.'"

I vse slushateli molcha nakloniali golovy v otvetnom privetstvii. (114)

[Grigorii read and the others listened seriously and answered with sincere feelings.

"'A Polish spy, Zluchkovskii, has been apprehended by our border guards!'" read Grigorii.

"Hang 'em by the nails!" decided the listeners with regard to the spy.

"'A powerful new lubricant factory has opened in Baku.'"

"The machines require grease. This is of the utmost necessity," said the workmen approvingly of the deed, empathizing with the machines.

"'The Kamchatka fur expedition of *Gostorg* sends greetings to the proletariat of the Soviet Union.'"

And all the listeners silently bowed their heads in a return greeting.]

The chronicle's closing scene features Pavel Egorovich, a pathetic fool who under the tutelage of a "conscious" wife transforms into a model citizen and leader, delivering an oration (in celebration of a successful fall harvest) that serves more to underscore his unchanged condition than exemplify the narrator's closing observation that "Pashka" serves as "living proof that stupidity is but a transient social condition":

"Ia—tovarishch Pashka—so vsemi vami, bedniakami i tovarishchami, dob'ius' togo, chtoby v SSSR nikogda ne smolkal rev gudkov industrializatsii, kak nad britanskim imperializmom nikogda ne zakhodit solntse. I dal'she togo: my dob'emsia, chtoby dym nashikh zavodov zastil solntse nad Britaniei! . . . My dolzhny v budushchem godu vziat' kakoi-nibud' geroicheskii zavod, daby polnost'iu snabzhat' ego iz nashego kolkhoza pshenichnym zernom,—pust' nash rabochii tovarishch ostavit chernyi kislyi khleb i kushaet nash pervyi pervach! Eto govoriu ia—tovarishch Pashka! . . ." (154)

["I, comrade Pashka, with all of you, poor peasants and comrades, will see to it that the roar of the whistles of industrialization never goes silent in the USSR, just as the sun never sets over British imperialism. And furthermore: we will see to it that the smoke from our factories obscures the sun over Britain! . . . We must, in the coming year, take some heroic factory (under our patronage—MSG) in order to supply it with the wheat grain of our collective farm—may our worker comrade set aside black, sour bread and eat the cream of our crop! It is I—comrade Pashka—who says this! . . ."]

Be it through bizarre attempts at resurrecting the revolutionary moment or through the rampant distortion—and then revitalization—of the language of the party, Platonov's narrative articulates the "dizziness" of the collectivization effort in a manner that makes it clear that the root of the problem is deeper than most would care to admit and naturalized on a most primitive linguistic level. As in "Che-Che-O," the perversions of the socialist ideal loom so large that they overshadow any evidence of positive inroads. The voice of the party is articulated almost entirely through the distorted formulations of the "general line," of class identity and affiliation, and of the canonical language proscribed for expressing them. Ironically, when forced to account for his perverse publication after it drew the ire of Stalin and the Politburo, Platonov acknowledged, in a confessional letter to Gorky, that the story had turned out to be "truly 'fraudulent' and antagonistic in a class sense [klassovo vrazhdebnaia]," but he then blamed language for the failure, claiming it was "negative quality of a technical order" that caused public misperception of the work.[69] Complaints in that same letter about the length of time and number of revisions he and his manuscript were forced to endure appear to contradict his line of verbal defense. Indeed, when viewed in light of the other major works he wrote during this period but that remained unpublished, one must rather conclude that his distorted voice was not so much an accidental result of haste as it was a masterful invention of an "organizational-philosophical" discourse that sought to highlight the fissures and fault lines of legitimacy, meaning, and truth that lay at the core of the canonical party voice.

. . .

Both through their successes and failures, these glimpses of the shifting language culture from within Soviet folklore, sketch writing, and the production novel demonstrate how models of revolutionary, popular, and proletarian modes of expression in fiction came to be eclipsed by the aestheticization of an "objective," "scientific," and easily reproduced party language—here in the form of the central newspapers, technical reports, and the "Stalinist word." Aided by these new speech genres, a well-established canon of written and rehearsed discourse and institutions for controlling and disseminating it provided an authoritative and obligatory expression of party-state truths. In that sense, the burden and urgency of communication had shifted entirely from the once-emerging state in need of legitimacy and authority to the dues-paying citizens who recognized that their comfort and mobility within the institutions of the party-state depended on the ability to master—and accept as one's own—its unbending code.[70]

One also finds a new set of dominant genres emerging. The production sketch—an essentially written mode of expression largely dependent on the transparent transmission of facts, data, and quoted canonical texts—replaced the orally oriented declamatory voice of the early revolutionary years and the *skaz* narrative of the 1920s as the genre of choice for low-level verbal production. The socialist-realist novel, in turn, brought this realist form of narrative to greater aesthetic heights, further validating the frequent invocation of official, nonliterary voices in the context of literary texts, and allowed for the aestheticization of the *glas naroda* in various stages of political enlightenment, marked with the appropriate positive and negative guideposts.[71] The mixing of voices and genres itself invoked the legacy of revolutionary innovation, but, unlike that earlier verbal dominant, reflected a clear hierarchy that privileged a storyteller who narrated fluently and transparently in the language of the party-state and exhibited firm narrative control over all the other voices. Be it in the folk reminiscence, the production sketch, or the socialist-realist novel, the end result was a similarly dominant narrative voice, one with clear authority and legitimacy grounded in the canonical discourse of the party-state but which exhibited clear traces and influences of the other competing models of writing and speech. Works that complicated this vocal synthesis or in any way contested the integrity of its underlying hierarchy did so at their own risk. The language culture of Stalinist Russia had little room for holy fools, but ample space for linguistic heretics.

EPILOGUE

THE POLITICS OF VOICE AT THE
MARGINS OF SOVIET HISTORY

Мы ему поставили пределом
Скудные пределы естества,
И, как пчелы в улье опустелом,
Дурно пахнут мертвые слова.

[We have placed upon it (the word—MSG) limits, the meager limits of nature. And, like bees in a deserted hive, dead words emit a nasty stench.]

—Nikolai Gumilev, "Slovo" (*The Word*, 1921)

Витёк взял вольвёшник. Взял и Вован. Вовандос весь версачах.
Вовандос весь в голде. Каков Вовандос! Во!

[Vityok took a Volvo. So did Vovan. Vovan's all Versaci. Vovan's all in gold. What a man, Vovan! Whoa!]

У Жеки джипец. Джипец у Жеки. У Жеки имижж. Джек-пот.
Блэк Джек. Жека нажрался в жопито.

[Jacko has a jeeplet. The jeeplet's with Jacko. Jacko has an image. Jack pot. Black Jack. Jacko got plastered.]

Мама мыла мерс
[Mama washed the Mercedes.]

—*The New Russian's ABC* (*Novyi russkii bukvar'*, 1998)

The crisis in authorship commonly identified with the literary culture of the 1920s finds, on the broader level of language culture, a corresponding crisis in voice. As demonstrated in the first part of this study, a number of factors may be identified as its cause. First, the Bolsheviks' tenuous hold on the reins of power in a period marked by social, political, and economic chaos placed an enormous burden on public discourse to communicate to a largely unsympathetic citizenry radically new ideas for change. This burden was further generated by a broad-based belief among political and cultural leaders that public discourse was in fact at their disposal to transform, and that every Soviet citizen ought to participate actively in the process of language reconstruction. Second, despite the belief in sociolinguistic engineering, the language that did begin to emerge in the early postrevolutionary years displayed a sometimes bizarre mix of influences—ranging from militarisms and neologisms to Marxist rhetoric and thieves' argot—that quickly assumed a life of their own beyond the control of revolutionary leaders. As it flooded political rallies, newspapers, classrooms, and contemporary fiction in unpredictable ways, the language of revolution gave rise to a substantial communication gap between the cultural and political elite (the producers of public discourse) and a largely nonreading, peasant population (that language's default consumers). In virtually all spheres strongly dependent on public discourse, it became quickly evident that the language was either incomprehensible to the reading and listening population or, still worse, substantially distorted by it.

In addition to establishing and elaborating on the various historical, cultural, and linguistic factors underlying the crisis in voice that defined the language culture of Russia after October 1917, this study has highlighted different voices, or speech genres, that enjoyed varying degrees of linguistic authority during the formative years of early Soviet Russia as well as examined the institutions that figured most actively in the process of redefining linguistic authority in the new era. I have been careful not to attempt any direct mapping of model to time period or institution, but a certain progression of shifting authority does emerge from the evidence. Most prominent in the language culture of the chaotic years just following October 1917 was the revolutionary penchant for innovation, the rejection of past authority, novelty of expression, and the spontaneity afforded by oral modes of communication. That trend was personified by the charismatic orator and civic poet, whose lines and slogans, when not recited, were plastered across newspaper pages and storefronts.

As the revolutionary fervor died, the language culture witnessed a shift in emphasis toward popularization, marked by the attempted assimilation of these charismatic forms of expression by the population at large. The inevitable process of routinization—if not distortion and reappropriation—of the charismatic tongues of the revolutionaries led, in the early to mid-1920s, to a shift in prominence from the lofty genres of the oratory and declamation to more prosaic forms of expression, such as the short story (and the prevalence in it of the *skaz* narrative) and the local news report, which gave a more privileged position in the hierarchy of discourses to the language of the people, the *glas naroda*, in its varied and often problematic permutations. Concurrent to the rise in linguistic capital of the vox populi was the gradual recognition of the serious problems of credibility and authority to which the shift in power gave rise, the realization that the voices of the worker and peasant did not necessarily echo the imagined writing and speech of a conscious proletariat. The gift of tongues became more a source of confusion and babble than a divine mode of universal comprehension.

The growing confusion resulting from the imperfect transfer of revolutionary authority boosted the symbolic influence of the voice of moderation, which sought to reestablish more stable sources of verbal authority passed on through the national tradition of letters. This voice, which was present throughout the decade but could be heard with increasing frequency and earnestness in the second half of the 1920s, cautioned against excessive verbal experimentation and the uncritical mimicking of the nonstandard speech practices of the people, and it advocated instead a return to the literary classics for linguistic authority. The shift from the revolutionary and popular models to the national one marked a more fundamental turning point in the process of forging a new language of state, where orally oriented models of writing and speech are eclipsed by models firmly established in a written tradition (however reinvented that tradition may have been). What was once an essentially revolutionary language culture, a culture bent on the rejection or at least transformation of the old, became a language culture of establishment, focused on securing rather than challenging linguistic authority. If the national voice articulated the formal foundation for that process, it was the voice of the party-state that provided the content.

With the shift in emphasis from oral to written, from revolution to state building, came parallel shifts in dominant speech genres. The charismatic orator had already spoken, the oratory now safely inscribed in canonical texts. It was now the duty of the agitator, writer, folklorist, linguist, teacher, and citizen to assimilate those texts, perpetuate them, and, where necessary, interpret them to fit the changing needs of the state. Infatuation with the vox populi and the *skaz* narrative, in all their creatively uttered imperfections and distortions, gave way to the more cautiously documented literary sketch and its more ambitious cousin, the socialist-realist novel, each more likely to quote the authoritative language of politics and science than ramble on in dangerous improvisation. The voices of charismatic revolutionaries, innovators, peasants, workers, and the literary classics all found resonance in the new language culture of Soviet Russia, but they were carefully subordinated to the canonical voice of the party-state, giving rise to a culture that emphasized language's function as a cue to membership rather than a tool for innovation, class empowerment, or national revitalization.

So is this process unique to early Soviet Russia? The need to establish verbal authority is real in all modern societies, and it is particularly acute in all modern periods of radical, if not revolutionary, social change.[1] Likewise, all modern political language cultures are fraught with communication gaps.[2] The particular language models and speech genres that become influential, moreover, if abstracted even further from their particulars, find resonance in other cultures as well. One need not look far for local examples of language innovators, populists, and nationalists. (It is perhaps not insignificant that "modern," "popular," "folk," and "classical" are all well-established categories of modern music.)[3] Unique to the Soviet experiment in this regard are notions of "proletarian" and "party" languages (which, I argue here, come to signify one and the same thing), but even here one can find parallels in modern single-party dictatorships, such as Nazi Germany or communist China. In the same way, the major institutional forces contributing to the formation of the new Soviet language—journalism, pedagogy, linguistics, and literature—can likewise be seen as central in other periods of Russian and non-Russian language culture reform, though the influence of any one institution will vary according to time period and other factors.

Finally, language, particularly that used in public, always functions as a cue to membership. Consciously or subconsciously, one of the primary means by which we place an individual into overlapping spheres of social, political, cultural, and geographical identity is by looking at how they write, listening to how they speak. The main difference here is one of degree and scope: the "official public sphere" in early Stalinist Russia came to include most forms of writing and speech outside of informal gatherings of friends (and oftentimes, sadly, even in those), and the "cue to membership" was quite specifically and narrowly construed to mean the language of the party-state, which was more or less required as the primary language for citizens who aspired to participate and advance in public life. There is no question that citizens could and did manipulate that language toward their own needs and ends, even within the permissible norms of official language culture, but few would also question that the risks were far greater, in the first instance, and the range of alternative voices, in the second, was far narrower—in both cases precisely because of the official language's narrowly construed vocabulary and broad scope of influence.

The uniqueness of this particular episode of language culture in transformation lies more in the particular combination of factors at play than in any one specifically "Soviet" feature. That the Bolsheviks assumed power of an enormous modernizing nation severely lagging and crippled by a series of wars, revolution, and famine meant that they had to depend almost entirely on the symbolic power of the word for legitimacy. What is more, they also faced the daunting task of communicating their message to a vast, diverse, and marginally literate rural population. The Bolsheviks' relatively early and gradually increasing control over the sources of information and the flow of communication was thus one of the more decisive factors in accounting for the contours of the language of state that came to be. Also significant to the story was the degree of control the state and its various representative organs came to exercise over those spheres most directly involved in issues of language culture—publishing, belles lettres, linguistics, journalism, and education, among the more influential.

Of no less importance was the success with which various levels of popular literacy efforts—at the front, in village and factory workshops, at the newspapers, and in the schools—transmitted the language and ideas of the state to citizens at least cognizant of the personal gain to be had upon mastering the basics of reading and writing. In this sense, the low levels of literacy worked to the advantage of the nascent state, easing the synthesis and assimilation of a new language and ideology. Coupled with that advantage was the equally essential cultural sensitivity toward the issue of language and the widely held belief that it could, in effect, be reengineered to better fit the changing dynamics of power and authority. Thus, a wide range of voices from a wide range of institutions were represented in the debates, and the topic of language was addressed in a highly explicit, self-conscious manner, with a "speech community" in mind that was unparalleled in size—at least in the history of Russian language culture.

One also finds uniqueness in the political ideology underlying the reforms: the vocabulary of Marxism and Leninism, and the ensuing sublexicons validated by the bureaucracy that put those ideologies into institutional practice, dramatically shaped public discourse from the early days of the revolution and remained central throughout—although even this vocabulary was susceptible to shifts in policies, canonical figures, and texts over the years. Finally, the traditionally high premium placed by Russians in the writing community as a source of moral and political authority likewise gives the story a particularly Russian flavor. That leading political figures such as Lenin, Trotsky, and Stalin were even entering into debates about literary policy, specific works of literature, and language itself testifies to the degree of sanctity the written word held in early Soviet Russia, indeed, in Russian cultural history in general. All the complications, contradictions, and convolutions of these competing models and the party-state resolution were nowhere so starkly reflected as in the wide diversity of narrative fiction produced during the period. From the verbal experiments of Pil'niak and Maiakovskii to the popular representations of Babel', Fedorchenko, Seifullina, and Zoshchenko, contemporary fiction brought to life the implied heroes and their language as no other verbal medium could. For each of the many defining episodes of the early Soviet state—revolution, civil war, reconstruction, the New Economic Policy, and collectivization, to name only the most obvious—a polyphony of narrative voices documented and represented the revolutionary, popular, national, and party-state myths that quickly enveloped them. The power of these voices to shape and define those myths (most importantly, the myth of the state) was not underestimated by contemporaries, and, as the central party-state gradually grew in power, so too did it take increasing control over the authoritative voice of narrative fiction.

In both literature and life, the voice that emerged dominant by the early 1930s was based on a notion of dual competency—mastering, on the one hand, the forms of the standard literary language and, on the other, the content of the party-state ideology. It marked, in addition to the end of a utopian mentality that saw an essential link between form and content and the possibility of the complete reinvention of a new language culture, the beginning of an age in which incantation, rather than innovation, became the guiding linguistic principle. Although it would be too simplistic to describe the language culture of Stalinist Russia as "monologic," there is no question that the diversity of public language became largely muted by the pressures for verbal conformity to the "magic word." It was a word that controlled public discourse even after the death of the Sorcerer himself and holds sway even today in some regions of the heteroglossic Babel of the post-Soviet world. Though competing discourses have since emerged, it takes little effort to recognize—be it in the rhetoric of a parliamentary debate or the eloquence of ultranationalist leaders—recourse taken to the well-established gift of tongues of the former party-state.

LANGUAGE CULTURE AFTER THE COLLAPSE

As the language institutions slowly change and diversify in post-Soviet Russia, so, too, do the forms and functions of public discourse, transformed still further through the organic forces of popular consumption. Much like its Bolshevik predecessor of eight decades ago, the new Russian state is in the midst of the daunting task of redefining itself. No small part of that process has involved formulating a public discourse that transmits both meaning and authority. While this is still largely a work in progress and the specific grammar and vocabulary of that new language remain to be seen, certain features and dynamics call attention to themselves in light of the foregoing discussion of the early Soviet language culture.

First, several clear differences distinguish this episode of transitional language culture from the one that defined the beginning of the Soviet era. The institutional landscape has shifted considerably since the opening decades of the twentieth century, most dramatically in the domination of television and radio over the print media in terms of public access and attention. These media themselves have undergone great changes since the days of central control under Gosteleradio (the central state agency responsible for oversight of television and radio in the Soviet era). One look at the television listings across the main channels is enough to confirm the broad spectrum of voices offered through the post-Soviet television—even if the channels still are subject to the oversight of either the state or the corporate and political interests of a select number of "oligarchs."[4] With the increase in the number of channels and growing access to cable broadcasts, Russians' options are only growing.

The print media sources to which citizens have access have diversified still more rapidly than television, especially since the days when *Pravda* and *Izvestiia* were the primary options available. Street vendors and open-access bookstores offer a far greater selection of titles, many of which had no place in the Soviet publishing world. A host of glossy magazines for women, men, youth, "new Russians," and scores of other reading audiences have established a foothold in the topsy-turvy market, as have romance novels, pulp and science fiction, and self-help manuals. The competition that all this presents for "big" literature has never been greater, giving rise to questions, in turn, about the authority of the writer in the post-Soviet era. Citizens are still seeking formal education, but one must ask the same question about the language models passed on through the other traditional standard-bearers for the national tongue—teachers. Is it enough? Finally and most obviously, the nature of the shift in dominant vocabularies is quite different during the fall of the empire in comparison to those of its formative years. The voice of the Soviet party-state now finds itself in the position of a largely discredited discourse of the "old regime," and new alternatives—the voices of capitalism, of democracy, of popular Western culture, and of Russian nationalism—have come to the fore.

Yet the closer monitoring of these new voices reveals compelling parallels with the language culture of early Soviet Russia. The dominant models themselves, on the ideal-typical level, bear striking resemblances to their early Soviet predecessors, with regard to not only the sources of authority they imply but also the function and place they occupy in the shifts in authority characteristic of a transitional language culture. The voices of democracy and capitalism, like that of Marxism and socialism, flooded the press, airwaves, and public rallies in the early days of glasnost, articulated by charismatic orators who urged the people to abandon the canonical scripts and texts of the Soviet regime and speak their minds. The vocabulary they offered for doing so was, like the language of Bolshevism, as mystifying as it was liberating for the average citizen and led to a variety of distortions that ranged in severity from minor mangling by broadcasters and parliamentarians to the use of slick Western-style advertisement campaigns, in the case of the pyramid-scheming investment group "MMM," to bilk thousands of unsuspecting citizens of their life savings.

Innovative postmodern writers from Lev Rubenshtein to Viktor Pelevin use the language in their avant-garde literature to poke fun at the paradoxes of Russian life and absence of meaning after the collapse. Pelevin's *Generation "P,"* for instance, portrays a post-Soviet political culture generated and maintained entirely by an elaborate virtual (and ethereal) reality concocted by slick admen, who, for all their mastery at manipulating symbolic authority, still find themselves at a loss for words when attempting to draft a concept and jingle for the "Russian Idea."[5] Supplying ample fodder for such futuristic parodies, politicians take advantage of a more free-flowing mass media to generate televisual forms of post-Soviet folklore, producing thinly veiled campaign ads bearing the time-honored title of *"Glas naroda."*[6] The voice of the people assumes similarly mythic proportions in the scores of dictionaries of vulgarisms, thieves' jargon, and prison-camp slang published in the fifteen years since the emergence of glasnost—a collective declaration (and highly lucrative one, at that) of the "right to citizenship" of the formerly suppressed, creative expressions of the masses.[7]

The impressive array of new vocabularies produced for and consumed by the Russian population has likewise given rise to a growing chorus of protests against the perversion of the Russian national language culture. These new Russian purists themselves occupy a range of ideological positions. On the more benign end, the Russian Orthodox Church has co-hosted a pseudoscholarly conference whose title, "In Defense of the Russian Language," recalls the linguistic treatises of émigré purists of old.[8] The distinguished writer Aleksandr Solzhenitsyn has published his *Russian Dictionary of Language Expansion,* a 270-page compilation of words and expressions that have disappeared "prematurely" from the "living language" and which, in the words of the compiler, "still deserve the right to live."[9] And in a similarly quixotic vein Russian parliamentarians have attempted to pass laws that would fine government officials who used obscenities on the job (under the category of "petty hooliganism").[10] On the more pernicious end of the purist spectrum, a small but vocal minority of Russian nationalists bitterly denounce what they perceive to be the linguistic contamination of the national bloodline by satanic forces in control of Russia's geographic, mental, and ethereal space.[11] Regardless of the tenor of the reaction, however, the search for a much-needed antidote to the contemporary verbal chaos is fixed on the past, rather than the present, adding to the time-honored authority of the classics the revitalized voice of Russian Orthodoxy.

With the 1998 collapse of the ruble, wars in Kosovo and Chechnya, and the election of Vladimir Putin all helping dampen the Yeltsin-era fashion for things (and words) Western, the linguistic capital of the purists is once again on the rise. Early efforts by Putin to consolidate power in the parliament and the media (under the curious, if not ominous, slogan of "Dictatorship of the Law"), together with signs of more recent political and economic stability, have increased the likelihood of growing moderation and synthesis among the voices competing for verbal authority. Recent state-initiated actions more directly linked to language policy likewise mark important new symbolic and financial investment in stabilizing the language culture—two of the more significant ones being the president's January 2000 revival of the Russian Language Council and the government's July 2001 approval of the comprehensive program "Russian Language" for 2002–2005. The latter boasts a budget of 80 million rubles and a broad range of plans that include the development of a new code of usage rules, a new generation of textbooks, technology-based methods and materials for teaching and learning, and a series of television and radio programs "propagandizing Russian language and culture."[12] All these shifts should strengthen the hand of the purists, who themselves have come to discover the power of mass communication (traditionally the object of their wrath) in bringing their message of language propriety to the general public.[13]

What can be said with certainty is that the post-Soviet language culture is taking shape under the influence of a complex web of ideological, institutional, and individual factors, which, in their diversity, should insulate it from overly zealous attempts at manipulation on the part of either the most respected guardian or the most feared tyrant or thug. At the same time, as the preceding analysis has shown, more subtle manipulation is possible and commonly practiced by language mavens and dilettantes of all political persuasions—be it in the form of writing, publishing, marketing, legislation, or metaphorically charged "talk about talk"—and such practices ultimately help forge a more stable set of language norms as well as more coherent narratives of national and state identity. The eventual dissipation of linguistic chaos during times of revolutionary change is as inevitable as the initial shock.

NOTES

INTRODUCTION

1. John E. Toews offers an eloquent word of caution against "the reduction of experience to the meanings that shape it" and condemns "the [intellectual] hubris of wordmakers who claim to be makers of reality" in "Intellectual History after the Linguistic Turn: The Autonomy of Meaning and the Irreducibility of Experience," *American Historical Review* 92 (1987): 906.

2. In his book on the French political culture of the eighteenth century, Keith Michael Baker underscores language's role in giving shape to political cultures: "Political authority is essentially a matter of linguistic authority: first, in the sense that political functions are defined and allocated within the framework of a given political discourse; and second, in the sense that their exercise takes the form of upholding authoritative definitions of the terms within that discourse." *Inventing the French Revolution: Essays on French Political Culture in the Eighteenth Century* (Cambridge: Cambridge University Press, 1990), 4–5.

3. Plato expressed grave suspicion of rhetoric for its power to deceive when detached from Truth, but he nevertheless acknowledged it as a necessary political instrument of persuasion. See *Gorgias,* trans. Terence Irwin (Oxford: Clarendon Press, 1979); and *Phaedrus,* in *Plato's* Phaedrus: *The Philosophy of Love,* ed. Graeme Nicholson (West Lafayette, Ind.: Purdue University Press, 1999).

4. Hans Aarsleff, *From Locke to Saussure: Essays on the Study of Language and Intellectual History* (Minneapolis: University of Minnesota Press, 1982), 278–92; Umberto Eco, *The Search for the Perfect Language,* trans. James Fentress (Oxford: Blackwell, 1995).

5. Aarsleff, *From Locke to Saussure,* 30–31, 278–92.

6. Karl Marx, "The Eighteenth Brumaire of Louis Bonaparte," in Robert C. Tucker, ed., *The Marx-Engels Reader,* 2d ed. (New York: W. W. Norton, 1978), 594–617.

7. For good overviews, see Claudia Crawford, *The Beginnings of Nietzsche's Theory of Language* (Berlin: Walter de Gruyter, 1988); and Sander L. Gilman, Carole Blaire, and David J. Parent, eds., *Friedrich Nietzsche on Rhetoric and Language* (New York: Oxford University Press, 1989).

8. All of the aforementioned theoretical sources have strongly influenced this book and will be cited in context over the course of discussion. Outside of my immediate field of Slavic studies, the list of "linguistically sensitive studies of culture" is too long for an endnote citation but would certainly include toward the top: Baker, *Inventing the French Revolution;* Roger Chartier, *The Cultural Origins of the*

French Revolution, trans. Lydia G. Cochrane (Durham, N.C.: Duke University Press, 1991); François Furet, *Interpreting the French Revolution,* trans. Elborg Forster (Cambridge: Cambridge University Press, 1981); Lynn Hunt, *Politics, Culture and Class in the French Revolution* (Berkeley: University of California Press, 1984); J. G. A. Pocock, *Politics, Language, and Time: Essays on Political Thought and History* (Chicago: University of Chicago Press, 1960); and James C. Scott, *Domination and the Arts of Resistance: Hidden Transcripts* (New Haven, Conn.: Yale University Press, 1990). Books that address language more specifically as a social, cultural, and historical construct also come primarily from outside Slavic studies and include: David E. Apter and Tony Saich, *Revolutionary Discourse in Mao's Republic* (Cambridge, Mass.: Harvard University Press, 1994); Steven Blakemore, *Burke and the Fall of Language: The French Revolution as Linguistic Event* (Hanover, N.H.: University Press of New England, 1988); Kenneth Cmiel, *Democratic Eloquence: The Fight over Popular Speech in Nineteenth-Century America* (New York: W. Morrow, 1990); R. D. Grillo, *Dominant Languages: Language and Hierarchy in Britain and France* (Cambridge: Cambridge University Press, 1989); Thomas Gustafson, *Representative Words: Politics, Literature, and the American Language, 1776–1865* (Cambridge: Cambridge University Press, 1992); Gareth Stedman Jones, *Language of Class: Studies in English Working Class History, 1832–1982* (Cambridge: Cambridge University Press, 1983); Victor Klemperer, *Die unbewältigte Sprache: Aus dem Notizbuch eines Philologen "LTI,"* (Darmstadt: Joseph Melzer Verlag, 1966); and Michael P. Kramer, *Imagining Language in America: From the Revolution to the Civil War* (Princeton: Princeton University Press, 1991).

9. Orlando Figes and Boris Kolonitskii, *Interpreting the Russian Revolution: The Language and Symbols of 1917* (New Haven, Conn.: Yale University Press, 1999). For a more detailed critique of this book, see my review essay in *Kritika: Explorations in Russian and Eurasian History* 1, no. 3 (2000): 597–602.

10. Jeffrey Brooks, *Thank You, Comrade Stalin! Soviet Public Culture from Revolution to Cold War* (Princeton, N.J.: Princeton University Press, 2000).

11. Stephen Kotkin, *Magnetic Mountain: Stalinism as a Civilization* (Berkeley: University of California Press, 1995), 220. The conflation of the two languages is particularly striking given one of Kotkin's other main theses—that Stalinism constitutes a coherent "set of values, a social identity, a way of life" (23).

12. Katerina Clark, *Petersburg: Crucible of Cultural Revolution* (Cambridge, Mass.: Harvard University Press, 1995), esp. chaps. 9–10. Clark's discussion of promethean linguistics features Lev Trotsky, Maksim Gorky, and Nikolai Marr.

13. Michael G. Smith, *Language and Power in the Creation of the USSR, 1917–1953* (Berlin: Mouton de Gruyter, 1998).

14. Other studies devoting particularly noteworthy attention to the intersection of language and politics in early Soviet Russia include M. O. Chudakova, *Poetika Mikhaila Zoshchenko* (1979), in *Izbrannye raboty,* vol. 1 (Moscow: Iazyki russkoi kul'tury, 2001), 79–244; Katerina Clark, *The Soviet Novel: History as Ritual* (Chicago: University of Chicago Press, 1981); Régine Robin, *Socialist Realism: An Impossible Aesthetic,* trans. Catherine Porter (Stanford, Calif.: Stanford University Press, 1992); Thomas Seifrid, *Andrei Platonov: Uncertainties of Spirit* (Cambridge: Cambridge University Press, 1992); Kevin M. F. Platt, *History in a Grotesque Key: Russian Literature and the Idea of Revolution* (Stanford, Calif.: Stanford University Press, 1997); Evgeny Dobrenko, *The Making of the State Reader: Social and Aesthetic Contexts of the Recep-*

tion of Soviet Literature, trans. Jesse M. Savage (Stanford, Calif.: Stanford University Press, 1997); Eric Naiman, *Sex in Public: The Incarnation of Early Soviet Ideology* (Princeton, N.J.: Princeton University Press, 1997); Gregory Carleton, *The Politics of Reception: Cultural Constructions of Mikhail Zoshchenko* (Evanston, Ill.: Northwestern University Press, 1998); Matthew E. Lenoe, "Agitation, Propaganda, and the 'Stalinization' of the Soviet Press, 1922–1930," *Carl Beck Papers in Russian and East European Studies,* no. 1305 (Pittsburgh: University of Pittsburgh, 1998); Daniel E. Collins, "The Tower of Babel Undone in a Soviet Pentecost: A Linguistic Myth of the First Five-Year Plan," *Slavic and East European Journal* 42, no. 3 (1998): 423–43; Igal Halfin, *From Darkness to Light: Class, Consciousness, and Salvation in Revolutionary Russia* (Pittsburgh: University of Pittsburgh Press, 2000); Lisa A. Kirschenbaum, *Small Comrades: Revolutionizing Childhood in Soviet Russia, 1917–1932* (New York: RoutledgeFalmer, 2001); and Mikhail Vaiskopf, *Pisatel' Stalin* (Moscow: Novoe literaturnoe obozrenie, 2002). For more descriptive (rather than cultural) studies of the language of Soviet Russia, see Bernard Comrie, Gerald Stone, and Maria Polinsky, *The Russian Language in the Twentieth Century* (New York: Oxford University Press, 1996); Françoise Thom, *Newspeak: The Language of Soviet Communism,* trans. Ken Connelly (London: Claridge Press, 1989); and Patrick Seriot, *Analyse du discours politique soviétique,* Cultures et sociétés de l'Est, 2 (Paris: Institut D'Études Slaves, 1985).

15. In addition to the works cited earlier, writings by Hayden White and Jerome Bruner offer compelling, albeit different, critiques on the role of language and narrative in making sense of reality—in White's case, with a stronger emphasis on power and authority; in Bruner's, on the formation and perpetuation of personal and cultural identities. See Hayden White, "The Value of Narrativity in the Representation of Reality," in W. J. T. Mitchell, ed., *On Narrative* (Chicago: University of Chicago Press, 1980), 1–23; and Jerome Bruner, *Acts of Meaning* (Cambridge, Mass.: Harvard University Press, 1990).

16. In the shorthand of contemporary cultural studies, this book performs a "linguistic turn" on language itself. For all the recent attention that has been given to "discourse" in the consolidation of power, the legitimation of authority, and the negotiation of identity, few studies have directly addressed the discourse on language itself—or the way in which debates over competing models of speaking and writing contribute to broader issues of authority and identity. As reductionist as this may initially seem, one must be prepared to entertain this dimension of the puzzle if one is to speak honestly or meaningfully about other types of "discourse." For discussions of the "linguistic turn," see William J. Bouwsma, "From History of Ideas to History of Meaning," *Journal of Interdisciplinary History* 12 (1981): 279–91; James Vernon, "Who's Afraid of the 'Linguistic Turn'? The Politics of Social History and Its Discontents," *Social History* 19 (1984): 81–97; John E. Toews, "Intellectual History after the Linguistic Turn"; and Victoria E. Bonnell and Lynn Hunt, eds., *Beyond the Cultural Turn: New Directions in the Study of Society and Culture* (Berkeley: University of California Press, 1999).

17. G. O. Vinokur, *Kul'tura iazyka,* 2d expanded ed. (Moscow: Federatsiia, 1929). Trained as a comparative linguist at Moscow State University, Grigorii Osipovich Vinokur (1896–1947) went on to make significant contributions to an impressively wide range of philological subdisciplines, including morphology, lexicography, language culture, stylistics, stage pronunciation, historical linguistics, literary

history and criticism, and biography. For a comprehensive bibliography of his published works, see G. O. Vinokur, *Filologicheskie issledovaniia: Lingvistika i poetika* (Moscow: Nauka, 1990), 405–14.

18. William H. Sewell, Jr., "The Concept(s) of Culture," in Bonnell and Hunt, eds., *Beyond the Cultural Turn*, 41.

19. Sewell, "Concept(s) of Culture," 47, 52.

20. V. M. Zhivov, *Iazyk i kul'tura v Rossii XVIII veka* (Moscow: Shkola 'Iazyki Russkoi Kul'tury', 1996), 124. See also Zhivov, "Azbuchnaia reforma Petra I kak semioticheskoe preobrazovanie," in *Semiotika prostranstva i prostranstvo semiotiki. Trudy po znakovym sistemam*, vol. 19 (Tartu: Uchenyi zapiski Tartuskogo gosudarstvennogo universiteta, 1986), 54–67.

21. Zhivov, *Iazyk i kul'tura v Rossii XVIII veka*, 74, 86. See also B. A. Uspenskii, *Kratkii ocherk istorii russkogo literaturnogo iazyka (XI-XIX vv.)* (Moscow: Gnosis, 1994), 115–20.

22. Significantly, both camps saw their projects as a form of linguistic purification—in the Shishkovites' case, of the impurities that lay outside a Russian language firmly rooted in a tradition of Old Church Slavonic; in the Karamzinists' case, of the impurities that lay outside of the Russian spoken by polite society. Both sides framed their arguments in terms of an opposition between "self" and "other" *(svoi—chuzhoi)* (Uspenskii, *Kratkii ocherk istorii russkogo literaturnogo iazyka*, 164–67). Also see Iu. Lotman and B. Uspenskii, "Spory o iazyke v nachale XIX v. kak fakt russkoi kul'tury ('Proisshestvie v tsarstve tenei, ili sud'bina rossiiskogo iazyka'— neizvestnoe sochinenie Semena Bobrova)," in *Trudy po russkoi i slavianskoi filologii, XXIV: literaturovedenie*, Uchenye zapiski Tartuskogo gosudarstvennogo universiteta, no. 358 (Tartu, 1975), 168–254; and Iurii Tynianov, "Arkhaisty i Pushkin," in *Arkhaisty i novatory* (Moscow: Priboi, 1929; rpt., Ann Arbor, Mich.: Ardis, 1985), 89–93.

23. See Scott Joseph Seregny, *Russian Teachers and Peasant Revolution: The Politics of Education in 1905* (Bloomington: Indiana University Press, 1988); and Christine Ruane, *Gender, Class, and the Professionalization of Russian City Teachers, 1860–1914* (Pittsburgh: University of Pittsburgh Press, 1994).

24. The most comprehensive study of the reading culture of prerevolutionary Russia remains Jeffrey Brooks, *When Russia Learned to Read: Literacy and Popular Literature, 1861–1917* (Princeton, N.J.: Princeton University Press, 1985).

25. Andrey Bely, "The Magic of Words," in Steven Cassedy, trans. and ed., *Selected Essays of Andrey Bely* (Berkeley: University of California Press, 1985), 93.

26. Bely, "Magic of Words," 96–98.

27. Andrey Bely, *Glossolaliia. Poema o zvuke* (1917; rpt., Tomsk: Izd. "Vodolei," 1994), 5.

28. Ibid., 95. The call for a revolution in poetic language, though less apocalyptic than in Bely, likewise appears in Viktor Shklovskii's 1914 essay on "The Resurrection of the Word" in W.-D. Stempel, ed., *Texte der rusischen Formalisten*, vol. 2 (1914; rpt., Munich: Wilhelm Fink Verlag, 1972), 2–16.

29. Quoted in Raymond Cooke, *Velimir Khlebnikov: A Critical Study* (Cambridge: Cambridge University Press, 1987), 81.

30. Cooke, *Velimir Khlebnikov*, 24–25, 44–52, chap. 3. *Zaumnyi iazyk*, or "transrational language," was a concept advanced foremost by Khlebnikov and the poet A. E. Kruchonykh. It referred to an experimental language consisting of neologisms built off of existing Russian phonemes, morphemes, and lexemes. For one of the more cogent discussions of *zaum* and its links to Bely, Potebnia, and Humboldt (among

others), see Gerald Janecek, *Zaum: The Transrational Poetry of Russian Futurism* (San Diego: San Diego State University Press, 1996), esp. 1–48.

31. In order of appearance, "revolution," "ideology," "agitation," "meeting," "proletariat," and "bourgeoisie."

32. For just a few examples, see A. Belina, *Slovotolkovatel' neponiatnykh slov, vstrechaiushchikhsia pri chtenii knig i gazet* (Moscow: Kniga i pravda, 1906); *Karmannyi slovar' Politicheskikh Terminov* (Kiev: Trud i znanie, 1906); and *Sovremennyi obshchestvenno-politicheskii i ekonomicheskii slovar'* (Moscow: tip. T-va I.D. Sytina, 1906). This genre of publication enjoyed a second, more pronounced boom in response to the changing political climate of 1917. See Orlando Figes, "The Russian Revolution of 1917 and Its Language in the Village," *Russian Review* 56 (1997), 327n.14.

33. Moshe Lewin, "The Social Background of Stalinism," in *The Making of the Soviet System: Essays in the Social History of Interwar Russia* (New York: Pantheon Books, 1985), 260. Commenting on the ambiguous dynamics of the postrevolutionary "class struggle," Sheila Fitzpatrick argues that both sides of the equation were essentially fictitious: "By 1920 . . . the great 'class struggle' was being waged by a surrogate proletariat (the Red Army and the Communist Party) against a surrogate bourgeoisie (the White Armies and the urban intelligentsia)." "New Perspectives on the Civil War," in Diane P. Koenker, William G. Rosenberg, and Ronald Grigor Suny, eds., *Party, State, and Society in the Russian Civil War: Explorations in Social History* (Bloomington: Indiana University Press, 1989), 6.

34. See Alec Nove, "Socialism, Centralised Planning, and the One-Party State," in T. H. Rigby, Archie Brown, and Peter Reddaway, eds., *Authority, Power, and Policy in the USSR: Essays Dedicated to Leonard Shapiro* (London: MacMillan, 1980), 77–97; and Maria Hirszowicz, "The Sovereign Bureaucracy as a New Social Phenomenon," in *The Bureaucratic Leviathan: A Study in the Sociology of Communism* (Oxford: M. Robertson, 1980), 13–47. T. H. Rigby has succinctly argued that a centralized command economy was in fact the only viable option for a leadership bent on building a single-party state, though there is little doubt that the experience of "war communism" helped make its implementation inevitable—even palatable. "Stalinism and the Mono-Organizational Society," in Robert C. Tucker, ed., *Stalinism* (New York: Norton, 1977), 53–76.

35. In fact, it is precisely at this time that debates over institutions of social "enlightenment" and control heightened markedly. Sheila Fitzpatrick offers a detailed account of the reorganization of the *Narkompros* in 1920–1921 in *Commissariat of Enlightenment* (Cambridge: Cambridge University Press, 1970), esp. 162–209. For a more recent study of the Bolshevik restructuring of higher education, see Michael David-Fox, *Revolution of the Mind: Higher Learning among the Bolsheviks, 1918–1929* (Ithaca, N.Y.: Cornell University Press, 1997). For a thorough discussion of the debate over the status of the *Proletcult* movement during this period, see Lynn Mally, *Culture of the Future: The Proletkult Movement in Revolutionary Russia* (Berkeley: University of California Press, 1990), esp. chap. 7.

36. *O partiinoi i sovetskoi pechati. Sbornik dokumentov* (Moscow: Pravda, 1954), 173.

37. Quoted from Mikhail Heller and Aleksandr Nekrich, *Utopia in Power: The History of the Soviet Union from 1917 to the Present* (New York: Summit Books, 1986), 174.

38. *Kommunisticheskaia partiia sovetskogo soiuza v rezoliutsiiakh i resheniiakh s''ezdov, konferentsii i plenumov TsK*, vol. 2 (Moscow: Izd. politicheskoi literatury, 1970), 360.

39. For a detailed study of the censorship industry in early Soviet Russia, see the companion volumes by A. V. Blium, *Za kulisami "Ministerstva pravdy": tainaia istoriia sovetskoi tsenzury, 1917–1929* (Sankt-Peterburg: Akademicheskii proekt, 1994); *Sovetskaia tsenzura v epokhu total'nogo terrora, 1929–1953* (St. Petersburg: Akademicheskii proekt, 2000); as well as T. M. Goriaeva, *Politicheskaia tsenzura v SSSR, 1917–1991* (Moscow: ROSSPEN, 2002).

40. According to Jeffrey Brooks, deficits in materials, funds, and experienced labor led to a full-fledged crisis in which the circulation of newspapers and journals dropped well below prerevolutionary levels. "The Breakdown in Production and Distribution of Printed Material, 1917–1927," in Abbott Gleason, Peter Kenez, and Richard Stites, eds., *Bolshevik Culture* (Bloomington: Indiana University Press, 1985), 151–74.

41. Ia. M. Shafir, *Gazeta i derevnia*, 2d expanded ed. (Moscow: Krasnaia nov', 1924), 112–13, 118. "Nepmen" was the term given, often disparagingly, to the entrepreneurs who took advantage of the more decentralized economic policies of the NEP. Shafir contributed extensively to the research on and debate over the contemporary language—in particular, the language of the newspaper. James C. Scott discusses the function of rumors and gossip in popular resistance in *Domination and the Arts of Resistance*, 142–48.

42. Shafir, *Gazeta i derevnia*, 113. The Russian word *slovesnost'* has a broader connotation than the English "literature," including in it folklore as well as poetry and prose fiction. A less polemical recognition of competing voices in the countryside can be found in the writing of the folklorist Iu. M. Sokolov, who, in the introduction to a 1926 collection of lore, acknowledged the overtly social, and often oppositional form, that contemporary *ustnaia slovesnost'* had taken, referring specifically to the "innumerable quantity of legends about antichrist-Bolsheviks, about the impending end of the world, about the cruel punishment of the godless, who have permitted themselves to disrupt the peace of holy forces, about commissars who have sealed up churches, about the repentance and conversion of the godless to the 'right path of faith,' about the five-pointed star as the stamp of the antichrist, etc. etc. . . . The whole, motley, multivoiced, contradictory life of revolutionary breakdown *[lomka]* has been reflected in capricious forms of oral literature *[ustnaia slovesnost']*" (Boris Sokolov and Iurii Sokolov, *Poeziia derevni. Rukovodstvo dlia sobiraniia proizvedenii ustnoi slovesnosti* [Moscow: Novaia Moskva, 1926], 12–13). Sources independent of Shafir go one step further and note how the reemergence of witchcraft, sorcery, and paganism in the villages was popularly associated with and attributed to the rise of Soviet power (V. G. Tan-Bogoraz, "Staryi i novyi byt," in *Staryi i novyi byt. Sbornik* [Leningrad: GIZ, 1924]). For an interesting discussion of the role of rumors in 1917 and the downfall of Kerensky in particular, see Figes and Kolonitskii, *Interpreting the Russian Revolution*, 1–29.

43. The literary critic Boris Arvatov described the "living newspaper" as a "review combined with a stage performance *(estrada)* with proletarian thematics—a flexible, nonpatronal *(vne-khramovaia)* traveling theater, capable of being as ideational as Shakespeare, as qualified as Sophocles, [and] exerting more influence than all the Shakespeares and Sophocles put together" ("Zhivaia gazeta, kak teatral'naia forma," *Zhizn' iskusstva* 25 [1925]: 2). The most notorious of these traveling groups was the "Blue Blouse" *(Siniaia bluza)* troupe, alternately castigated and praised for its more entertainment-oriented performances (for a negative review of *Siniaia bluza* and praise for living newspapers in Leningrad, see "Zhivye gazety,"

Zhizn' iskusstva 2 [1925]: 18). For a recent study of agitational and other forms of amateur theater, see Lynn Mally, *Revolutionary Acts: Amateur Theater and the Soviet State* (Ithaca, N.Y.: Cornell University Press, 2000), esp. chap. 2.

44. "Kak ia ustroil 'zhivuiu' gazetu," *Krasnyi zhurnalist* 2–3 (12 Sept. 1920): 66.

45. John Reed, *Ten Days that Shook the World* (New York: International Publishers, 1926), 14–15.

46. F. Zelinskii, "Znachenie oratorskogo iskusstva," in Konst. Erberg, ed., *Iskusstvo i narod. Sbornik* (Peterburg: Kolos, 1922), 171–75.

47. Vladimir Dal', in fact, used one in the very title of his four-volume *Interpretive Dictionary of the Living Great-Russian Language (Tolkovyi slovar' zhivogo velikorusskogo iazyka*, 2d ed., 4 vols. [1880; rpt., Moscow: Russkii iazyk, 1978]), where he defined it as the "language spoken currently by the people" and "a language full of life—warm, boiling, and natural." In the context of revolution, both terms came to be synonymous with innovative, oral, and even colloquial speech employed in the advancement of the Bolshevik cause. For a good example of the revolutionary recasting, see the opening editorial to first issue of *Vestnik agitatsii i propagandy* (1 [1920]; renamed *Kommunisticheskaia revoliutsiia* beginning 1 August 1922).

48. Gosudarstvennyi arkhiv Rossiiskoi Federatsii (GARF), f. A2306, op. 18, d. 290, l. 11, 35. For a full listing of courses, curricula, and research goals, see *Zapiski Instituta Zhivogo Slova* (Peterburg, 1919).

49. *Zapiski Instituta Zhivogo Slova*, 13, 20, 22.

50. "From the time of the Revolution a shift in the direction of the *living word* has been witnessed here in Russia, as if it has broken through the dam and spread in a mighty flow through the country." Nikolai Pashkov, "O nedostatkakh rechi," *Rodnoi iazyk v shkole* 7 (1925): 165.

51. For evidence of storytelling circles for adults, see GARF, f. A-2313, op. 6, d. 298, l. 20; f. A-2314, op. 5, d. 5, l. 5; for evidence of the politicization of gradeschool storytelling, see Nauchnyi Arkhiv Rossiiskoi Akademii Obrazovaniia (NA RAO), f. 5, op. 1, dd. 44, 54, 61, 62, 79, 81, 83, 90, 92.

52. I. Ustinov, *Razvitie rechi. K voprosu o metodakh zaniatii v shkolakh vzroslykh i na komandnykh kursakh* (Moscow: Gosizdat., 1922), 21.

53. *Rodnoi iazyk i literatura v fabzavuche i profshkole. Metodicheskoe pis'mo,* Biblioteka rabochego obrazovaniia, no. 20 (Moscow: ORO and IP Glavprofobra NKP RSFSR [Gosizdat.], 1928), 13.

54. This is not to say, however, that the movement succeeding in producing a new breed of "proletarian writer." It was arguably more successful in the production of amateur stage performances. See Edward J. Brown, *The Proletarian Episode in Russian Literature, 1928–1932* (New York: Columbia University Press, 1953); Mally, *Culture of the Future;* and Mally, *Revolutionary Acts.*

55. Groshik, "Invalidy," *Griadushchee* 4 (1918): 11.

56. Zoia Aspii, "Miatezhnyi gorod. (Ocherki)," *Griadushchee* 1 (1919): 5.

57. Iak. Okunev, "Ulybka," *Plamia* 1 (1918): 6.

58. V. N. Alferov, *Vozniknovenie i razvitie rabsel'korovskogo dvizheniia v SSSR* (Moscow: Izd. Mysl', 1970), 85. Trade journals geared toward the new correspondents carried regular sections coaching them on appropriate themes (e.g., "Kak i o chem pisat'," *Rabkor Zheleznodorozhnik* 1 [1925]: 10–14; "O chem pisat'?" *Rabsel'kor* 11–12 [1926]; "Kak rabsel'kory dolzhny otvetit' Chemberlenu?" and "Kak pisat' o khoroshikh i plokhikh kooperativakh," *Raboche-krest'ianskii Korrespondent* 12

[1927]: 1–2, 8–10). The editorial board of the paper *Gudok* sent circulars to new *rabkory* instructing them to "follow the newspaper and take note of instructional articles and the mailbox, where [they] could find out which issues in Union life were currently the most burning *(zlobodnevnye)* and in need of illumination from the peripheries *(s mest)*" (Rossiiskii gosudarstvennyi arkhiv sotsial'no-politicheskoi istorii [RGASPI], f. 17, op. 60, ed. khr. 907, l. 4).

59. According to Alferov, worker and village correspondents numbered in the hundreds by 1923 and rose to 500,000 by 1928 (*Vozniknovenie i razvitie rabsel'korovskogo dvizheniia*, 91, 118). Peter Kenez offers similar numbers, though he wisely advises caution in interpreting them (*The Birth of the Propaganda State: Soviet Methods of Mass Mobilization, 1917–1929* [Cambridge: Cambridge University Press, 1985], 235). For two more recent and detailed historical studies of the correspondents movement during the 1920s, see Jennifer Clibbon, "The Soviet Press and Grass-roots Organization: The Rabkor Movement, NEP to the First Five-year Plan" (Ph.D. diss., University of Toronto, 1993); and Steven Robert Coe, "Peasants, the State, and the Languages of NEP: The Rural Correspondents Movement in the Soviet Union, 1924–1928" (Ph.D. diss., University of Michigan, 1993). The "Pioneers" were the communist version of the Cub Scouts, only coeducational.

60. By "popular" language I mean the "language of the *narod*," a term used loosely and subjectively by contemporaries to refer to a preconceived notion of nonintellectual, rank-and-file members of the peasantry and working class. The demographic makeup of the correspondents is itself somewhat ambiguous. Jeffrey Brooks offers a cogent argument for the prerevolutionary roots of this model of the "intellectual from the people," and he notes that they were not at all strictly workers and peasants ("Competing Modes of Popular Discourse: Individualism and Class Consciousness in the Russian Print Media, 1880–1928," in Marc Ferro, Sheila Fitzpatrick, Sydney Monas, and Jutta Scherrer, eds., *Culture et Révolution* [Paris: Martine Godet, 1989], 71–81). Edward Hallet Carr similarly claims that, especially in the early years in the villages, there were not enough literate peasants to recruit for the *sel'kor* ranks and that many of the rural correspondents were "party officials or workers sent on duty to the country" (*Socialism in One Country, 1924–1926,* 3 vols. [New York: MacMillan, 1958–1964], 1:196). Anecdotal statistics from both regional and central organizations suggest that perhaps even a majority of contributors came not from workers or peasants but from the so-called "service sector" *(sluzhashchie)* (e.g., *Rabkor Zheleznodorozhnik* 6 [1925], 30; RGASPI, f. 17, op. 60, ed. khr. 907, l. 6). This is supported by published complaints from working-class correspondents that their ranks were watered down by such nonworker elements, many of whom had never picked up a hammer or sickle in their lives: because they were "service sector" workers, wrote one, they should be distinguished apart from the *rabkory* by the separate title *sluzhkor* ("Korrespondenty sovetskie sluzhashchie—sluzhkory," *Raboche-krest'ianskii Korrespondent* 22 [1927]: 17–19).

61. Under the more recent influence of Ferdinand de Saussure, Gustav Shpet, and others, but also harking back to the linguistic thought of Wolfgang von Humboldt and Aleksandr Potebnia, an increasing number of Russian linguists were turning against the traditions of the neo-grammarians and historical linguists that had dominated the field in the decades surrounding the turn of the century and were beginning to recognize the need to examine language in a more sociolinguistic context. For background on the nineteenth-century trend of viewing language as

an organic entity and its study more akin to a natural science, see Aarsleff, *From Locke to Saussure*, 3–41, 293–334. For a more detailed discussion of Shpet's contribution to the linguistics of early Soviet Russia, see Smith, *Language and Power in the Creation of the USSR*, chap. 3.

62. Institut russkogo iazyka (IRIa), f. 20, op. 14, pp. 340–41.

63. 17 and 25 May 1919 (IRIa, f. 20, op. 2, pp. 28–29, 49–50). One of the legends summarized by Jakobson and illustrating what the linguist called an "eschatological conceptualization of events" tells of a Serpukhov worker and Bolshevik agitator who "delivers eschatological speeches where the analogy is made between the current events and the Second Coming (Lenin). His speech makes a strong impression, especially on women" (17 May 1919 [IRIa, f. 20, op. 2, p. 29, 49–50]). Clearly, the "oral literature" referred to earlier by Shafir was not only antagonistic to the Bolshevik cause.

64. For a full list of talks delivered, see IRIa, f. 20, op. 2, p. 52ob. The discussion of the archive took place on 25 April 1920 (IRIa, f. 20, op. 3, p. 94). Jakobson and M. M. Königsberg were the initiators of the project, described as "an archive for the collection of various phenomena in the area of the contemporary living language and other fields relating to language culture and language policy." They divided the proposed archive into four sections ("material on the language of minor nationalities and language policy, material on language pedagogy, new phenomena in the area of the Russian language, and urban folklore") and assigned different members to investigate each.

65. The personal archive of G. O. Vinokur, who was designated the keeper and director of the archive at that same meeting, contains a list of "contemporary acronyms and new formations" compiled by Ushakov (Rossiiskii Gosudarstvennyi Arkhiv Literatury i Iskusstva [RGALI], f. 2164, op. 1, ed. khr. 367). The circle had even broader plans for such work, according to an account of its activity for the years 1924–1925. In addition to "the influence of war and revolution on Russian," a list of specific topics under the major heading of "the study of the contemporary Russian language" included "the language of Soviet acronyms," "the language of contemporary newspapers, posters, slogans, etc.," "stylistics of Soviet oratorical and literary speeches, stylistic peculiarities of speeches of leaders of the Russian revolution," and "the issue of renamings . . . of streets, cities, institutions" (RGALI, f. 2164, ed. khr. 1). By this point, however, significant differences of opinion over the goals and functions of the circle had arisen that contributed to its dissolution during that same year. See IRIa, f. 20, op. 5 (protocols from the 21 Mar., 4 Apr., and 22 Oct. 1922 meetings), for documentation of the fractious discussions on the future direction of the circle. E. A. Toddes and M. O. Chudakova also refer to the split in their article "Pervyi russkii perevod *Kursa obshchei lingvistiki* F. de Sossiura i deiatel'nost' Moskovskogo Lingvisticheskogo Kruzhka (Materialy k izucheniiu bytovaniia nauchnoi knigi v 1920-e gody)," in *Fedorovskie chteniia 1978* (Moscow: Nauka, 1981), 229–49. For evidence of circle members' interest in the language of the Bolshevik revolution, see discussions of Grigorii Vinokur's work in chapter 2 as well as the following: Roman Jakobson, "Vliv revoluce na rusky jazyk: Poznamky ke knize André Mazona 'Lexique de la guerre et de la révolution en Russie' (Paris, 1920)," *Nové Atheneum* Roc. II, sv. III (1920–1921) 3:111–14, 5:200–212, 6:250–55, 7:310–18. R. O. Shor (1894–1939), a linguist and literary historian who was also active in the circle at the time of the archive's conception, published

descriptive commentaries on contemporary language change as well as the period's most popular introduction to sociolinguistics, *Language and Society*. See "O neologizmakh revoliutsionnoi epokhi," *Russkii iazyk v sovetskoi shkole* 1 (1929): 50–56; and *Iazyk i obshchestvo* (Moscow: Rabotnik prosveshcheniia, 1926).

66. GARF, f. A2306, op. 18, ed. khr. 290, pp. 12–12ob.

67. The Academy *(Gosudarstvennaia Akademiia Khudozhestvennykh Nauk)* was founded in 1924 and continued work in a variety of disciplines up until its reorganization in 1930. Active participants in the Academy's work in the field of public speaking included several members of the Moscow Linguistics Circle (G. O. Vinokur, O. M. Brik, A. M. Peshkovskii, D. N. Ushakov) and many other prominent participants in the language and literary debates of the day (A. V. Lunacharskii, P. S. Kogan, V. F. Pereverzev, V. P. Polonskii). Meetings for the first commission were held from 1925–1930 and were attended by up to forty-five scholars, including the likes of Kogan, Peshkovskii, Ushakov, and Vinokur. They addressed historical, contemporary, and theoretical issues, including "The Orator and Actor in Ancient and Modern Performances," "Interdependence of Form and Content in the Living Word," "Collective Declamation," "From the Stylistics of Contemporary Speech (Verb or Noun)," and "Poets—the Lyric as Declamator" (RGALI, f. 941, op. 6, d. 39, 40, 51, 66, 80, 81, 108, 109). The second commission met between 1925 and 1926 in the Academy's Physio-Psychology Division (RGALI, f. 941, op. 12, d. 20, l. 36).

68. RGALI, f. 941, op. 12, ed. khr. 20, p. 36.

69. "Vnushenie kak kharakternaia osobennost' podsoznatel'noi deiatel'nosti," RGALI, f. 941, op. 12, ed. khr. 20, p. 8.

70. Brooks, "Breakdown in Production and Distribution of Printed Material," 151–74.

71. In his influential study of the origins of nationalism, Benedict Anderson singles out the newspaper and the novel as the two most influential forums for the creation and maintenance of what he calls "imagined communities" (*Imagined Communities: Reflections on the Origin and Spread of Nationalism* [London: Verso Editions, 1983]). Antonio Gramsci, by comparison, lists eight "sources of diffusion" that are most responsible for creating a "national linguistic conformism": the education system; newspapers; artistic writers and popular writers; theater and sound films; radio; public meetings; verbal interaction between more- and less-educated strata of the population; and local dialects ("Sources of Diffusion of Linguistic Innovations in the Tradition and of a national Linguistic Conformism in the Broad National Masses," in William Boelhower, trans., and David Forgacs and Geoffrey Nowell-Smith, eds., *Selections from Cultural Writings* [Cambridge, Mass.: Harvard University Press, 1985], 183). The role of radio in the shaping of a new language culture in early Soviet Russia is an understudied topic particularly worthy of closer examination. For the most comprehensive study to date, see T. M. Goriaeva, ed., *Istoriia sovetskoi radio–zhurnalistiki: Dokumenty, teksty, vospominaniia, 1917–1945* (Moscow: Izdatel'stvo Moskovskogo universiteta, 1991).

72. V. N. Voloshinov, *Marxism and the Philosophy of Language*, trans. Ladislav Matejka and I. R. Titunik (Cambridge, Mass.: Harvard University Press, 1986).

73. For more recent discussions of the cultural authority of linguists and linguistics, see Deborah Cameron, *Verbal Hygiene* (London: Routledge, 1995); Tony

Crowley, *The Politics of Discourse: The Standard Language Question in British Cultural Debates* (London: Macmillan, 1989); and Susan Gal and Kathryn A. Woolard, "Constructing Languages and Publics: Authority and Representation," *Pragmatics* 5 (1995): 129–38.

74. Limitations in time and scope restrict my attention in this regard to linguistic discussions that speak directly to the early Soviet language culture. More general studies in the origins and philosophy of language, while highly deserving of further historical elucidation, figure into my discussion only in the cases where either they had some practical application to the language debates or they provide theoretical illumination of my main points. Nikolai Marr's ideas on the origin and nature of language, for this reason, while highly influential in shaping contemporary language policy with respect to non-Russian nationalities, figure into this discussion only tangentially. At the same time, although Bakhtin's work had little impact on the contemporary language debates, they do offer profound insight into the dynamics of a language culture in flux—hence his feature role in this work as interpretive guide. The need for elaborating on the wealth of ideas about the origin and nature of language produced during this period in Soviet Russia has been alleviated somewhat by a number of thoughtful studies, among them Gary Saul Morson and Caryl Emerson, *Mikhail Bakhtin: Creation of a Prosaics* (Stanford, Calif.: Stanford University Press, 1990); V. M. Alpatov, *Istoriia odnogo mifa: Marr i marrizm* (Moscow: Nauka, 1991); Smith, *Language and Power in the Creation of the USSR*, 51–102; Galin Tikhanov, *The Master and the Slave: Lukács, Bakhtin, and the Ideas of Their Time* (Oxford: Oxford University Press, 2000). For a thorough analysis of Bakhtin's reception in Russia, see Caryl Emerson, *The First Hundred Years of Mikhail Bakhtin* (Princeton, N.J.: Princeton University Press, 1977).

75. Applying Sewell's bipartite definition of culture, Victoria Bonnell and Lynn Hunt describe narrative's import as lying in its ability to "provide a link between culture as system and culture as practice," as "an arena in which meaning takes form, in which individuals connect to the public and social world, and in which change therefore becomes possible" (*Beyond the Cultural Turn*, 17).

76. For commentary on the special regard for the writer and the intelligentsia in general, see Gary Saul Morson, "Introduction: Literary History and the Russian Experience," in Gary Saul Morson, ed., *Literature and History: Theoretical Problems and Russian Case Studies* (Stanford, Calif.: Stanford University Press, 1986), 14–27.

77. In his study of Russian modernism, Victor Erlich contemplates the fruitfulness of a study "probing the interrelationship between style and worldview" (*Modernism and Revolution: Russian Literature in Transition* [Cambridge, Mass.: Harvard University Press, 1994], 12).

78. This is not to claim either that *all* writers felt compelled to engage the emerging language of state in their literature or that *all* state authorities were keen on literature's importance in state building and the symbolic representation of authority and identity. The discussion that follows will make amply clear, however, the remarkable prevalence of this mutual sensitivity.

79. I use the term "ideal type" as it was first introduced by Max Weber in his essay, "'Objectivity' in Social Science," in *The Methodology of the Social Sciences* (Free Press: New York, 1949). When used in the context of these types, I employ the terms "language" and "voice" more or less synonymously to refer to what in

contemporary cultural studies has come to be referred to as "discourse"—a term I try to avoid, because of its overuse and misuse. My use of all of these terms closely resembles the "discourse" analyzed by John Toews, who, in following J. G. A. Pocock, ascribes to it three interlocking dimensions of meaning—structural, communicative (or action-oriented), and experiential. Elaborating on the structural dimension, Toews writes that "languages embody the rules that define a communicative world, determining what counts as reality and limiting the possible ways in which realities can be connected. Many such languages may and usually do coexist . . . in the public space of political struggle and discussion at any particular historical moment, and any given text may participate in a number of languages and relate them to each other implicitly or explicitly in a variety of ways, occasionally developing 'meta-languages' or secondary languages in order to do so. The first task of the historian of discourse is to identify and reconstruct such languages, to demonstrate their 'paradigmatic' force or organizing power in various texts and to construct their implicit forms into an explicit 'ideal type' or hypothetical model that can then become an instrument for identifying a particular language in other texts and contexts." "Intellectual History after the Linguistic Turn," 891.

80. Mikhail Bakhtin characterizes a "speech genre" as a "typical form of utterance" and underscores the degree to which it reflects a particular perception of the world: "In the genre the word acquires a particular typical expression. Genres correspond to typical situations of speech communication, typical themes, and consequently, also to particular contacts between the *meanings* of words and actual concrete reality under certain typical circumstances." Bakhtin argues that, in any given social and historical context, there exist both distinguishable and dominant styles of speaking and writing that extend across disciplines, that rise and fall in importance over time, and that are closely linked to issues of identity, authority, and ideology. See M. M. Bakhtin, "The Problem of Speech Genres," in Vern W. McGee, trans., and Caryl Emerson and Michael Holquist, eds., *Speech Genres and Other Late Essays* (Austin: University of Texas Press, 1986), 87.

81. My use of the terms "linguistic capital" and "cultural capital" come from Pierre Bourdieu, *Language and Symbolic Power,* trans. Gino Raymond and Matthew Adamson and ed. John B. Thompson (Cambridge, Mass.: Harvard University Press, 1991), esp. 43–89.

82. Acts 2:1–14, New International Bible.

83. William J. Samarin, *Tongues of Men and Angels: The Religious Language of Pentecostalism* (New York: Macmillan, 1970), xvii.

84. See Gen. 11.

1: THE CONTOURS OF THE COMMUNICATION GAP

1. A. Barannikov, "Iz nabliudenii nad razvitiem russkogo iazyka v poslednie gody," in *Uchenye zapiski Samarskogo Universiteta,* vol. 2 (Samara: Tip. Sredvolsoiuza no. 1, 1919), 64–84; Jakobson, "Vliv revoluce na rusky jazyk," 3:111–14, 5:200–212, 6:250–55, 7:310–18; S. O. Kartsevskii, *Iazyk, voina i revoliutsiia* (Berlin: Russkoe Universal'noe Izd., 1923); André Mazon, *Lexique de la guerre et de la révolution en Russie (1914–1918),* Bibliothéque de L'Institut Français de Petrograd, vol. 4 (Paris: Librairie Anciènne Honoré Champion, Edouard Champion, 1920); E. D. Polivanov, "O literaturnom (standartnom) iazyke sovremennosti," *Rodnoi iazyk v shkole* 1 (1927):

225–35; A. M. Selishchev, *Iazyk revoliutsionnoi epokhi: iz nabliudenii nad russkim iazykom poslednikh let (1917–1926)* (1928; rpt., Letchworth-Herts, England: Prideaux Press, 1971); P. Ia. Chernykh, "Russkii iazyk i revoliutsiia," in *I. Sovremennye techeniia v lingvistike. II. Russkii iazyk i revoliutsiia* (Irkutsk: [Vlast' truda], 1929). These works will henceforth be referred to by author and page number only. Numerous other article-sized features appeared over the decade, the most noteworthy of which include the submissions to the "open discussion" conducted on the pages of the professional journal *The Journalist [Zhurnalist]* (no. 2 [1925]: 5–10), which included comments by Shcherba, Iakubinskii, Bernshtein, and Ushakov as well as Selishchev's article, "Vyrazitel'nost' i obraznost' iazyka revoliutsionnoi epokhi," (1927; reprinted in *Izbrannye trudy* [Moscow: Prosveshchenie, 1968]: 141–46). A. M. Selishchev (1886–1942), a linguist trained in Slavic languages and professor of historical linguistics and dialectology at Moscow State University from 1922, dedicated a considerable portion of his career to the study of contemporary changes in the Russian literary language. His 1928 description of the language of the revolutionary epoch remains unmatched to this day.

2. It is not my intent to repeat or expand on the formal linguistic descriptions of Russian in the revolutionary period; what follows is a critical overview of the contemporary descriptions. As my analysis is more concerned with the cultural impact of the language changes, and the debates and representations of those changes, my goal here is to provide a menu of the formal features of the language that were commonly cited as "sociolinguistic facts" and most frequently served as the verbal objects of the contemporary debates and fictional portraits. Specific words, forms, or stylistic features will be discussed when appropriate to this broader, cultural context. Among contemporary analyses of the formal aspects of the language changes of early Soviet Russia, two of the more detailed include Comrie, Stone, and Polinsky, *Russian Language in the Twentieth Century;* and Seriot, *Analyse du discours politique soviétique.* For a more sociolinguistic orientation, see Wilhelm von Timroth's *Russian and Soviet Sociolinguistics and Taboo Varieties of the Russian Language,* rev. and enlarged ed., Slavistische Beiträge, vol. 205, trans. Nortrud Gupta (München: Verlag Otto Sagner, 1986). For a post-Soviet lexicographic interpretation of the language of the Soviet state, see V. M. Mokienko and T. G. Nikitina, eds., *Tolkovyi slovar' iazyka Sovdepi* (St. Petersburg: Folio-press, 1998).

3. Approximate English equivalents, in the order in which they are listed (groups separated by semicolon): "tsar," "prince," "count," "zemstvo," "Senate," "Synod," "gymnasium"; "policeman" —> "militia man," "minister" —> "commissar," "bureaucrat" —> "Soviet service employee," "soldier" —> "Red Army man," "salary" —> "work payment (shortened from *zarabotnaia plata*)," "servant" —> "household worker" (f.), "holiday" —> "day of rest."

4. "Sir," "comrade," "baron," "party," "[member of the] bourgeoisie" (derogatory), "intellectual," "[cultural] chief," "[party] cell," "purge."

5. "Demonstration," "revolution," "agitation," "meeting" (as in "rally"), "mandate," "resolution," "deputy," "delegate," "commune," "proletariat," "bourgeoisie," "boycott," "discussion," "platform," "privilege," "repression," "slogan," "strike breaker," "de-classed" (i.e., dispossessed of or otherwise excluded from one's social class), "constitute," "Fordization."

6. "Front," "struggle," "line," "army," "weapon," "mobilization," "offensive" (n.), "shock" (adj.). Kartsevskii (31) and Jakobson attribute the influx of military

language into civilian spheres to the civil war, as it was "a political struggle fought with weapons." Note also that Selishchev (95–96) attributes the frequent use of categorical expressions (*iasno* [clearly], *opredelenno* [definitely], *fakt* [fact], *nichego podobnogo* [nothing of the kind]) to the language of the war period and war communism.

7. "Emergency commission for the struggle against counterrevolution, sabotage, and speculation," "Russian Soviet Federative Socialist Republic," "Socialist Revolutionary," "Union of Soviet Socialist Republics," "Central Committee"; "Ukrainian Press Bureau," "General Directorate for Military Training Institutions," "General Directorate for Military Engineering," "Moscow Department of Public Education," "New Economic Policy," "Council for Labor and Defense," "Central Executive Committee"; "General Directorate for the Paper Industry," "Executive Committee," "*Gubernia* Food Committee," "Communist International, Comintern," "Division Commander," "National Education Committee," "worker correspondent," "Proletarian Culture," "National Economic Council." I have taken the terms "literal" and "syllabic" from Mazon (1–4); Bernard Comrie and Gerald Stone introduce the term "stump-compound" to describe the splicing together of usually single syllables of the two or more words making up a phrase or, most commonly, an institutional name or occupation (e.g., *Narodnyi Kommissariat Prosveshcheniia* —> *Narkompros*) (*The Russian Language Since the Revolution* [Oxford: Oxford University Press, 1978], 100). For a comprehensive list of acronyms and stump-compounds, see Selishchev (158–64).

8. From the last group, "agricultural," "anarchism," "bureaucracy," "democracy," "quorum," "collective," "slogan," "(party) committee," "mandate," "orator." Selishchev (15–22) has an extended discussion of the language characteristic of the French Revolution. He notes the pervasiveness of oratory, the marked expressiveness and emotionality of this genre, and the sharp increase in language activity in general. Note also the German influence manifested in such common phrases as *v obshchem i tselom* (Ger. *im grossen und ganzen*), *tselikom i pol'nost'iu* (*ganz und voll*), *segodniashnii den'* (*der heutige Tag*) (Selishchev, 38–39).

9. "Lensk Gold Association," "Society for the Sale of Russian Metal Products." Kartsevskii (30) and Barannikov (78) also refer to the use of acronyms and stump-compounds in the "secret language" of prerevolutionary merchants and traders.

10. "Red Army man," "Leninist," "Kornilovist"; "Bolshevik," "mass operative" (one who works with the masses), "school child," "shockworker"; "Kolchakism," "Kerenskyism," "White-guardism"; "20-ruble note (introduced into circulation under Kerenskii in 1917)," "leaflet," "chat session"; "compromiser, yes-man"; "activist," "communist," "Trotskyist," "Chekist," "Bolshevism," "Tsarism," "speculator," "saboteur," "agitator," "liquidator"; "to speculate," "to mobilize," "to chekaize" (subject to the force of Cheka); "to hold a rally," "to nationalize," "to proletarianize," "to agitate," "to sovietize." Mazon (36–37).

11. Polivanov (226); Chernykh (57).

12. Shcherba (1925:6); Ushakov (1925:9–10); Chernykh (46).

13. Kartsevskii (70–71); Iakubinskii (8); Selishchev (1927:143). For a discussion of the phenomenon of "leveling" in revolutionary Russia—in language as well as other aspects of daily life—see Richard Stites, *Revolutionary Dreams: Utopian Vision and Experimental Life in the Russian Revolution* (New York: Oxford University Press, 1989), 124–35.

14. Polivanov (229); Selishchev (69–84); Chernykh (55–57); Selishchev (59).

15. Selishchev (1925:121–55); Chernykh (58).

16. Barannikov, 19. The third case of paronomastic inversion substitutes "left-" for "rev-olution" and, the fourth, "perelet-" ("fly through" or "overshoot") for "prolet-ariat."

17. Selishchev, *Iazyk revoliutsionnoi epokhi*, 198–209, 210–18. After the introductory discussion of spheres of linguistic influence, Selishchev unsurprisingly collected all of his data from one of three different sources—factory meetings, factory newspapers, and contemporary fiction portraying factory life.

18. Later he refers to this latter group specifically as party and Komsomol members (198).

19. Selishchev, *Iazyk revoliutsionnoi epokhi*, 203–8.

20. Ibid., 80.

21. See N. Markovskii, "Za kul'turu komsomol'skogo iazyka," *Molodoi Bol'shevik* 15–16 (1926), for an example of the political ire such teen experimentation evoked.

22. V. Straten, "Ob argo i argotizmakh," *Russkii iazyk v sovetskoi shkole* 5 (1929): 39–53. Selishchev acknowledges this link directly, supporting the notion of interdependence between youth and thieves' jargon and the emerging language of state (69–82).

23. Indeed, few of her examples of coarsening and distortion could be traced directly to the new public discourse. A three-page list of examples included such colorful school slang such as *na fig* (a rough equivalent of "up yours," accompanied by a extended fist with thumb thrust between index and middle fingers), *shit'sia* ("to go with," "hang out with") and *ryzhii* ("fool") as well as jargon traditionally used by thieves and sailors (*grubó* ["bitchin'"], *shámat'* ["to chow"], *kolotít'* ["to thrash, drub"], *zeks* [exclamation of warning, used in case of approaching militiaman or teacher]). M. Rybnikova, "Ob iskazhenii i ogrubenii rechi uchashchikhsia," *Rodnoi iazyk v shkole* 1 (1927): 243–46.

24. Ibid., 248.

25. Ibid., 246, 250. Another contributor to the same journal argued that the language of the street and newspapers influenced children even more than the literary language they encountered in school (A. Sletova, "Kul'tura rechi uchashchikhsia kak obshchaia zadacha shkoly," *Russkii iazyk v sovetskoi shkole* 3 [1929]: 88). Alan Ball documents the surge in numbers of *besprizornye* over the first half-decade of Bolshevik rule and the negative social repercussions in his book, *And Now My Soul Is Hardened: Abandoned Children in Soviet Russia, 1918–1930* (Berkeley: University of California Press, 1994).

26. Rybnikova, "Ob iskazhenii i ogrubenii," 250, 254.

27. Iu. I. Kazhdanskaia, "Sotsial'no-politicheskie predstavleniia deteishkol'nikov pervogo kontsentra trudovykh shkol gor. Odessa," *Pedalogiia*, bk. 2, ser. B (1928): 90, 93–94. The lone fact that such studies existed and even increased over the course of the First Five-Year Plan suggests that there was concern over the efficacy of the state's communication with its emerging citizenry. Larry E. Holmes documents the inefficacy of the curricular reforms at least through the late 1920s (*The Kremlin and the Schoolhouse: Reforming Education in Soviet Russia, 1917–1931* [Bloomington: Indiana University Press, 1991], 93–97). That little changed over the next three years is supported by data from a similar study conducted by researchers at the "Scientific Research Program-Methodology Institute" of the Narkompros in 1931. It measured the associations that seven- and eight-year-old "working-class"

schoolchildren had with such keywords as "Lenin," "rabochii," "burzhui," "revoliutsiia," "piatiletka," and "nerusskii" and showed a fairly wide range of comprehension—from next to nothing, to accurate, albeit formulaic, interpretations (NA RAO, f. 8, d. 215, ll. 1–13).

28. S. Abakumov, "Rabota nad slovarem i frazoi v novykh uchebnykh posobiiakh po tekhnike i kul'ture rechi," *Russkii iazyk v sovetskoi shkole* 1 (1929): 82.

29. I. N. Shpil'rein, *Iazyk krasnoarmeitsa* (Moscow: Gosizdat., 1928). The study was commissioned by the Agitational Division of the publishing house "Proletariat at the Wheel" ("PUR") and the Moscow Committee of the Communist Party. For shorter accounts of similar studies, see also S. Ryss, "Issledovanie slovaria kr-tsev," *Sputnik politrabotnika* 1 (1924): 51–58; and Kudrin, "Kak vosprinimaet gazetu riadovoi krasnoarmeets," *Krasnaia Pechat'* 6 (1924): 5–9.

30. Shpil'rein, *Iazyk krasnoarmeitsa,* 56. For a discussion of the Bolsheviks' hopes and aspirations for Red Army soldiers as "proletarians," see Sheila Fitzpatrick, "New Perspectives on the Civil War," 391–92; and Mark Von Hagen, *Soldiers in the Proletarian Dictatorship: The Red Army and the Soviet Socialist State, 1917–1930* (Ithaca, N.Y.: Cornell University Press, 1990).

31. Shpil'rein, *Iazyk krasnoarmeitsa,* 115.

32. Ibid., 116.

33. Ibid., 80.

34. Ibid., 27.

35. Ibid., 118.

36. Shafir, *Gazeta i derevnia.* The main results of his study came out in 1923; this and all further citations are from the 1924 reprint, which has some additional chapters, none of which are referred to here.

37. Group readings were conducted by having one of the participants read an article (which in some cases appeared to be selected on the spot), during the course of which both the reader and the listener-participants would discuss the meaning of individual words, phrases, and sentences.

38. Shafir, *Gazeta i derevnia,* 15.

39. For the present discussion, Shafir's book is of interest as much as a historical document as it is a contemporary sociological study. Despite its loose methodology (by current standards), it gave rise to a lively debate over the form, function, and future of public discourse that lasted well through the 1920s. Contemporaries viewed Shafir's data with more than "purely linguistic" concern. The newspaper, as the chief mouthpiece of the emerging Soviet state, bore a heavy political and ideological function. It is within the context of this larger issue of state building that these rural responses to the emerging language of state acquire interpretive validity and import.

40. "Element," "categorically," *gubernia zemel'noe upravlenie* ("*gubernia* land bureau"), *sel'skokhoziaistvennaia mashina* ("farm machine"), *gosudarstvennyi sel'skokhozaistvennyi sklad* ("state agricultural storage facility") (Shafir, *Gazeta i derevnia*). All further citations to Shafir's work appear parenthetically in the text and refer to his 1924 expanded edition.

41. Following Michel de Certeau, they can often be seen as re-readings, or "tactics," rather than misreadings, executed in the fashion of guerrilla warfare on the part of a population engaged in a lopsided struggle against the dominant ideology of the state (*The Practice of Everyday Life* [Berkeley: University of California Press, 1984], esp. 1–42).

42. Ernst Cassirer, *The Myth of the State* (New Haven, Conn.: Yale University Press, 1946), 45.

43. One should also resist presumptions of widespread political activism on the part of the peasantry in the civil war. As Leopold H. Haimson writes, "While the peasants did display an occasional willingness to fight and die to defend their own interests and way of life, they did not, by and large, articulate any conception of a political and social order encompassing other groups of the body politic, nor indeed any aspirations to rule it. What they did act out was a profound urge to be left alone." "Civil War and the Problem of Social Identities in Early Twentieth-Century Russia," in Koenker, Rosenberg, and Suny, eds., *Party, State, and Society in the Russian Civil War*, 44–45.

44. William Sewell offers a note of caution against overestimating the power of popular resistance: "It is important to remember that much cultural practice is concentrated in and around powerful institutional nodes—including religions, communications media, business corporations, and, most spectacularly, states. These institutions, which tend to be relatively large in scale, centralized, and wealthy, are all cultural actors; their agents make continuous use of their considerable resources in efforts to order meanings. Studies of culture need to pay at least as much attention to such sites of concentrated cultural practice as to the dispersed sites of resistance that currently predominate in the literature" ("Concept(s) of Culture," 55–56). James C. Scott himself notes the only "marginal effects over the state of things" that such acts of resistance have—not to mention the fact that the peasantry does not have a monopoly on these weapons (*Weapons of the Weak: Everyday Forms of Peasant Resistance* [New Haven, Conn.: Yale University Press, 1985], 29–30).

45. For an excellent discussion of this phenomenon, see B. I. Kolonitskii, "'Revolutionary Names': Russian Personal Names and Political Consciousness in the 1920s and 1930s," *Revolutionary Russia* 6, no. 2 (1993): 210–28.

46. Surnames listed are derived, in order, from the Russian words for "May," "October," "Lenin," "machine," "combine," and "fighter." The source for all of the name changes mentioned here is A. M. Selishchev, "Smena familii i lichnykh imen," in *Trudy po znakovym sistemam 5: Pamiati Vladimira Iakovlevicha Proppa* (Tartu, 1971), 493–500.

47. Surnames derived, in order, from the Russian words for "dog," "cow," "rat," "cockroach," "savage," "scoundrel," "fool," "fat," "saliva," "navel *[pup]*," "coolie wench," "varmint wench," and "blabbermouth wench." Selishchev also documents the common practice of discarding surnames that had become politically incorrect (e.g., *Kulak, Bogach, Zhandarmov, Arkhangel'skii, Bogov, Voskresenskii, Moliboga, Monakhov* [derived from, in order, "rich peasant," "rich man," "gendarme," "archangel," "God," "Resurrection," "pray-to-God," "monk"]).

48. The first surnames listed are derived from names of Russian writers or fictional characters (Pushkin, Tolstoy, Onegin) and geographical references (Neva, *gora* ["mountain"], Amur, Urals). In the "before —> after" examples, Anis'ia Khliupina rejects a surname evocative of "sloshing" or "slogging" (e.g., through the mud) for one that recalls a pine forest (acquiring a more classical, high-society given name for good measure), a "self-made fool" becomes "the polar one," and "Chickenman" becomes "Eagleton."

49. I. E. Babel', "Moi pervyi gus" (1923), in *Konarmiia* (1928), in *Detstvo i drugie rasskazy* (Jerusalem: Biblioteka-Alia, 1979), 132. English translations here and

in subsequent quotes appearing in this section, come, with minor modifications, from Walter Morison, trans. and ed., *Isaac Babel: The Collected Stories* (New York: Penguin, 1955), 76. Isaak Emmanuilovich Babel' (1894–1940), best known for his prose fiction, served as a war correspondent and propagandist during the civil war, where he gathered the bulk of the material for the *Red Cavalry* tales, most of which were published separately in various literary journals between 1923–1925. Though recognized broadly as among the more talented Soviet writers in the 1920s, Babel' came under increasing criticism in the more restrictive literary and political climate of the 1930s and was ultimately arrested and shot, allegedly for being "an agent for French and Austrian intelligence." *Russkie pisateli 20 veka: Biograficheskii slovar'* (Moscow: Nauchnoe izdatel'stvo "Bol'shaia rossiiskaia entsiklopediia," Izdatel'stvo "Randevu-AM," 2000), 58–60.

50. As in many other spheres, Lenin was used as an ideal model for various interests in the domain of language—a point that will be addressed at greater length in chapter 3. See also Yuri K. Shcheglov, "Some Themes and Archetypes in Babel's *Red Cavalry*," *Slavic Review* 53 (1994): 658.

51. S. Budennyi, "Babizm Babelia iz *Krasnoi novi*'," *Oktiabr'* 3 (1924): 196. For a counterargument, see V. Veshchnev's commentary in "Poeziia banditizma," *Molodaia gvardiia* 7/8 (1924): 274–80. Also note A. Voronskii's response to such accusations in his article "Babel', Seifullina," *Krasnaia nov'* 5 (1924), esp. 284–90.

52. See Figes, "Russian Revolution of 1917," 323–45.

53. Shafir, *Gazeta i derevnia*, 63.

54. Ibid., 63. Emphasis in original.

55. A. A. Zhdanov, [Opening speech to the First All-Union Congress of Soviet Writers], *Pervyi vsesoiuznyi s"ezd sovetskikh pisatelei, 1934. Stenograficheskii otchet* (1934; rpt., Moscow: Sovetskii pisatel', 1990), 4; Robin, *Socialist Realism*. Katerina Clark elaborates on this "dual modality" and its manifestations in socialist-realist fiction in *The Soviet Novel*, esp. 36–45.

56. Shafir's study is referred to by several of the speakers and comes to serve as a shorthand reference to the problem.

57. Detailed transcripts of the conference appeared in *Pravda*, 17–28 Nov. 1923.

58. L. S. Sosnovskii (1886–1937), a journalist and government official, was active in the revolutionary movement beginning in 1903. He was a prominent figure in Soviet journalism and state affairs in the early 1920s, until 1927, when he was stripped of his party membership for active opposition to Stalin's programs. He was sentenced to death for antiparty activities in 1937.

59. *Pravda*, 21 Nov. 1923.

60. *Pravda*, 22 Nov. 1923.

61. Note that the "working class" is reduced to the position of genitive quantifier in the phrase "party of the working class."

62. Some effort was made to gauge language of different newspapers to better speak to their intended reading audiences. See Smith, *Language and Power in the Creation of the USSR*, 39.

63. *Pravda*, 22 Nov. 1923. This position on public discourse closely resembles Bukharin's general attitude toward the New Economic Policy. See Stephen F. Cohen, *Bukharin and the Bolshevik Revolution: A Political Biography, 1888–1938* (New York: A. A. Knopf, 1973).

64. *Pravda*, 23 Nov. 1923.

65. Edward Shils, "Center and Periphery," in *The Constitution of Society: Essays in Macrosociology* (Chicago: University of Chicago Press, 1982), 93–109.

2: THE REVOLUTIONARY VOICE AND THE RESURRECTION OF MEANING

1. On the essentially utopian nature of attempts to create new modes of writing, Roland Barthes writes: "Feeling permanently guilty of its own solitude, it [literary writing] is none the less an imagination eagerly desiring a felicity of words, it hastens towards a dreamed-of language whose freshness, by a kind of ideal anticipation, might portray the perfection of some new Adamic world where language would no longer be alienated. The proliferation of modes of writing brings a new Literature into being in so far as the latter invents its language only in order to be a project: Literature becomes the Utopia of language." *Writing Degree Zero* (1953), in *Writing Degree Zero and Elements of Semiology*, trans. Annette Lavers and Colin Smith (Boston: Beacon Press, 1970), 88.

2. It is no accident that what I call the "revolutionary" voice in the language debates bears close resemblance to attitudes toward art commonly found among representatives of Russian modernism. This is especially true when this latter term is understood, as Victor Erlich proposes, in the broader sense of "a discernible sensibility or impulse underlying and informing various disparate, indeed conflicting, literary currents of the modern era"—key features of which include an "awareness of a profound crisis, of a radical discontinuity with the past," a recognition of an "improbable, disturbing fragmented world," a "cult of novelty," a sense of "dislocation," "turmoil," "fragmentation," and a penchant for "blurring the traditional boundaries between art and reality" (*Modernism and Revolution: Russian Literature in Transition* [Cambridge, Mass.: Harvard University Press, 1994], 2–8). My "revolutionary voice," however, is more specifically related to the concern its representatives demonstrate for the social impact that language has on the reshaping of state and citizens. Hence, although writers such as Andrei Bely and Velimir Khlebnikov are important voices of modernism, their contribution to the revolutionary model of public discourse is less directly significant compared, for instance, to Vladimir Maiakovskii's. Given its primarily aesthetic foundations, modernism would likewise be an unlikely label used in conjunction with the likes of Trotsky and Vinokur—two of the more interesting representatives of my "revolutionary voice."

3. G. O. Vinokur, "Iazyk gazety," in *Kul'tura iazyka*, 188–89 (first published as "Gazetnyi iazyk," *Lef* 2 [1924]: 117–40).

4. G. O. Vinokur, "O revoliutsionnoi frazeologii," *Lef* 2 (1923): 108, 110.

5. Ibid., 110.

6. Ibid., 111. Cf. Shklovskii, "Voskreshenie slova"; and "Iskusstvo kak priem," in *Sbornik po teorii poeticheskogo iazyka*, vol. 2 (Petrograd, 1917), 3–14.

7. Vinokur, "O revoliutsionnoi frazeologii," 112.

8. The emphasis here is original and quite typical of the declamatory style of the *Lef* critics. Vinokur, "O revoliutsionnoi frazeologii," 113–14.

9. "Iazyk Nep'a," in *Kul'tura iazyka*, 125–26.

10. "Iazyk Nep'a," 128, 139.

11. Gregory Freidin discusses the tradition of the poet as an object of verbal,

public emulation in Russian culture in *A Coat of Many Colors: Osip Mandelshtam and His Mythologies of Self-Presentation* (Berkeley: University of California Press, 1987), esp. chap. 1.

12. *[Sdelat' iazyk ulitsy . . . neizbezhnym stremleniem preodolet' kosnoiazychie massy]*. Vinokur, "Futuristy—stroiteli iazyka," 206–7.

13. Ibid., 207–8. Emphasis in original. A similar though less guarded view of the role of poetry in revitalizing the language of the streets can be found in the writings of the avant-garde literary critic, Boris Arvatov, who viewed poetry as the "masked laboratory of the living language" and, in the hands of "the enemies," "a weapon for the distortion of speech" (B. I. Arvatov, "K marksistskoi poetike," in *Sotsiologicheskaia poetika* [Moscow: Federatsiia, 1928], 24–25).

14. In fact, Vinokur's declaration about the insignificance of the difference between "poetic" and "practical language," if anything, was more pronounced in his later discussions of the issue. Cf. "Rechevaia praktika Futuristov," where he notes: "In recent years no too few swords have been crossed in order to prove that the system of poetic language differs at root from practical language. To a large extent I consider this issue an idle one; in any case we have observed here just the opposite: between the word in general and the poetic word, we found several points of contiguity which even allowed us to evaluate poetry itself from the point of view of the technical and practical possibilities potentially contained within it" (304). For an extended discussion of this issue, see M. I. Shapir's commentary on the reprint of "Futuristy—stroiteli iazyka," in *Filologicheskie issledovaniia: lingvistika i poetika* (Moscow: Nauka, 1990), 263–71.

15. Vinokur, "O revoliutsionnoi frazeologii," 117.

16. Ibid., 117. With equal emphasis, Vinokur asserted the crucial position of the philologist in the process of establishing a "reading culture" in an article on that theme: "*Philology has enormous and inexhaustible cultural-educational significance.* Philological studies train one to read in a manner in which *no doubt remains as to the meaning of that which has been read*" (emphasis in original). "Kul'tura chteniia," in *Kul'tura iazyka*, 335.

17. Here I will concentrate on the articles by V. B. Shklovskii, B. M. Eikhenbaum, Iu. N. Tynianov, L. P. Iakubinskii, and B. V. Tomashevskii, though B. Kazanskii was also a contributor and sympathetic to the OPOIaZ group. In general, I prefer to avoid the term "formalism" in this discussion, first, because it means and meant different things to different people (see, for example, Eikhenbaum, "Vokrug voprosa o 'Formalistakh'," *Pechat' i revoliutsiia* 5 [1924]: 1–12; also see Peter Steiner, *Russian Formalism: A Metapoetics* [Ithaca, N.Y.: Cornell University Press, 1984], chap. 1) and, second, because it clouds important distinctions in attitudes and focuses on language held by the OPOIaZ group and the Moscow Linguistics Circle and of their individual members (see Toddes and Chudakova, "Pervyi russkii perevod *Kursa obshchei lingvistiki*," 229–49).

18. Several other contemporaries wrote books or articles on Lenin's language (see A. Kruchenykh, *Iazyk Lenina: Odinnadtsat' priemov Leninskoi rechi* [Moscow: Vserossiiskii Soiuz Poetov, 1925]; and Aleksandr Finkel', *O iazyke i stile V. I. Lenina*, vyp. 1 [Moscow: Proletarii, 1925]). A report in the "Chronicle" section of the monthly journal *The Press and Revolution* likewise notes the plans for collection on Lenin's language through the Institute of Linguistics and the History of Literature, with Selishchev, Ushakov, Shor, and others contributing (*Pechat' i revoliutsiia* 3

[1925]: 312–13). Descriptions also commonly appeared in contemporary language textbooks (see Ia. Shafir, *Voprosy gazetnoi kul'tury* [Moscow: Gosizdat., 1927], 156–68). There is little doubt that the journal's editors saw the discussion's publication as politically beneficial. It is interesting to note, however, that, although most of those who took part in the language issue used Lenin's comments *about* language in their own defense, few besides this collection of writers subjected Lenin's language itself to a critical stylistic analysis. In a sense, the *Lef* discussions of Lenin's language legitimated two of Vinokur's basic presumptions at once: first, that the differences between "poetic" and "practical" language were much hazier and less significant than their underlying similarities; and, second, that the language of the great "poets" (here, orator-poet) provided solid stylistic models for new directions in public discourse. On a deeper level, of course, they sought to give legitimacy to a third assumption of Vinokur's—that the philologist enjoyed a privileged position of power by virtue of his or her ability to rationalize, organize, and generally "make sense" out of the complex and chaotic discursive environment of contemporary life.

19. Boris Tomashevskii, "Konstruktsiia tezisov," *Lef* 1 (1924): 140–41. In a separate article, Lev Iakubinskii also addressed the growing significance of public speaking in Soviet society and the acute need for a coherently organized discipline for training future participants in public life. "O snizhenii vysokogo stilia u Lenina," *Lef* 1 (1924): 72.

20. Tomashevskii went so far as to declare that "sociopolitical works," typified by the verbal production of Lenin, constituted "the most significant sphere of contemporary prose." "Konstruktsiia tezisov," 141.

21. Iakubinskii, "O snizhenii vysokogo stilia u Lenina," 72.

22. Viktor Shklovskii, "Lenin, kak dekanonizator," *Lef* 1 (1924): 55.

23. Their contemporary E. I. Zamiatin (1884–1937), both a modernist writer and former Bolshevik, elaborated on the relationship between revolution and energy in his article "On Literature, Revolution, Entropy, and Other Matters" (1923) (in *A Soviet Heretic: Essays by Yevgeny Zamyatin*, trans. and ed. Mirra Ginsburg [Chicago: University of Chicago Press, 1970], 107–12).

24. Shklovskii, "Lenin, kak dekanonizator," 56. His *use* of language notwithstanding, Lenin's own *attitudes* toward it and the issue of standards were much less revolutionary than the *Lef* analyses might imply, as will be discussed in chap. 5.

25. Iu. N. Tynianov, "Slovar' Lenina-polemista," *Lef* 1 (1924): 98–99.

26. Ibid., 91, 89. The Russian word *byt* has no direct equivalent in English, but it invokes something along the lines of "the mundane reality of everyday life."

27. Ibid., 102. Emphasis in original.

28. For a more literary discussion of the "laying bare of the device" *(obnazhenie priema)*, see Viktor Shklovskii, *O teorii prozy* (Moscow: Federatsiia, 1929; rpt., Ann Arbor, Mich.: Ardis, 1985).

29. Tynianov, "Slovar' Lenina-polemista," 96.

30. Like Vinokur, Eikhenbaum likens Lenin in this respect to the futurist writers ("Osnovnye stilevye tendentsii v rechi Lenina," 70 *Lef* 1 [1924]: 57–70).

31. Iakubinskii, "O snizhenii vysokogo stilia u Lenina," 76–80.

32. Tynianov, "Slovar' Lenina-polemista," 106.

33. As did many of the leading critics and writers of the day, Shklovskii participated actively in various aspects of popular education, especially the training of

novice writers. See, for example, his writing manual, *Tekhnika pisatel'skogo remesla* (Moscow: Molodaia Gvardiia, 1928); see also the collection of similarly aimed articles by contemporary writers: Andrei Belyi et al., *Kak my pishem?* (1930; rpt., Moscow: Kniga, 1989).

34. L. D. Trotskii, *Voprosy kul'turnoi raboty* (Moscow: Gosizdat., 1924); and *Voprosy byta: epokha "kul'turnichestva" i ee zadachi* (Moscow: Gosizdat., 1925).

35. Katerina Clark offers an insightful discussion of Trotsky's views on language in *Petersburg*, 207–12.

36. Trotskii, "Zadachi voennoi pechati. (Rech' na s"ezde rabotnikov voennoi pechati 10 maia 1924 g.)," in *Voprosy kul'turnoi raboty*, 20. "Leninizm i bibliotechnaia rabota. (Rech' na 1–om Vsesoiuznom s"ezde bibliotekarei 3 iiulia 1924 g.)," in ibid., 100.

37. Trotskii, "Leninizm i bibliotechnaia rabota," 89.

38. Trotskii, "Rabkor i ego kul'turnaia rol' (Rech' na konferentsii Sokol'nicheskogo raikoma, posviashchennoi vypusku raionnykh kursov rabkorov i vystavke stennykh gazet)," in *Voprosy kul'turnoi raboty*, 53–54.

39. Ibid., 55.

40. Trotskii, "Zadachi voennoi pechati," 34–35.

41. See also Trotsky's comment on the ease with which citizens (himself included) repeated revolutionary slogans "almost automatically," in "Leninizm i bibliotechnaia rabota," 100.

42. Trotskii, "Gazeta i ee chitatel'," in *Voprosy byta*, 28.

43. Ibid., 27. It is an attitude that later in the 1920s and early 1930s became one of the main sources for broad attacks on Trotsky and "Trotskyism," chiefly from proponents of what I refer to here as the "party-state" model of public discourse.

44. Trotskii, "Rabkor i ego kul'turnaia rol'," 52.

45. Trotskii, "Gazeta i ee chitatel'," 25.

46. Ibid., 29.

47. Trotskii, "Zadachi voennoi pechati," 42–43. Shklovskii takes the idea one step further when he writes, "A formula, when it appears in the agitational work of Lenin's, is organized such that it won't become fixed" ("Lenin, kak dekanonizator," 55).

48. Trotskii, "Leninizm i bibliotechnaia rabota," 103.

49. See, for example, Trotsky's attack on the misguided perception that *Rosta*, the central news agency, had a "dictatorship over information" and functioned as a "legislator of style." ("Zadachi voennoi pechati," 23.)

50. For a thoughtful discussion of the psychology of crowds, see Elias Canetti, *Crowds and Power*, trans. Carol Stewart (New York: Penguin, 1981).

51. Max Weber, *Economy and Society: An Outline of Interpretive Sociology*, ed. Guenther Roth and Claus Wittich, 2 vols. (Berkeley: University of California Press, 1978), 1:243. Weber describes "charisma" as "a certain quality of an individual personality by virtue of which he is considered extraordinary and treated as endowed with supernatural, superhuman, or at least specifically exceptional powers or qualities." He explains that "the power of charisma rests upon the belief in revelation and heroes, upon the conviction that certain manifestations—whether they be of a religious, ethical, artistic, scientific, political or other kind—are important and valu-

able; it rests upon 'heroism' of an ascetic, military, judicial, magical or whichever kind. Charismatic belief revolutionizes men 'from within' and shapes material and social conditions according to its revolutionary will" (1116).

52. Ibid., 2:1121.

53. The parallel between linguistic and political philosophy becomes still more compelling when considering that Stalin's response to Trotsky's doctrine, the idea of "socialism in one country," essentially paved the way for a more trenchant state (and linguistic) bureaucracy. See Trotsky, *Permanent Revolution*, trans. Max Shachtman (New York: Pioneer Publishers, 1931); and Isaac Deutscher, *The Prophet Unarmed: Trotsky, 1921–1929* (London: Oxford University Press, 1959).

54. That is, assuming they retain their ties to the charismatic source. In his speech to the military correspondents, Trotsky describes the potential scenario of the newly enlightened Red Army soldier returning to his home village and, owing to his isolation, transforming into a *kulak* much more terrible than the illiterate, icon-toting *kulak* of traditional Russia, namely, a "Europeanized kulak" ("Zadachi voennoi pechati," 29–30). The image attests to the degree of faith Trotsky placed in the transformational power of popular education as well as the degree to which he viewed this as a process of modernization.

55. Trotskii, "Rabkor i ego kul'turnaia rol'," 75, 58–59.

56. In addition to Vinokur's discussions cited earlier, see Boris Arvatov, "Sintaksis Maiakovskogo," *Pechat' i revoliutsiia* 1 (1923): 84–102 (also the source for the second epigraph to this chapter).

57. Unless otherwise noted, all parenthetical citations refer to volumes and page numbers from Vladimir Maiakovskii, *Polnoe sobranie sochinenii v trinadtsati tomakh* (Moscow: Gosudarstvennoe izdatel'stvo khudozhestvennoi literatury, 1955).

58. Tynianov, "Literaturnyi fakt," in *Arkhaisty i novatory*, 5–29.

59. E.g., "Oda revoliutsii" (2:12–13).

60. D. El'kina, N. Bugoslavskaia and A. Kurskaia, *Doloi negramotnost'. Bukvar' dlia vzroslykh* (Moscow: Izd. Vserossiiskoi Chrezvychainoi Komissii po likvidatsii bezgramotnosti, 1920), 7. The affinities between modernist language innovation and children's language play are compelling but remain understudied (for a brief discussion with regard to *zaum*, see Janecek, *Zaum*, 21–26). It is not coincidental that many of the writers with roots in this movement at some point turned to children's literature as a creative outlet—Maiakovskii, Iurii Olesha, and Daniil Kharms, to name only a few.

61. Among the more metalinguistic *Rosta* texts was the following jingle cajoling workers to use the language of guns and cannons in response to proposals of entente: "*Rabochie,/ zabud'te diplomaticheskii iazyk./ Vash iazyk—/ pushechnyi zyk!/ Razgovory—erunda,/ razgovory—nul'!/ Iazyk rabochego—/iazyk pul'!/ Rech' odna v polozhen'i takom—/ ne iazykom vertet',/ a shtykom!*" (3:107 [1920]) ["Workers, forget the diplomatic language. Your language is the roar of the cannon! Conversations are nonsense, conversations are zilch! The worker's language is the language of bullets! Just one thing can be said in such a situation: twirl your sword, not your tongue!"].

62. Quoted in *V. Maiakovskii v vospominaniiakh sovremennikov.* Seriia literaturnykh memuarov (Moscow: Gosudarstvennoe izdatel'stvo khudozhestvennoi literatury, 1963), 187.

63. *V. Maiakovskii v vospominaniiakh sovremennikov*, 196. One of the more detailed memoir accounts of the energy and creativity Maiakovskii devoted to the ROSTA windows comes from Rita Rait, also in ibid., 236–78.

64. During the period of the NEP, Maiakovskii applied his poetic voice and authority to the realm of advertising, writing text for commercial concerns that included department stores, cigarette companies, chewing gum, and even baby pacifiers.

65. *Novyi Lef* 3 (1928): 2–3.

66. O. V. Gzovskaia, "Moi vstrechi s poetom," in *V. Maiakovskii v vospominaniiakh sovremennikov*, 156.

67. Rita Rait, *Tol'ko vospominaniia*, quoted in *V. Maiakovskii v vospominaniiakh sovremennikov*, 257.

68. I. V. Il'inskii, "S Maiakovskim," in *V. Maiakovskii v vospominaniiakh sovremennikov*, 289. Iurii Tynianov attested to the oratorical might of Maiakovskii's verse by citing the poet as a modern-day example of his thesis regarding the ode's status as an oratorical genre. See "Oda kak oratorskii zhanr," in *Arkhaisty i novatory*, 48–86.

69. According to Goriaeva, Maiakovskii was among the more noteworthy writers to perform their works on the live airwaves, making more than fifteen appearances on the popular program "Radio Newspaper" ("Radiogazeta") between 1925 and 1930 (*Politicheskaia tsenzura v SSSR*, 94–95).

70. For a critique of Fedor Gladkov's *Cement*, see "Podozhdem obviniat' poetov," 12:66–80. On worn-out tropes, see "Stikhi s primechaniiami," 12:171–75; and "Vystuplenie na dispute 'Lef ili Blef?'" 12:325–26. Maiakovskii saw more promise in the germinating literature of the *rabkory* and factory workers than in that of the more established "proletarian" writers such as Gladkov, Dem'ian Bedny, Aleksandr Serafimovich, and Iurii Libedinskii (e.g., 12:268, 288).

3: AWKWARD AMBIGUITIES OF THE SOVIET VOX POPULI

1. V. Astrov, "Kak ne nuzhno pisat' peredovuiu," *Krasnyi zhurnalist* 2–3 (1920): 263–64; S. Smirnov, "Poproshche," *Krasnyi zhurnalist* 4–5–6 (1920): 247–50; Kh. Rakovskii, "Desiat' zapovedei rabochei gazety," *Zhurnalist* 6 (1923): 23–26; Ia. Shafir, "Iazyk gazety," *Zhurnalist* 9 (1924): 8–12; V. N—skii, "O chem i kak pisat'," *Zhurnalist* 14 (1924): 41; M. Gus, Iu. Zagorianskii, and N. Kaganovich, *Iazyk gazety* (Moscow: Rabotnik prosveshcheniia, 1926); F. Raskol'nikov, "Rabkory i proletarskaia literatura," *Na postu* 1(6) (1925): 105–12. Brooks identifies this negative attitude toward the discourse of the old intelligentsia as one of the defining features of the "new intelligentsia" and their prerevolutionary predecessors ("Competing Modes of Popular Discourse," 71–81). In his study of Marxist philosophy in the Russian revolution, Igal Halfin argues that the anti-intelligentsia strain became dominant, though not unqualified, in postrevolutionary Bolshevik discourse (*From Darkness to Light*, 149–204, 394–99).

2. Shafir, *Voprosy gazetnoi kul'tury*, 129–30. Shafir went so far as to claim that bourgeois writers were incapable of re-creating the language of the masses, that all attempts at doing so came across as false and contrived ("Iazyk gazety," 12).

3. Shafir, *Voprosy gazetnoi kul'tury*, 166.

4. RGASPI, f. 17, op. 60, ed. khr. 935, ll. 21–22.

5. J. Alexander Ogden provides a thorough exegesis of the term "voice of the people" in Russian culture and Western civilization in his research on peasant poets

in Russia—tracing its more reverential link to national identity back to the German thinker, Johann Gottfried Herder. See, for example, Ogden's "Romantic National-ism and Peasant Poets: The Search for a 'Voice of the People'" (paper delivered at the Southern Conference on Slavic Studies, Daytona Beach, Fla., March 2002).

6. Igal Halfin documents a similar plasticity with regard to notions of "prole-tariat" in his discussion of the "language of class statistics" in Soviet universities (*From Darkness to Light*, 246–55).

7. *Khlyst. Sekty, literatura i revoliutsiia* (Moscow: Novoe literaturnoe obozrenie, 1998), 4.

8. *Krasnaia nov'* 1–13 (1921–1923). Factors contributing to this new emphasis included the lingering prominence of Socialist Revolutionary sentiments among Russian intellectuals, modernist literary trends exploring alternative voices, and the social, political, and economic realities of war communism.

9. E.g., A. Semenovskii, "Sovremennaia chastushka," *Krasnaia nov'* 1 (1921): 53–61; Vsev. Ivanov, "Altaiskie skazki," *Krasnaia nov'* 2 (1921): 3–11; L. Seifullina, "Muzhitskii skaz o Lenine," *Krasnaia nov'* 1 (1924): 162–69; Vasilii Kniazev, *Sovre-mennye chastushki, 1917–1922* (Moscow-Petrograd: GIZ, 1924); Khrebes, *Sovremen-naia derevnia v chastushkakh i pesenkakh revoliutsionnoi molodezhi* (Moscow-Leningrad: Molodaia gvardiia, 1925). For ethnographic studies, see *Sibirskaia zhivaia starina. Etnograficheskii sbornik*, vols. 1–2 (Irkutsk: Vostochno-Sibirskii Otdel Russkogo Geograficheskogo Obshchestva, 1923); V. G. Tan-Bogoraz, ed. *Revoliutsiia v derevne. Ocherki* (Moscow-Leningrad: Krasnaia nov', 1924); and Tan-Bogoraz, ed., *Staryi i novyi byt*.

10. *Narod na voine: Frontovye zapisi* (Kiev: Izd. Izdatel'skogo Podotdela Komiteta Iugo-Zap. Fronta Vseros. Zemskogo Soiuza, 1917); *Narod na voine*, Bib-lioteka sovremennikov (Moscow: Novaia Moskva, 1923). Fedorchenko organized her second volume around the theme of revolution and provided no preface or in-troduction to the only complete edition of it published during her lifetime (*Narod na voine. T. II: Revoliutsiia* [Moscow: Nikitinskie subbotniki, 1925]). The third vol-ume, dedicated to the civil war, appeared only in excerpted form in journal publi-cations (*Novyi mir* 3–4, 6 [1927]; *Oktiabr'* 6 [1927]; *Ogonek* 27 [1927]). It was pub-lished in full only in 1983 (*Literaturnoe nasledstvo*, vol. 93 [Moscow: Nauka, 1983]). All three volumes first appeared together, and in full, in 1990 (*Narod na voine* [Moscow: Sovetskii pisatel', 1990]). For thematic reasons, my discussion here will focus exclusively on the material from the third volume. I use her introduction to the first as it is the most detailed description of her methods of collection, and the one that led to substantial controversy several years later. Her introduction to the civil war material (in *Novyi mir* 3 [1927]) makes similar (though less detailed) claims, and the contents are nearly identical in structure, style, and voice.

11. Fedorchenko, *Narod na voine. Frontovye zapisi*, 3. Her even briefer intro-duction to the journal publication of excerpts from vol. 3 invites similar assump-tions, though it offers more by way of categorization of her "subjects": "All the ma-terial for this book [consists of] conversations about selves and others, fates, facts, tales, [and] songs collected by me between 1917 and 1922 . . . in Ukraine, Novorossiia, the northern Caucasus, and the Crimea. Here are [represented] various insurgents, bandits, greens, reds, whites, and a variety of others." *Novyi mir* 3 (1927): 82 (cited in N. A. Trifonov, "Introduction" to Sof'ia Fedorchenko, *Narod na voine. Kniga tret'ia: grazhdanskaia voina* [*Literaturnaia nasledstvo* 93:9]). After the

early success of her "fieldnotes," Sof'ia Zakharovna Fedorchenko (1880–1959) dedicated the remainder of her life to writing literature (children's literature and historical novels), but the later scandal surrounding *Narod na voine* led to a significant drop in her literary output (and reputation) (*Russkie pisateli 20 veka,* 713–14).

12. Fedorchenko, *Narod na voine: Frontovye zapisi* (1917), 3.

13. In a 1928 *Izvestiia* article acrimoniously titled "Fal'sifikatory i mistifikatory—ne literatory" ("Falsifiers and Mystifiers are not Literati"), Bednyi lashed out at Fedorchenko for leading her audience astray and misrepresenting the sacred *glas naroda,* and he declared her books "not worth a brass farthing" *(lomanogo grosha ne stoit).* More levelheaded reactions from the likes of Maxim Gorky and Kornei Chukovskii went unheeded, and Fedorchenko's collection gradually disappeared from the public eye. For a complete account of the events leading up to the revelation and the ensuing scandal, see N. Trifonov's introductory article, "Nespravedlivo zabytaia kniga," in Fedorchenko, *Narod na voine* (1990), 10.

14. It did elicit some questions of ethnographic authenticity from certain professional ethnographers suspicious of her lack of attributions. For references to both, see V. I. Glotser, "K istorii knigi S. Fedorchenko *Narod na voine," Russkaia literatura* 1 (1973): 148–55.

15. Barthes sheds light on the power of the preterite tense, used seldomly in the Fedorchenko narratives, in bringing order to reality: "Allowing as it does an ambiguity between temporality and causality, it calls for a sequence of events, that is for an intelligible Narrative. This is why it is the ideal instrument for every construction of a world; it is the unreal time of cosmogonies, myths, History and Novels. It presupposes a world which is constructed, elaborated, self-sufficient, reduced to significant lines, and not one which has been sent sprawling before us, for us to take or leave. Behind the preterite there always lurks a demiurge, a God or a reciter. The world is not unexplained since it is told like a story; each one of its accidents is but a circumstance, and the preterite is precisely this operative sign whereby the narrator reduces the exploded reality to a slim and pure logos, without density, without volume, without spread, and whose sole function is to unite as rapidly as possible a cause and an end" (*Writing Degree Zero,* 30–31). In Fedorchenko's narratives, where the preterite rarely appears, reality appears in all its haphazard "multiplicity of experiences," offering neither narrator nor reader even a hint of intelligibly constructed order.

16. L. M. Kleinbort, *Ocherki narodnoi literatury (1880–1923). Belletristy* (Leningrad, 1924), 119.

17. Ibid.

18. Kleinbort attributed this paradox to the beginning phases of the proletarian writers' movement, and he envisioned the worker-writer eventually being able to do both well at once (ibid., 162). The perceived opposition between the "good" and the "beautiful," which had strong prerevolutionary roots, would reappear in full force during the debates over socialist realism in 1931–1932.

19. G. Seryi, "Blizhaishaia zadacha," in *Proletariat i literatura: Sbornik statei* (Leningrad: Gosizdat., 1925), 127. The adjective *seryi* in Russian means "gray." The poet A. I. Bezymenskii similarly claimed that the first step to the successful literary depiction of the working class was the acquisition of the worker's language ("O tvorcheskikh putiakh," *Na postu* 1[5] [1924]: 121–28).

20. For a discussion of the "Smithy" group, see Herman Ermolaev's *Soviet Literary Theories, 1917–1934: The Genesis of Socialist Realism,* University of California

Publications in Modern Philology, vol. 69 (Berkeley: University of California Press, 1963), 19–26.

21. L. M. Kleinbort, *Russkii chitatel'-rabochii. Po materialam, sobrannym avtorom* (Leningrad: Izd. Len. Gub. Soveta Prof. Soiuzov, 1925), 16.

22. Ibid., 257.

23. The terminological elasticity outlined here mirrors the constant need, noted by Kotkin and others, to "reinvent" class-based politics in the 1920s and earlier, as "no existing working class anywhere had the kind of characteristics, especially the mental outlook, that the Bolsheviks deemed 'natural' for such a class" (Kotkin, *Magnetic Mountain*, 490n.13). See also Fitzpatrick, "New Perspectives on the Civil War," 12. In a compelling twist to the "linguistic turn," however, Figes and Kolonitskii argue that the very ambiguity of the basic terms of class also gave them the flexibility necessary for serving as a viable and lasting discourse of power (*Interpreting the Russian Revolution*, 104–26).

24. A. Kraiskii, *Chto nado znat' nachinaiushchemu pisateliu* (Leningrad: Krasnaia gazeta, 1927), 38. The recommendation here to introduce them into authorial speech, presented as a further means of empowerment, is particularly noteworthy in light of the numerous contemporary works that, in doing so, wound up bringing the very "authority" of the implied author into question.

25. "Neitralitet ili rukovodstvo? (K discussii o politike RKP v khudozhestvennoi literature)," *Pravda*, 19 Feb. 1924, reprinted in T. Gromova, ed., *V tiskakh ideologii: Antologiia literaturno-politicheskikh dokumentov, 1917–1927* (Moscow: Knizhnaia palata, 1992), 202–7.

26. G. Lelevich, "Partiinaia politika v iskusstve," *Na postu* 4 (1923): 40.

27. A. V. Lunacharskii, "Nashi zadachi v oblasti khudozhestvennoi zhizni," *Krasnaia nov'* 1 (1921): 146–57 (quoted from Gromova, ed., *V tiskakh ideologii*, 88, 87, 90).

28. Ia. Iakovlev, "O 'proletarskoi kul'ture' i Proletkul'te" (1922) (quoted from Gromova, ed., *V tiskakh ideologii*, 124).

29. Gromova, ed., *V tiskakh ideologii*, 126.

30. Voronskii became editor of *Krasnaia nov'* upon its inception in 1921 and remained there until 1927, when he was ousted for what by then became perceived as ideological laxness. For an in-depth discussion of Voronskii and his journal, see Robert A. Maguire's *Red Virgin Soil: Soviet Literature in the 1920s* (Princeton, N.J.: Princeton University Press, 1968).

31. A. K. Voronskii, "O proletarskom iskusstve i khudozhestvennoi politike nashei partii," *Krasnaia nov'* 7 (1923): 257–76 (quoted here from Gromova, ed., *V tiskakh ideologii*, 172–73).

32. Leon Trotsky, "Proletarian Culture and Proletarian Art," in *Literature and Revolution* (New York: Russell & Russell, 1957), esp. 200–204.

33. Trotsky, *Literature and Revolution*, 57.

34. The term came to be used extremely fluidly in scope and levels of suspicion. Trotsky did not mention either Babel' or Seifullina, but these two were commonly so labeled in the broader discussions of contemporary literature.

35. Boris Pil'niak, *Golyi god. Roman* (Nikola-na-Posad'iakh: [published privately by the author], 1923).

36. Vsevolod Ivanov, "Bronepoezd No. 14-69," *Krasnaia nov'* 1 (1922): 75–124.

37. Lidiia Seifullina, "Peregnoi," *Sibirskie ogni* 5 (1922): 3–49; Seifullina,

"Virineia," *Krasnaia nov'* 4 (1924): 26–96. Her short piece entitled "Muzhitskii skaz o Lenine" features popular folk accounts of Lenin, all steeped in the colloquial language of a modern folktale.

38. See M. M. Zoshchenko, *Rasskazy Nazara Il'icha gospodina Sinebriukhova* (Petrograd, 1922).

39. The pejorative, abstracting suffix "*-shchina*" combined with the slang for the equivalent of a peasant "good ol' boy," or even "redneck" *(muzhik)*.

40. "K voprosu o politike RKP(b) v khudozhestvennoi literature" (9–10 May 1924) (quoted from Gromova, ed., *V tiskakh ideologii*, 247).

41. Gromova, ed., *V tiskakh ideologii*, 254.

42. Ibid., 225.

43. Richard Stites describes the *smychka* as "a kind of 'to the people' movement in the context of a revolutionary state—with all the strengths and distortions attendant upon it" *(Revolutionary Dreams*, 116).

44. Most prominent among the "peasant writers" were Sergei Esenin, Nikolai Kliuev, Sergei Klychkov, and Petr Oreshin. In the present discussion, I will concentrate on debates concerning the fellow-travelers for three reasons: first, they were the most productive prose writers of the day; second, the question of their role in contemporary literature occupied a central position in the literary debates; and, finally, it was the *poputchiki*, more than any other group, who most approximated in narrative style the popular and proletarian discourses identified at the outset of this chapter.

45. It should be noted that few of these writers were themselves of strictly peasant origin. Therefore, when used in reference to them, the notion of *smychka* carried more a figurative than a literal meaning, referring more to *style* than class origin.

46. Gromova, ed., *V tiskakh ideologii*, 228.

47. I. Vareikis, "O nashei linii v khudozhestvennoi literature i o proletkul'-takh," in *Voprosy kul'tury pri diktature proletariata* (Moscow, 1925) (quoted from Gromova, ed., *V tiskakh ideologii*, 349).

48. "O politike partii v oblasti khudozhestvennoi literatury (Rezoliutsiia TsK RKP[b] ot 18 iiunia 1925 g.)" (quoted from Gromova, ed., *V tiskakh ideologii*, 378). For a detailed catalog of the evolving policies toward literature in the political and literary culture of the 1920s and early 1930s, see Karl Eimermacher, *Politika i kul'-tura pri Lenine i Staline. 1917–1932* (Moscow: AIRO-XX, 1998).

49. Semen Pod"iachev, "Boliashchii," *Krasnaia nov'* 3 (1921): 3. All further references to this work will appear parenthetically in the text. Semion Pavlovich Pod"iachev (1866–1934) was born and raised in a poor family of former serfs from the Moscow provinces and received little formal education beyond his village school training. Discovered by Vladimir Korolenko in 1901, he began publishing his literary works (which filled more than eleven volumes by the end of his life), joined the Communist Party in 1918, and served on the executive committee of the Peasant Writers Union from 1926–1929 (*Russkie pisateli 20 veka*, 560–61).

50. Seifullina, "Peregnoi," 3–49. A native of western Siberia and daughter of a Russian Orthodox priest, Lidiia Nikolaevna Seifullina (1889–1954) was a staunch supporter of the Socialist-Revolutionary party after the February revolution but later renounced the S-Rs during the civil war. She worked as a librarian and village schoolteacher before dedicating herself entirely to writing, publishing numerous stories, short novels, and plays depicting life in the village under Soviet rule (*Russkie pisateli 20 veka*, 626–27). My choice of translations for Seifullina's short

novel, pronounced *hyu-mus,* refers to the organic mix of "partially or wholly de-cayed vegetable or animal matter that provides nutrients to plants and increases the ability of soil to retain water" (*American Heritage Dictionary of the English Language,* 3d ed.).

51. *Sovnarkom—Sovet Narodnykh Kommissarov* (The Council of People's Commissars); *ispolkom—ispolnitel'nyi komitet* (executive committee); *sovdepy—Sovet rabochikh, krest'ianskikh i krasnoarmeiskikh deputatov* (Council of workers, peasants, and Red Army deputies).

52. *Predsedatel' volostnogo ispol'nitel'nogo komiteta* (chairman of the *volost'* executive committee).

4: MODELS OF PROLETARIAN LANGUAGE ACQUISTION

1. For an excellent discussion of "proletarianization" and the cultivation of a "new intelligentsia" in the early Soviet universities, see Halfin, *From Darkness to Light,* chap. 4.

2. "Rezoliutsiia, predlozhennaia tov. Ia. Iakovlevym i priniataia Soveshchaniem pri Otdele pechati TsK RKP(b)" (1924) (quoted from Gromova, ed., *V tiskakh ideologii,* 279).

3. Gromova, ed., *V tiskakh ideologii,* 271.

4. L. Averbakh, "O politike partii v oblasti khudozhestvennoi literatury (Doklad vo fraktsii RKP pravleniia VAPP i MAPP i kollektiva MAPP)" (1925) (quoted from Gromova, ed., *V tiskakh ideologii,* 400).

5. This was particularly the case among the advocates of a "proletarian" literature. Other critics, however, such as Voronskii, dismissed the *rabkor* movement as a literary force, saying that it was too narrow in focus, too derivative in style, and generally too amateur to make a unique contribution to contemporary literature. (A. K. Voronskii, "Khudozhestvennaia literatura i rabkory. [O prostykh istinakh i prostom pisatele]," in *Literaturnye zapisi* [Moscow: Krug, 1926], 101–9).

6. For conflicting statements on the role of the *rabkor,* see "Rabochie korrespondenty posle s'ezda," *Zhurnalist* 5 (1923): 42; S. Uritskii, "Kak byt' s rabkorami?" *Zhurnalist* 8 (1923): 29; and *Rabkor Zheleznodorozhnik* 1 (Moscow: Izd. "Gudok," 1925): 1.

7. Raskol'nikov, "Rabkory i proletarskaia literatura," 111. Cf. the anonymous advice to worker correspondents in the trade journal *Rabkor-Railroad worker:* "Workers should write only in their own, worker's language *(rabochii iazyk)*—and no other. . . . [E]ven the practical, the everyday language of the worker is sufficiently colorful and expressive. . . ." ("Azbuka prozy," *Rabkor Zheleznodorozhnik* 2 [1925]: 42).

8. *Khrestomatiia rabochego korrespondenta* (Kiev: Otdel Rabochei Zhizni gazety "Proletarskaia Pravda," 1923), 8–9, 18. Similar collections include F. Lukoianov and M. Rafail, eds., *Rabkory o smerti Il'icha. Sbornik pisem, statei i zametok rabkorov, sel'korov i voenkorov o smerti V.I. Lenina* (Moscow: "Krasnaia zvezda," 1925); and Ia. Selikh and I. Grinevskii, eds., with preface by M. Gor'kii, *Krest'iane o sovetskoi vlasti* (Moscow: Gosizdat., 1929).

9. *Khrestomatiia rabochego korrespondenta,* 46–47.

10. The fact that the author depicts workers who are still separate (by their position and their interests) from the "red directorship" while at the same time creating distance between himself and the workers (by placing, for instance, quotation marks around such terms as *kompaneiskaia* and *s dymom*) supports Brooks's

contention that, at least in this earlier period, the "new intellectual" did not completely identify discursively with *either* group ("Competing Modes of Popular Discourse," 77, 80).

11. *Khrestomatiia rabochego korrespondenta,* 49.

12. "Kakim iazykom nado razgovarivat' s massovym chitatelem," *Zhurnalist* 3 (1925): 14.

13. According to Bakhtin, a hybrid is "an utterance that belongs, by its grammatical (syntactic) and compositional markers, to a single speaker, but that actually contains mixed within it two utterances, two speech manners, two styles, two 'languages,' two semantic and axiological belief systems" (M. M. Bakhtin, "Discourse in the Novel," in Caryl Emerson and Michael Holquist, trans., and Michael Holquist, ed., *The Dialogic Imagination* [Austin: University of Texas Press, 1981], 304).

14. Bourdieu, *Language and Symbolic Power,* 52.

15. See also Seifullina's "Muzhitskii skaz o Lenine," 162–69; and Ivanov's *Golubye peski,* in *Sobranie sochinenii,* vol. 5 (Moscow: Gosizdat, 1929), 101–300.

16. M. M. Zoshchenko, "O sebe, o kritikakh i o svoei rabote," in *Mastera sovremennoi literatury,* no. 1, ed. B. V. Kazanskii and Iu. N. Tynianov (Leningrad: "Academia," 1928), 11. Chudakova nicely captures the sociological dimension of Zoshchenko's early language program when she explains that "the language of Zoshchenko's prose is borne, in essence, out of the intersection of two factors; the writer is unable not to take into account new linguistic phenomena and changes to the linguistic consciousness, nor can he help but consider it in full seriousness— not as exotica, not as an ornament. At the same time, he is unable to convince himself of the full authority of any speech environment of the day" (*Poetika Mikhaila Zoshchenko,* 149). One of the most popular satirical writers of the 1920s and 1930s, Mikhail Mikhailovich Zoshchenko (1894–1958) published his feuilletons and short stories in a wide variety of newspapers, journals, and separate volumes. For an excellent study of Zoshchenko's complex attitude toward power and authority, see A. K. Zholkovskii, *Mikhail Zoshchenko: Poetika nedoveriia* (Moscow: Shkola "Iazyki russkoi kul'tury," 1999), 58–79.

17. "Obez'ianii iazyk," in *Mikhail Zoshchenko: Sobranie sochinenii,* vol. 1 (Leningrad: "Khudozhestvennaia literatura," 1986), 265.

18. "Pisatel'," in *Mikhail Zoshchenko,* 1:157. A sketch submitted by a *rabkor* to the *Workers' Newspaper (Rabochaia gazeta)* in 1927 suggests that Zoshchenko's mock-poeticality was not completely contrived. It begins, *"Utrom, kogda kosye luchi i ne dumali eshche progliadyvat' skvoz' osennie tuchi, kogda chut'-chut' zabryzzhet rassvet, dvenadtsat' tysiach tekstilei, s ozabochennym vidom speshat k svoim stankam, veretenam, chtoby nachat' svoi trudovoi den'."* ["In the morning, when the crooked rays had not yet even thought of peeping through the autumn storm clouds, when dawn was just barely splashing, twelve thousand textile workers rush to their workbenches with a preoccupied look, in order to begin their work day."] (RGASPI, f. 610, op. 1, ed. khr. 185, l. 4).

19. My understanding of *skaz* most closely resembles that forwarded by Bakhtin in *Problemy poetiki Dostoevskogo,* 3d ed. (Moscow: Izd. khudozhestvennaia literatura, 1972), 326–29. For a detailed analysis that rightly highlights the protean nature of the device (both in function and form), see Carleton, *Politics of Reception,* esp. 31–59.

20. The Russian term *iskazhenie,* which I translate in this discussion as "dis-

tortion" or "perversion," nicely reflects the degree to which the act is rooted in language or narration (as suggested by the root -SKAZ-). The term was commonly employed by contemporary critics who complained of the postrevolutionary mangling of the Russian language, Soviet ideology, or both. See Rybnikova, "Ob iskazhenii i ogrubenii," 243–55; Shpil'rein, *Iazyk krasnoarmeitsa*, 118.

21. The power of the editorial pen should not be underestimated. The passages quoted from the *Anthology of Worker Correspondents* no doubt passed through stages of editorial "refinement" (in style, if not content), whereas the Papoviants text retains evidence of a low level of literacy. Not surprisingly, archival copies of original *rabkor* and *sel'kor* letters exhibit a greater degree of illiteracy than the letters that wound up in separate collections and on the pages of at least the larger, central newspapers. See, for example, letters submitted to the *Workers' Newspaper* in RGASPI, f. 610, op. 1, ed. khr. 10, 50, 185.

22. Bourdieu accounts for the likelihood of this editor-writer power play when he notes that the authority of "legitimate language" rests not in the language itself but "in the social conditions of production and reproduction" and "the distribution between the classes of the knowledge" of that language (*Language and Symbolic Power*, 113). That direct access to the market of literary production was restricted also finds indirect proof in letters to Zoshchenko from new writers (one a *rabkor*) seeking the author's patronage, if not the clout of his name itself (*Pis'ma k pisateliu* [Leningrad: Izd. "Pisatelei v Leningrade," 1929], 15–16, 115–16).

23. In Maiakovskii, *Sobranie sochinenii v tridtsati tomakh*, 25:400. See also "Rabkoram 'Pravdy'" (1926), in *Sobranie sochinenii*, 24:262–63; "[Eshche rabsel'koram]" (1928), in *Sobranie sochinenii*, 24:313–18; "O pol'ze gramotnosti" (1928), in Maksim Gor'kii, *Stat'i o literature i literaturnoi tekhnike* (Leningrad: Gosizdat. khudozhestvennoi literatury, 1931), 3–9; "O nachinaiushchikh pisateliakh" (1928), in *Stat'i o literature*, 17–26; and "Pis'ma nachinaiushchim literatoram" (1930), in *Stat'i o literature*, 87–112.

24. *Krasnaia nov'* 8 (1926): 167–93; 10 (1926): 88–110; 11 (1927): 69–97. A more complete version of the *Diary* appeared in Ognev's *Sobranie sochinenii*, vols. 1, 3 (Moscow, 1928–1929), from which all further references in this discussion will be taken. Generally sympathetic to the revolutionary cause, Nikolai Ognev (pseudonym of Mikhail Grigor'evich Rozanov, 1888–1938) worked as an agitator, civil war correspondent, and schoolteacher in the years just following October 1917 and participated in a variety of writers' organizations through the 1920s and 1930s (Constructivists, "Pereval," the All-Russian Writers' Union [VSSP], and the Soviet Writers Union). By far his most well-known work, the *Diary* was the first and most successful part of a triology, the sequels to which addressed Kostia's university experiences (*Iskhod Nikpetozha* [1928]) and his earliest grade-school years (*Tri izmereniia* [1929]). Despite its earlier positive reception, Ognev's fiction went unpublished and unmentioned for nearly three decades after his death.

25. B. O., *Kniga i profsoiuzy* 5 (1927): 47.

26. Ognev elaborates on Kostia's preschool years in a later work, *Tri izmereniia* (Moscow: Gos. izd-vo khudosz. lit-ra, 1933).

27. For historical documentation of both positive and negative manifestations of the idea of pupil self-government, see Sheila Fitzpatrick, *Education and Social Mobility in the Soviet Union, 1921–1934* (Cambridge: Cambridge University Press, 1979), 25–29.

28. Aleksandr Voronskii notes Kostia's general disregard for authority in his complementary introduction to Ognev's collected works ("N. Ognev," in Ognev, *Sobranie sochinenii*, 1:14).

29. "Razboinichii forpost," in Ognev, *Sobranie sochinenii*, 3:243–96. The section carries its own epigraph and date (1928), suggesting it was written as a separate continuation to the previous three parts of the *Diary*. Although missing from the earliest publications of the *Diary*, this fourth section appears in all editions beginning with the 1928 version.

30. For ambiguous categorizations of Ognev as a writer, see Georgii Gorbachev, who calls him a "new fellow-traveler" and one of the more talented of recent writers (*Sovremennaia russkaia literatura* [Moscow: Priboi, 1929], 192–93; also "M. Sh.," "Massovaia biblioteka 'Molodoi gvardii,'" *Zemlia sovetskaia* 12 [1929], 58). Ognev himself makes ambivalent reference to his perceived status as *poputchik* in a personal letter to Boris Pil'niak, observing that it can only be something for history to judge (RGALI, f. 370, d. 128, l. 1).

31. D. A. Gorbov, "Pisateli o molodezhi," in *U nas za rubezhom: Literaturnye ocherki* (Moscow: Krug, 1928), 188.

32. M. Bochachev, "Rasstrel individualizma (O tvorchestve N. Ogneva)," *Khudozhestvennaia literatura* 30 (1932): 5, 10.

33. For Gorky's assessment of the diary, see "Pamiati N. Ogneva," *Detskaia literatura* 14 (1938): 3.

34. With the exception of the one critic already mentioned, who was confused by the voice, most praised Ognev's use of *skaz* (e.g., Gorbov, "Pisateli o molodezhi," 174–76; Gorbachev, *Sovremennaia russkaia literatura*, 192; a review of the *Diary* by Gennadii Fish in *Zvezda* 4 [1927]: 167; and A. Riden, "Sovetskii podrostok i shkola v khudozhestvennoi literature," *Narodnyi uchitel'* 7–8 [1927]: 139). The very genre of the diary no doubt helps expand the permissible limits of verbal disjunction and play. As a less formal and more spontaneous writing medium, ostensibly intended for an audience of one (the diarist), it can afford to take and reflect greater linguistic and ideological risks.

35. L. S. Vygotskii, *Myshlenie i rech'* (1934; rpt., Moscow, Labarint, 1996), esp. chaps. 2–3.

36. Zh. I. Shif, *Razvitie nauchnykh poniatii u shkol'nika. Issledovanie k voprosu umstvennogo razvitiia shkol'nika pri obuchenii obshchestvovedeniiu* (Moscow-Leningrad: Gosudarstvennoe uchebnoe pedagogicheskoe izd., 1935).

37. Quoted in René Van der Veer and Jaan Valsiner, *Understanding Vygotsky: A Quest for Synthesis* (Oxford: Blackwell, 1993), 271.

38. Vygotskii described the tendency somewhat differently, arguing that "concepts" were perceived more concretely by younger subjects than adults—an observation that helps account for Kostia Riabtsev's occasional misapplication of the language of state (*Myshlenie i rech'*, 129–34).

39. Van der Veer and Valsiner, *Understanding Vygotsky*, 274; see also Vygotskii, *Myshlenie i rech'*, 264–65.

40. Vygotskii, *Myshlenie i rech'*, 268–69. Vygotskii also characterized everyday language as more "spontaneous" and readily accessible, in contrast to scientific language, which was more complicated—a distinction that not only contributes to a developmentally based understanding of Kostia Riabtsev's use of language but also

clearly echoes the opposition between "elemental" and "conscious" so prevalent in the public discourse of early Soviet Russia (see Clark, *The Soviet Novel*, 15–24).

41. None of the aforementioned studies directly considers the possibility that young speakers and writers ignored the emerging language of state altogether, however implied it may be in their conclusions. The few examples of "authentic" children's diaries from this period suggest that, in fact, this was quite a common scenario. See V. Sinaiskaia-Finkel'shtein, *Nerastsvetshaia (Istoriia iunoi dushi)*, ed. N. Chukovskii, intro. Maksamilian Voloshin (Moscow, 1924); Anna Grigoreva, *Zapiski uchenitsy* (Moscow, 1928); and M. M. Rubinshtein, *Iunost' po dnevnikam i avtobiograficheskim zapisiam* (1928), esp. 151–94.

42. With fewer linguistic registers to fall back on, less-educated citizens are particularly dependent on the language imposed on them by state-controlled institutions such as the schools and the press. See Claus Mueller, *The Politics of Communication: A Study in the Political Sociology of Language, Socialization, and Legitimation* (New York: Oxford University Press, 1973), 13–17.

43. Voloshinov, *Marxism and the Philosophy of Language*, 19.

44. Voronskii, "N. Ognev," 12–13, 17; Riden, "Sovetskii podrostok i shkola v khudozhestvennoi literature," 140; Gorbov, "Pisateli o molodezhi," 188.

45. "Tol'ko cherez massu," in Al. Tolstoi et al., *Pisatel' ob iskusstve i o sebe* (Moscow, 1921), 162.

46. Ibid. Particularly in this light, it is interesting to note that the sequel to the *Diary, The End of Nikpetozh*, shows a significant decline in linguistic "invention" and playfulness in Kostia's university diary. Perhaps not accidentally, it also received far less favorable reviews (e.g., *Sovremennaia russkaia literatura*, 192; M. Bochachev, "Rasstrel individualizma [O tvorchestve N. Ogneva]," *Khudozhestvennaia literatura* 30 [1932]: 10).

47. "j" here refers to the Cyrillic "short i" or "i-kratkoe."

48. *Metodicheskii spravochnik po obucheniiu negramotnykh krasnoarmeitsev po kompleksnomu metodu* (Moscow: Politupravleniia M. V. O., 1922), 26–28. Emphasis in original. Oddly, two of the three letters mentioned in the course of the instructions as objects of instruction, "j" and "p," appear just once in the featured slogan.

49. Larry Holmes discusses this relative conservatism in *Kremlin and the Schoolhouse*. See also N. V. Kotriakhov and L. E. Holmes, *Teoriia i praktika trudovoi shkoly v Rossii (1917–1932 gg.)* (Kirov: Kirovskii gosudarstvennyi pedagogicheskii institut im. V. I. Lenina, 1993).

50. Brooks, "Breakdown in Production and Distribution of Printed Material"; Kenez, *Birth of the Propaganda State*; Von Hagen, *Soldiers in the Proletarian Dictatorship*.

51. Weber, *Economy and Society*, 1134.

52. "Strada. Zapiski T. A. Zabytogo," *Krasnaia nov'* 2 (1921): 26–51 (*Zabytyi*, in Russian, means "The Forgotten One"). Voronskii frequently cited Arosev as one of the more promising "proletarian writers" (A. K. Voronskii, "O proletarskom iskusstve i khudozhestvennoi politike nashei partii," *Krasnaia nov'* 7 [1923]: 257–76 [cited here from Gromova, ed., *V tiskakh ideologii*, 172, 182, 185, 189]). Aleksandr Iakovlevich Arosev (1890–1937) was an active participant in the revolutionary movement and held various government posts, including diplomat and supreme court judge, under Soviet rule. He enjoyed a fairly successful writing career, partly with the support of Voronskii, into the 1930s, but perished in the Stalin purges.

Nikolai Tkachenko, "Sled na zemle" (introductory article) in A. Ia. Arosev, *Belaia lestnitsa: Roman, povesti, rasskazy* (Moscow: Sovremennik, 1989), 3–17.

53. The device in Russian literature dates back at least to Pushkin's *Povesti pokoinogo Ivana Petrovicha Belkina* (1831) and was used by other writers ranging from Gogol' and Turgenev to Babel' and Zoshchenko.

54. Iu. N. Libedinskii, *Nedelia*, in *Nashi dni* 2 (1922): 61–144. All further references to this work are cited parenthetically in the text. Iurii Nikolaevich Libedinskii (1898–1959) joined the Communist Party in 1920 and played an active part in various "proletarian" writers' groups throughout the 1920s and early 1930s. Despite controversies surrounding two of his works from the 1930s, leading to his temporary exclusion from the party from 1937–1939 and the banning of all his pre-1937 prose, Libedinskii remained a prolific contributor to Soviet letters through the final decades of his life (*Russkie pisateli 20 veka*, 409–10).

55. Gornykh represents the realization of a model introduced earlier in the form of a rhetorical query by the author-narrator, who had contemplated the unfair practice within party ranks of giving positions of responsibility to those who were "able to chair *(predsedatel'stvovat')*, speak eloquently, and conduct meetings," rather than to those who, although inarticulate, spoke with fewer "loud phrases" and a deeper understanding of "the class struggle and basic party principles" [117–18].

56. As William J. Chase puts it, "The restoration of the proletariat began to give way to its dilution as increasing numbers of inexperienced and unskilled rural migrants secured factory employment" (*Workers, Society, and the Soviet State: Labor and Life in Moscow, 1918–1929* [Urbana: University of Illinois Press, 1987], 103). See also Sheila Fitzpatrick, "The Bolsheviks' Dilemma: The Class Issue in Party Politics and Culture," in *The Cultural Front: Power and Culture in Revolutionary Russia* (Ithaca, N.Y.: Cornell University Press, 1992), 16–36.

57. The character Gleb Chumalov of Fedor Gladkov's *Cement* offers an even more brash, less polished version of this straight-talking organizational model, particularly in contrast to the long-winded bureaucratic hacks of the local *Sovnarkom*. See especially the closing scene, where the ringing rhetoric of Bad'in is contrasted to Gleb's brief, reluctant, and unpolished speech—prefaced by his rhetorical query, "Why talk when everything is clear without words?" (in *Sobranie sochinenii*, vol. 2 [Moscow: Zemlia i fabrika, 1927], 315–17).

58. *Sputnik agitatora* 3 (1925): 49–50.

59. E. Khersonskaia (starshaia), *Publichnye vystupleniia. Posobie dlia nachinaiushchikh*, 2d corrected and expanded ed. (Moscow: Krasnaia nov' [Glavpolitprosvet], 1923), 9–11. Chase argues that the policy shifts and dashed hopes brought on by the civil war and war communism gave rise to a growing "estrangement" between the state and the working class—a rift no doubt contributing to the dissolution of "revolutionary pathos" (*Workers, Society, and the Soviet State*, 11–72).

60. A. Abolin, "Vnimanie postanovke agitatsii," *Komunisticheskaia revoliutsiia* 6 (1925): 14.

61. The first term, a deverbal noun created from an already derivative verb *(miting -> mitingovat' -> mitingovanie)* carries a distinctly (and overly) bureaucratic flavor; the second, by virtue of the *-shchina* suffix, is plainly derogatory, an abstract noun roughly denoting an overzealous penchant for holding needless and pointless rallies.

62. K. Mal'tsev, "Formy massovoi agitatsii. (Stat'ia 3–ia.)," *Sputnik agitatora* 16 (1925): 28, 30.

63. E.g., V. Galenkina, "Neskol'ko slov o formakh massovoi agitatsii," *Sputnik agitatora* 13 (1925): 53. Khersonskaia also advises that the *beseda*, rather than the rally, is "the best means for working out *methodical thought* on social issues" (*Kak besedovat' so vzroslymi po obshchestvennym voprosam*, Pedagogicheskie kursy na domu, no. 18 [Moscow: Rabotnik prosveshcheniia, 1924], 11).

64. A. V. Mirtov, *Umen'e govorit' publichno: teoriia, zadachi, uprazhneniia*, 5th reworked and expanded ed. (Moscow: Doloi negramotnost', 1927), 22.

65. The opposition itself goes back in Russian revolutionary thought at least to N. G. Chernyshevskii (see *Antropologicheskii printsip v filosofii* [1860] [Moscow: OGIZ, Gospolitizdat, 1948]).

66. A. Adzharov, *Oratorskoe iskusstvo: Prakticheskoe posobie dlia molodezhi* (Moscow: Molodaia gvardiia, 1925), 25.

5: THE CLEANSING AUTHORITY OF THE RUSSIAN NATIONAL VOICE

1. I use the term "culturist" here in the sense described by Jeffrey Brooks in *When Russia Learned to Read*, that is, "the perception on the part of many educated Russians that they had a moral obligation to influence and contribute to the cultural development of the newly literate and to the widely shared belief that Russian literature could serve as a bridge between the classes" (317). Brooks notes that many educated, westernized Russians of the late nineteenth and early twentieth century viewed cultural identity, rather than political or religious affiliations, as the primary indicator of national identity.

2. The full passage from Turgenev, which has served as a battle call for purists throughout the twentieth century, reads: *"Vo dni somnenii, vo dni tiagostnykh razdumii o sud'bakh moei rodiny—ty odin mne podderzhka i opora o velikii, moguchii, pravdivyi i svobodnyi russkii iazyk! Ne bud' tebia—kak ne vpast' v otchaianie pri vide vsego, chto sovershaetsia doma? No nel'zia verit', chtoby takoi iazyk ne byl dan velikomu narodu!"* ["In days of doubt, in days of burdensome reflection about the fate of my homeland, you alone are my support and my buttress, oh great, mighty, honest, and free Russian language! Without you, how could one not fall into desperation at the sight of all that is transpiring at home? But it is impossible to believe that such a language was not given to a great people!"] "Russkii iazyk" (1882), in Ivan Sergeevich Turgenev, *Polnoe sobranie sochinenii i pisem v tridtsati tomakh*, vol. 10 (Moscow: Nauka, 1982), 172.

3. In 1922, A. G. Gornfel'd noted the tension between the revolutionary "innovators" and the so-called "purists," although he cited only one incomplete reference to contemporary representatives of the purist camp (a certain "A. K." in an unspecified issue of *Vestnik literatury*) (*Novye slovechki i starye slova. [Rech' na s"ezde prepodavatelei russkogo iazyka i slovesnosti v Peterburge 5 sentiabria 1921 g.]* [Petrograd: KOLOS, 1922]). In 1923, Vladimir Azov decried the spoiling of the Russian language, as evidenced by such forms as *izviniaius', poka*, and the confusion of *odevat'sia* and *nadet'*. He blamed as the source of the problem the large influx of "refugees" from the outlying regions, including non-Russian territories such as Poland ("Otkrytoe pis'mo Akademii Nauk, Narkomu prosveshcheniia A. V. Lunacharskomu, Ak-tsentru, Gubpolitprosvetu, Sorabisu, Upravleniiu Akademicheskikh teatrov, mestkomam chastnykh teatrov i vsem gramotnym russkim liudiam," *Zhizn' iskusstva* 43 [1923]: 8).

4. V. I. Lenin, *Polnoe sobranie sochinenii,* 5th ed., 55 vols. (Moscow: Izd. Politicheskoi literatury, 1970), 40:49.

5. Emphasis in original (18 January 1920) (*Polnoe sobranie sochinenii,* 51:121–22). Although a prolific fiction writer, Vladimir Dal' (1801–1872) is best known today for his four-volume *Tolkovyi slovar' zhivogo velikorusskogo iazyka* (1863–1866). A new comprehensive dictionary did emerge, but only fifteen years after Lenin's original proposal—and under markedly different linguistic and cultural conditions.

6. See Edward J. Brown, *Russian Literature since the Revolution,* rev. and enlarged ed. (Cambridge, Mass.: Harvard University Press, 1982), 31, 34, 106–8.

7. According to Vinokur, language purism is a kind of mood or disposition most often grounded in dogma or a (frequently false) sense of tradition and directed against any sort of novelty in language form. Viktor Zhivov offers valuable background from the history of the Russian literary language on the purely conventional nature not only of the concept of language purism but of the idea of a standard literary language itself (see *Iazyk i kul'tura v Rossii XVIII veka,* 41–52, 171–84). That the underlying social implications of this particular struggle between language purism and innovation was linked to the issue of national identity is well demonstrated by Lotman and Uspenskii in "Spory o iazyke v nachale XIX v. kak fakt russkoi kul'tury."

8. For more on purism's role in identity politics, particularly during periods of social transformation, see Björn H. Jernudd and Michael J. Shapiro, eds., *The Politics of Language Purism,* Contribution to the Sociology of Language, vol. 54 (Berlin: Mouton de Gruyter, 1989), esp. 1–28.

9. See Bourdieu, "The Production and Reproduction of Legitimate Language," in *Language and Symbolic Power,* 43–65.

10. "Khaltura," *Poslednie Novosti* (Paris, 3 Feb. 1922), in S. I. Kartsevskii, *Iz lingvisticheskogo naslediia* (Moscow: Iazyki russkoi kul'tury, 2000): 210–14.

11. "Iazyk Lenina" (1924), in John Malmstad and Robert Hughes, eds., *Sobranie sochinenii,* vol. 2 (Ann Arbor, Mich.: Ardis, 1990), 349–52.

12. Militsa Grin, ed., *Ustami Buninykh. Dnevniki Ivana Alekseevicha i Very Nikolaevny i drugie arkhivnye materialy,* 3 vols. (Frankfurt am Main: Posev, 1977), 1:245, 2:63; I. A. Bunin, *Sobranie sochinenii v shesti tomakh* (Moscow: Khudozhestvennaia literatura, 1988), 6:423, 410, 400–401.

13. Bunin, *Sobranie sochinenii,* 6:630, 642, 422, 418–19.

14. "Pamiati sil'nogo cheloveka" (1894), in Bunin, *Sobranie sochinenii,* 6:590. Emphasis in original.

15. Blium, *Sovetskaia tsenzura,* 181.

16. A. Volkonskii, "O zaimstvovannykh inoiazychnykh slovakh," in *V zashchitu russkogo iazyka. Sbornik statei* (Berlin: Izd. "Mednyi Vsadnik," 1928), 59. Emphasis in original.

17. Ibid., 34, 42, 59.

18. S. Volkonskii, "O russkom iazyke," in *V zashchitu russkogo iazyka,* 11.

19. Ibid., 1–12.

20. Ibid., 21–22, 32; "O zaimstvovannykh inoiazychnykh slovakh," 36, 47, 49, 63; A. Volkonskii, "O nekotorykh grammaticheskikh oshibkakh," in *V zashchitu russkogo iazyka,* 73.

21. Volkonskii, "O zaimstvovannykh inoiazychnykh slovakh," 60.

22. A. Volkonskii, "Imia i iazyk," in *V zashchitu russkogo iazyka*, 102.

23. Referring to the next generation, they write, "May it preserve the indestructible, multidimensional name 'Russian' and watch over the purity of the Russian language; may it see the dawn of the revival that we, already old, will not live to see" (*V zashchitu russkago iazyka*, 6).

24. P. Bitsilli, a Russian émigré living in Sofia and an occasional contributor to the journal *Sovremennyia Zapiski*, offered an in-depth discussion on the essential link between language and national identity ("Natsiia i iazyk," *Sovremennyia Zapiski* 40 [1929]: 403–26). Although he made no mention of events in Soviet Russia, he discussed how language and culture, as the most basic, organic, and "irrational" components of national identity, were the first to suffer in the highly rationalized process of modern state building.

25. A. A. Surkov, *Kratkaia literaturnaia entsiklopediia* (Moscow: Sovetskaia entsiklopediia, 1962), 2:285.

26. Gorky, in fact, was quite clear in his disdain for at least those expatriates who, while bemoaning the doomed experiment taking place in the homeland, were themselves rapidly loosing a feel for the language (e.g., 1927 letter to M. M. Prishvin, in Andrew Barratt and Barry P. Scherr, trans. and eds., *Maksim Gorky: Selected Letters* [New York: Oxford University Press, 1997], 282–83).

27. In this respect, Gorky shared the attitude of Trotsky, Voronskii, and others, who openly recognized that behind most urban laborers stood a person of peasant stock. See "O pisateliakh-samouchkakh" (1911), in *Sobranie sochinenii v 30-i tomakh* (Moscow: Gosizdat. khudozhestvennoi literatury, 1953), 24:99–137; and "Predislovie k 'Sborniku proletarskikh pisatelei'" (1914), in *Sobranie sochinenii*, 24:168–72.

28. "Rabkoram 'Pravdy'" (1926), in *Sobranie sochinenii*, 24:262–63; "[Eshche rabsel'koram]" (1928), in *Sobranie sochinenii*, 24:313–18; "O pol'ze gramotnosti" (1928), in *Stat'i o literature*, 3–9; "O nachinaiushchikh pisateliakh" (1928), in *Stat'i o literature*, 17–26.

29. "Pis'ma nachinaiushchim literatoram" (1930), in *Stat'i o literature*, 87–112; "O nachinaiushchikh pisateliakh," in ibid., 19.

30. According to Blium, Bunin was commonly considered a "classic" until 1928, whereupon the publication of his work sharply curtailed. In contrast, Gorky's work benefited markedly during the First Five-Year Plan, accounting for roughly 19 million of the approximately 244 million copies of literary works published from 1929–1933 (that is, approximately 1 out of every 12). Blium, *Sovetskaia tsenzura*, 77, 182–86.

31. "O tom, kak ia uchilsia pisat'" (1928), in *Stat'i o literature*, 80; "Pis'ma nachinaiushchim literatoram," in ibid., 99; "O pol'ze gramotnosti," in ibid., 9.

32. "O pol'ze gramotnosti," in ibid., 8–9.

33. Ibid., 7. Emphasis in original.

34. The "canonization" process, as Brooks and others show, began in the final decades of the nineteenth century ("Russian Nationalism and Russian Literature: The Canonization of the Classics," in Ivo Banac, John G. Ackerman, and Roman Szporluk, eds., *Nation and Ideology: Essays in Honor of Wayne S. Vucinich* [New York: Columbia University Press, 1981], 315–34; see also Stephen Moeller-Sally, "Parallel Lives: Gogol''s Biography and Mass Readership in Late Imperial Russia," *Slavic Review* 54 [1995]: 62–79). It is also worth noting that the "statization" and

"nationalization" of the classics can be traced back to the "Decree on the State Publishing House" of 29 December 1917, which gave the state a monopoly on publishing Russian classics. What, exactly, constituted a "classic" depended largely on the "aesthetic tastes" of the Bolshevik leaders in power at the time. See Blium, *Sovetskaia tsenzura*, 150–52.

35. "Rabochii klass dolzhen vospitat' svoikh masterov kul'tury" (1929), in *Stat'i o literature*, 31.

36. In this sense, Gorky's view on language standards echoed those of Antonio Gramsci, who viewed a "unified national language" that was "organically tied to tradition" rather than the perpetuation or elevation of separate dialects or the creation of something utterly new, as the best way of securing political and cultural hegemony for the proletariat (cf. Gramsci, *Selections from Cultural Writings*, 183–88, 26–34).

37. *Maksim Gorky: Selected Letters*, 258.

38. "Pis'ma nachinaiushchim literatoram," in *Stat'i o literature*, 108–9.

39. Ibid., 103; "O literature" (1930), in *Stat'i o literature*, 39. The important issue of latinizing and russifying the alphabets of non-Russian ethnic minorities lies outside the scope of this book but is thoroughly discussed in Michael G. Smith's *Language and Power in the Creation of the USSR*.

40. *Maksim Gorky: Selected Letters*, 281.

41. Maksim Gor'kii, "O rabote neumeloi, nebrezhnoi, nedobrosovestnoi, i t.d." (1931), in *O literature: Stat'i i rechi 1928–1935 gg* (Moscow: Gosizdat. Khudozhestvennaia literatura, 1935), 84. Gorky also predicted gleeful derision from the "spite-mongers and enemies of worker-peasant power" as a result of such indications of illiteracy (76).

42. Edward J. Brown observes that, in contrast to literary representatives of the Proletcult, the leaders of these proletarian groups consistently held a more conservative approach to issues of style and voice; but the classical orientation intensified in the late 1920s with the group's "Learn from the Classics" campaign (*Proletarian Episode*, 12–16, 66–69). Beginning in 1933, Gorky's own literary journal, *Literaturnaia ucheba*, featured a regular section dedicated to writing skills under the rubric "Learning from the classics" *("Ucheba u klassikov")*.

43. Institut Mirovoi Literatury (IMLI), f. 40, op. 1, d. 563, ll. 2, 4; RGALI, f. 1638, op. 1, d. 45, l. 2.

44. E. Troshchenko, "Literaturnaia konsul'tatsiia RAPP'a i ee korrespondenty," *Na literaturnom postu* 16 (1929): 33–39. This author also notes the predominantly *rural* origins of most of the manuscripts received (34).

45. IMLI, f. 40, op. 1, d. 577a, l. 7.

46. Nik. Smirnov, "Khudozhestvennoe tvorchestvo rabkorov (Po povodu odnogo al'manakha)," *Novyi mir* 4 (1929): 204.

47. "Izuchenie iazyka i slovesnogo tvorchestva detei i podrostkov v GAKhN," *Russkii iazyk v sovetskoi shkole* 1 (1930): 169. By way of explanation the author of the report notes: "The commission has not set age limits for the authors of the works under study. Its interest is directed to primitive, undeveloped literary forms."

48. The readjustment described here took place within the broader context of secondary school curriculum reform during the middle years of the decade. Increasingly frustrated with the overambitious methodological experiments of the *Narkompros* (and the "complex method," in particular), teachers and local school

systems returned to more traditional methods of instruction and curricular organization. For a discussion of the "compromise" between teachers and the *Narkompros* in 1926–1927, see Holmes, *Kremlin and the Schoolhouse*, esp. 69–83.

49. "Lit. khronika," *Rodnoi iazyk v shkole* 2 (1927): 93.

50. A. Mirtov, "Sem' urokov vezhlivosti na zaniatiiakh russkim iazykom (Evfemisticheskie uprazhneniia.)," *Rodnoi iazyk v shkole* 2 (1927): 276.

51. *Rodnoi iazyk v shkole* 2 (1927): 95. It was in this same year that a critical essay on the language of the Soviet newspapers appeared in the influential journal *Pechat' i revoliutsiia* calling for a general purification of the language from the various foreign loanwords and nonstandard colloquialisms that had come to dominate their pages (A. Smirnov-Kutacheskii, "Iazyk i stil' sovremennoi gazety," *Pechat' i revoliutsiia* 1 [1927]: 5–18, 2 [1927]: 16–24).

52. M. N. Peterson, "Russkii iazyk, kak predmet prepodavaniia," *Rodnoi iazyk v shkole* 3 (1927): 126–27. A prominent voice of dissent in this praise of the classics and condemnation of the newspaper as the speech genre of choice came from the journal *Novyi Lef*, the contributors of whom generally espoused the modern voice discussed in chap. 3. This later period of the journal is distinguished—with respect to language—precisely by its embrace of the newspaper as the modern day "epos," the "Bible of our day," the ideal genre (in contrast to the misguided hunt for a "New Lev Tolstoi") for realizing the fact-based mission that language is to play in the contemporary society—an aesthetic they came to call "factography" (S. Tret'iakov, "Novyi Lef Tolstoy," *Novyi Lef* 1 [1927]: 34–38).

53. Smith points to evidence of pedagogues from the earlier part of the 1920s who advocated the "native approach"—"recognizing territorial dialects as useful standards of teaching"—but even this, Smith notes, was always with a "higher" end in mind: "Education was to begin with the lower orbits of language and culture, the simple and accessible, in order to reach the higher orbits, the complex and remote fundamentals of the literary language, with greater ease." *Language and Power in the Creation of the USSR*, 112–13.

54. S. Abakumov, "Rabota nad slovarem i frazoi v novykh uchebnykh posobiakh po tekhnike i kul'ture rechi," *Russkii iazyk v sovetskoi shkole* 1 (1929): 81.

55. A. Sletova, "Kul'tura rechi uchashchikhsia kak obshchaia zadacha shkoly," *Russkii iazyk v sovetskoi shkole* 3 (1929): 88.

56. I. Veksler, "Literatura v srednei shkole," *Russkii iazyk v sovetskoi shkole* 3 (1930): 34, 37.

57. All programs discussed here were developed by the *Narkompros* for the fifth through seventh grades, which at that time roughly corresponded to ages twelve through fourteen or fifteen. The following remarks concerning the 1926 list are based on *Programmy dlia vtorogo kontsentra shkoly semiletki (V, VI i VII gody obucheniia)* (Moscow: MONO, 1926), 251–71. Although the programs changed in format from year to year, the language and literature listings usually appeared together under the heading "Native language and literature." Programs from the early 1920s openly stated their status as *recommended* lists, to be modified at the discretion of the teacher (see, for example, *Primernaia programma po literature dlia shkoly II-i stupeni* [Moscow: Gosizdat., 1921], 3). This nonbinding status was compounded by relatively small printings of the early programs. Toward the end of the 1920s, however, the programs took on a more obligatory status and enjoyed broader distribution (see Holmes, *Kremlin and the Schoolhouse*, 71–75).

58. The thematic groupings reflect the influence of the "complex method," which sought a more integrated approach to learning. It is also worthy of note that, unlike the 1927 list, this one contained several works by difficult modernist writers (Blok, Bely, Briusov) as well as works by foreign authors (Heine, Hugo, Sinclair, Zola, and others).

59. *Programmy* (1926), 260.

60. Ibid., 263, 264, 266.

61. Ibid., 267.

62. The following remarks concerning the 1927 list are based on *Programmy i metodicheskie zapiski edinoi trudovoi shkoly. Vypusk tretii. 1–kontsentr gorodskoi shkoly, II stupeni* (Moscow: Gosizdat., 1927), 61–98.

63. *Programmy* (1927), 62.

64. Ibid., 83.

65. Ibid., 74.

66. Ibid., 76–80.

67. K. B. Barkhin, *Kul'tura slova. Metodicheskoe posobie dlia prepodavatelei II stupeni*, 2d ed. (Moscow: Rabotnik prosveshcheniia, 1930), 3–4. The preface from which this quote is taken is dated 1928.

68. "Klassiki-poputchiki—proletpisateli (peredovaia)," *Na literaturnom postu* 5–6 (1927): 5. The All-Russian Association of Proletarian Writers (VAPP) became the Russian Association of Proletarian Writers (RAPP) beginning with the All-Union Congress of Proletarian Writers in April 1928. For a more detailed description of the various battles and reorganizations of the literary groups during this time, see Brown's *Proletarian Episode*.

69. V. Ermilov, "Problema zhivogo cheloveka v sovremennoi literature i *Vor* L. Leonova," *Na literaturnom postu* 5–6 (1927): 70. Although ostensibly an article about Leonov's *Vor*, Ermilov likewise singles out Fadeev's *Razgrom* as another example of this positive quality (71). The literary aesthetic here, of course, makes some explicit assumptions about not only the role of literature and the manner in which it is consumed but also about what, in the Russian tradition, constituted a "classic."

70. A. Zonin, "Proletarskii realizm (O *Razgrome* A. Fadeeva) (Okonchanie)," *Na literaturnom postu* 8 (1927): 20. A Communist Party member and prose writer from the early days of Bolshevik rule, Aleksandr Aleksandrovich Fadeev (1901–1956) served in central leadership positions in the Russian Association of Proletarian Writers (RAPP) and, later, in the Soviet Writers' Union (*Russkie pisateli 20 veka*, 706–7).

71. Barthes, *Writing Degree Zero*, 67–69.

72. A. Zonin, "O starykh lozungakh i novykh zadachakh," *Oktiabr'* 11 (1927): 183–91.

73. In addition to Babel''s *Konarmiia* stories, Vsevolod Ivanov's *Armored Train No. 14-69* (*Bronepoezd 14-69*, 1922), Dmitrii Furmanov's *Chapaev* (1923), and Aleksandr Serafimovich's *Iron Flood* (*Zheleznyi potok*, 1924) are some of the more influential works from the 1920s that highlight the civil war theme. While a comprehensive study of Soviet civil war fiction has yet to be written, Edward J. Brown's (*Russian Literature since the Revolution*) and Katerina Clark's (*The Soviet Novel*) observations on most of the more influential works remain among the best to date.

74. Brown, *Russian Literature since the Revolution*, 136.

75. Calls for the depiction of "the living person" came from certain factions of proletarian writers, headed by Libedinskii and Fadeev, in reaction to the prevail-

ing view among other proletarian colleagues that literature ought to engage in the creation of "positive heroes" with the goal of changing, rather than simply reflecting, reality. See Brown, *Proletarian Episode*, esp. 66–86.

76. A. Zonin, "Proletarskii realizm (O *Razgrome* A. Fadeeva) (Okonchanie)," 20.

77. N. Berkovskii, "Stilevye problemy proletarskoi prozy," *Na literaturnom postu* 24 (1927): 14–15.

78. Although this argument finds resonance in Ernest Gellner's idea that nationalism involves "the general imposition of a high culture on society, where previously low cultures had taken up the lives of the majority, and in some cases of the totality, of the population," it more closely resembles Gal and Woolard's claim that strategies which minimize "intertextual gaps" and underscore the continuity of a contemporary language or voice with those of the past are, in fact, most effective at constructing history, and, through it, authenticity and legitimacy. Ernest Gellner, *Nations and Nationalism* (Ithaca, N.Y.: Cornell University Press, 1983), 57; Gal and Woolard, "Constructing Languages and Publics," 135. In his short essay on Nikolai Marr, Iurii Murashov likewise observes a shift from an "avant-garde, revolutionary orientation on oral discourse to the socialist realist cult of the letter," but he restricts it primarily to Stalinist culture of the 1930s ("Pis'mo i ustnaia rech' v diskursakh o iazyke 1930-x godov: N. Marr," in *Sotsrealisticheskii kanon* [St. Petersburg: Gumanitarnoe Agenstvo "Akademicheskii proekt," 2000], 599–608).

79. Barthes, *Writing Degree Zero*, 19.

6: CANONIZATION OF THE PARTY-STATE VOICE

1. For a discussion of the appropriateness of the term "party-state" in the context of Stalinist Russia, see Kotkin, *Magnetic Mountain*, 286–98.

2. I borrow the notion of "patristic texts" from Katerina Clark, who argues that it was a certain group of canonical works, more than stylistic or ideological features, that defined socialist realism as a genre. See *The Soviet Novel*, 3ff.

3. Weber, *Economy and Society*, 1121.

4. See especially Bourdieu, *Language and Symbolic Power*, 37–102; and Mueller, *Politics of Communication*.

5. Weber, *Economy and Society*, 1122.

6. In their study of revolutionary discourse in Mao's China, Apter and Saich likewise argue that the shift from oral to written modes marks a process of canonization, characterizing the transcription of speeches, in particular, as a form of *writ*ualization: "The relationship of orality to writing was the act of creating texts as *writ*uals, the conversion requiring the listeners to become readers. Doing so put education at the center of the redeeming project." See Apter and Saich, *Revolutionary Discourse in Mao's Republic*, 87.

7. Andrei Siniavskii likens the Soviet Union as a whole under Stalin to a "Church-State." For his comments on language in this regard, see *Soviet Civilization: A Cultural History*, trans. Joanne Turnbull (New York: Arcade, 1988), 111–12.

8. V. Rozhitsyn, *Kak vystupat' na sobraniiakh s dokaldami i rechami* (Khar'kov: Proletarii, 1928), 6. The editor of a later manual changes the relative weight of these two factors in a similar manner, noting that it is most important for the agitator to be "prepared politically, . . . armed with the dialectic method, with Marxist-Leninist theory." Only then do the more technical or mechanical

aspects of oratory come into play (V. M. Kreps and K. A. Erberg, eds. *Praktika oratorskoi rechi. Sbornik statei*, Nauchno-Issledovatel'skii Institut Rechevoi Kul'tury Laboratoriia Publichnoi Rechi [Leningrad: Izd. Inst-ta Agitatsii im. Volodarskogo, 1931], 5–6).

9. Rozhitsyn, *Kak vystupat' na sobraniiakh*, 6. Emphasis added. This process of "internalization" coincided with the purging of the old intelligentsia and heavy recruitment of new party cadres under Stalin during the "Cultural Revolution" (see Fitzpatrick, "Stalin and the Making of a New Elite," in *The Cultural Front*, 149–82).

10. Rozhitsyn, *Kak vystupat' na sobraniiakh*, 41. Nina Tumarkin describes the Stalinist reappropriation and institutionalization of Lenin, his works, and the "cult" formed around him in *Lenin Lives! The Lenin Cult in Soviet Russia* (Cambridge, Mass.: Harvard University Press, 1983), 207–51.

11. Rozhitsyn, *Kak vystupat' na sobraniiakh*, 42–43.

12. Ibid., 83.

13. Vladimir Maiakovskii, *Vladimir Il'ich Lenin* (1924), in *Polnoe sobranie sochinenii*, 6:233.

14. Viktor Gofman, *Slovo oratora: ritorika i politika* (Leningrad: Izd-vo Pisatelei v Leningrade, 1932) 71, 193, 227.

15. Gofman, *Slovo oratora*, 228.

16. Boris Groys offers a compelling, though not uncontroversial, argument for avant-garde legacies in socialist-realist aesthetics in *Total Art of Stalin: Avant-Garde, Aesthetic Dictatorship, and Beyond*, trans. Charles Rougle (Princeton, N.J.: Princeton University Press, 1992).

17. Gofman, *Slovo oratora*, 254–55. Cf. Siniavskii's alternative characterization of the result of total control by the party language: "Words replace knowledge: it's enough to know a specific set of words to feel on top of the situation" (*Soviet Civilization*, 195).

18. Both Holmes and Sheila Fitzpatrick document the growing politicization of the school programs from the beginning of the First Five-Year Plan, linking it in part to the changing of the old guard at *Narkompros* (*Kremlin and the Schoolhouse*, 115–17; *Education and Social Mobility in the Soviet Union*, 136–57).

19. The introductory remarks to the 1930 grade-school program proclaimed, "The programs must not only contain several elements of polytechnism, they must be polytechnized to a maximal degree and have the tendency of pushing the school onto the path of further . . . developing polytechnic upbringing and education" (*Programmy Fabrichno-Zavodskoi Semiletki* [Moscow: Gosizdat., 1930], 15; see also 3–5). Though still outnumbered by the general-education schools, the polytechnic schools (Factory Seven-Year Schools and Schools for Collective Farm Youth) saw an increase in both number and enrollments and enjoyed growing priority in state and local school planning (Holmes, *Kremlin and the Schoolhouse*, 121–36).

20. *Programmy i metodicheskie zapiski shkol kolkhoznoi molodezhi*, vyp. I (Moscow: Gosizdat., 1930), 5; *Programmy Fabrichno-Zavodskoi Semiletki* (Moscow: Gosizdat., 1930), 6.

21. *FZS: Programmy russkogo iazyka i literatury* (Leningrad: Leningradskii gorodskoi otdel narodnogo obrazovaniia, 1932), 37.

22. V. Neboliubov, "Iz nabliudenii nad stilem V. I. Lenina," *Russkii iazyk v sovetskoi shkole* 1 (1930): 33.

23. *FZS: Programmy russkogo iazyka i literatury* (1932), 6–14.

24. Ibid., 13.

25. Ibid., 15.

26. Ibid., 13.

27. It likewise avoided the dangerous proximity of some versions of the national model to formal and ideological "purism," by distinguishing between "international words" (especially those with "social economic bases"), which represented a positive, progressive trend, and "foreign pandering" *(inostranshchina)*—the excessive (and pernicious) use of foreign words ("without discretion," in Lenin's words) (*FZS: Programmy russkogo iazyka i literatury* [1932], 13).

28. Ibid., 15–17.

29. Ibid., 42–43.

30. In discussing the dual importance of these two processes, Ernest Gellner observes, "Both memory and forgetfulness have deep social roots; neither springs from historical accident" (*Culture, Identity, and Politics* [Cambridge: Cambridge University Press, 1987], 17). For an excellent discussion of the emergence of the cult of Stalin, see Brooks, *Thank You, Comrade Stalin!*, 54–82.

31. Il. Vardin, "Voprosy pechati na XII s'ezde RKP," *Zhurnalist* 6 (1923): 8; S. Uritskii, "Kak byt' s rabkorami?" *Zhurnalist* 8 (1923): 27–29.

32. The violence brought against the worker and village correspondents is well documented in period journals, particularly in 1922 and 1924, when the high-profile assassinations of the *rabkor* Spiridonov and the *sel'kor* Malinovskii led to high-level denunciations and vows for greater protection (see Kenez, *Birth of the Propaganda State,* 233–37). The trade journal for *Pravda* correspondents, the *Worker-Peasant Correspondent (Raboche-krest'ianskii Korrespondent),* even had a regular section entitled "Persecutions" *(Presledovaniia),* reporting on various acts against correspondents (frequent subheadings included "Murders," "Assassination attempts," "Beatings," and "Layoffs").

33. "O perestroike rabsel'korovskogo dvizheniia (Postanovlenie ot 16.IV.1931)," in *O partiinoi i sovetskoi pechati,* 409.

34. Ibid., 411. The combined oversight of the state-run editorial boards and internal party members reflects the state of "dual-subordination" that has been cited as one of the distinctive institutional features of the single-party state. See Hirszowicz, "Sovereign Bureaucracy as a New Social Phenomenon," 13–47.

35. "O perestroike rabsel'korovskogo dvizheniia," in *O partiinoi i sovetskoi pechati,* 410. This combination of increased party-state oversight and greater potential for upward mobility supports Sheila Fitzpatrick's more general thesis regarding working-class upward mobility in "The Bolsheviks' Dilemma," 559–613.

36. See Kenez, *Birth of the Propaganda State,* 233–37.

37. A. Meromskii, *Iazyk sel'kora* (Moscow: Federatsiia, 1930), 19. Matthew Lenoe points to the training of younger and more militant party members with no ties to prerevolutionary journalism as one of the key features leading to the shift in newspaper discourse during the First Five-Year Plan. "Agitation, Propaganda, and the 'Stalinization' of the Soviet Press," 58–76.

38. I. Bas, *Iazyk bol'shevistskoi gazety* (Moscow: Vsesoiuznyi Kommunisticheskii Institut Zhurnalistiki im. Pravdy, 1934), 44–45.

39. Meromskii, *Iazyk sel'kora*, 10.

40. "O pechati," in *O partiinoi i sovetskoi pechati*, 305. Emphasis in original.

41. *O partiinoi i sovetskoi pechati*, 263. Brooks describes this shift as one from persuasion to compulsion in his discussion of the early Soviet press (*Thank You, Comrade Stalin!*, chaps. 1–3).

42. Trotskii, "Gazeta i ee chitatel'," 29.

43. P. Ia. Khavin, "Za bol'shevistskii iazyk v raionnoi gazete," *Literaturnaia ucheba* 5 (1932): 37–38, 42.

44. *Iazyk krest'ianskoi gazety* (Moscow: Krest'ianskaia gazeta, 1933), 13 (emphasis added). I. Bas, in his own discussion of the Soviet press, also cited this feature of truth telling as one of the distinctive ones of the Bolshevik newspapers (*Iazyk bol'shevistskoi gazety*, 34).

45. Another feature that marked the strength of the language of the party-state, the inseparable link between word and deed, reflects the influence of the proletarian model. "In the Bolshevik newspaper," commented one analyst, "the word must not part ways with the deed." This notion of words that led to deeds was contrasted to the idea of "phrasemongering" *(frazerstvo)* criticized in the popular and modern models alike. *Iazyk bol'shevistskoi gazety*, 38.

46. Ibid., 14. Emphasis added.

47. A. M. Selishchev, "O iazyke sovremennoi derevni," *Zemlia Sovetskaia* 9 (1932): 120–33.

48. Nikolai Iakovlevich Marr (1864–1934) began his linguistic career with comparative and historical studies of the languages of the Caucasus but became famous for his Japhetic theory, later developed into a full-blown "new theory of language"—an unapologetic graft of Marxist ideology onto his own colorful views on the nature and origin of language. Despite their scholarly speciousness and lack of productivity, Marr's theories and followers came to dominate Soviet linguistics for more than two decades, until they were refuted by the linguist Stalin himself in *Marksizm i voprosy iazykoznaniia* (Moscow: Gosudarstvennoe izdatel'stvo politicheskoi literatury, 1950), a treatise that first appeared in serial form in *Pravda*. For details on Marr's ideas, their influence in Soviet linguistics, the trumped charges against Selishchev and other anti-Marr linguists, and Selishchev's eventual arrest and expulsion from the Scientific Research Institute for Linguistics in what has become known as the "Slavists' Affair," see F. D. Ashnin and V. M. Alpatov, *Delo Slavistov: 30-e gody* (Moscow: Nasledie, 1994); Alpatov, *Istoriia odnogo mifa*; and Smith, *Language and Power in the Creation of the USSR*, 80–102. Smith also offers a detailed discussion of Stalin's foray into linguistics in *Language and Power in the Creation of the USSR*, 161–73.

49. Selishchev, "O iazyke sovremennoi derevni," 130.

50. Ibid., 120–21. Recall that Shafir reported just the opposite attitude, that is, a keen perception by peasants of a discursive gap between "our language" and the "language of power."

51. Ibid., 124–25, 130.

52. Ibid., 126.

53. Ibid., 127–28. There is little doubt that the term *aktivist* had specifically political connotations. At least by the mid-twenties, it came to imply not only "political activism" but activism on behalf of the Communist Party and Soviet state, if not by a member of the Communist Party, then at least by a strong sympathizer of

it. A 1926 supplemental glossary to *The Peasant Newspaper* offered the following definition of the term: "Activist: precisely, this word means an ally of decisive action. In our time, activists usually refer to Communists or *Komsomol* members who conduct responsible work, or citizens in general who actively bring about the construction of the Soviet state" (*Krest'ianskii slovarik [Ob'iasnenie neponiatnykh slov]*, Besplatnoe prilozhenie k ural'skoi oblastnoi "Krest'ianskoi Gazete" [Sverdlovsk, 1926], 7.)

54. Selishchev, "O iazyke sovremennoi derevni," 131. In the manuscript for an unpublished book titled "Studies in the Russian Language of the Contemporary Period," Selishchev includes extended passages from such petitions and meetings, passages that offer striking confirmation of his point. Only selected chapters of the manuscript, including this 1932 scaled-down version of the chapter "In the Village," ever made it to publication. The manuscript includes linguistic material up through the late 1930s and would be useful for a study of the language of state beyond the earlier state-building years (A. M. Selishchev, RGALI, f. 2231, ed. khr. 24–25; esp. ed. khr. 24, pp. 359–63.)

55. A later study of the language of the village, in fact, convincingly documents villagers' ability to switch between the two registers, depending on the context and interlocutor, attesting to the still-formidable role of the traditional village discourse. N. M. Karinskii, *Ocherki iazyka russkikh krest'ian. Govor derevni Vanilovo* (Moscow: Gosud. sotsial'no-ekonomicheskoe izdatel'stvo, 1936), 7–8.

56. In addition to Selishchev's and Karinskii's work, see also P. Ia. Chernykh's *Russkii iazyk v Sibiri* (Irkutsk: OGIZ Vostochnosibirskoe oblastnoe izd., 1937). The absence of similar studies of the proletariat was noted perhaps most astutely by the linguist B. Larin, who pointed rather innocently to what for more concerned party-state sympathizers posed a serious theoretical and methodological lacuna, namely, the fact that no discrete linguistic register could be identified for what in essence was, in Voronskii's words, a "literary type" ("O lingvisticheskom izuchenii goroda," in L. V. Shcherba, ed., *Russkaia rech'*, vol. 3 [Leningrad: Academia, 1928], 61–74).

57. The rubric begins to appear with the third issue of 1933.

58. He embraces, in fact, the standard Russian national language as his formal model.

59. L. Iakubinskii, "Stat'ia chetvertaia. Klassovyi sostav sovremennogo russkogo iazyka. Iazyk krest'ianstva," part 1, *Literaturnaia ucheba* 4 (1930): 80–92.

60. Ibid., 89–92.

61. L. Iakubinskii, "Stat'ia chetvertaia. Klassovyi sostav sovremennogo russkogo iazyka. Iazyk krest'ianstva," part 2, *Literaturnaia ucheba* 6 (1930): 51–66.

62. L. Iakubinskii, "Stat'ia piataia. Klassovyi sostav sovremennogo russkogo iazyka. Iazyk proletariata," *Literaturnaia ucheba* 7 (1931): 22–33.

63. In fact, he identifies a separate "language of workers" that is characterized precisely by a combination of "the remnants *[perezhitki]* of local peasant dialects" and the Russian national language. Ibid., 30.

64. Ibid., 32. Emphasis in original.

65. Ibid.

66. Ibid., 32–33.

67. He actually reviews in detail Lenin's argument and conclusions regarding the working-class's "trade-unionist" mentality in *What Is to Be Done?* (ibid., 27–29).

68. In a subsequent article, Iakubinskii discusses Stalin's policies on nationalism and national languages at length ("Russkii iazyk v epokhu diktatury proletariata

[Part I]," *Literaturnaia ucheba* 9 [1931]: 66–76). Like those of Bukharin and Trotsky, Stalin's position on language finds close parallels in his political views, particularly that concerning "socialism in one country" (Carr, *Socialism in One Country,* esp. 2:36–51).

69. Maksim Gor'kii, *O russkom krest'ianstve* (Berlin: Izd. I. P. Ladyzhnikov, 1922), 43–44. Gregory Freidin goes so far as to link the intensification of the "war against the peasantry" to Gorky's return to Soviet Russia, first in 1928, and finally in 1931 ("Romans into Italians: Russian National Identity in Transition," *Stanford Slavic Studies* 7 [1993]: 263–68).

70. G. Vasil'kovskii, "O tret'ei knige *Bruskov* Fedora Panferova," *Literaturnyi kritik* 4 (1933): 39–56. The first three volumes of the novel appeared between 1928 and 1933, initially in the journal *Oktiabr',* and then under separate cover. Accentuating the ideologically charged nature of the debate with Gorky was the fact that Fedor Ivanovich Panferov (1896–1960) was one of the leading members of RAPP as well as the editor of *Oktiabr'* beginning in 1931.

71. Two exceptions to the general trend of praise included P. Neznamov, "Derevnia krasivogo opereniia," *Novyi Lef* 8 (1928): 2–9; and D. Tal'nikov, "Literaturnye zametki," *Krasnaia nov'* 1 (1929): 237–42. More "proletarian"-minded journals lavished the novels with praise, dedicating considerable space to its analysis and reception (e.g., *Na literaturnom postu* 12 [1930]: 29–32, 75–80; and "O 'Bruskakh' F. Panferova," *Oktiabr'* 2 [1934]: 188–225).

72. "Po povodu odnoi diskussii," *Literaturnaia gazeta* (28 January 1934).

73. A. S. Serafimovich, "O pisateliakh 'oblizannykh' i 'neoblizannykh,'" *Literaturnaia gazeta* (12 Feb. 1934). Serafimovich (1863–1949) was five years Gorky's elder and the author of the highly acclaimed *Iron Flood* (*Zheleznyi potok,* 1924).

74. Maksim Gor'kii, "Otkrytoe pis'mo A. S. Serafimovichu," *Literaturnaia gazeta* (14 Feb. 1934) (quoted from *Sobranie sochinenii,* 27:148).

75. Ibid., 152, 151. Serafimovich's response to this telling rejects Gorky's word choice in defending the use of "popular speech" *(narodnaia rech')* as a necessary reflection of the changing language culture in Soviet Russia ("Otvet A. M. Gor'komu," *Literaturnaia Gazeta* [1 Mar. 1934]). In her own thoughtful discussion of the controversy surrounding *Bruski,* Régine Robin describes Gorky's position as a (successful) attempt at establishing a more "monologic," "authoritarian" literary language (*Socialist Realism,* 165–90).

76. Other established writers who sided with Gorky include Aleksei Tolstoi ("Nuzhna li muzhitskaia sila?," *Literaturnaia gazeta* [6 Mar. 1934]); Mikhail Sholokhov (who parenthetically acknowledged his own past "misuse of local expressions," in "Za chestnuiu rabotu pisatelia i kritika," *Literaturnaia gazeta* [18 Mar. 1934]); Leonid Leonov ("Prizyv k muzhestvu," *Literaturnaia gazeta* [16 Apr. 1934]); Marietta Shaganian ("Diskussiia o iazyke," *Literaturnaia gazeta* [18 Apr. 1934]); and Ol'ga Forsh.

77. "'Za zdorov'e preosviashhennogo!'" *Literaturnaia gazeta* (2 Apr. 1934).

78. M. Serebrianskii, "K diskussii o *Bruskakh,*" *Literaturnaia gazeta* (28 Mar. 1934).

79. A. Derman, "Problema zhivoi rechi v khudozhestvennoi literature," *Novyi mir* 5 (1931): 161.

80. N. Kovarskii, "Spor o iazyke," *Literaturnyi sovremennik* 4 (1934): 112. Gorky made the same point in his article "On language," claiming that "littering"

the literary language signified a negative attitude toward the social group being reflected ("O iazyke," *Pravda* 76 [1934], quoted from *Sobranie sochinenii*, 27:166.)

81. "Slovo chitatelia," *Literaturnaia gazeta* (28 Mar. 1934) (cf. Toporov, *Krest'iane o pisateliakh*, 182–201). Such "popular" surveys, especially when cited in isolation, must be taken with a grain of salt. It was common practice for all sides of such debates to invoke the voice of the people in support of their cause. For contrasting invocations of the vox populi in the Panferov case, cf. "Obsuzhdaem *Bruski* F. Panferova. Golos chitatelia," *Na literaturnom postu* 12 (1930): 75–80. For excellent discussions of what still remains a sound, though at times overstated, thesis—that the style of socialist-realist novels was simplified largely because of reader demands—see Robin, "Popular Literature of the 1920s," 253–67; and Dobrenko, *Making of the State Reader*, esp. 82–145.

82. Dal', *Tolkovyi slovar' russkogo iazyka*.

83. Ibid., 1:3, 5.

84. P. Khavin, "Bol'shevistskaia publitsistika i literaturnyi iazyk," *Literaturnaia ucheba* 8 (1934): 77–78. Compare this refinement of the notion of "simplicity" with the "wise simplicity of the Bolsheviks" posited by F. I. Panferov, himself at the First Writers' Congress in 1934 (*Pervyi vsesoiuznyi s"ezd sovetskikh pisatelei, 1934*, 275).

85. Kovarskii, "Spor o iazyke," 113.

86. Viktor Gofman, "Stil', iazyk i dialekt," in *Iazyk literatury: ocherki i etiudy* (Leningrad: Gosizdat. "khud. lit", 1936), 149–50. See also Khavin, "Bol'shevistskaia publitsistika i literaturnyi iazyk," 86.

87. Khavin, "Bol'shevistskaia publitsistika i literaturnyi iazyk," 86. Using a similar formulation, Khavin contested Panferov's defense of his language play as a reflection of the influence of the revolution on Russian by claiming that revolution in language was not a matter of formal innovation but rather a revolution in content—one, more specifically, that "enriched and enriches language first of all by bringing new Socialist content into it" (86).

88. A. Selivanovskii, "Nakanune bol'shikh sporov," *Literaturnaia gazeta* 17 (1934).

89. P. Chernykh, "Literaturnyi iazyk na rasput'i," *Budushchaia Sibir'* 4 (1934): 87. Later he embraced the same notion of "revolutionary purism" as a cure for several other diseases: "oversimplification" *(uproshchenchestvo)*, "the multifarious forms of verbal idle talk *[pustozvonstvo]*, concocting new and extraordinary words when one could get by with old ones, using foreign words without discretion, verbosity, syntactic tightrope-walking, hazy similes, and fanciful metaphors, etc." (91).

90. *Pervyi vsesoiuznyi s"ezd sovetskikh pisatelei, 1934*, 4.

91. Khavin, "Bol'shevistskaia publitsistika i literaturnyi iazyk," 76–78.

92. K. Fedin, "Iazyk literatury," *Literaturnaia ucheba* 3–4 (1933): 111; Khavin, "Bol'shevistskaia publitsistika i literaturnyi iazyk," 75. Even Panferov, the object of criticism for his overuse of rural colloquial speech, was careful to describe the leaders of the revolution as the strongest influence on the language of the revolution. In his address to the First Writers' Congress, he remarked, "Our authentic revolutionary leaders, through speeches, articles, books, influence the general language of the masses; the language of the revolution thus comes from the best and most valued part of the language of the *narod*, and the language of the leaders of the revolution" (*Pervyi vsesoiuznyi s"ezd sovetskikh pisatelei, 1934*, 174).

93. For a penetrating study of the style of Stalin's writing, particularly with

regard to its logical structure, its folkloric, pagan, and Christian roots, and its transformation of the myth of Lenin, see Vaiskopf, *Pisatel' Stalin*.

7: NARRATING THE PARTY-STATE

1. As Kotkin puts it, "[T]he Civil War not only gave the daring, opportunistic Bolsheviks a modus operandi and helped solidify their still amorphous identity as the consummate builders of a socially oriented, powerful state; it also furthered the process whereby the Bolsheviks' being in power came to be identified with the cause of 'the revolution.'" *Magnetic Mountain*, 14.

2. Citing Soviet sources, Lewin offers the following demographic breakdown of Red Army soldiers: peasants, 77 percent; workers, 14.8 percent; others, 8.2 percent. "The Civil War: Dynamics and Legacy," in Koenker, Rosenberg, and Suny, eds., *Party, State, and Society in the Russian Civil War*, 420n.13.

3. See Von Hagen, *Soldiers in the Proletarian Dictatorship*, 50–66, for a discussion of the state's increased concern for and monitoring of the numerous bands of partisan fighters who fought against both White and Red Armies in 1918–1919. Von Hagen argues that the movement was a response by rural peasant communities to the power vacuum in the countryside, in an effort to defend their local interests.

4. Dm. Furmanov, *Chapaev* (Moscow: Gosizdat., 1923), 12. This and subsequent quotes from *Chapaev* are taken from this first-edition volume. Page numbers will appear in parentheses following the text. All translations of *Chapaev* are my own.

5. Most reviews, in fact, characterize the work as being more akin to a journalistic memoir than a work of fiction. See [G. Kor.], "Chapaev," *Na postu* 4 (1923): 195; A. V. Lunacharskii, "Desiat' knig za desiat' let revoliutsii," *Sobranie sochinenii v vos'mi tomakh: literaturovedenie, kritika, estetika*, vol. 2 (Moscow: Khudozhestvennaia literatura, 1964), 359; and A. Kamegulov, "*Chapaev* Dm. Furmanova. Frontovye zapiski," *Literaturnaia ucheba* 6–7 (1933): 39. All reviews listed here cite this feature as a positive one, the last one in particular praising it, because it permitted Furmanov to "interrupt the picture of the artistic display of the civil war with . . . commentaries on military-strategic and political themes" (42–43).

6. For discussions of the criticism of folklore from writers' groups such as the Proletcult and RAPP, see Dana Prescott Howell, *Development of Soviet Folkloristics* (New York: Garland, 1992.), 73–81; Frank J. Miller, *Folklore for Stalin: Russian Folklore and Pseudofolklore of the Stalin Era* (Armonk, N.Y.: M. E. Sharpe, 1990), 6–7; and Iu. Sokolov, "Osnovnye linii razvitiia sovetskogo fol'klora," *Sovetskii fol'klor* 7 (1940): 38–53. For an example of urban folklore studies, see P. Sobolev, "Sovremennyi fabrichno-gorodskoi fol'klor," *Pechat' i revoliutsiia* 6 (1929): 89–98.

7. Sokolov's full statement reflects the degree to which the language of state had dominated academic spheres by the early 1930s: "The oral creative work of the masses, despite the sharp class struggle that is reflected in and transmitted by it, remains in an elemental state and is, for the most part, devoid of any systematic ideological or artistic guidance. It is essential to do away with this indifferent attitude toward folklore and—as a counterbalance to the old, noble-romantic, and bourgeois-populist theories that have defended the 'inviolability of the people's creative work'—to lay down the limit of elementalness, actively intervene in the folklore process, to sharpen the struggle against all that is hostile to socialist construction, against *kulak*, vulgar and petit-bourgeois folklore, and to support the growth of a

healthy proletarian and *kolkhoz* oral poetry" (*Fol'klor. Biulleten' fol'klornoi sektsii Instituta antropologii i etnografii AN SSSR* 1–2 [1934]: 17). Compare this to his 1926 description of folklore as a "living chronicle" of the mood of the village: "Oral literature must be seen as a living and poetic chronicle of a swift-flowing life. Herein lies its social meaning. It eases the understanding of the popular moods and the changes that have occurred and still occur in popular everyday life." (Sokolov and Sokolov, *Poeziia derevni,* 13).

8. A recent study of the "Sokolov school" of folkore studies meticulously traces these unfortunate transformations within the field, documenting both the pressures for "modernization" placed on it from the outside and the great ambivalence (and, later, regret) with which Sokolov and other specialists regarded the shifts (and their participation in them) toward more mass-collected and artificially engineered folklore. See V. A. Bakhtina, *Fol'kloristicheskaia shkola brat'ev Sokolovykh. Dostoinstvo i prevratnosti nauchnogo znaniia* (Moscow: Nasledie, 2000), esp. 217–92.

9. The collection and publication of contemporary *chastushki*—particularly those with themes and motifs relevant and sympathetic to recent political and social transformations—became something of a cottage industry in the 1920s and 1930s. Similar to the trends in changing voice I discuss here in relation to oral civil war narratives, one finds a wider range of discursive models in the earlier representations of *chastushki* and a more uniform, politically "conscious" (and pro-Soviet) voice in the collections appearing later in the 1920s and early 1930s. For a representative range, see A. Semenovskii, "Sovremennaia chastushka," *Krasnaia nov'* 1 (1921): 53–61; A. M. Smirnov-Kutacheskii, "Proiskhozhdenie chastushki," *Pechat' i revoliutsiia* 2 (1925): 42–60; "Khuliganskaia chastushka sovremennoi derevni," *Pechat' i revoliutsiia* 7 (1925): 128–32; Kniazev, *Sovremennye chastushki; Chastushki krasnoarmeiskie i o krasnoi armii* (Moscow: GIZ, 1925); and Khrebes, *Sovremennaia derevnia v chastushkakh.* What most of the discussions fail to note, however, is that *chastushki* relating to current political and social events made up a relatively small proportion of those in popular circulation at any one time, the majority of which were dedicated instead to themes of love and romance (N. Morev i N. Sh., "Sovremennaia chastushka," in Tan-Bogoraz, ed., *Staryi i novyi byt,* 117–25).

10. Semen Mirer and Vasilii Borovik, *Revoliutsiia: Ustnye rasskazy ural'skikh rabochikh o grazhdanskoi voine* (Moscow, 1931). This was the first in a series of three "oral histories" compiled by Mirer and Borovik. The following two were dedicated to the shockworker campaign and a celebration of Lenin: *Delo chesti: Ustnye rasskazy rabochikh o sotsialisticheskom sorevnovanii* (Moscow, 1931); *Rasskazy rabochikh o Lenine* (Moscow, 1934).

11. The collector of a separate collection of civil war narratives describes the import of her material in a similar manner, claiming that the stories "give the masses new artistic material of great revolutionary significance. . . . [O]ne of our leading tasks is to support and stimulate the creation, development, and widespread dissemination of an authentically revolutionary epos" (A. M. Astakhova, "Fol'klor grazhdanskoi voiny" in *Sovetskii fol'klor. Stat'i i materialy,* vol. 1 [Leningrad: Izd. AN SSSR, 1934], 38–39).

12. "Recorded on a steamship from Perm' to Cherdyn' from the words of a forty year-old worker from Pozhvinsk" (56). Appended to this narrative is an extensive quote from the storyteller in which, among other things, he shares his intention to "compile a novel" (57).

13. For a thorough discussion of the role of such remembrances, and of the place of narrative in the making of history, see Frederick Corney's "Writing October: Memory and the Making of the Bolshevik Revolution" (unpublished book manuscript).

14. "From the words of a thirty-two-year-old alpine storeman of the Kiseltrest mines' northern group, by origin from the workers of the Alexandrovsk factory. Served in the military from ages 17–26. Reads newspapers and books, but is able to study little. Good-natured and responsive. Narrates with great excitement, engaging listeners" (75–76).

15. "P. K. Lar'kov, about thirty years old. A volunteer since March 1918, participant at the Turkistani, eastern and southern fronts" (199). That some of these "oral stories" could have assumed a written form from the start is certainly not out of the question. For a brief, but insightful, discussion of the various public "meetings" conducted on the pages of newspapers and edited collections, see Platt, *History in a Grotesque Key*, 136–39. Recent archival publications have confirmed long-standing suspicions that published collections of the *glas naroda*—particularly beginning in the late 1920s—constituted an ideologically controlled representation of a much more complicated, confused discursive environment. See V. V. Kabanov et al., "'Sotsializm—eto rai na zemle' (Krest'ianskie predstavleniia o sotsializme v pis'makh 20–x godov)," in *Neizvestnaia Rossiia. XX vek* (Moscow: Istoricheskoe nasledie, 1993), 3:199–226; *Golos naroda. Pis'ma i otkliki riadovykh sovetskikh grazhdan o sobytiiakh 1918–1932 gg.* (Moscow: ROSSPEN, 1998); and *Pis'ma vo vlast', 1917–1927. Zaiavleniia, zhaloby, donosy, pis'ma v gosudarstvennye struktury i bol'shevistskim vozhdiam* (Moscow: ROSSPEN, 1998).

16. Among the more prominent researchers into the genre of the "worker autobiography" was the pedagogue N. A. Rybnikov, whose *Aftobiografii rabochikh i ikh izuchenie* (Moscow, 1930) stands out as the most comprehensive discussion of the field and includes the most detailed bibliography. For examples of collective public testimonies, see Lukoianov and Rafail, eds., *Rabkory o smerti Il'icha;* and Selikh and Grinevskii, eds., *Krest'iane o sovetskoi vlasti.*

17. One must not underestimate the importance of the context in which these respective sets of narratives were gathered. Although fraught with imprecision, the respective introductions do safely suggest that the setting in Fedorchenko's case was primarily private and informal, whereas that in the case of Mirer and Borovik was substantially more public, formal, and official (perhaps even in the form of the "evenings" that were widespread by this time).

18. Even by the early 1930s, however, the more coherent and politically conscious reminiscences were still inadequate for telling the authoritative history of the civil war in the eyes of Maxim Gorky, who had undertaken the compilation of a popular, multivolume *History of the Civil War*. Explaining his rationale and plans in a 1929 letter to Stalin, Gorky wrote that "the peasants do not understand that history because they do not know its full extent. The peasant needs to know the motives that inspired the working class to begin this war; he needs to know that the workers saved the country from slavery and conquest by foreign capital; he needs to know what bloodshed and loss of life, what economic damage—in figures and pictures—were caused in the land. . . ." Most telling was Gorky's plan to enlist leading Soviet writers of the day (he suggests Aleksei Tolstoi, Mikhail Sholokhov, and Iurii Libedinskii) to transform the assembled "raw material . . . into literary

form" and publish the book "in a mass edition, so that there would be a copy in every village, where it would be read like a novel" (*Maksim Gorky: Selected Letters*, 319–20). The two volumes of *History of the Civil War* appeared in 1937 and 1942.

19. Basic root meanings include "delineation, depiction, portrayal," with nearly all words formed off of the root containing some link to the act of taking pen to paper; e.g., *chertit'* (draft, sketch), *ochertit'* (trace, draw, sketch, describe), *nachertat'* (trace, inscribe, write), *podcherknut'* (underline), *zacherknut'* (cross out). Catherine A. Wolkonsky and Marianna A. Poltoratzky, comps., *Handbook of Russian Roots* (New York: Columbia University Press, 1961), 397–98.

20. All of the titles come from sketches appearing in *Novyi mir* in the late 1920s. By early 1930 the journal ran a regular section of sketches under the less rurally oriented title "People and Facts." An equal number of sketches appeared in the journal *Oktiabr'* under titles such as "Notes of a Rural Correspondent," "How the Workers Live," and "Life in Motion."

21. A. Belyi, "Kul'tura kraevedcheskogo ocherka," *Novyi mir* 3 (1933): 257–73.

22. L. Korelin, "Ocherki kollektivizatsii. Obzor ocherkov v broshiurakh i gazetakh," *Na literaturnom postu* 9 (1930): 49.

23. Indicative of this emphasis was the shift in rubric for sketches beginning with the 1929 issues of *Novyi mir* from the village-oriented titles cited above to "People and Facts."

24. For the contrast between "fact" and "fantasy," and the recommended inclusion of various documentary data, see Mikh. Bekker, "Problema khudozhestvennogo ocherka," *Na literaturnom postu* 13 (1929): 55. On the inappropriateness of fabrication, see V. Bobryshev, "Ocherk—bol'shaia literatura," *Nashi dostizheniia* 5 (1934): 115.

25. A. Isbakh, "O rabote v nizovykh kruzhkakh (Opyt kolomzavodskogo kruzhka 'Dizel'')," *Na literaturnom postu* 15–16 (1930): 101.

26. I. Zhiga, "Promezhutochnyi zhanr," *Literaturnaia gazeta* (15 June 1930).

27. V. Bobryshev, "Ob ocherke," *Nashi dostizheniia* 8 (1933): 94.

28. L. Korelin, "Ocherk i fel'eton v gazete," *Na literaturnom postu* 10 (1930): 57; B. Galin, "Za deistvennost' ocherka," *Na literaturnom postu* 4 (1931): 18ff.; Bobryshev, "Ob ocherke," 114; "Itogi soveshchaniia rabochikh-ocherkistov," *Literaturnaia gazeta* (30 May 1931).

29. S. Tret'iakov, "Evoliutsiia zhanra," *Nashi dostizheniia* 7–8 (1934): 161; Bekker, "Problema khudozhestvennogo ocherka," 55; Korelin, "Ocherk i fel'eton v gazete," 57; M. Luzgin, "Za boevoi proletarskii ocherk," *Na literaturnom postu* 4 (1931): 14.

30. Luzgin, "Za boevoi proletarskii ocherk," 17; Korelin, "Ocherki kollektivizatsii," 50.

31. Originating out of the avant-garde journal *Novyi Lef*, "factography" held, among other things, that nonliterary genres such as the newspaper and ethnography had superseded belles lettres as the linguistic dominant in Soviet times because of their special ability to convey the critical facts of labor production in the workplace and countryside free of all aesthetic trappings. Characteristic of this position is Boris Kushner's statement that "in Soviet literature the fact and document are winning for themselves a more and more dominant position, decisively pushing aside and supplanting allegory, euphemism, and analogous forms of literary fabrication" ("Ocherk o zarubezhnykh stranakh," *Nashi dostizheniia* 5 [1934]: 140). For

an excellent collection of articles outlining the *New LEF* critics' idea of "factography" and their defense of the generic superiority of the newspaper ("the Bible of our day"), see N. F. Chuzhak, ed., *Literatura fakta. Pervyi sbornik materialov rabotnikov LEFa* (1929; rpt., Moscow: Zakharov, 2000). For critiques of such claims, see Bekker, "Problema khudozhestvennogo ocherka," 54–55; Luzgin, "Ob ocherke," 95–98; and V. Stavskii, "Ob ocherke i ocherkiste," *Na literaturnom postu* 4 (1931): 16–17.

32. Korelin, "Ocherki kollektivizatsii," 47–52; Luzgin, "Ob ocherke," 102, 106.

33. Luzgin, "Ob ocherke," 103–5, 111.

34. B. Kuz'min, "Ocherki Ivana Zhigi," *Na literaturnom postu* 11 (1931): 36; V. Bor, "Ocherk—eto 'razvedka boem'. Na vserossiiskom proizvodstvennom soveshchanii ocherkistov RAPP," *Literaturnaia gazeta* (14 Jan. 1931).

35. Aleksandr Mar'iamov, "Put' k geroiu," *Nashi dostizheniia* 7–8 (1934): 186–87.

36. Isbakh, "O rabote v nizovykh kruzhkakh," 104; M. Luzgin, "Za boevoi proletarskii ocherk," 16; V. Bobryshev, "O rodimykh piatnakh," *Nashi dostizheniia* 7–8 (1934) 155–56.

37. I. Evdokimov, quoted by the head of the State Publishing House in "V bor'be za novogo avtora. beseda s zav. OGIZ tov. Khalatovym," *Literaturnaia gazeta* (25 Sept. 1931).

38. Bobryshev, "Ob ocherke," 93; "Ocherk—sredstvo pokaza geroev sotsialisticheskogo truda," *Literaturnaia gazeta* (30 May 1931); "Ob itogakh proizvodstvennogo soveshchaniia ocherkistov," *Na literaturnom postu* 10 (1931): 38–39.

39. Bekker, "Problema khudozhestvennogo ocherka," 53, 57–58.

40. V. Pertsov, "Kuda vedet ocherk?" *Literaturnaia gazeta* (16 June 1930). See also Bobryshev, "Ocherk—bol'shaia literatura," 114. Gorky was perhaps one the advocates' strongest exemplars, but they remained largely mute about the awkward fact that his forays were almost all of a memoiristic form—looking back in time—rather than at the productivity of the glorious present and radiant future.

41. M. Gor'kii, L. Averbakh and S. Firin, eds., *Belomorsko-Baltiiskii Kanal imeni Stalina. Istoriia stroitel'stva* (Moscow: Gosudarstvennoe izdatel'stvo 'Istoriia fabrik i zavodov', 1934).

42. Among the thirty-six writers listed on the title page are Averbakh, Gorky, Zoshchenko, Vsevolod Ivanov, Valentin Kataev, A. Tolstoi, and Shklovskii.

43. Cynthia A. Ruder, *Making History for Stalin: The Story of the Belomor Canal* (Gainesville: University Press of Florida, 1998).

44. Even Zoshchenko's prose style, however, undergoes a significant transformation in the direction of clarity and simplicity toward the middle of the 1930s. For an excellent analysis of the complicated nature of this change, see Chudakova, *Poetika Mikhaila Zoshchenko*, 160–80.

45. Ruder, *Making History for Stalin*, 105–14.

46. The book's appendix includes an extended list of field transcripts, notes, and texts—ranging from local newspapers to transcripts of interviews with prisoners—all of which served as "raw material" for the drafting of its sections.

47. V. P. Kataev, *Vremia, vpered!* (Moscow: Sovetskaia literatura, 1933), 12–13 (all further references to this novel appear parenthetically in the text). Stalin's speech is published in I. V. Stalin, "O zadachakh khoziastvennikov" (4 Feb. 1931), in *Sochineniia* (Moscow: Gosizdat. politicheskoi literatury, 1951), 13:29–42. Among the more prominent Soviet novelists, Valentin Petrovich Kataev (1897–1986) wrote

Time, Forward! following a trip to Magnetigorsk, Stalin's model city for the industrial and social ideals of the First Five-Year Plan.

48. Compare this diversion of discourse to Trotsky's own abandonment of a prepared speech—only in that case to articulate the immediate unspoken needs of the crowd.

49. Iakov Il'in, *Bol'shoi konveier* (Moscow: OGIZ, Molodaia gvardiia, 1934), 160–61. Earlier descriptions in the scene have Stalin "seizing hold of the very issues that were disturbing and could not but disturb the delegates" and running through the details of his argument "patiently as always, with precise and finished phrases, like mathematical formulas, [while] the audience carefully followed him, still unable to catch the main thread on which those formulas were being strung" [159–60]. Newspaper excerpts and other official documents play a particularly prominent role in Vasilii Il'enkov's *Driving Axle* (1932), beginning with the epigraph from Engels and the *Pravda* report "For the Mobilization of Internal Resources" and continuing with key appearances and references throughout. Even the leading local party official, Vartan'ian—the most fluent in the party language, and through whom "the party speaks to the thousands"—speaks with a heavy Georgian accent (*Vedushchaia os'*, bk. 1 [Moscow: Gosizdat. khudozhestvennoi literatury, 1932], 3, 22, 56–57, 91, 168–78, 244, 323, 373–75, 395–97, 427).

50. Kataev, *Vremia, vpered!*, 301–2.

51. N. Ostrovskii, *Kak zakalialas' stal'* (Moscow: Izvestiia, 1965), 344–65. The title of the novella, *Rozhdennye burei*, is identical to that of Ostrovskii's own next literary project, the first volume of which was published in 1936.

52. The first title appeared as *Krasnoe derevo* in *Krasnoe derevo i drugie* (Berlin: Petropolis, 1929). The second first appeared as *Volga vpadaet v Kaspiiskoe more* (Moscow: Nedra, 1930). Unless otherwise noted, parenthetic page references to the second novel come from a reproduction of the first edition by Russian Language Specialties (Russian Studies Series, no. 79) (Pullman, Mich., 1973). Boris Andreevich Pil'niak, born Vogau (1894–1938), was among the more well-known and controversial writers of early Soviet letters, in part owing to the innovative style of his prose, in part owing to its unconventional (albeit revolutionary) subject matter. His refusal to compromise his literary and moral standards led to his ultimate arrest and death sentence on false charges of having committed state crimes (*Russkie pisateli 20 veka*, 553–55).

53. Gary Browning discusses at length the growing intensity of attacks on Pil'niak over the second half of the 1920s, culminating in the scandal over *Mahogany*, in *Boris Pilniak: Scythian at a Typewriter* (Ann Arbor, Mich.: Ardis, 1985), 29–76. Here Browning also disputes the long-held belief that Pil'niak reshaped the first into the second primarily out of political motivation—to appease criticism of an ideological nature—arguing instead that Pil'niak's main motivations were aesthetic. Whether Pil'niak actually intended the novel to be exemplary of the socialist realist variety is also secondary to this discussion. Even if he had not, its close affinities to that genre were sufficient to invite such a reading by nearly all of his critics.

54. N. Artiukhin, "Volga vpadaet v kaspiiskoe more'," *Na literaturnom postu* 13–14 (1930): 105.

55. The Greek derivation of *okhlomon*—*okhlos* ("mob") plus *monos* ("alone")

rendering "alone from the mob" or "outcast"—was first posited by Vera Reck in her translation of Pil'niak stories in *Mother Earth and Other Stories* (New York: Anchor Books, 1968), 71 (cited here in Browning, *Boris Pilniak*, 218–19n.86).

56. R. Azarkh, "Savanarolla s Tverskogo bul'vara. Kuda vpadaet Volga . . . Pil'niaka," *Na literaturnom postu* 4 (1931): 20–27.

57. The foldout page appears between pages 250 and 251 in the book's first edition.

58. E. Blium, "Roman o chestnom, no beskrovnom stroitel'stve," *Literatura i iskusstvo* 1 (1930): 117.

59. The newspaper insert, the critic claims, is the only place, in fact, where one can find the true, "unbloodless material—competition, *udarnichestvo*," but, he adds, it is "neither in plot nor in any general way connected to the novel" (117).

60. E.g., "Lenin" (1920), in *Andrei Platonov: Vozvrashchenie* (Moscow: Molodaia gvardiia, 1989), 9–10; "Remont zemli" (1920), in ibid., 10–12.

61. "Che-Che-O" first appeared in *Novyi mir* (no. 12 [1928]: 249–58) and listed Boris Pil'niak as coauthor. All references to the story here are cited from Andrei Platonov and Boris Pil'niak, "ChE-ChE-O. Oblastnye organizatsionno-filosofskie ocherki," in *Andrei Platonov: Vozvrashchenie*, 75–92.

62. Comprising commonly used components, these stump-compounds, if not entirely fictitious, are mildly comical in their euphonic combinations. In order, "Chairman of the regional union for consumers' cooperatives," "Director of the people's trade commission," "District executive committee," "District labor soviet," and the particularly odd "District town."

63. A. Selivanovskii, "V chem 'somnevaetsia' Andrei Platonov," *Literaturnaia gazeta* (10 June 1931), reprinted in N. V. Kornienko and E. D. Shubina, eds., *Andrei Platonov: Mir tvorchestvo* (Moscow: Sovremennyi pisatel', 1994), 269. On multiple occasions after the scandal surrounding the story, Platonov describes Pil'niak's role in its creation as primarily editorial in nature. See Elena Tolstaia-Segal, "'Stikhiinye sily': Platonov i Pil'niak (1928–1929)," in Kornienko and Shubina, eds., *Andrei Platonov: Mir tvorchestvo*, 84–104; and "Stenogramma tvorcheskogo vechera Andreia Platonova vo Vserossiiskom Soiuze sovetskikh pisatelei 1 fevralia 1932 g.," in N. V. Kornienko and E. D. Shubina, eds., *Andrei Platonov: Vospominaniia sovremenikov, Materialy k biografii* (Moscow: Sovremennyi pisatel', 1994), 295, 301–2.

64. "Vprok (Bediatskaia khronika)" first appeared in *Krasnaia nov'* 9 (1931): 3–39. Pages cited in this discussion come from *Andrei Platonov: Vozvrashchenie*, 92–154. For an account of the story's negative impression on Stalin, leading in turn to a public denunciation of the piece by Fadeev, see the text, introduction, and commentary by E. Shubina to A. Fadeev, "Ob odnoi Kulatskoi khronike," in Kornienko and Shubina, eds., *Andrei Platonov: Mir tvorchestva*, 272–78. Fadeev's denunciation appeared in two prominent periodicals, *Kranaia nov'* 5–6 (1931) and *Izvestiia* (3 July 1931).

65. See p. 109. Thomas Seifrid notes the likeness of such passages to Platonov's journalism and technical reports from the early 1920s (*Andrei Platonov*, 139).

66. For a thorough treatment of Platonov's language, see Seifrid's *Andrei Platonov*.

67. Contrasting Platonov to Zoshchenko, Chudakova notes that, whereas Zoshchenko presented in his *skaz* narrator a "real" portrait of the new speaking proletarian, with all its deficiencies on clear display, Platonov portrayed a more ide-

alized context for the proletarian voice, where there was no palpable authority gap between narrator and author (*Poetika Mikhaila Zoshchenko*, 150–53). For a broader comparison of Platonov's narrative voice with the *skaz* and modernist narratives of the 1920s, see Seifrid, *Andrei Platonov*, 84–90.

68. Seifrid makes a similar comparison in passing in *Andrei Platonov*, 88–89. See also E. Shubina's characterization of Platonov's *"iurodstvuiushchaia fraza"* in "Sozertsatel' i delatel' (1899–1926)," in Kornienko and Shubina, eds., *Andrei Platonov: Vospominaniia sovremennikov*, 147.

69. A. Platonov, [Pis'mo k A. M. Gor'komu], in Kornienko and Shubina, eds., *Andrei Platonov: Mir tvorchestva*, 279–80. The letter is dated 24 July 1931.

70. The shift is not dissimilar to that noted by Emmet Kennedy in parliamentary discourse in the decade following the French Revolution: "The role of rhetoric as persuasion, with consensus as its goal, was superseded by a discourse in which consensus was the premise and its celebration the end" (*A Cultural History of the French Revolution* [New Haven, Conn.: Yale University Press, 1989], 303).

71. In his address to the First Congress of Soviet Writers, the writer Ilya Erenburg lists sketches, confessions, and even protocols and stenographic notes as genres that are contributing to the creation of a "new form" for the Soviet novel (*Pervyi vsesoiuznyi s"ezd sovetskikh pisatelei, 1934*, 185).

EPILOGUE

1. For an extended discussion of this thesis, see Gellner, *Nations and Nationalism*.

2. As Keith Michael Baker puts it, "In practice, meanings (and those who depend upon them) are always implicitly at risk. Any utterance puts the authority of the speaker, and the place from which he or she speaks, potentially in question. . . . Individual acts and utterances may therefore take on meanings within several different fields of discourse simultaneously, redounding upon one another in often unpredictable ways. Thus language can say more than any individual actor intends; meanings can be appropriated and extended by others in unanticipated ways. At the limit, no one is safe from the potential play of discursivity." *Inventing the French Revolution*, 6–7.

3. I am indebted to Richard Stites for pointing out this connection.

4. Indeed, since the beginning of his presidency, Putin has largely impeded the normal operations of the few remaining major television stations not structurally beholden to the state, first NTV, and then TV 6, with regular raids by the tax police, jailings of key executives, and wholesale restructuring.

5. Viktor Pelevin, *Generation 'P.' Roman* (Moscow: VAGRIUS, 1999).

6. More recently the title of an award-winning television talk show, the phrase was first adopted for a series of campaign promotions broadcast during the 1996 presidential elections. Each episode would feature 15–20 everyday citizen-orators, who were given a minute to record their opinions before a camera in a portable booth (referred to in the Gorbachev days as the *budka glasnosti*, or "glasnost booth"). While the citizens were free to speak their minds on any issue whatsoever, the vast majority spoke out about politics, and did so strongly in favor of Yeltsin's reforms and reelection—again, testimony to the powerful rhetorical force, and equally powerful mythologization, of the *glas naroda*.

7. For an excellent discussion of this phenomenon, see Aleksei Plutser-Sarno,

"Russkii vorovskoi slovar' kak kul'turnyi fenomen," *Logos* 2, no. 23 (2000): 208–17. In this same volume, Plutser-Sarno provides an exhaustive bibliography of such dictionaries published in Russia through the nineteenth and twentieth centuries ("Bibliografiia slovarei 'vorovskoi,' 'ofenskoi,' 'razboinich'ei,' 'tiuremnoi,' 'blatnoi,' 'lagernoi,' 'ugolovnoi' leksiki, izdannykh v Rossii i za rubezhom za poslednie dva stoletiia," *Logos* 2, no. 23 [2000]: 222–26.) For one of the more astute discussions of the role of argot in Russian society, see V. S. Elistratov, "Argo i kul'tura," in *Slovar' russkogo argo (materaly 1980–1990-kh gg.)* (Moscow: Russkie slovari, 2000), 574–692.

8. For a report on the conference proceedings, see "Zashchitu rodnogo slova," *Moskva* 8 (1994): 145–53.

9. A. I. Solzhenitsyn, comp., *Russkii slovar' iazykovogo rasshireniia* (Moscow: Nauka, 1990).

10. The bill was introduced by State Duma Deputy (Unity) Kaadyr-Ool Bilcheldei in June 2001.

11. Cf. Iurii Makarov, "Otvet'te mne oral'no, pristebyvaia gubami (Otkrytoe pis'mo diktoru radio rossii T. Vizbor)," *Molodaia gvardiia* 5 (1996): 249. For an analysis of the full range of the purist spectrum in the contemporary language debates, see my article "*Natsiia ili snikerizatsiia?* Identity and Perversion in the Language Debates of Late- and Post-Soviet Russia," *Russian Review* 59 (2000): 614–29.

12. Pravitel'stvo Rossiiskoi Federatsii, Press-tsentr, Soobshcheniia dlia pechati, no. 865 (www.pravitelstvo.gov.ru/2001/07/03/994164012.html).

13. Together with the radio show "We speak Russian" ("Govorim po-russki"), a weekly talk show dedicated to general issues of language usage, policy, and history that is broadcast on the popular radio station, "Ekho, Moskvy," most notable in this respect is the internet portal "Russkii iazyk" (www.gramota.ru), a virtual mediator of a wide range of language-related resources, including official documents and decisions, scholarly papers, national contests, conference announcements and reports, informal chat forums, and an extensive catalog of online resources, jointly sponsored by the Russian Language Council and the Federal Ministry of the Press, Television, and Mass Media.

SELECT BIBLIOGRAPHY

ARCHIVAL SOURCES

Gosudarstvennyi Arkhiv Rossiiskoi Federatsii (GARF) (formerly Tsentral'nyi Gosudarstvennyi Arkhiv [TsGA])

Fond A-1575. Opis' 10. Glavnoe upravlenie sotsial'nogo vospitaniia i politicheskogo obrazovaniia detei (Glavsotsvos) Narkompros RSFSR. Otdel edinnoi shkoly.

Fond A-2306. Opis' 18. Narodnyi Komissariat Prosveshcheniia (Narkompros). Otdel Vysshikh Uchebnykh Zavedenii.

Fond A-2313. Opis' 2. Narkompros RSFSR. Glavnyi politiko-prosvetitel'nyi komitet Respubliki (Glavpolitprosvet). Otdel agitatsii. Podotdely agitatorov. Otdelenie agitpunktov.

———. Opis' 3. Narkompros RSFSR. Glavnyi politiko-prosvetitel'nyi komitet Respubliki (Glavpolitprosvet). Propagandistskii otdel. Podotdel klubnyi.

———. Opis' 6. Narkompros RSFSR. Glavnyi politiko-prosvetitel'nyi komitet Respubliki (Glavpolitprosvet). Khudozhestvennyi otdel. Literaturnyi podotdel.

Fond A-2314. Vserossiiskaia chrezvychainaia komissiia po likvidatsii bezgramotnosti (VChKLB).

Fond A-2330. Opis' 1. Narkompros RSFSR. Tsentral'naia kollegiia agitatsionnykh punktov.

Fond A-4655. Opis' 1. Naucho-issledovatel'skii institut iazykovedeniia i istorii literatury pri RANINKhIRK. Institut iazyka i literatury.

Institut Mirovoi Literatury (IMLI)

Fond 40. Rossiiskaia assotsiatsiia proletarskogo iskusstva (RAPP).

Fond 155. Vsesoiuznaia assotsiatsiia proletarskogo iskusstva (RAPP).

Fond 156. Vsesoiuznaia organizatsiia krest'ianskikh pisatelei (VOKP).

Fond 158. Moskovskaia assotsiatsiia proletarskogo iskusstva (MAPP).

Institut Russkogo Iazyka pri Akademii Nauk (IRIa)

Fond 20. Moskovskii Lingvisticheskii Krug (MLK).

Nauchnyi Arkhiv Rossiiskoi Akademii Obrazovaniia (NA RAO)

Fond 5. Nauchno-pedagogicheskii institut metodov vneshkol'noi raboty.

Fond 8. Nauchno-issledovatel'skii programmno-metodicheskii institut NKR RSFSR.

Fond 17. Tsentral'naia Pedagogicheskaia Laboratoriia Narkomprosa RSFSR. Sektsiia russkogo iazyka.

Fond 47. Arkhiv N. A. Rybnikova.

Rossiiskii gosudarstvennyi arkhiv sotsial'no-politicheskoi istorii (RGASPI) (formerly Rossiiskii Tsentr Khraneniia i Izucheniia Dokumentov Noveishei Istorii [RTsKhIDNI])
Fond 17. Opis' 60: TsK RKP(b) otdel agitatsii i propagandy.
Fond 610. Opis' 1: Gazeta "Rabochaia Moskva."

Rossiiskii Gosudarstvennyi Arkhiv Literatury i Iskusstva (RGALI)
Fond 483. Sokolov, Iu. M., and B. M. Sokolov
Fond 941. Opis' 6. Gosudarstvennaia Akademiia Khudozhestvennykh Nauk
(GAKhN). Literaturnaia sektsiia.
————. Opis' 12. GAKhN. Fiziko-psikhologicheskoe otdelenie.
————. Opis' 13. GAKhN. Sotsiologicheskoe otdelenie.
————. Opis' 14. GAKhN. Filosofskoe otdelenie.
————. Opis' 16. GAKhN. Kabinet po izucheniiu khudozhestvennoi agitatsii i
propagandy.
Fond 1230. Tsentral'nyi komitet Vserossiiskogo Soveta proletarskikh kul'-
turno-prosvetitel'nykh organizatsii (Proletkul't).
Fond 1418. Baranov, E. Z.
Fond 1538. Iurgin, N. N.
Fond 1638. Vsesoiuznoe Obshchestvo proletarskikh pisatelei "Kuznitsa."
Fond 2164. Vinokur, G. O.
Fond 2231. Selishchev, A. M.

BOOKS AND ARTICLES

Aarsleff, Hans. *From Locke to Saussure: Essays on the Study of Language and Intellectual History.* Minneapolis: University of Minnesota Press, 1982.
Alferov, V. N. *Vozniknovenie i razvitie rabsel'korovskogo dvizheniia v SSSR.* Moscow: Izd. Mysl', 1970.
Alpatov, V. M. *Istoriia odnogo mifa: Marr i marrizm.* Moscow: Nauka, 1991.
Anderson, Benedict. *Imagined Communities: Reflections on the Origin and Spread of Nationalism.* London: Verso Editions, 1983.
Apter, David E., and Tony Saich. *Revolutionary Discourse in Mao's Republic.* Cambridge, Mass: Harvard University Press, 1994.
Arosev, A. Ia. "Strada. Zapiski T. A. Zabytogo." *Krasnaia nov'* 2 (1921): 26–51.
————. *Belaia lestnitsa: Roman, povesti, rasskazy.* Moscow: Sovremennik, 1989.
Arvatov, B. I. *Sotsiologicheskaia poetika.* Moscow: Federatsiia, 1928.
Ashnin, F. D., and V. M. Alpatov. *Delo Slavistov: 30-e gody.* Moscow: Nasledie, 1994.
Averbakh, L. *Nashi literaturnye raznoglasiia.* Leningrad: Priboi, 1927.
Azov, Vl. "Otkrytoe pis'mo Akademii Nauk, Narkomu prosveshcheniia A. V. Lunacharskomu, Ak-tsentru, Gubpolitprosvetu, Sorabisu, Upravleniiu Akademicheskikh teatrov, mestkomam chastnykh teatrov i vsem gramotnym russkim liudiam." *Zhizn' iskusstva* 43 (1923): 8.
Babel', I. E. "Aftobiografiia." 1924. In *I. E. Babel': stat'i i materialy.* Mastera sovremennoi literatury, no. 2, edited by B. V. Kazanskii and Iu. N. Tynianov, 6–9. Leningrad: Academia, 1928.
————. *Detstvo i drugie rasskazy.* Jerusalem: Biblioteka-Alia, 1979.
Baker, Keith Michael. *Inventing the French Revolution: Essays on French Political Culture in the Eighteenth Century.* Cambridge: Cambridge University Press, 1990.

Bakhtin, M. M. *Problemy poetiki Dostoevskogo*. 3d ed. Moscow: Izd. khudozhestven-naia literatura, 1972.

———. "Discourse in the Novel." In *The Dialogic Imagination*, translated by Caryl Emerson and Michael Holquist and edited by Michael Holquist, 259–422. Austin: University of Texas Press, 1981.

———. "The Problem of Speech Genres." In *Speech Genres and Other Late Essays*, translated by Vern W. McGee and edited by Caryl Emerson and Michael Holquist, 60–102. Austin: University of Texas Press, 1986.

Bakhtina, V. A. *Fol'kloristicheskaia shkola brat'ev Sokolovykh. Dostoinstvo i prevratnosti nauchnogo znaniia*. Moscow: Nasledie, 2000.

Ball, Alan. *And Now My Soul Is Hardened: Abandoned Children in Soviet Russia, 1918–1930*. Berkeley: University of California Press, 1994.

Barannikov, A. "Iz nabliudenii nad razvitiem russkogo iazyka v poslednie gody." In *Uchenye zapiski Samarskogo Universiteta*, vol. 2, 64–84. Samara: Tip. Sredvol-soiuza no. 1, 1919.

Barthes, Roland. *Writing Degree Zero*. 1953. In *Writing Degree Zero and Elements of Semiology*, translated by Annette Lavers and Colin Smith, 1–88. Boston: Beacon Press, 1970.

———. *The Rustle of Language*, translated by Richard Howard. New York: Hill and Wang, 1986.

Bas, I. *Iazyk bol'shevistskoi gazety*. Moscow: Vsesoiuznyi Kommunisticheskii Institut Zhurnalistiki im. Pravdy, 1934.

Bely, Andrey. *Selected Essays of Andrey Bely*. Translated and edited by Steven Cassedy. Berkeley: University of California Press, 1985.

———. *Glossolaliia. Poema o zvuke*. 1917. Reprint, Tomsk: Izdatel'stvo "Vodolei," 1994.

Bendix, Reinhard. *Nation-Building and Citizenship*. New York: Wiley, 1974.

Bezymenskii, A. "O tvorcheskikh putiakh." *Na postu* 1(5) (1924): 121–28.

Bitsilli, P. "Natsiia i iazyk." *Sovremennyia zapiski* 40 (1929): 403–26.

Blakemore, Steven. *Burke and the Fall of Language: The French Revolution as Linguistic Event*. Hanover, N.H.: University Press of New England, 1988.

Blium, A. V. *Za kulisami "Ministerstva pravdy": tainaia istoriia sovetskoi tsenzury, 1917–1929*. Sankt-Peterburg: Akademicheskii proekt, 1994.

———. *Sovetskaia tsenzura v epokhu total'nogo terrora, 1929–1953*. St. Petersburg: Akademicheskii proekt, 2000.

Bloch, M., ed. *Political Language and Oratory in Traditional Society*. London: Academic Press, 1975.

Bonnell, Victoria E. *Iconography of Power: Soviet Political Posters under Lenin and Stalin*. Berkeley: University of California Press, 1997.

Bonnell, Victoria E., and Lynn Hunt, eds. *Beyond the Cultural Turn: New Directions in the Study of Society and Culture*. Berkeley: University of California Press, 1999.

Bourdieu, Pierre. *Language and Symbolic Power*. Translated by Gino Raymond and Matthew Adamson and edited by John B. Thompson. Cambridge, Mass.: Harvard University Press, 1991.

Bouwsma, William J. "From History of Ideas to History of Meaning." *Journal of Interdisciplinary History* 12 (1981): 279–91.

Brooks, Jeffrey. "Russian Nationalism and Russian Literature: The Canonization of the Classics." In *Nation and Ideology: Essays in Honor of Wayne S. Vucinich*, edited by Ivo Banac, John G. Ackerman, and Roman Szporluk, 315–34. New York: Columbia University Press, 1981.

———. "The Breakdown in Production and Distribution of Printed Material, 1917–1927." In *Bolshevik Culture*, edited by Abbott Gleason, Peter Kenez, and Richard Stites, 151–74. Bloomington: Indiana University Press, 1985.

———. *When Russia Learned to Read: Literacy and Popular Literature, 1861–1917*. Princeton, N.J.: Princeton University Press, 1985.

———. "Competing Modes of Popular Discourse: Individualism and Class Consciousness in the Russian Print Media, 1880–1928." In *Culture et Révolution*, edited by Marc Ferro, Sheila Fitzpatrick, Sydney Monas, and Jutta Scherrer, 71–81. Paris: Martine Godet, 1989.

———. *Thank You, Comrade Stalin! Soviet Public Culture from Revolution to Cold War*. Princeton, N.J.: Princeton University Press, 2000.

Brown, Edward J. *The Proletarian Episode in Russian Literature, 1928–1932*. New York: Columbia University Press, 1953.

———. *Russian Literature since the Revolution*. Rev. and enlarged ed. Cambridge, Mass.: Harvard University Press, 1982.

Browning, Gary. *Boris Pilniak: Scythian at a Typewriter*. Ann Arbor, Mich.: Ardis, 1985.

Bruner, Jerome. *Acts of Meaning*. Cambridge, Mass.: Harvard University Press, 1990.

Budennyi, S. "Babizm Babelia iz *Krasnoi novi*." *Oktiabr'* 3 (1924): 196–97.

Bukharin, N. *O rabkor i sel'kor*. 2d ed. Moscow: Pravda, 1926.

Bunin, I. A. *Sobranie sochinenii v shesti tomakh*. Moscow: Khudozhestvennaia literatura, 1988.

Cameron, Deborah. *Verbal Hygiene*. London: Routledge, 1995.

Canetti, Elias. *Crowds and Power*. Translated by Carol Stewart. New York: Penguin, 1981.

Carleton, Gregory. *The Politics of Reception: Cultural Constructions of Mikhail Zoshchenko*. Evanston, Ill.: Northwestern University Press, 1998.

Carr, Edward Hallett. *Socialism in One Country, 1924–1926*. 3 vols. New York: Macmillan, 1958–1964.

Cassirer, Ernst. *The Myth of the State*. New Haven, Conn.: Yale University Press, 1946.

Certeau, Michel de. *The Practice of Everyday Life*. Berkeley: University of California Press, 1984.

Chartier, Roger. *The Cultural Origins of the French Revolution*. Translated by Lydia G. Cochrane. Durham, N.C.: Duke University Press, 1991.

Chase, William J. *Workers, Society, and the Soviet State: Labor and Life in Moscow, 1918–1929*. Urbana: University of Illinois Press, 1987.

Chernykh, P. Ia. "Russkii iazyk i revoliutsiia." In *I. Sovremennye techeniia v lingvistike. II. Russkii iazyk i revoliutsiia*. Irkutsk: [Vlast' truda], 1929.

———. *Sovremennye techeniia v lingvistike*. In *I. Sovremennye techeniia v lingvistike. II. Russkii iazyk i revoliutsiia*. Irkutsk, 1929.

———. "Literaturnyi iazyk na rasput'i." *Budushchaia Sibir'* 4 (1934): 86–96.

———. *Russkii iazyk v Sibiri*. Irkutsk: OGIZ Vostochnosibirskoe oblastnoe izd., 1937.

Chto chitaiut vzroslye rabochie i sluzhashchie po belletristike. Materialy vyborochnogo obsledovaniia chitatel'skikh formuliarov moskovskikh profsoiuznykh bibliotek. Moscow: Izd. MGSPS "Trud i kniga," 1928.

Chudakova, M. O. *Poetika Mikhaila Zoshchenko* (1979). In *Izbrannye raboty*, vol. 1, 79–244. Moscow: Iazyki russkoi kul'tury, 2001.

Chuzhak, N. F., ed. *Literatura fakta. Pervyi sbornik materialov rabotnikov LEFa*. 1929. Reprint, Moscow: Zakharov, 2000.

Clark, Katerina. *The Soviet Novel: History as Ritual*. Chicago: University of Chicago Press, 1981.

———. *Petersburg: Crucible of Cultural Revolution*. Cambridge, Mass.: Harvard University Press, 1995.

Clibbon, Jennifer. "The Soviet Press and Grass-roots Organization: The Rabkor Movement, NEP to the First Five-Year Plan." Ph.D. diss., University of Toronto, 1993.

Cmiel, Kenneth. *Democratic Eloquence: The Fight over Popular Speech in Nineteenth-Century America*. New York: W. Morrow, 1990.

Coe, Steven Robert. "Peasants, the State, and the Languages of NEP: The Rural Correspondents Movement in the Soviet Union, 1924–1928." Ph.D. diss., University of Michigan, 1993.

Cohen, Stephen F. *Bukharin and the Bolshevik Revolution: A Political Biography, 1888–1938*. New York: A. A. Knopf, 1973.

Collins, Daniel E. "The Tower of Babel Undone in a Soviet Pentecost: A Linguistic Myth of the First Five-Year Plan." *Slavic and East European Journal* 42, no. 3 (1998): 423–43.

Comrie, Bernard, Gerald Stone, and Maria Polinsky. *The Russian Language in the Twentieth Century*. New York: Oxford University Press, 1996.

Cooke, Raymond. *Velimir Khlebnikov: A Critical Study*. Cambridge: Cambridge University Press, 1987.

Crawford, Claudia. *The Beginnings of Nietzsche's Theory of Language*. Berlin: Walter de Gruyter, 1988.

Crowley, Tony. *The Politics of Discourse: The Standard Language Question in British Cultural Debates*. London: Macmillan, 1989.

David-Fox, Michael. *Revolution of the Mind: Higher Learning among the Bolsheviks, 1918–1929*. Ithaca, N.Y.: Cornell University Press, 1997.

Derman, A. "Problema zhivoi rechi v khudozhestvennoi literature." *Novyi mir* 5 (1931): 144–62.

Deutscher, Isaac. *The Prophet Unarmed: Trotsky, 1921–1929*. London: Oxford University Press, 1959.

Dobrenko, Evgenii. *The Making of the State Reader: Social and Aesthetic Contexts of the Reception of Soviet Literature*. Translated by Jesse M. Savage. Stanford, Calif.: Stanford University Press, 1997.

Eco, Umberto. *The Search for the Perfect Language*. Translated by James Fentress. Oxford: Blackwell, 1995.

Eikhenbaum, B. "Osnovnye stilevye tendentsii v rechi Lenina." *Lef* 1 (1924): 57–70.

———. "Vokrug voprosa o 'Formalistakh'." *Pechat' i revoliutsiia* 5 (1924): 1–12.

Eimermacher, Karl. "Sovietskaia literaturnaia politika mezhdu 1917-m i 1932-m." In *V tiskakh ideologii: Antologiia literaturno-politicheskikh dokumentov, 1917–1927*, edited by T. Gromova, 3–61. Moscow: Knizhnaia palata, 1992.

———. *Politika i kul'tura pri Lenine i Staline. 1917–1932*. Moscow: AIRO-XX, 1998.

Elistratov, V. S. "Argo i kul'tura." In *Slovar' russkogo argo (materialy 1980–1990-kh gg.)*, 574–692. Moscow: Russkie slovari, 2000.

Emerson, Caryl. *The First Hundred Years of Mikhail Bakhtin.* Princeton, N.J.: Princeton University Press, 1997.

Erlich, Victor. *Modernism and Revolution: Russian Literature in Transition.* Cambridge, Mass.: Harvard University Press, 1994.

Ermolaev, Herman. *Soviet Literary Theories, 1917–1934: The Genesis of Socialist Realism.* University of California Publications in Modern Philology, vol. 69. Berkeley: University of California Press, 1963.

Etkind, A. *Khlyst. Sekty, literatura i revoliutsiia.* Moscow: Novoe literaturnoe obozrenie, 1998.

Fedin, K. "Iazyk literatury." *Literaturnaia ucheba* 3–4 (1933): 110–16.

Fedorchenko, S. *Narod na voine: Frontovye zapisi.* Kiev: Izd. Izdatel'skogo Podotdela Komiteta Iugo-Zap. Fronta Vseros. Zemskogo Soiuza, 1917.

———. *Narod na voine.* 3 vols. Moscow: Sovetskii pisatel', 1990.

Figes, Orlando. "The Russian Revolution of 1917 and Its Language in the Village." *Russian Review* 56 (1997): 323–45.

Figes, Orlando, and Boris Kolonitskii. *Interpreting the Russian Revolution: The Language and Symbols of 1917.* New Haven, Conn.: Yale University Press, 1999.

Finkel', Aleksandr. *O iazyke i stile V. I. Lenina.* Moscow: Proletarii, 1925.

Fitzpatrick, Sheila. *Commissariat of Enlightenment.* Cambridge: Cambridge University Press, 1970.

———. *Education and Social Mobility in the Soviet Union, 1921–1934.* Cambridge: Cambridge University Press, 1979.

———. "The Bolsheviks' Dilemma: Class, Culture, and Politics in Early Soviet Years." *Slavic Review* 47 (1988): 559–613.

———. "New Perspectives on the Civil War." In *Party, State, and Society in the Russian Civil War: Explorations in Social History,* edited by Diane P. Koenker, William G. Rosenberg, and Ronald Grigor Suny, 3–23. Bloomington: Indiana University Press, 1989.

———. *The Cultural Front: Power and Culture in Revolutionary Russia.* Ithaca, N.Y.: Cornell University Press, 1992.

———. *Stalin's Peasants: Resistance and Survival in the Russian Village after Collectivization.* New York: Oxford University Press, 1994.

Fol'klor. Biulleten' fol'klornoi sektsii Instituta antropologii i etnografii AN SSSR. Leningrad, 1934.

Foucault, Michel. *The Archaeology of Knowledge and the Discourse on Language.* New York: Pantheon Books, 1972.

Freidin, Gregory. "Authorship and Citizenship." *Stanford Slavic Studies* 1 (1987): 361–78.

———. *A Coat of Many Colors: Osip Mandelshtam and His Mythologies of Self-Presentation.* Berkeley: University of California Press, 1987.

———. "Isaac Babel." In *European Writers: The Twentieth Century,* edited by George Stade, 1885–1914. New York: Scribner's, 1990.

———. "Romans into Italians: Russian National Identity in Transition." *Stanford Slavic Studies* 7 (1993): 241–74.

Fueloep-Miller, René. *The Mind and Face of Bolshevism: An Experimentation of Cultural Life in Soviet Russia.* 1927. Reprint, Harper revised ed. New York, 1962.

Furet, François. *Interpreting the French Revolution.* Translated by Elborg Forster. Cambridge: Cambridge University Press, 1981.

Furmanov, D. A. *Chapaev.* Moscow: Gosizdat., 1923.

———. *Iz dnevnika pisatelia.* OGIZ: Molodaia gvardiia, 1934.

Gal, Susan, and Kathryn A. Woolard. "Constructing Languages and Publics: Authority and Representation," *Pragmatics* 5 (1995): 129–38.

Geertz, Clifford. "Art as a Cultural System." In *Local Knowledge: Further Essays in Interpretive Anthropology*, 94–120. New York: Basic Books, 1983.

Gellner, Ernest. *Nations and Nationalism*. Ithaca, N.Y.: Cornell University Press, 1983.

———. *Culture, Identity, and Politics*. Cambridge: Cambridge University Press, 1987.

Gilman, Sander L., Carole Blaire, and David J. Parent, eds. *Friedrich Nietzsche on Rhetoric and Language*. New York: Oxford University Press, 1989.

Gladkov, F. *Tsement*. In *Sobranie sochinenii*, vol. 2. Moscow: Zemlia i fabrika, 1927.

Glotser, V. I. "K istorii knigi S. Fedorchenko *Narod na voine.*" *Russkaia literatura* 1 (1973): 148–55.

Gofman, Viktor. *Slovo oratora: ritorika i politika*. Leningrad: Izd-vo Pisatelei v Leningrade, 1932.

———. *Iazyk literatury: ocherki i etiudy*. Leningrad: Gosizdat. "khud. lit", 1936.

Golos naroda. Pis'ma i otkliki riadovykh sovetskikh grazhdan o sobytiiakh 1918–1932 gg. Moscow: ROSSPEN, 1998.

Golos rabochego chitatelia. Sovremennaia sovetskaia khudozhestvennaia literatura v svete massovoi rabochei kritiki. Leningrad, 1929.

Gorbachev, Georgii. *Sovremennaia russkaia literatura*. Moscow: Priboi, 1929

Goriaeva, T. M. *Politicheskaia tsenzura v SSSR, 1917–1991.* "Kul'tura i vlast' ot Stalina do Gorbacheva. Issledovaniia." Moscow: ROSSPEN, 2002.

———. ed. *Istoriia sovetskoi radio-zhurnalistiki: Dokumenty, teksty, vospominaniia, 1917–1945.* Moscow: Izdatel'stvo Moskovskogo universiteta, 1991.

Gor'kii, Maksim. *O russkom krest'ianstve*. Berlin: Izd. I. P. Ladyzhnikov, 1922.

———. *Stat'i o literature i literaturnoi tekhnike*. Leningrad: Gosizdat khudozhestvennoi literatury, 1931.

———. "O iazyke." 1934. In *Sobranii sochinenii v 30-i tomakh*, 27:164–70. Moscow: Gosizdat. khudozhestvennoi literatury, 1953.

———. "Otkrytoe pis'mo A. S. Serafimovichu." 1934. In *Sobranii sochinenii v 30-i tomakh*, 27:147–52. Moscow: Gosizdat. khudozhestvennoi literatury, 1953.

———. "Po povodu odnoi diskussii." 1934. In *Sobranii sochinenii v 30-i tomakh*, 27:138–41. Moscow: Gosizdat. khudozhestvennoi literatury, 1953.

———. *O literature: Stat'i i rechi 1928–1935 gg*. Moscow: Gosizdat. Khudozhestvennaia literatura, 1935.

———. *Sobranie sochinenii v 30-i tomakh*. Vols. 24–27. Moscow: Gosizdat. khudozhestvennoi literatury, 1953.

———. *Maksim Gorky: Selected Letters*. Translated and edited by Andrew Barratt and Barry P. Scherr. New York: Oxford University Press, 1997.

Gor'kii, Maksim, L. Averbakh, and S. Firin, eds. *Belomorsko-Baltiiskii Kanal imeni Stalina. Istoriia stroitel'stva*. Moscow: Gosudarstvennoe izdatel'stvo 'Istoriia fabrik i zavodov', 1934.

Gornfel'd, A. G. *Novye slovechki i starye slova. (Rech' na s"ezde prepodavatelei russkogo iazyka i slovesnosti v Peterburge 5 sentiabria 1921 g.)*. Petrograd: KOLOS, 1922.

Gramsci, Antonio. *Selections from Cultural Writings*. Translated by William Boelhower and edited by David Forgacs and Geoffrey Nowell-Smith. Cambridge, Mass.: Harvard University Press, 1985.

Grillo, R. D. *Dominant Languages: Language and Hierarchy in Britain and France*. Cambridge: Cambridge University Press, 1989.

Grin, Militsa, ed. *Ustami Buninykh. Dnevniki Ivana Alekseevicha i Very Nikolaevny i drugie arkhivnye materialy*, 3 vols. Frankfurt am Main: Posev, 1977.

Gromova, T., ed. *V tiskakh ideologii: Antologiia literaturno-politicheskikh dokumentov, 1917–1927*. Moscow: Knizhnaia palata, 1992.

Groys, Boris. *Total Art of Stalin: Avant-Garde, Aesthetic Dictatorship, and Beyond*. Translated by Charles Rougle. Princeton, N.J.: Princeton University Press, 1992.

Gus, M., Iu. Zagorianskii, and N. Kaganovich. *Iazyk gazety*. Moscow: Rabotnik prosveshcheniia, 1926.

Gustafson, Thomas. *Representative Words: Politics, Literature, and the American Language, 1776–1865*. Cambridge: Cambridge University Press, 1992.

Haimson, Leopold H., "Civil War and the Problem of Social Identities in Early Twentieth-Century Russia." In *Party, State, and Society in the Russian Civil War: Explorations in Social History*, edited by Diane P. Koenker, William G. Rosenberg, and Ronald Grigor Suny, 24–47. Bloomington: Indiana University Press, 1989.

Halfin, Igal. *From Darkness to Light: Class, Consciousness, and Salvation in Revolutionary Russia*. Pittsburgh: University of Pittsburgh Press, 2000.

Heller, Mikhail. *Cogs in the Wheel: The Formation of Soviet Man*. New York: Knopf, 1988.

Heller, Mikhail, and Aleksandr Nekrich. *Utopia in Power: The History of the Soviet Union from 1917 to the Present*. New York: Summit Books, 1986.

Hirszowicz, Maria. "The Sovereign Bureaucracy as a New Social Phenomenon." In *The Bureaucratic Leviathan: A Study in the Sociology of Communism*, 13–47. Oxford: M. Robertson, 1980.

Holmes, Larry E. *The Kremlin and the Schoolhouse: Reforming Education in Soviet Russia, 1917–1931*. Bloomington: Indiana University Press, 1991.

Howell, Dana Prescott. *Development of Soviet Folkloristics*. New York: Garland, 1992.

Humboldt, Wilhelm von. *On Language: The Diversity of Human Language-Structure and Its Influence on the Mental Development of Mankind*. 1836. Translated by Peter Heath. Cambridge: Cambridge University Press, 1988.

Hunt, Lynn. *Politics, Culture, and Class in the French Revolution*. Berkeley: University of California Press, 1984.

Hunter, Lynette. "A Rhetoric of Mass Communication: Collective or Corporate Public Discourse." In *Oral and Written Communication: Historical Approaches*, edited by Richard Leo Enos, 216–61. Written Communication Annual: An International Survey of Research and Theory, vol. 4. Newbury Park, Calif.: Sage Publications, 1990.

Iakubinskii, L. P. "O snizhenii vysokogo stilia u Lenina." *Lef* 1 (1924): 71–80.

———. "O rabote nachinaiushchego pisatelia nad iazykom svoikh proizvedenii. (Stat'ia pervaia.)" *Literaturnaia ucheba* 1 (1930): 34–43.

———. "Stat'ia chetvertaia. Klassovyi sostav sovremennogo russkogo iazyka. Iazyk krest'ianstva." Part 1. *Literaturnaia ucheba* 4 (1930): 80–92.

———. "Stat'ia chetvertaia. Klassovyi sostav sovremennogo russkogo iazyka. Iazyk krest'ianstva." Part 2. *Literaturnaia ucheba* 6 (1930): 51–66.

———. "F. de-Sossiur o nevozmozhnosti iazykovoi politiki." *Iazykovedenie i materializm* 2:91–104. Moscow: Gos. sotsial'no-ekonomicheskoe izdatel'stvo, 1931.

———. "Russkii iazyk v epokhu diktatury proletariata." Part 1. *Literaturnaia ucheba* 9 (1931): 66–76.

————. "Stat'ia piataia. Klassovyi sostav sovremennogo russkogo iazyka. Iazyk pro-letariata." *Literaturnaia ucheba* 7 (1931): 22–33.

Iazyk krest'ianskoi gazety. Moscow: Krest'ianskaia gazeta, 1933.

Il'enkov, V. *Vedushchaia os',* bk. 1. Moscow: Gosizdat. khudozhestvennoi literatury, 1932.

Il'in, Iakov. *Bol'shoi konveier.* Moscow: OGIZ, Molodaia gvardiia, 1934.

Ivanov, Vsevolod. "Bronepoezd No. 14-69." *Krasnaia nov'* 1 (1922): 75–124.

Jakobson, R. O. "Vliv revoluce na rusky jazyk: Poznamky ke knize André Mazona 'Lexique de la guerre et de la révolution en Russie' (Paris, 1920). *Nové Atheneum* Roc. II, sv. III (1920–1921) 3:111–14; 5:200–212; 6:250–55; 7:310–18.

Janecek, Gerald. *Zaum: The Transrational Poetry of Russian Futurism.* San Diego: San Diego State University Press, 1996.

Jones, Gareth Stedman. *Language of Class: Studies in English Working Class History, 1832–1982.* Cambridge: Cambridge University Press, 1983.

Kabanov, V. V. et al. "'Sotsializm—eto rai na zemle' (Krest'ianskie predstavleniia o sotsializme v pis'makh 20–x godov)." In *Neizvesntaia Rossiia. XX vek,* 3:199–226. Moscow: Istoricheskoe nasledie, 1993.

Kamegulov, A. "*Chapaev* Dm. Furmanova. Frontovye zapiski." *Literaturnaia ucheba* 6–7 (1933): 39–57.

Karinskii, N. M. *Ocherki iazyka russkikh krest'ian. Govor derevni Vanilovo.* Moscow: Gos. sotsial'no-ekonomicheskoe izdatel'stvo, 1936.

Kartsevskii, S. I. "Khaltura." *Poslednie Novosti* (3 Feb. 1922).

————. *Iazyk, voina i revoliutsiia.* Berlin: Russkoe Universal'noe Izd., 1923.

————. *Iz lingvisticheskogo naslediia.* Moscow: Iazyki russkoi kul'tury, 2000.

Kataev, V. P. *Vremia, vpered!* Moscow: Sovetskaia literatura, 1933.

Katsis, L. F. *Vladimir Maiakovskii. Poet v intellektual'nom kontekste epokhi.* Moscow: Iazyki russkoi kul'tury, 2000.

Kazanskii, B. "Rech' Lenina. (Opyt ritoricheskogo analiza)." *Lef* 1 (1924): 111–39.

Kazanskii, B. V., and Iu. N. Tynianov, eds. *Mastera sovremennoi literatury,* no. 1 (M. M. Zoshchenko). Leningrad: "Academia," 1928.

Kenez, Peter. *The Birth of the Propaganda State: Soviet Methods of Mass Mobilization, 1917–1929.* Cambridge: Cambridge University Press, 1985.

Kennedy, Emmet. *A Cultural History of the French Revolution.* New Haven, Conn.: Yale University Press, 1989.

Khavin, P. Ia. "Za bol'shevistskii iazyk v raionnoi gazete." *Literaturnaia ucheba* 5 (1932): 37–44.

————. "Bol'shevistskaia publitsistika i literaturnyi iazyk." *Literaturnaia ucheba* 8 (1934): 75–91.

Khrebes. *Sovremennaia derevnia v chastushkakh i pesenkakh revoliutsionnoi molodezhi.* Moscow-Leningrad: Molodaia gvardiia, 1925.

Khrestomatiia rabochego korrespondenta. Kiev: Otdel Rabochei Zhizni gazety "Prole-tarskaia Pravda," 1923.

Kirschenbaum, Lisa A. *Small Comrades: Revolutionizing Childhood in Soviet Russia, 1917–1932.* New York: RoutledgeFalmer, 2001.

Kleinbort, L. M. *Ocherki narodnoi literatury (1880–1923). Belletristy.* Leningrad, 1924.

————. *Russkii chitatel'-rabochii. Po materialam, sobrannym avtorom.* Leningrad: Izd. Len. Gub. Soveta Profsoiuzov, 1925.

Klemperer, Victor. *Die unbewältigte Sprache: Aus dem Notizbuch eines Philologen "LTI."* Darmstadt: Joseph Melzer Verlag, 1966.

Kniazev, Vasilii. *Sovremennye chastushki, 1917–1922.* Moscow-Petrograd: GIZ, 1924.

———. *Chastushki krasnoarmeiskie i o krasnoi armii.* Moscow: GIZ, 1925.

Kochin, Nikolai. *Zapiski sel'kora.* Moscow: Federatsiia, 1930.

Koenker, Diane P., William G. Rosenberg, and Ronald Grigor Suny, eds. *Party, State, and Society in the Russian Civil War: Explorations in Social History.* Bloomington: Indiana University Press, 1989.

Kolonitskii, B. I. "'Revolutionary Names': Russian Personal Names and Political Consciousness in the 1920s and 1930s." *Revolutionary Russia* 6, no. 2 (1993): 210–28.

Kolosov, M. *Komsomol'skie rasskazy.* Moscow: Molodaia gvardiia, 1925.

Kommunisticheskaia partiia sovetskogo soiuza v rezoliutsiiakh i resheniiakh s"ezdov, konferentsii i plenumov TsK. Vol. 2. Moscow: Izd. politicheskoi literatury, 1970.

Kornienko, N. V., and E. D. Shubina, eds. *Andrei Platonov: Mir tvorchestvo.* Moscow: Sovremennyi pisatel', 1994.

———. *Andrei Platonov: Vospominaniia sovremenikov, Materialy k biografii.* Moscow: Sovremennyi pisatel', 1994.

Kotkin, Stephen. *Magnetic Mountain: Stalinism as a Civilization.* Berkeley: University of California Press, 1995.

Kotriakhov, N. V., and L. E. Holmes. *Teoriia i praktika trudovoi shkoly v Rossii (1917–1932 gg.).* Kirov: Kirovskii gosudarstvennyi pedagogicheskii institut im. V. I. Lenina, 1993.

Kovarskii, N. "Spor o iazyke." *Literaturnyi sovremennik* 4 (1934): 107–26.

Kramer, Michael P. *Imagining Language in America: From the Revolution to the Civil War.* Princeton, N.J.: Princeton University Press, 1991.

Kruchenykh, A. *Fonetika teatra.* Moscow, 1923.

———. *Iazyk Lenina: Odinnadtsat' priemov Leninskoi rechi.* Moscow: Vserossiiskii Soiuz Poetov, 1925.

Larin, B. A. "O lingvisticheskom izuchenii goroda." In *Russkaia rech',* edited by L. V. Shcherba, 3:61–74. Leningrad: Academia, 1928.

Lelevich, G. "Partiinaia politika v iskusstve." *Na postu* 4 (1923).

Lenin, V. I. "The Workers' Party and the Peasantry." In *Alliance of the Working Class and the Peasantry,* 11–19. Moscow: Foreign Languages Publishing House, 1959.

———. *Polnoe sobranie sochinenii,* 5th ed. 55 vols. Moscow: Izd. Politicheskoi literatury, 1970.

———. *Lenin on Language.* Moscow: Raduga Publishers, 1983.

Lenoe, Matthew E. "Agitation, Propaganda, and the 'Stalinization' of the Soviet Press, 1922–1930." *Carl Beck Papers in Russian and East European Studies,* no. 1305. Pittsburgh: University of Pittsburgh, 1998.

Lewin, Moshe. "The Social Background of Stalinism." In *The Making of the Soviet System: Essays in the Social History of Interwar Russia.* New York: Pantheon Books, 1985.

———. "The Civil War: Dynamics and Legacy." In *Party, State, and Society in the Russian Civil War: Explorations in Social History,* edited by Diane P. Koenker, William G. Rosenberg, and Ronald Grigor Suny, 399–423. Bloomington: Indiana University Press, 1989.

Libedinskii, Iu. N. *Nedelia. Nashi dni* 2 (1922): 61–144.

————. "Kak ia pisal svoiu pervuiu povest'." In *Ob uvazhenii k literature: stat'i, retsenzii, vospominaniia*, 21–44. Moscow: Sovetskii pisatel', 1965.

Lotman, Iu., and B. Uspenskii. "Spory o iazyke v nachale XIX v. kak fakt russkoi kul'tury ('Proisshestvie v tsarstve tenei, ili sud'bina rossiiskogo iazyka'—neizvestnoe sochinenie Semena Bobrova)." In *Trudy po russkoi i slavianskoi filologii, XXIV: literaturovedenie*, 168–254. Uchenye zapiski tartuskogo gosudarstvennogo universiteta, no. 358. Tartu, 1975.

Lukoianov, F., and M. Rafail, eds. *Rabkory o smerti Il'icha. Sbornik pisem, statei i zametok rabkorov, sel'korov i voenkorov o smerti V. I. Lenina*. Moscow: Krasnaia zvezda, 1925.

Lunacharskii, A. V. "Desiat' knig za desiat' let revoliutsii." In *Sobranie sochinenii v vos'mi tomakh: literaturovedenie, kritika, estetika*, 2:359–61. Moscow: Khudozhestvennaia literatura, 1964.

Maguire, Robert A. *Red Virgin Soil: Soviet Literature in the 1920s*. Princeton, N.J.: Princeton University Press, 1968.

Maiakovskii, Vladimir. *Polnoe sobranie sochinenii v trinadtsati tomakh*. Moscow: Gosudarstvennoe izdatel'stvo khudozhestvennoi literatury, 1955.

Mally, Lynn. *Culture of the Future: The Proletkult Movement in Revolutionary Russia*. Berkeley: University of California Press, 1990.

————. *Revolutionary Acts: Amateur Theater and the Soviet State*. Ithaca, N.Y.: Cornell University Press, 2000.

Mandel'shtam, O. E. "O prirode slova." 1921. In *O. E. Mandel'shtam: Sobranie sochinenii v chetyrekh tomakh*, edited by G. P. Struve and B. A. Filippov, 2:241–59. Moscow: Terra, 1991.

————. "Slovo i kul'tura. 1921. In *O. E. Mandel'shtam: Sobranie sochinenii v chetyrekh tomakh*, edited by G. P. Struve and B. A. Filippov, 2:267–68. Moscow: Terra, 1991.

Mannheim, Karl. *Ideology and Utopia: An Introduction to the Sociology of Knowledge*. Translated by Louis Wirth and Edward Shils. New York: Harcourt Brace Jovanovich, 1936.

Marx, Karl. "The Eighteenth Brumaire of Louis Bonaparte." In *The Marx-Engels Reader*, 2d ed., edited by Robert C. Tucker, 594–617. New York: W. W. Norton, 1978.

Matejka, Ladislav. "On the First Russian Prolegomena to Semiotics." In V. N. Voloshinov, *Marxism and the Philosophy of Language*. 1929. Reprint, Cambridge, Mass.: Harvard University Press, 1973.

Mazon, André. *Lexique de la guerre et de la révolution en Russie (1914–1918)*. Bibliothéque de L'Institut Français de Petrograd, vol. 4. Paris: Librairie Anciènne Honoré Champion, Edouard Champion, 1920.

Meromskii, A. *Iazyk sel'kora*. Moscow: Federatsiia, 1930.

Miller, Frank J. *Folklore for Stalin: Russian Folklore and Pseudofolklore of the Stalin Era*. Armonk, N.Y.: M. E. Sharpe, 1990.

Mirer, Semen, and Vasilii Borovik. *Delo chesti: Ustnye rasskazy rabochikh o sotsialisticheskom sorevnovanii*. Moscow, 1931.

————. *Revoliutsiia: Ustnye rasskazy ural'skikh rabochikh o grazhdanskoi voine*. Moscow, 1931.

————. *Rasskazy rabochikh o Lenine*. Moscow, 1934.

Mitchell, W. J. T., ed. *On Narrative*. Chicago: University of Chicago Press, 1980.

Morson, Gary Saul, "Introduction: Literary History and the Russian Experience." In *Literature and History: Theoretical Problems and Russian Case Studies*, edited by Gary Saul Morson, 1–30. Stanford, Calif.: Stanford University Press, 1986.

Morson, Gary Saul, and Caryl Emerson. *Mikhail Bakhtin: Creation of a Prosaics*. Stanford, Calif.: Stanford University Press, 1990.

Mueller, Claus. *The Politics of Communication: A Study in the Political Sociology of Language, Socialization, and Legitimation*. New York: Oxford University Press, 1973.

Murashov, Iurii. "Pis'mo i ustnaia rech' v diskursakh o iazyke 1930-x godov: N. Marr." In *Sotsrealisticheskii kanon*, edited by Hans Gunther and Evgenii Dobrenko, 599–608. St. Petersburg: Gumanitarnoe Agenstvo "Akademicheskii proekt," 2000.

Naiman, Eric. *Sex in Public: The Incarnation of Early Soviet Ideology*. Princeton, N.J.: Princeton University Press, 1997.

Nemirovskii, M. Ia. *Sovremennoe iazykoznanie i ego ocherednaia zadacha*. Vladikavkaz: Izd. Gorskogo Pedagogicheskogo Instituta, 1926.

Nove, Alec. "Socialism, Centralised Planning, and the One-Party State." In *Authority, Power, and Policy in the USSR: Essays Dedicated to Leonard Shapiro*, edited by T. H. Rigby, Archie Brown, and Peter Reddaway, 77–97. London: MacMillan, 1980.

Ognev, Nikolai. *Sobranie sochinenii*. Vols. 1, 3. Moscow, 1928–1929.

———. *Tri izmereniia*. Moscow: Gos. izd-vo khudosz. lit-ra, 1933.

Ong, Walter J. *Orality and Literacy: The Technologizing of the Word*. London: Routledge, 1990.

O partiinoi i sovetskoi pechati. Sbornik dokumentov. Moscow: Pravda, 1954.

Ostrovskii, N. *Kak zakalialas' stal'*. Moscow: Izvestiia, 1965.

Pervyi vsesoiuznyi s''ezd sovetskikh pisatelei, 1934. Stenograficheskii otchet. 1934. Reprint, Moscow: Sovetskii pisatel', 1990.

Peterson, M. N. "Iazyk kak sotsial'noe iavlenie." *Uchenye zapiski RANION po Institutu iazyka i literatury*. Vol. 1. [N.p.], 1927.

Pil'niak, Boris. *Golyi god. Roman*. Nikola-na-Posad'iakh: [published privately by the author], 1923.

———. *Krasnoe derevo*. In *Krasnoe derevo i drugie*. Berlin: Petropolis, 1929. Reprint, Russian Study Series, no. 65. Chicago: Russian Language Specialities, 1968.

———. *Volga vpadaet v Kaspiiskoe more*. Moscow: Nedra, 1930. Reprint, Russian Studies Series, no. 79. Pullman, Mich.: Russian Language Specialties, 1973.

Pis'ma vo vlast', 1917–1927. Zaiavleniia, zhaloby, donosy, pis'ma v gosudarstvennye struktury i bol'shevistskim vozhdiam. Moskva: ROSSPEN, 1998.

Plato. *Gorgias*. Translated by Terence Irwin. Oxford: Clarendon Press, 1979.

———. *The Republic*. Translated by Robin Waterfield. Oxford: Oxford University Press, 1993.

———. *Plato's Phaedrus: The Philosophy of Love*. Edited by Graeme Nicholson. West Lafayette, Ind.: Purdue University Press, 1999.

Platonov, A. P. "Kul'tura proletariata." 1920. In *Andrei Platonov: Vozvrashchenie*, 21–32. Moscow: Molodaia Gvardiia, 1989.

———. "Proletarskaia poeziia." 1922. In *Andrei Platonov: Vozvrashchenie*, 44–49. Moscow: Molodaia Gvardiia, 1989.

Platonov, A. P., and Boris Pil'niak. "ChE-ChE-O. Oblastnye organizatsionno-filosof-skie ocherki," in *Andrei Platonov: Vozvrashchenie*, 75–92. Moscow: Molodaia Gvardiia, 1989.

Platt, Kevin M. F. *History in a Grotesque Key: Russian Literature and the Idea of Revolution*. Stanford, Calif.: Stanford University Press, 1997.

Plutser-Sarno, Aleksei. "Bibliografiia slovarei 'vorovskoi', 'ofenskoi', 'razboinich'ei', 'tiuremnoi', 'blatnoi', 'lagernoi', 'ugolovnoi' leksiki, izdan-nykh v Rossii i za rubezhom za poslednie dva stoletiia." *Logos* 2, no. 23 (2000): 222–26.

———. "Russkii vorovskoi slovar' kak kul'turnyi fenomen." *Logos* 2, no. 23 (2000): 208–17.

Pocock, J. G. A. *Politics, Language, and Time: Essays on Political Thought and History*. Chicago: University of Chicago Press, 1960.

Pod"iachev, Semen. "Boliashchii," *Krasnaia nov'* 3 (1921): 3–12.

Polivanov, E. D. "O literaturnom (standartnom) iazyke sovremennosti." *Rodnoi iazyk v shkole* 1 (1927): 225–35.

———. "Krug sovremennykh problem sovremennoi lingvistiki." *Russkii iazyk v sovetskoi shkole* 1 (1929): 57–62.

Preobrazhenskii, E. A., and N. I. Bukharin. *Azbuka kommunizma*. Moscow, 1921.

Raskol'nikov, F. "Rabkory i proletarskaia literatura." *Na postu* 1(6) (1925): 105–12.

Read, Christopher. *Culture and Power in Revolutionary Russia*. London: Macmillan, 1990.

Reed, John. *Ten Days that Shook the World*. New York: International Publishers, 1926.

Rigby, T. H. "Stalinism and the Mono-Organizational Society." In *Stalinism*, edited by Robert C. Tucker, 53–76. New York: Norton, 1977.

Roberts, Graham. *The Last Soviet Avant-Garde: OBERIU—Fact, Fiction, Metafiction*. Cambridge: Cambridge University Press, 1997.

Robin, Régine. "Popular Literature of the 1920s: Russian Peasants as Readers." In *Russia in the Era of NEP: Explorations in Soviet Society and Culture*, edited by Sheila Fitzpatrick, Alexander Rabinowitch, and Richard Stites, 253–67. Bloomington: Indiana University Press, 1991.

———. *Socialist Realism: An Impossible Aesthetic*. Translated by Catherine Porter. Stanford, Calif.: Stanford University Press, 1992.

Ruder, Cynthia A. *Making History for Stalin: The Story of the Belomor Canal*. Gainesville: University Press of Florida, 1998.

Russkie pisateli 20 veka: Biograficheskii slovar'. Moscow: Nauchnoe izdatel'stvo "Bol'shaia rossiiskaia entsiklopediia," Izdatel'stvo "Randevu-AM," 2000.

Rybnikov, N. A. *Iazyk rebenka*. Moscow: Biblioteka pedagoga, 1926.

———. *Aftobiografii rabochikh i ikh izuchenie*. Moscow, 1930.

Rybnikova, M. "Ob iskazhenii i ogrubenii rechi uchashchikhsia." *Rodnoi iazyk v shkole* 1 (1927): 243–55.

Samarin, William J. *Tongues of Men and Angels: The Religious Language of Pentecostal-ism*. New York: Macmillan, 1970.

Scott, James C. *Weapons of the Weak: Everyday Forms of Peasant Resistance*. New Haven, Conn.: Yale University Press, 1985.

———. *Domination and the Arts of Resistance: Hidden Transcripts*. New Haven, Conn.: Yale University Press, 1990.

Seifrid, Thomas. *Andrei Platonov: Uncertainties of Spirit.* Cambridge: Cambridge University Press, 1992.

———. "Khaidegger i russkie o iazyke i bytii." *Novoe literaturnoe obozrenie* 53 (2002): 64–74.

Seifullina, Lidiia. "Peregnoi." *Sibirskie ogni* 5 (1922): 3–49.

———. "Muzhitskii skaz o Lenine." *Krasnaia nov'* 1 (1924): 162–69.

———. "Virineia." *Krasnaia nov'* 4 (1924): 26–96.

Selikh, I., and I. Grinevskii, eds. *Krest'iane o sovetskoi vlasti.* With preface by M. Gor'kii. Moscow: Gosizdat, 1929.

Selishchev, A. M. "Vyrazitel'nost' i obraznost' iazyka revoliutsionnoi epokhi." 1927. Reprinted in *Izbrannye trudy,* 141–46. Moscow: Prosveshchenie, 1968.

———. *Iazyk revoliutsionnoi epokhi: iz nabliudenii nad russkim izykom poslednikh let (1917–1926).* 1928. Reprint, Letchworth-Herts, England: Prideaux Press, 1971.

———. "O iazyke sovremennoi derevni." *Zemlia Sovetskaia* 9 (1932): 120–33.

———. "Smena familii i lichnykh imen." In *Trudy po znakovym sistemam 5: Pamiati Vladimira Iakovlevicha Proppa,* 493–500. Tartu, 1971.

Selivanovskii, A. "Nakanune bol'shikh sporov." *Literaturnaia gazeta* 17 (1934).

Serafimovich, A. S. "O pisateliakh 'oblizannykh' i 'neoblizannykh.'" *Literaturnaia gazeta* (12 Feb. 1934).

———. "Otvet A. M. Gor'komu." *Literaturnaia Gazeta* (1 Mar. 1934).

Seriot, Patrick. *Analyse du discours politique soviétique.* Cultures et sociétés de l'Est, 2. Paris: Institut D'Études Slaves, 1985.

Seryi, G. "Blizhaishaia zadacha." In *Proletariat i literatura: Sbornik statei,* 122–32. Leningrad: Gosizdat., 1925.

Sewell, Jr., William H. "The Concept(s) of Culture." In *Beyond the Cultural Turn: New Directions in the Study of Society and Culture,* edited by Victoria E. Bonnell and Lynn Hunt, 35–61. Berkeley: University of California Press, 1999.

Shafir, Ia. *Gazeta i derevnia.* 2d expanded ed. Moscow: Krasnaia nov', 1924.

———. "Iazyk gazety." *Zhurnalist* 9 (1924): 8–12.

———. *Voprosy gazetnoi kul'tury.* Moscow: Gosizdat., 1927.

Shcherba, L. V., ed. *Russkaia rech': Sborniki statei.* Petrograd: Izd. Foneticheskogo Instituta Prakticheskogo Izucheniia Iazykov, 1923.

Shils, Edward. *The Constitution of Society: Essays in Macrosociology.* Chicago: University of Chicago Press, 1982.

Shklovskii, Viktor. "Voskreshenie slova." In *Texte der rusischen Formalisten,* vol. 2, ed. W.-D. Stempel, 2–16. 1914. Reprint, Munich: Wilhelm Fink Verlag, 1972.

———. "Iskusstvo kak priem." In *Sbornik po teorii poeticheskogo iazyka,* vol. 2. Petrograd, 1917.

———. "I. Babel': Kriticheskii romans." *Lef* 2 (1924): 152–55.

———. "Lenin, kak dekanonizator." *Lef* 1 (1924): 53–56.

———. *O teorii prozy.* Moscow: Federatsiia, 1929. Reprint, Ann Arbor, Mich.: Ardis, 1985.

Shkur, Peter. *Rasskazy prostogo rabochego.* Translated by B. Gimel'farb. Moscow: Izd. MGSPS "Trud i kniga," 1925.

Shor, R. O. *Iazyk i obshchestvo.* Moscow: Rabotnik prosveshcheniia, 1926.

———. "Krizis sovremennoi lingvistiki." *Iafeticheskii sbornik* 5 (1927): 32–71.

Shpil'rein, I. N. *Iazyk krasnoarmeitsa.* Moscow: Gosizdat., 1928.

Sibirskaia zhivaia starina. Etnograficheskii sbornik. Vols. 1–2. Irkutsk: Vostochno-Sibirskii Otdel Russkogo Geograficheskogo Obshchestva, 1923.

Siniavskii, Andrei. *Soviet Civilization: A Cultural History.* Translated by Joanne Turnbull. New York: Arcade, 1988.

Slukhovskii, M. I. *Kniga i derevnia.* Moscow: Gosizdat, 1928.

Smirnov-Kutacheskii, A. "Iazyk i stil' sovremennoi gazety," *Pechat' i revoliutsiia* 1 (1927): 5–18, 2 (1927): 16–24.

Smith, Michael G. *Language and Power in the Creation of the USSR, 1917–1953.* Berlin: Mouton de Gruyter, 1998.

Sokolov, Boris, and Iurii Sokolov. *Poeziia derevni. Rukovodstvo dlia sobiraniia proizvedenii ustnoi slovesnosti.* Moscow: Novaia Moskva, 1926.

Solzhenitsyn, A. I., comp. *Russkii slovar' iazykovogo rasshireniia.* Moscow: Nauka, 1990.

Sovietskii fol'klor. Stat'i i materialy. Vol. 1. AN SSSR: Trudy fol'klornnoi sektsii instituta antropologii i etnografii. Leningrad: Izd. AN SSSR, 1934.

Spravochnaia kniga rabkora. Moscow: Moskovskii rabochii, 1926.

Stalin, I. *Marksizm i voprosy iazykoznaniia.* Moscow: Pravda, 1950.

Steiner, Peter. *Russian Formalism: A Metapoetics.* Ithaca, N.Y.: Cornell University Press, 1984.

Stevens, Jennie A. "Children of the Revolution: Soviet Russia's Homeless Children *(Besprizorniki)* in the 1920s." *Russian History* 9, nos. 2 and 3 (1982): 242–64.

Stites, Richard. *Revolutionary Dreams: Utopian Vision and Experimental Life in the Russian Revolution.* New York: Oxford University Press, 1989.

Straten, V. "Ob argo i argotizmakh." *Russkii iazyk v sovetskoi shkole* 5 (1929): 39–53.

Tan-Bogoraz, V. G., ed. *Revoliutsiia v derevne. Ocherki.* Moscow-Leningrad: Krasnaia nov', 1924.

———. *Staryi i novyi byt. Sbornik.* Leningrad: GIZ, 1924.

Thom, Françoise. *Newspeak: The Language of Soviet Communism.* Translated by Ken Connelly. London: Claridge Press, 1989.

Thomas, Lawrence. *The Linguistic Theories of N. Ja. Marr.* Berkeley: University of California Press, 1957.

Tikhanov, Galin. *The Master and the Slave: Lukács, Bakhtin, and the Ideas of Their Time.* Oxford: Oxford University Press, 2000.

Timroth, Wilhelm von. *Russian and Soviet Sociolinguistics and Taboo Varieties of the Russian Language.* Slavistische Beiträge, vol. 205. Rev. and enlarged ed. Translated by Nortrud Gupta. München: Verlag Otto Sagner, 1986.

Toddes, E. A., and M. O. Chudakova. "Pervyi russkii perevod *Kursa obshchei lingvistiki* F. de Sossiura i deiatel'nost' Moskovskogo Lingvisticheskogo Kruzhka (Materialy k izucheniiu bytovaniia nauchnoi knigi v 1920-e gody)." In *Fedorovskie chteniia 1978,* 229–49. Moscow: Nauka, 1981.

Toews, John E. "Intellectual History after the Linguistic Turn: The Autonomy of Meaning and the Irreducibility of Experience." *American Historical Review* 92 (1987): 879–907.

Tolstaia-Segal, Elena. "'Stikhiinye sily': Platonov i Pil'niak (1928–1929)." In *Andrei Platonov: Mir tvorchestvo,* 84–104. Moscow: Sovremennyi pisatel', 1994.

Tomashevskii, Boris. "Konstruktsiia tezisov." *Lef* 1 (1924): 140–48.

Toporov, A. M. *Krest'iane o pisateliakh: opyt, metodika i obraztsy krest'ianskoi kritiki sovremennoi khudozhestvennoi literatury.* Moscow: Gosizdat., 1930.

Trifonov, N. "Nespravedlivo zabytaia kniga." In *Narod na voine,* by S. Fedorchenko, 3–23. Moscow: Sovetskii pisatel', 1990.

Trotskii, L. D. "Kak pisat'? (Iz doklada tov. Trotskogo)." *Zhurnalist* 14 (1924): 39.

———. "Kul'tura, gazeta i kniga. (Iz doklada tov. Trotskogo)." *Zhurnalist* 13 (1924): 28–29.

———. "Leninizm i bibliotechnaia rabota. (Rech' na 1–om Vsesoiuznom s"ezde bibliotekarei 3 iiulia 1924 g.)." In *Voprosy kul'turnoi raboty,* 89–117. Moscow: Gosizdat., 1924.

———. "Rabkor i ego kul'turnaia rol'. (Rech' na konferentsii Sokol'nicheskogo raikoma, posviashchennoi vypusku raionnykh kursov rabkorov i vystavke stennykh gazet)." In *Voprosy kul'turnoi raboty,* 44–76. Moscow: Gosizdat., 1924.

———. *Voprosy kul'turnoi raboty.* Moscow: Gosizdat., 1924.

———. "Zadachi voennoi pechati. (Rech' na s"ezde rabotnikov voennoi pechati 10 maia 1924 g.)." In *Voprosy kul'turnoi raboty,* 20–43. Moscow: Gosizdat., 1924.

———. "Bor'ba za kul'turnost' rechi." In *Voprosy byta: epokha "kul'turnichestva" i ee zadachi,* 70–75. Moscow: Gosizdat., 1925.

———. "Gazeta i ee chitatel'." In *Voprosy byta: epokha "kul'turnichestva" i ee zadachi,* 19–30. Moscow: Gosizdat., 1925.

———. *Voprosy byta: epokha "kul'turnichestva" i ee zadachi.* Moscow: Gosizdat., 1925.

———. *Moia zhizn': opyt avtobiografii.* Vol. 2. Berlin: Granit, 1930.

———. *Permanent Revolution.* Translated by Max Shachtman. New York: Pioneer Publishers, 1931.

———. *Literature and Revolution.* New York: Russell & Russell, 1957.

Tucker, Robert C. *The Marx-Engels Reader.* 2d ed. New York: W. W. Norton, 1978.

Tumarkin, Nina. *Lenin Lives! The Lenin Cult in Soviet Russia.* Cambridge, Mass.: Harvard University Press, 1983.

Tynianov, Iu. N. "Slovar' Lenina-polemista." *Lef* 1 (1924): 81–110.

———. "Arkhaisty i Pushkin." In *Arkhaisty i novatory,* 87–227. Moscow: Priboi, 1929. Reprint, Ann Arbor, Mich.: Ardis, 1985.

———. "Oda kak oratorskii zhanr." In *Arkhaisty i novatory,* 48–86. Moscow: Priboi, 1929. Reprint, Ann Arbor, Mich.: Ardis, 1985.

Uspenskii, B. A. *Kratkii ocherk istorii russkogo literaturnogo iazyka (XI-XIX vv.).* Moscow: Gnosis, 1994.

V. Maiakovskii v vospominaniiakh sovremennikov. Seriia literaturnykh memuarov. Moscow: Gosudarstvennoe izdatel'stvo khudozhestvennoi literatury, 1963.

Vaiskopf, Mikhail. *Pisatel' Stalin.* Moscow: Novoe literaturnoe obozrenie, 2002.

Van der Veer, René, and Jaan Valsiner. *Understanding Vygotsky: A Quest for Synthesis.* Oxford: Blackwell, 1993.

Vernon, James. "Who's Afraid of the 'Linguistic Turn'? The Politics of Social History and Its Discontents." In *Social History* 19 (1984): 81–97.

Veshchnev, V. "Poeziia banditizma." *Molodvaia gvardiia* 7/8 (1924): 274–80.

Vinokur, G. O. "Futuristy—stroiteli iazyka." *Lef* 1 (1923): 204–13.

———. "Kul'tura iazyka (zadachi sovremennogo iazykoznaniia)." *Pechat' i revoliutsiia* 5 (1923): 100–11.

———. "O revoliutsionnoi frazeologii." *Lef* 2 (1923): 104–18.

———. "Poetika. Lingvistika. Sotsiologiia. (Metodologicheskaia spravka)." *Lef* 3 (1923): 104–13.

———. "Gazetnyi iazyk." *Lef* 2 (1924): 117–40.

———. "Iazyk gazety". In *Kul'tura iazyka*, 166–217. Moscow: Federatsiia, 1929.

———. "Iazyk 'NEPA'." In *Kul'tura iazyka*, 115–39. Moscow: Federatsiia, 1929.

———. "Kul'tura chteniia." In *Kul'tura iazyka*, 314–35. Moscow: Federatsiia, 1929.

———. *Kul'tura iazyka*. 2d expanded ed. Moscow: Federatsiia, 1929.

———. "Poeziia i prakticheskaia stilistika." In *Kul'tura iazyka*, 261–83. Moscow: Federatsiia, 1929.

———. "Rechevaia praktika futuristov." In *Kul'tura iazyka*, 304–18. Moscow: Federatsiia, 1929.

———. *Filologicheskie issledovaniia: lingvistika i poetika*. Edited by G. B. Stepanov and V. P. Neroznak and compiled by T. G. Vinokur and M. I. Shapir. Moscow: Nauka, 1990.

Vitberg, F. A. "Revniteli russkogo sloga prezhniago vremeni," St. Petersburg, 1899

Volkonskii, Sergei, and Aleksandr Volkonskii. *V zashchitu russkago iazyka. Sbornik statei*. Berlin: Izd. "Mednyi Vsadnik," 1928.

Voloshinov, V. N. *Marxism and the Philosophy of Language*. 1929. Translated by Landislav Matejka and I. R. Titunik. Cambridge, Mass.: Harvard University Press, 1973.

Von Geldern, James. *Festivals of the Revolution, 1917–1920*. Berkeley: University of California Press, 1993.

Von Hagen, Mark. *Soldiers in the Proletarian Dictatorship: The Red Army and the Soviet Socialist State, 1917–1930*. Ithaca, N.Y.: Cornell University Press, 1990.

Voronskii. A. K. "Babel', Seifullina." *Krasnaia nov'* 5 (1924): 276–301.

———. *Literaturnye zapisi*. Moscow: Krug, 1926.

Vygotskii, L. S. *Myshlenie i rech'*. 1934. Reprint, Moscow: Labirint, 1996.

Waiskopf, Mikhail. *Vo ves' logos: Religiia Maiakovskogo*. Moscow: Salamandra, 1996.

Weber, Max. *The Methodology of the Social Sciences*. New York: Free Press, 1949.

———. *Economy and Society: An Outline of Interpretive Sociology*. Edited by Guenther Roth and Claus Wittich. 2 vols. Berkeley: University of California Press, 1978.

White, Hayden. "The Value of Narrativity in the Representation of Reality." In *On Narrative*, edited by W. J. T. Mitchell, 1–23. Chicago: University of Chicago Press, 1980.

———. *The Content of the Form: Narrative Discourse and Historical Representation*. Baltimore: Johns Hopkins University Press, 1987.

Zamiatin, E. I. "On Literature, Revolution, Entropy, and Other Matters." 1923. In *A Soviet Heretic: Essays by Yevgeny Zamyatin*, translated and edited by Mirra Ginsburg, 107–12. Chicago: University of Chicago Press, 1970.

Zhdanov, A. A. [Opening speech to the First All-Union Congress of Soviet Writers.] *Pervyi vsesoiuznyi s"ezd sovetskikh pisatelei, 1934. Stenograficheskii otchet*. 1934. Reprint, Moscow: Sovetskii pisatel', 1990.

Zhiga, I. *Dumy rabochikh, zaboty, dela. Zapiski rabkora*. Leningrad: Rabochee izdatel'stvo "Priboi," 1927.

Zhivov, V. M. "Azbuchnaia reforma Petra I kak semioticheskoe preobrazovanie." In *Semiotika prostranstva i prostranstvo semiotiki. Trudy po znakovym sistemam*, 19:54–67. Tartu: Uchenyi zapiski Tartuskogo gosudarstvennogo universiteta, 1986.

———. *Iazyk i kul'tura v Rossii XVIII veka*. Moscow: Shkola 'Iazyki Russkoi Kul'tury', 1996.

Zholkovskii, A. K. *Mikhail Zoshchenko: Poetika nedoveriia*. Moscow: Shkola "Iazyki russkoi kul'tury," 1999.

Zholkovskii, A., and M. V. Iampol'skii. *Babel'/Babel*. Moscow: Carte Blanche, 1994.

Zoshchenko, M. M. *Rasskazy Nazara Il'icha gospodina Sinebriukhova*. Petrograd, 1922.

———. "O sebe, o kritikakh i o svoei rabote." In *Mastera sovremennoi literatury*, no. 1, ed. B. V. Kazanskii and Iu. N. Tynianov, 5–11. Leningrad: Academia, 1928.

———. *Pis'ma k pisateliu*. Leningrad: Izd. "Pisatelei v Leningrade," 1929.

———. "Obez'ianii iazyk." In *Mikhail Zoshchenko: Sobranie sochinenii*, vol. 1, 264–66. Leningrad: "Khudozhestvennaia literatura," 1986.

———. "Pisatel'." In *Mikhail Zoshchenko: Sobranie sochinenii*, vol. 1, 155–57. Leningrad: "Khudozhestvennaia literatura," 1986.

PERIODICALS

Etnografiia (1927)
Griadushchee (1918–1921)
Iazyk i literatura (1926–1931)
Khudozhestvennyi fol'klor (1926–1929)
Kommunisticheskaia revoliutsiia (1922–1935)
Krasnaia nov' (1921–1934)
Krasnaia pechat' (1924)
Krasnyi bibliotekar' (1926–1928)
Krasnyi zhurnalist (1920–1921)
Lef (1923–1925)
Listok rabsel'kora i stengazet (1925)
Literatura i iazyk v politekhnicheskoi shkole (1932)
Literatura i iskusstvo (1930–1931)
Literatura i marksism (1928–1931)
Literaturnaia gazeta (1929–1936)
Literaturnaia ucheba (1930–1935)
Literaturnyi kritik (1933–1935)
Literaturnyi sovremennik (1933–1935)
Na literaturnom postu (1926–1932)
Na postu (1923–1925)
Nashi dostizheniia (1931–1934)
Novyi Lef (1927–1928)
Novyi mir (1925–1933)
Oktiabr' (1924–1934)
Pechat' i revoliutsiia (1921–1930)
Pedalogiia (1928–1932)
Plamia (1918–1920)
Proletarskaia kul'tura (1918–1921)
Rabkor Zheleznodorozhnik (1925)
Raboche-krest'ianskii korrespondent (1927)
Rabochii chitatel' (1925)
Rabsel'kor (1926)
Revoliutsiia i kul'tura (1928–1930)

Rodnoi iazyk v shkole (1914–1927)
Russkii iazyk i literatura v srednei shkole (1934)
Russkii iazyk v sovetskoi shkole (1929–1931)
Sibirskie ogni (1922–1927)
Sputnik agitatora (1925–1926)
30 dnei (1925–1928)
Vestnik agitatsii i propagandy (1920–1922)
Vestnik kommunisticheskoi akademii (1922–1927)
Zvezda (1924–1926)
Zhurnalist (1922–1925)

INSTRUCTIONAL MANUALS FOR WRITING AND SPEAKING

Adzharov, A. *Oratorskoe iskusstvo: Prakticheskoe posobie dlia molodezhi.* Moscow: Molodaia gvardiia, 1925.

Belyi, Andrei, et al. *Kak my pishem?* 1930. Reprint, Moscow: Kniga, 1989.

Chernyshev, V. *Pravil'nost' i chistota russkoi rechi. Opyt russkoi stilisticheskoi grammatiki.* 3d ed. S. Peterburg, 1914.

Iurskii, N. *Literatura, kak faktor obshchestvenno-organizatsionnoi raboty. (Lektsionnaia i kruzhkovaia rabota po literature v klubakh i domakh prosveshcheniia.)* Petrograd: Kniga, 1923.

Khersonskaia (starshaia), E. *Publichnye vystupleniia. Posobie dlia nachinaiushchikh.* 2d corrected and expanded ed. Moscow: Krasnaia nov', 1923.

Kraiskii, A. *Chto nado znat' nachinaiushchemu pisateliu.* Leningrad: Krasnaia gazeta, 1927.

Kreps, V. M., and K. A. Erberg, eds. *Praktika oratorskoi rechi. Sbornik statei.* Leningrad: Izd. Instituta Agitatsii im. Volodarskogo, 1931.

Mirtov, A. V. *Umenie govorit' publichno: teoriia, zadachi, uprazhneniia,* 5th reworked and expanded ed. Moscow: Doloi negramotnost', 1927.

Rozhitsyn, V. *Kak vystupat' na sobraniiakh s dokaldami i rechami.* Khar'kov: Proletarii, 1928.

Shklovskii, V. B. *Tekhnika pisatel'skogo remesla.* Moscow: Molodaia gvardiia, 1928.

Sidorov, E. A., et al. *Delovaia rech'.* Moscow: Rabotnik prosveshcheniia, 1927.

Ustinov, I. *Razvitie rechi. K voprosu o metodakh zaniatii v shkolakh vzroslykh i na komandnykh kursakh.* Moscow: Gosizdat., 1922.

TEXTBOOKS AND PRIMERS FOR RUSSIAN LANGUAGE AND LITERATURE

Abakumov, S. I. *Russkii iazyk. Rabochaia kniga dlia shestogo goda obucheniia.* Moscow: Gosizdat., 1930.

Abakumov, S. I., and N. Nikol'skii. *Uchebnik po russkomu iazyku.* Moscow, 1933.

Barkhin, K. B. *Razvitie rechi i izuchenie khudozhestvennykh proizvedenii. Rabochaia kniga po metodike rodnogo iazyka dlia uchashchikhsia pedtekhnikumov i uchitelei.* 2d ed. Moscow: Rabotnik prosveshcheniia, 1928.

———. *Kul'tura slova. Metodicheskoe posobie dlia prepodavatelei II stupeni.* 2d ed. Moscow: Rabotnik prosveshcheniia, 1930.

———. *Sbornik uprazhnenii po stilistike. Uchebnik dlia 5–7-go klassov nepolnoi srednei i srednei shkoly.* 2d ed. Moscow: Uchpedgiz, 1936.

Blekher, F. N. *Nasha knizhka*. Posobie po gramote dlia nulevoi gruppy i detsada. Leningrad, 1932.

Boborykin, N. *Gramotnyi, obuchi negramotnogo. Metodicheskoe posobie dlia lits, zhelaiushchikh obuchat' gramote vzroslykh negramotnykh*. Khabarovsk: Izd. Dal'ono, 1925.

Chernyshev, V. *Pravil'nost' i chistota russkoi rechi. Opyt russkoi stilisticheskoi grammatiki*. 3d ed. S. Peterburg, 1914.

Danilov, V. V. *Kontsentricheskii kurs russkogo iazyka. (Po formal'nomu metodu). 1–y god kontsetra*. Petrograd, 1923.

Diubinskaia, S., et al. *Svoimi silami*. Moscow, 1925.

Dosycheva, E. I., ed. *Voprosy iazyka i stilia v V i VI gruppakh II stupeni. Sb. statei*. Moscow: Gosizdat., 1929.

El'kina, D., N. Bugoslavskaia, and A. Kurskaia. *Doloi negramotnost'. Bukvar' dlia vzroslykh*. Moscow: Izd. Vserossiiskoi Chrezvychainoi Komissii po likvidatsii bezgramotnosti, 1920.

———, ed. *Likvidatoram negramotnosti. Prakticheskoe rukovodstvo. (Kollektivnaia rabota kursantov vserossiiskikh kursov po likvidatsii negramotonosti.)* Vserossiiskaia chrezvychainaia komissiia po likvidatsii bezgramotnosti. Moscow: Gosizdat., 1921.

Golant, E., and E. Vissel'. *Budem uchit'sia. Gorodskoi bukvar' dlia vzroslykh*. 2d corrected and expanded ed. Moscow: Gosizdat., 1929.

Gurevich, A., A. Sletova, M. Sokolova, and M. Ianchevskaia. *Kul'tura rechi v obraztsakh i zadaniiakh dlia samostoiatel'noi prorabotki. Rabochaia kniga dlia shkol II-oi stupeni, rabfakov, komvuzov, partshkol i pedtekhnikumov*. Leningrad: Brokgauz-Efron, 1929.

Iordanskaia, E. *Rasskazyvanie v doshkol'nykh uchrezhdeniiakh. Metodika i khrestomatiia*. Leningrad: Gosizdat., 1925.

———. *Chto chitat' i rasskazyvat' malen'kim detiam*. Leningrad: Rabochee izdatel'stvo Priboi: 1926.

Iordanskaia, E., et al., eds. *V pomoshch' rasskazchiku*. Material dlia khudozhestvennogo rasskazyvaniia. Petrograd: Izd. Mysl', 1923.

Krugliasheva, R.A., et al. *Malen'kim kolkhoznikam. Bukvar' dlia sel'skoi shkoly*. Moscow-Sverdlovsk: OGIZ, 1931.

Lavrov, A. Ia. *Rabochaia kniga po rodnomu iazyku. Grammatika, pravopisanie, razvitie rechi, stil'. Dlia VI i VII godov obucheniia*. 2d rev. and expanded ed. Moscow: Gosudarstvennoe uchebno-pedagogicheskoe izdatel'stvo, 1931.

Lebedev, V. *Uchenie—svet. Russkii Bukvar'*. Moscow, 1916.

Mel'nikov, M. A., comp. *Novyi put'. Kniga 3-ia dlia sel'skoi shkoly*. Moscow: Gosizdat., 1928.

Metodicheskii spravochnik po obucheniiu negramotnykh krasnoarmeitsev po kompleksnomu metodu. Moscow: Politupravleniia M. V. O., 1922.

Nikol'skii, N. D., and V. M. Chistiakov. *Rodnye slova. Grammatika i pravopisanie v sviazi s razvitiem rechi. 4-i god obucheniia*. Moscow: Gosizdat., 1929.

Ostrogorskii, A. *Zhivoe slovo*. St. Petersburg, 1913.

Peshkovskii, A. M., M. N. Andreevskii, and A. P. Gubskaia. *Pervye uroki russkogo iazyka. 4-i god obucheniia*. Moscow: Gosudarstvennoe uchebno-pedagogicheskoe izdatel'stvo, 1931.

Petrenko, A., A. Finkel', and M. Samarin. *Russkii iazyk. Shestoi god obucheniia*. Khar'kov: Gosizdat. Ukrainy, 1930.

Popova, N. V., and A. N. Sokolov. *Russkii iazyk. Uchebnik dlia piatogo goda FZS i pervogo goda ShKM.* Moscow: Uchpedgiz, 1932.

Smushkov, V. V. *Raboche-krest'ianskii bukvar' dlia vzroslykh.* Moscow: Gosizdat., 1920.

Solov'eva, E. E., et al. *V novoi shkole. Kniga dlia raboty vo vtoroi gruppe gorodskoi shkoly.* Moscow: Gosizdat., 1929.

Ssorin, N. *Sputnik likvidatora negramotnosti. Prakticheskoe rukovodstvo po organizatsionnym i metodicheskim voprosam likvidatsii negramotnosti i malogramotnosti.* Moscow: Doloi negramotnost', 1925.

Sychev, D. *Krasnoarmeets. Bukvar' dlia krasnoarmeitsev i doprizyvnikov. Politicheskoe upravlenie raboche-krest'ianskoi krasnoi armii.* 3d ed. Moscow-Leningrad: Gosizdat., 1929.

Ustinov, I. *Tekhnika razvitiia ustnoi i pis'mennoi rechi.* 2d rev. and expanded ed. Moscow: Izd. Krasnaia nov', Glavpolitprosvet, 1924.

Vakhterov, V. P. *Novyi russkii bukvar'.* Moscow: Gosizdat., 1922.

Vengrov, N., and N. Osmolovskii. *My v shkole. Vtoraia kniga posle bukvaria.* 4th ed. Novosibirsk: Sibkraiizdat, 1929.

———. *My v shkole. Bukvar' dlia shkol sibiri. Vesenii semester.* Novosibirsk, 1931.

Zakozhnikov, S. et al. *Svoimi silami.* Part 1. Moscow, 1925.

GRADE-SCHOOL RUSSIAN LANGUAGE AND LITERATURE CURRICULA

Primernaia programma po literature dlia shkoly II-i stupeni. Moscow: Gosizdat., 1921.

Programma po russkomu iazyku. Rostov-na-Don: Gosizdat., 1922.

Novye programmy dlia edinoi trudovoi shkoly. Vypusk 1. Moscow: Gosizdat., 1923.

Programmy dlia shkol semiletok. Ekaterinburg: Uralkniga, 1924.

Programmy dlia pervogo kontsentra shkol vtoroi stupeni. Moscow: Gosizdat., 1925.

Programmy dlia vtorogo kontsentra shkoly semiletki (V, VI i VII gody obucheniia). Moscow: MONO, 1926.

Programmy i metodicheskie zapiski edinoi trudovoi shkoly. Vypusk tretii 1-kontsentr gorodskoi shkoly, II stupeni. Moscow: Gosizdat., 1927.

Programmy i metodicheskie zapiski shkol krest'ianskoi molodezhi. Moscow: Gosizdat., 1928.

Rodnoi iazyk i literatura v fabzavuche i profskole. Metodicheskoe pis'mo. Biblioteka rabochego obrazovaniia, no. 20. Moscow: ORO and IP Glavprofobra NKP RSFSR (Gosizdat.), 1928.

Programmy i metodicheskie zapiski edinoi trudovoi shkoly. Moscow: Gosizdat., 1929.

Programmy Fabrichno-Zavodskoi Semiletki. Moscow: Gosizdat., 1930.

Programmy Shkol Kholkhoznoi Molodezhi. Vypusk 2. Moscow: Gosizdat., 1930.

Proekt novykh programm FZS. Vypusk tretii. Obshchestvedenie (sovremennost' i istoriia), geografiia, literatura i russkii iazyk, obshchestvennaia rabota. Moscow: Narkompros RSFSR, 1931.

Programma krasnoarmeiskogo literaturnogo kruzhka. Moscow, 1931.

Programmy shkol kolkhoznoi molodezhi. Vypusk tretii. Obshchestvedenie (sovremennost' i istoriia), geografiia, literatura i russkii iazyk, obshchestvennaia rabota. "Uchebno-metodicheskii sektor NKP RSFSR." Moscow—Leningrad: Narkompros RSFSR, 1931.

FZS: Programmy russkogo iazyka i literatury. Leningrad: Leningradskii gorodskoi otdel narodnogo obrazovaniia, 1932.

Programmy srednei shkoly (gorodskoi i sel'skoi) 5–8 goda obucheniia. Vypusk tretii. Istoriia, Russkii iazyk, literatura, inostrannyi iazyk. Moscow: Narkompros RS-FSR, Uchepdgiz, 1933.

Programmy srednoi shkoly, 8, 9 i 10 god obucheniia literatury. Moscow: Narkompros, Uchpedgiz, 1933.

Programmy srednei shkoly (goroorskoi i sel'skii). 5–8 goda obucheniia i ukazaniia k programmam nachal'noi shkoly. Vpusk Istoriia, russkaia iazyk, literatura, inostrannyi iazyk. 2d ed. Zapadno-Sibirskoe kraevoe izdatel'stvo. Novosibirsk, 1934.

DICTIONARIES, GLOSSARIES, AND OTHER REFERENCE WORKS

Belina, A. *Slovotolkovatel' neponiatnykh slov, vstrechaiushchikhsia pri chtenii knig i gazet.* Moscow: Kniga i pravda, 1906.

Dal', Vladimir. *Tolkovyi slovar' zhivogo velikorusskogo iazyka.* 2d ed. 4 vols. 1880. Reprint, Moscow: Russkii iazyk, 1978.

Karmannyi slovar' Politicheskikh Terminov. Kiev: Trud i znanie, 1906.

Kii. *Narodnyi tolkovyi slovar' (Posobie pri chtenii gazet i zhurnalov).* Tashkent: Turkestanskoe gosizdat., 1920.

Kratkii politicheskii slovar' (v pomoshch' chitateliu gazet i knig). Artemovsk: Rabochii Donbasa, 1925.

Krest'ianskii slovarik (Ob'iasnenie neponiatnykh slov). Besplatnoe prilozhenie k ural'skoi oblastnoi Krest'ianskoi Gazete. Sverdlovsk, 1926.

Sakharov, Iv. *Obshchenarodnyi slovar'—politicheskikh i maloponiatnykh slov. Neobkhodimoe posobie pri samoobrazovanii i chtenii gazet.* Moscow, 1917.

Slovar' voshedshikh v obikhod sokrashchennykh nazvanii. Vladivostok: Tipo-lit. Iosif Korot', 1924.

Sovremennyi obshchestvenno-politicheskii i ekonomicheskii slovar'. Moscow: Tipografiia T-va I. D. Sytina, 1906.

Ushakov, D. N. *Tolkovyi slovar' russkogo iazyka.* 4 vols. Moscow, 1935.

INDEX